AGENTS OF CHANGE

A Study in Police Reform

HANS TOCH
J. DOUGLAS GRANT
RAYMOND T. GALVIN

Foreword by Charles R. Gain

A SCHENKMAN PUBLICATION

HALSTED PRESS DIVISION

JOHN WILEY & SONS

New York—London—Sydney—Toronto

The opinions expressed herein are those of the project staff and do not reflect those of the Oakland Police Department or the Research Foundation of the State University of New York, nor those of the National Institute of Mental Health.

Library of Congress Catalog Card Number: 73-78120

Printed in the United States of America

Library of Congress Cataloging in Publication Data

Toch, Hans.
   Agents of change: a study in police reform.

   "A Schenkman publication."
   1. Oakland, Calif. — Police. 2. Public relations — Police. I. Grant, James Douglas, 1917–   joint author. II. Galvin, Raymond T., joint author. III. Title.
HV8148, 025T63   363.2   73-78120
ISBN 0-470-87606-9
ISBN 0-470-87607-7 (pbk.)

Contents

Part II

New Programs and Organization Change
Impact on Other Officers
Discussion

12 What Did We Learn? 332

A Role for Everyone
Being Your Own Man
Culture vs. Counter Culture
Carrying the Torch
Beyond the Project
Who Runs the Show?
Selection
Study Group Structure
Study Group Process
Staff Roles
Input from the Outside
Where Are We Now?
Epilogue
Prologue

Appendices

I Information Bulletins 350

Violence Prevention Program
Field Training Program
Family Crisis Intervention Program
Landlord-Tenant Intervention Program (LTIP)

II Other Departmental Documents 369

Special Order No. 1400
Critical Incident Questionnaire
The Violence Prevention Unit
Positions Created as a Result
of the Training Program

III Patrolmen Opinion Survey Relating to the Family Crisis Unit 379

IV Detailed Analysis of Critical Incident Questionnaire Results 381

The Revised Questionnaire
Distribution of Responses by Incident
Reliability and Validity
Incident Clusters
Summary

FOREWORD

In the past decade, the negative consequences of urban concentration and decay resulted in much of the public's recognition of the limited ability and resources of the government, particularly local government. Poverty, pollution, under-and un-employment, inadequate education and housing, and poor public transportation have placed what seems to be an insurmountable burden on our governmental system. A part of this governmental system, the police, specifically the municipal police, find themselves attempting to cope with the crime and other forms of social disorganization that are very often the end product of this litany of urban ills.

The police were not, and are not now, prepared for so severe a challenge. For a century or so, the vast majority of municipal police agencies have suffered from either malignant political interference or neglect. Even those few agencies that rose above the commonplace developed only a narrow professionalism which reflected a technical competence in the area of crime control, but displayed very little sensitivity to the complexities of modern urban living.

The civil rights movement of the late 50's and the 60's, and the urban upheavals of the mid and late 60's, focused public attention on the police and their shortcomings. In reaction, a series of federal, state and local study commissions were established and pinpointed police problems through their analysis, and called for a massive revitalization and reorganization of urban policing. While the police response was less than enthusiastic, and even hostile in some quarters, a considerable number of public and police officials seized upon this impetus to move forward with police reform. They felt that at long last, public support would be forthcoming.

Unfortunately, where there was a will to change, the police did not always possess either the solutions to their most pressing problems or the skills required to implement the necessary changes. The natural response to such a situation would be to seek assistance elsewhere outside police ranks but, traditionally, the police have fostered an aura of secretiveness insofar as their operations are concerned. Outsiders were generally suspect and external analysis was discouraged.

Such self-enforced isolation was, and is, detrimental to the police and a disservice to the public. The police must open their organizational windows to let in fresh new ideas. They must be prepared to solicit help whenever and wherever it may be found, conditioned only by their responsibilities to their clientele: the public.

The project described in this book is an excellent example of a cooperative endeavor between a university community and a municipal police department. Under a grant from the National Institute of Mental Health, the U. S. Department of Health, Education and Welfare, the School of Criminal Justice, State University of New York at Albany, and the Oakland Police Department undertook a three-year relationship in an attempt to reduce the amount of interpersonal violence in police-citizen contacts. The direct result of this effort is documented within the covers of this volume.

But possibly more important than the project's impact on police-citizen contacts is the fact that this program has resulted in a series of significant organizational changes which touched such diverse activities as communications, patrol and training. It conditioned departmental procedures for dealing with family and landlord-tenant disputes, and it may eventually bring about a significant change in performance evaluation techniques. *The effort truly let in the sunlight.* And while the project brought light, it also generated some heat. As noted before, police and university personnel are generally not used to working with each other. Occasionally, their differences in philosophy, perspective and style cause conflict, and delicate negotiations are required to keep such a project on track. Nevertheless, the end product becomes well worth the momentary disruptions — and even here, the experience can be educational for both police officer and professor alike.

Most of the credit for the project's success belongs to Dr. Hans Toch, J. Douglas Grant, Raymond T. Galvin and to the Oakland police officers who participated in the project. They worked long and hard to improve the quality of police service provided to the citizens of Oakland. Their initial and continued efforts resulted in a restructured, meaningful recruit training program, a field training officers program, more effective radio communication methods and, most importantly, a permanent Conflict Management Section.

It should be recognized that such a project does not take place in a vacuum. It occurs in a dynamic, urban environment. It affects many people, and many individuals leave their imprint upon it, so acknowledgement should be given in general to personnel of the Oakland Police Department for their willingness to cooperate with the project staff even though such cooperation caused occasional inconvenience. In particular, I want to acknowledge former City Manager Jerome Keithley for his professional support and guidance, for his understanding, and for providing an administrative atmosphere which encouraged experimentation despite the risks involved. Credit is also due to the citizens of Oakland for their goodwill and meaningful support, without which none of our endeavors could succeed.

Charles R. Gain
Chief of Police
Oakland, California

Acknowledgments

This volume is based on work done in the Oakland Police Department between 1969 and 1971 under a training grant (MH 12068) from the Center for Studies in Crime and Delinquency of the National Institute of Mental Health. We are grateful for this sponsorship and support.

It is impossible to acknowledge the assistance of individual members of the Oakland department. We discuss the key role of Chief Gain later, in context; the Chief speaks for himself in the Foreword to this volume.

The seven patrolmen with whom we began work are our main creditors. These men—whose thoughts comprise the bulk of this book—have earned our thanks. They deserve more. If the project has merit, these seven may be pioneers in policing. Their real names are John Dixon, Roy Garrison, Carl Hewitt, Larry Murphy, Mike Nordin, Robert Prentice, and Mike Weldon. Working with these officers has not only been a privilege, but a real partnership.

Hans Toch

PART I

1 • Strategy and Rationale

Several years ago a group of us became concerned about violence. We embarked on research and published our findings.[1] We were tempted to move on, hoping that others — including practitioners — would find our work of use.

Somehow, we did not move on. We became dissatisfied with the idea that inquiry must be impotent, and action undocumented. We have remained to implement some of our recommendations, to test some of our assumptions. As a matter of conscience, we have become campaigners of sorts in the war on violence.

We have begun our work in the Oakland Police Department — mostly for practical reasons. Oakland has a professional force, with an enlightened, change-oriented chief. What happens in Oakland is likely to be reviewed and adopted elsewhere. We knew the setting and had collected data there. We felt welcome and at home.

Having decided to work with the police, we shaped our aims to accommodate our hosts. Our effort became one of devising and implementing strategies to reduce violence between police and members of the public.

The task is complex, because police conduct is multi-dimensional. Each officer must perform with a style of temperament, emotional expression, and communication which extends into his private life and reflects him as a human being. He must act as a product of police training and influence, filtered through pre-existing conceptions and expectations. He works within an organization that faces him with pressures and demands, whose perception is reflected (positively or negatively) in his encounters. He relates to his partner, assesses his opponent, and may be angry or upset because he missed his lunch, resents his wife, suspects his mistress, and worries about his pre-school child. And he faces a suspect who represents a civilian counterpart of equivalent determinants in a game which has a life of its own.

If we could work intensively with an officer to neutralize some of these forces, we would be engaged in a gargantuan effort with limited results. At best we should achieve one reformed officer — a man better able to face adversity with equanimity, more aware of his biases, less responsive to destructive influence. The problem of physical confrontation between police and civilians would be minimally affected.

The second strategy — to attack a general problem dimension — has similar liabilities. Better police selection or training, for instance, leaves untouched the norms of the locker room, the dilemmas of the police role and the dynamics of confrontation. It would reduce incidence by accounting for some predisposing variance, as long as our reforms (in the shape of screening and special training) remained in force. But the impact is temporary, or tends not to affect individual dispositions to violence.

The challenge is to find change strategies that are both generalized in their impact and potent as resocializers. Such strategies should reshape people; they should also extend change-inducing influence beyond their immediate target; they should address the problem over time, and prevent future outbreaks or manifestations.

Can this requirement be met? It can, as long as "correction," "therapy," "retraining" or "resocialization" are not regarded as ends in themselves. Primary change efforts must become vehicles for further change or "handles" to more comprehensive change. Problem persons must help us to understand and to cope with organizational problems and other problem persons like themselves.

If the regeneration of problem-persons is only the first step in lasting change, what are the other steps? This question will occupy us in the remainder of this volume. We shall examine this issue empirically, with regard to problem-policemen and police-problems.

The premise we shall test is that change can be perpetuated and passed on by enlisting change-targets and change-clients as allies and partners-in-change. We assume that passive change is terminal change; that for change to take root and grow, change targets must become a force that can counter-attack its problems. Persons who have been shaped by destructive influences must not only escape their fate, but must learn to deal positively with its implications. If this can occur, the fulcrums of problem-producing pressures can become centers of "problem-solving" activity.

Is this picture utopian? Not if we think of change as involving people as opposed to objects. Human change targets are not passive arenas for ministrations; they are self-reflecting and active, and can take roles beyond their regeneration. They have relevant experience and skills, and reason to care. Thus, the police officer who has over-eagerly responded to hostile citizens accumulates experience with degenerating contacts. If we can induce such an officer to adopt a more sophisticated perspective, he can draw upon a wealth of data about human interactions not possessed by less aggressive officers. Moreover, he may be uniquely able to see the point of the violence prevention effort. He can think back to his own narrow escapes — the near-riots, injuries, courtroom inquisitions, and repri-mands from superiors. He can recall the necessary deceptions and their risks.[2]

Moreover, the literature on change suggests that "participa-tion" models produce change more completely, effectively and per-manently than other styles of intervention.[3] Lewin and his col-leagues initiated a tradition in which persons who are the targets of change are converted into agents of change.[4] Dietary habits have been modified by enlisting recalcitrant housewives as dietary re-formers; change resistant assembly-line workers have become plan-ners — and executors — of new production techniques. Therapists (in particular, behavior modification advocates) have recruited patients and pathogenic agents as therapeutic aids.[5] Illiterates have become teachers; delinquents and incarcerated offenders have been converted into street workers and providers of human services.[6] Self-help groups of deviant persons have kept themselves sober, drug-free, sane or slim by regenerating others like themselves.[7]

Our strategy departs from this tradition by expanding on it. We advocate not only the enlistment of problem people as problem solvers, but also the creation of organizational vehicles and com-munity supports to enhance and expand on the forces they initiate. We advocate a change in orientation from *passive* to *active* on the level of the individual, the organization, and the community. In this sense, ours is a venture which seeks to reverse the trend of alien-ation — the process whereby a man sees himself helpless in the grip of pressures and institutions which he cannot understand or control. Our emphasis rests on the assumption that as long as alienation exists, meaningful, permanent change is precluded.

The Concept of Alienation

To argue that our strategy represents an effort to neutralize alienation may seem pretentious. Alienation, after all, has been the plaything of giants. It has figured as a key concept in the writings of Marx, Weber, Durkheim, Fromm, and Mills.[8] It has also — as Seeman tells us in a classic paper — several distinct and separable connotations.

Seeman points out that the chief connotation of alienation is *powerlessness*. He defines powerlessness as the person's feeling that he cannot determine the consequences of his acts, nor achieve desirable ends. Seeman includes in this definition the premise that one is subject to the whims of others, and manipulated by one's environment. The second (related) connotation is *meaninglessness*, which amounts to being unclear about what one can believe, and assuming that one can't predict future fate. *Normlessness* borders on traditional sociology. It means that one must play outside the rules of the game (play dirty) to win. Other connotations cover such items as not caring, feeling isolated and estranged, and depending on material rewards for incentive.[9]

Other writers have coined similar (if less elaborate) definitions. Nettler characterizes the alienated as "one who has been estranged from, made unfriendly toward, his society and the culture it carries."[10] Srole sums up the condition in five items. These proclaim that a man feels that his superiors are indifferent to him, his peers non-dependable, the world unpredictable, his fate inhospitable, and his goals unrealizable.[11] Freud and Marx, each in his own way, stressed the assumption that alienated persons have no investment or stake in their work.

The concept of alienation is a key link between problems of individual mental health, organizational effectiveness and community welfare. On an individual level, the forms taken by alienation include apathy, unhappiness and frustration-motivated conduct, ineffectiveness (in relation to organizations) and poor citizenship (in relation to the community). Organizations which comprise alienated members or workers are unable to communicate their goals, and experience poor morale, high absenteeism and low quantities and/or qualities of production. Communities with high levels of alienation breed conflict, deviance and high drop-out rates, or apathy and stagnation.

It is fashionable to ascribe alienation (as Durkheim did) to confusing or unattainable norms or goals. These, in turn, are blamed on modernization, increasing organizational complexity, increased impersonality, specialization of roles, urbanization, and other side-products of social and industrial development. Although there is little doubt that contemporary forms of alienated reactions are shaped by the types of liabilities built into contemporary personal environments, this is not equivalent to the claim that the phenomenon of alienation itself is of current vintage, nor that alienation is an inevitable price we must pay for large-scale progress. W. E. Moore, in discussing Oscar Lewis, notes:

> Even in small tribal societies . . . there is no reason to suppose that the denizens lead lives troubled only by coping with the nonhuman environment. The human environment, even in seemingly simple societies, is wondrously complex and cannot fail to bear down on individuals with an uneven and, from time to time, impossibly peremptory hand . . . The simple, uncomplicated life of primitive people or of the historic past must be a fictitious, wishful reconstruction.[12]

Students of social history have cited forms of alienation as preconditions to revolutionary uprisings, religious upheavals and other forms of unrest in every day and age. It was alienated audiences who listened to the preachings of Christ, Luther, and Buddha; embarked on crusades, pogroms, and lynchings; constituted the membership of new sects; swelled the ranks of mobs and yielded to forms of collective hysteria in settings as diverse as imperial China and medieval France.[13] Alienation has also been diagnosed as the source of societal stagnation, and as the most universal resistance to planned change and innovation.

The common denominator of definitions of alienation is that they presume to deal with a general phenomenon, basic to personal fate, which can be diagnosed independently of organizational particulars and individual characteristics. To be sure, students of alienation in one type of context tend to be relatively uninterested in the functionally equivalent forms of their subject of study. Experts on alienated youth, for instance, are unlikely to compare their subjects to the lower middle class businessmen who backed Senator McCarthy, to the unemployed who elected Hitler, or (for that matter) to the contemporary alienation problem among American blue-collar workers.

In a sense, there is good reason for presuming generality but concentrating on specifics. This approach is wise, because the formal similarities among forms of alienation exist side by side with unique manifestations. The assembly line worker may be as bored as the student in a large lecture hall, but he is listening (or failing to listen) to a different drummer. The slum youth who plays truant is manifesting his displeasure in equivalent ways to that of his teacher who calls in sick, but they are reacting to different sets of determinants. Thus the teacher may be responding not only to the rituals of her supervisor — such as demands for lesson plans — but also to the behavioral problems of her disaffected students; the truant may be reacting not only to discontinuity between street and classroom, but also to the impatience, disinterest, and hostility of his disaffected teacher. It is part of the definition of alienation that each group sees others as representatives of the alienating system; and they do this with consistent mutuality. Leaders complain about apathetic followers, who in turn point to inflexible leaders; leaders and followers grouse about middle management, which feels pressed from above and below. The situation is reminiscent of the Aleichem story in which marriage partners accuse each other to their rabbi, who tells each that he (or she) is right. In the story, the rabbi's wife demurs, but possibly she shouldn't have.

Not only would it be incorrect to attribute reactions of various parties to a common deficit in the general system to which they are subjected, but it may become obvious that one set of alienated individuals may be always responsible for the alienation of another. It may not be far-fetched to suggest that alienation always breeds more of itself, although different components of an alienated system manifest qualitative differences. Thus the absent worker and his pressured supervisor, the hippie son of the discontent middle-class parent, the student and teacher, produce and re-cycle each other. What strikes us at first blush as structural or formal determinants (which thus *a priori* seem unmodifiable) are to a large measure interpersonal phenomena which remain unchanged *because* of alienation and which could be modified to the benefit of all the participants involved.

The content of the alienated state of mind provides clues to both the nature of the difficulty and the direction of possible interventions. Recurrently, the alienated proclaim their status as each others' helpless pawns, as well as their inability to affect their human environment and the circumscription (by others) of their sphere of activity or discretion. Almost always, they proclaim that they have "given up" on their organizational milieu or membership group and that they must operate on its margin or in isolation — or that they must play a passive or passively resistant role. They diagnose in this fashion problem areas having to do with limited communication, ambiguity of defined functions, limitations of discretion, failures to inventory and compensate, and failures to permit the individual to make policy decisions and thereby to direct his own fate. These are not inevitable consequences of societal or organizational structure but properties of specific interpersonal networks, which are amenable to change.

Alienation and the Police

One of the groups in American society today which is profoundly alienated, and whose alienation is of critical importance to social welfare, is found among the police. The forms taken by alienation in a police context share some of the attributes of blue collar discontent in general; thus, alienated police show increasing interest in trade union organization.[14] Police alienation shares features with middle class alienation; it can express itself in cynical political philosophy or protest oriented ideology.[15] Police alienation also shares some feelings of alienated minorities, including the traditional clients of enforcement.

We have written elsewhere:

> The police, like the black community, feel themselves discriminated against and unpopular. They feel themselves stigmatized by indices of status. They feel their ambitions thwarted and their objectives misunderstood. They feel impotent and without recourse. They feel hated and persecuted. And they sense that the situation is steadily degenerating into a future of complete hopelessness and utter helplessness. "We are damned on every side" is a favorite police maxim, stated with feeling.

> Militant police officers — like militant blacks — react with the premise that they can no longer operate within the system. They feel that, to make themselves heard and respected, they must by-pass the strictures imposed by an insensitive, or even malevolent, power structure. In a sense, this goes beyond the routine gambit of positive minorityism. It represents a super-defensive reaction, which arises when

standard group defenses fail. It is found among those members of a minority — mainly the young — who sense beyond the self-delusion of their fellows an unresolved, permanent impotence. What they demand is the removal of social institutions that enforce impotence; these, unfortunately, may include competing minorities.[16]

What is the alienated police officer like? He may be many things. He is likely to view himself as misunderstood and rejected; he may feel that others (particularly in the criminal justice system) bend their efforts to undoing his work. He may feel unappreciated, uncompensated and disrespected by both his clients and his superiors. He may also have little respect for large numbers of citizens (whom he may characterize as intrinsically evil and incorrigible) and may have contempt for his superiors (whom he may view as removed from police work, subject to political manipulation and imprisoned by community concerns).

The alienated officer may be inactive and corruptible. He may view himself as "doing time," and going through motions. Conversely, he may see himself engaged in a thankless crusade, unappreciated by others, which necessitates disguising his conduct, deceiving and prevaricating, and compartmentalizing his "official" activity from the reality of required acts.

Within standard classification of police orientations, the alienated officer is likely to be a blue collar militant; within the well-known typology of Wilson, he's apt to operate as "Watchman" or "Legalistic,"[17] and in both cases will tend toward the extreme. He's apt to have come to the notice of internal investigations personnel, and to be viewed by his clients as lazy or unresponsive or dishonest or brutal. His morale is apt to be low and his organizational status tenuous.

Contemporary efforts at police reform have increasingly addressed themselves to the problems of this type of officer, or to the problems created by him for the police organization and the community.

In this connection, reformers have tended to make the assumption that a more positive police role would neutralize the causes or the consequences of alienation. Traditional emphasis on enforcement or arrests can widen the gap between police and public, between city management and front line police personnel. It places the officer in opposition to agencies that stress reform, social service, or crime prevention and anchors the police at one end of a polarized spectrum.

Most police reform stresses the need for positive, meaningful contacts between police and public. These contacts integrate the officer in the community, and give him a sense of participation and vested interest in a larger social order.

Police Reform

Many of the experiments in police reform have resulted from a redefinition of the police role. In the mid-1950's the American Bar Foundation[18] undertook a study of the American criminal justice process. During their efforts they documented the fact that the police perform a variety of tasks, which, while related to the criminal justice process, are due to the decision not to invoke the criminal justice process, and are not criminal in nature.[19] Family disputes, landlord-tenant disagreements, and other interpersonal conflicts are generally disposed of without utilizing arrest powers. The same was true in the handling of some victimless crimes such as drunkenness.

The recognition given to this kind of police activity resulted in an extended discussion of the police role. Many police officials and some scholars utilized the debate to attempt to encourage the police to withdraw from activity which, in their opinion, detracted from the performance of the real police role, the prevention and control of serious crime. On the other side, the President's Commission on Law Enforcement and the Administration of Justice,[20] with the support of some scholars and a very few police officials, urged the police not only to continue to perform in this area, but to seek more and better alternatives for decriminalizing their work.

Bittner,[21] Goldstein and Remington,[22] and James Q. Wilson[23] all have defended the involvement of the police in non-enforcement activities, with Wilson describing the area as order maintenance. Police scholars have encouraged such efforts because they believe that positive contacts between the police and the public cannot but help improve police and community relations and may provide the police with the opportunity to prevent crime in a meaningful way.

Taking their lead from this philosophy of policing, a number of specific projects have been implemented. For example, in New York City, the Vera Institute and a number of other organizations have worked with the police department in the development and execution of a misdemeanor citation program. This program, which has led to similar programs in numerous cities including New Haven, San Francisco and Oakland, provides an alternative to arrest and incarceration. Certain types of offenders receive written citations rather than being arrested and are thus relieved of the stigma of arrest and the burden associated with spending time behind bars.

Working with the New York City Police Department, the institute also engaged in a pilot project to rehabilitate the chronic alcoholic. The Bowery Project attempted to deal with public drunkenness in a different way from the endless revolving door of arrest, incarceration, release, arrest, *ad infinitum*. It called for the interjection of treatment into the cycle. The St. Louis Police Department undertook a similar project and established a detoxification center directly under police control where chronic alcoholics who came into contact with the police were given treatment, including counseling, instead of a night in the "tank."[24]

It is interesting to note that a number of states have recently eliminated the crime of public drunkenness and are requiring the police to take such persons to detoxification centers. It should also be noted that there are not enough such centers to cope with the problem.

Another project begun in New York City was the Family Crisis Intervention Program. Dr. Morton Bard, working in one precinct of the city, selected and trained police officers to staff and operate a unit which specialized in the handling of family disputes.[25] The unit experienced a considerable degree of success and although it did not survive the experimental period, it did serve as the model for other departments. Further, it provided the impetus for the recognition of the family dispute as a serious police problem, and stimulated training for police officers in this area.

Police training in general is starting to reflect the newly adopted service orientation. The best police training programs have previously emphasized the development of technical competence in crime control and strict discipline, often through the application of stress techniques, and the majority of them still do, but there is a growing awareness of the need to improve their abilities in coping with people problems. Where casual community relations presentations were once offered, depth analyses are now given stressing the acquisition of a concrete understanding of the various police clients and their unique problems.

Of particular importance is the fact that the expanded subject matter has been complemented by the application of a variety of new training methods.[26] The Dayton Police Department has been particularly inventive in this field. It employs group discussions, role playing, and planned field experiences. Dayton and Covina, California, have gone so far as to utilize brief immersions in the community as a training technique.

In an attempt to reduce the regimentalism in police training some departments have cut down on drills and the military manner of instruction. Even the Los Angeles County Sheriff's Department, which has long been known for its stress training for recruits, has, after careful study, eliminated the stress atmosphere.

The unfortunate state of police and community relations, coupled with the availability of federal and state grant money, has also given an impetus to service oriented police programs. Community relations units were established, campaigns to recruit minority officers were designed and executed, and attempts were made to begin the police-community dialogue. While each of these techniques met with only limited success, some programs did broaden the police perspective. For example, in Winston-Salem, North Carolina, the police-community relations program undertook the functions of an emergency aid center. If it could not refer people and help was required, the officers did the job themselves. They obtained temporary housing, purchased and distributed food, and even located heating fuel if such was necessary.

In reaction to a series of disturbances, the Dayton Police Department established a Conflict Management Unit which focused on the prevention of such occurrences. Specially selected and trained officers take to the streets whenever there seems to be a problem. In numerous cases they have successfully "cooled" the situation.

Poor police and community relations have also brought about attempts at community participation in, and even community control of the police process. Although there has been a total rejection of police review boards and community control efforts such as the one suggested in Berkeley, California, many police advisory groups have been set up, more and more police agencies are willingly accepting and investigating citizen complaints, and some departments are experimenting with organizational forms which foster public involvement in police matters and focus upon specific community problems.

Most of these projects have been labeled neighborhood or team policing. New York City, Detroit, and Los Angeles are all experimenting with programs which assign individual officers to a permanent team which meets and works with local residents on local problems.

Similar but more ambitious projects have been implemented in

Dayton, Cincinnati, and Holyoke, Massachusetts. The Holyoke model is particularly innovative. With the support of both the Law Enforcement Assistance Administration and HUD's model cities, John Angell's[27] democratic organizational model was partially established in Holyoke. A small team of police officers were given the responsibility for policing the model cities area. They were given a great deal of freedom in formulating their methods of operations and even had a major part in choosing and purchasing their equipment and uniforms. They worked out of a store in the model cities neighborhood, encouraging drop-ins, working enthusiastically with kids and generally promoting the service aspect of policing. While the Team Policing Unit, as it is called, has generated considerable political opposition, it seems to have community support.

There is, of course, another side to the picture. Not all police reform has concerned itself with the newly emphasized service orientation of the police. Probably the greatest amount of money has been expended in an attempt to improve police efficiency in crime prevention and control. Literally millions have been poured into the applications of computer technology. Police departments now have available the technology to implement sophisticated manpower deployment systems. Response time can be significantly reduced, command and control systems are feasible and communications capabilities have been greatly enhanced.

Such developments are tangential to our concerns. While they improve law enforcement technology, they stipulate law enforcement roles. To the extent to which the police role, traditionally defined, molds armies of alienated technicians, this trend may be exacerbated by narrow professionalization.

Our Strategy

As a police reform venture, our project hoped to build a violence-oriented problem-solving component into the Oakland department. We wanted officers to address the problem of violence, and to do so in an objective, documented way. We wanted the officers to deal with the problem constructively, evolving means to counter the causes of violence plausibly and effectively. And we wanted them to monitor the results of their efforts, realigning strategies as dictated by impact.

We wanted the effort to be initiated by officers who themselves had been responsible for the problem. We felt that in the course of problem-solving these men would begin to see themselves as autonomous and self-directed, and would be liberated from destructive forces which their alienated stance would otherwise have stipulated.

We wanted this program to proceed through cumulative, gradually re-cycling, stages. We would start (in the tradition of "organizational development" teams) with a small group of men who would (1) inform themselves about parameters of the problem and devise an initial set of problem-solving strategies; in this context (2) we would prepare the men to take on roles as leaders for a larger problem-solving group, who would extend the effort further. This second group (or its sub-groups) could then expand the first team's effort, while engaged in both objective and self-directed inquiry. Ultimately, the larger group was expected to set up institutional arrangements in the form of a permanent problem-solving body within the department.

Our first group was to be composed of officers defined as "strong" problem solvers; only some of these men were to be derived from the violence-experienced pool. The second generation was to be composed exclusively of violence-prone officers. This generation was to be selected randomly out of the high-risk population, with provisions for a control group, to test the hypothesis that the program would affect behavior on the street.

We projected a sequence of development in which the first stage would consist of general inquiry into the violence problem. This inquiry was to focus on relatively non-controversial parameters, and to profit from the analysis of personal experiences. Formal research inquiry was to be initiated relatively early in this context. Subsequent phases were to center increasingly on the police role in promoting or sanctioning violence; self-analysis would complete this stage of inquiry.

Our first team was to proceed from problem definition, through research, to the creation of problem-solving groups. They would help us shape the second phase of the study, and would evolve into group leaders. The second generation would consist of these officers as "staff," our staff as consultants, and the violence-prone patrolmen as "trainees." The new men would be divided into groups, each with "co-leaders." They would proceed from problem-definition, to research, to self-analysis — and ultimately to organizational reform.

Research as Police Reform

Although our project includes "positive police role definition," and stresses the exercise of patrolman discretion, it is not equivalent to other interventions. For instance, it combines resocialization with organizational reform. In most programs, change leverage is associated with quality, strategic position, or demonstrated potential. Non-producers or mis-producers are cast as change resisters, attracted to the bandwagon, shamed into support, ignored, by-passed or weeded out. Their alienation is stipulated, and it becomes the waste-product of change. Left-over "legalists" in a service-reoriented department, non-team-selected men in team policing, officers non-interested in newly defined functions (such as family crisis management) drift in the wake of the ship of progress. By contrast, our strategy starts with such men and seeks to involve them preferentially and early. We pose the test case: If the course of alienation can be *reversed*, does it not follow that it can be neutralized?

Our project stresses self-study and research. The self-study component (which we have discussed elsewhere)[28] makes the person's own problems and experiences the starting point of inquiry. These experiences can be discussed within a problem-solving framework, permitting constructive (rather than dysfunctional) extrapolations. The stress on scientific inquiry (research) is the vehicle of transformation. We assume — as do most schools of psychotherapy — that solutions evolve from documented consequences of past conduct. As the person learns (through non-threatening exploration) that his behavior has failed or strayed from goals, he can explore and experience goal-directed options. These options can be personal, organization-directed, or (usually) both.

Our stress on violence is almost incidental. We know that violence is multi-dimensional. The corollary is that violence is one of several themes which reflect and concretize various malfunctions. These include defective personal adjustment, role-playing, and organizational pressures and supports. Violence thus provides an arena of inquiry, and — if our assumptions are valid — a handle for change.

1. Hans Toch, *Violent Men: An Inquiry into the Psychology of Violence* (Chicago: Aldine, 1969).

2. Hans Toch, "Change Through Participation (and Vice Versa)" *J. Res. in Crime and Delinquency* 7 (1970) p. 199.

3. W. G. Bennis, K. D. Benne and R. Chin, eds., *The Planning of Change* (New York: Holt, Rinehart and Winston, 1969); R. Lippitt, Jeanne Watson and B. Westley, *The Dynamics of Planned Change* (New York: Harcourt Brace, 1958).

4. K. Lewin, "Forces Behind Food Habits and Methods of Change," National Research Council Bulletin CVIII (1943); K. Lewin, "Frontiers in Group Dynamics," *Human Relations* I (1947) pp. 5-41.

5. A. Bandura, *Principles of Behavior Modification* (New York: Holt, Rinehart and Winston, 1969) pp. 104 ff.; B. G. Guerney, ed., *Psychotherapeutic Agents: New Roles for Nonprofessionals, Parents and Teachers* (New York: Holt, Rinehart, and Winston, 1969).

6. See, for example: *Experiment in Culture Expansion* (Proceedings of a Conference at Norco, California, 1963); *The Offender as a Correctional Manpower Resource* (Sacramento: Inst. Study Crime and Delinquency, Undated).

7. E. Sagarin, *Odd Man In: Societies of Deviants in America* (Chicago: Quadrangle Books, 1969).

8. Whereas Durkheim, Weber, Merton, and sociological students of deviants deal with "anomie" as descriptive of a societal condition, the concept we refer to relates to individual psychological states.

9. M. Seeman, "On the Meaning of Alienation," *Amer. Sociol. Review* 24 (1969) pp. 783-91.

10. Gwynn Nettler, "A Measure of Alienation," *Amer. Sociol. Review* 22 (1957) p. 671.

11. L. Srole, "Social Integration and Certain Corollaries: An Exploratory Study," *Amer. Sociol. Review* 21 (1956) pp. 709-16.

12. W. E. Moore, "Social Structure and Behavior" in G. Lindzey and E. Aronson, eds., *Handbook of Social Psychology* vol. IV (Reading: Addison-Wesley, 1969) p. 294.

13. Hans Toch, *The Social Psychology of Social Movements* (Indianapolis: Bobbs Merrill, 1965).

14. W. Turner, *The Police Establishment* (New York: G. P. Putnam's, 1968).

15. A. Niederhoffer, *Behind the Shield: The Police in Urban Society* (New York: Doubleday, Anchor, 1969) pp. 95 ff.

16. Hans Toch, "Cops and Blacks: Warring Minorities," *The Nation* (April 21, 1969) p. 491.

17. James Q. Wilson, *Varieties of Police Behavior* (Cambridge: Harvard Univ. Press, 1968).

18. American Bar Foundation, *The Administration of Criminal Justice in the United States: Plan for Survey* (Chicago: American Bar Foundation, 1955), pp. 1-21.

19. Wayne R. LaFave, *Arrest: The Decision to Take a Suspect into Custody* (Boston: Little, Brown and Company, 1965), pp. 61-153.

20. The President's Commission on Law Enforcement and the Administration of Justice, *Task Force Report: The Police* (Washington, D. C.: Government Printing Office, 1967), pp. 13-38.

21. Egon Bittner, *The Functions of the Police in Modern Society* (Chevy Chase, Maryland: Center for Studies of Crime and Delinquency, National Institute of Mental Health, 1970), pp. 1-122.

22. The President's Commission on Law Enforcement and the Administration of Justice, *Op. cit.*, pp. 13-38.

23. James Q. Wilson, *Op. cit.*, pp. 17-34.

24. The *St. Louis Detoxification and Diagnostic Evaluation Center* (Washington, D. C.: Government Printing Office, 1970), pp. 1-98.

25. Morton Bard, "Family Intervention Police Teams as a Community Mental Health Resource," *The Journal of Criminal Law, Criminology, and Police Science*, IX Number 2 (1969), pp. 247-250.

26. "Quiet Revolution Underway in Police Training, Education," *Information Bulletin* (Oakland Police Department, 1972), pp. 1-8.

27. John E. Angell, "Toward an Alternative to the Classic Police Organizational Arrangements," *Criminology*, IX, Numbers 2-3 (August-November, 1971) pp. 185-206.

28. *New Careers Development Project: Final Report* (Sacramento: Institute for the Study of Crime and Delinquency 1967) (Mimeo) pp. 6, ff.

2 • First Generation Change-Agents

The first phase of our project called for the creation of a group of change-agents. We set about finding (and training) seven patrolmen to initiate efforts that could reduce conflict and violence on the streets of Oakland. Our next task was to help our group to shoulder its burden and define its mission. The present chapter deals with this phase of the study.

In late June of 1969, two staff members and a consultant conducted group interviews designed to select members for the group. Some 80 officers were interviewed. These were drawn from four sources: (1) officers who had been included in an NIMH-sponsored violence study in 1966-67; (2) officers drawn from recent high-incidence lists of "resisting arrest"; (3) officers recommended by superiors as "good officers"; (4) officers suggested by peers as promising group members.

The object of the selection process was to locate men with violence-related experience, who were held in high regard by other officers. The interview was designed to select individuals most likely to be contributing group members. Candidates were chosen on the basis of ratings of quantity and quality of contribution to the interview situation. All interviewees were contacted after the interviews were completed. Those who had been chosen were invited to participate. All agreed to join.

The seven officers who were included in the group ranged in age from 26 to 41, with a mean age of 31. Their time with the department varied from 1½ to 18 years, with mean service of 6 years. Three had been subjects in our previous study of violence-prone officers; four were secured through other sources.

The group first convened on Wednesday, July 2, 1969. Each officer remained on his beat three days a week, and worked on the project two consecutive working days. During these two days the group met from 4 p.m. to midnight. The last half hour of each meeting was reserved for tape recorded summary statements. In addition to these sessions, staff and group were variously involved in project-related activities. Staff met to review progress, to plan subsequent sessions and to make administrative arrangements. Officers collected data, made individual arrangements for interviews, and tape recorded incidents on the street.

During the summer, the group met for eleven weeks — a total of 176 hours of meeting time. The group continued on a less ambitious schedule between mid-September and June of 1970. Generally, it put in eight hours every two weeks, except for more intensive planning sessions in December and April. In the summer of 1970, the seven officers designed and conducted the second phase of the project, which we shall describe later in the report.

The Induction Process

As soon as the group convened, it listened to a talk by one of the staff outlining the nature of the project. This introduction included a presentation of rationale, stressing the group's role as trainers and changers of others. The selection procedure was fully described, and the session format was outlined. The staff member pointed out that the men would have freedom in determining their area of activity, and that staff would provide resources and help. The group was told that it would face unfamiliar work and problems of trust. It was assured of confidentiality and was promised impact and self-development.

After this statement, the group moved to substantive discussions. As their first exercise, the men listed ten types of incidents likely to produce violence. They then selected one category — the family dispute — for intensive analysis. The analysis included isolating "cues" available to the officer as to the likelihood of violence, listing various opening police-moves and civilian counter-moves, and discussion of response-styles among officers.

The group went on to address areas of organizational functioning that could play a role in promoting violence. Among these was recruit training, dispatching, and communication — in particular, communication between patrolmen and their supervisors.

During the course of the first session, several officers demonstrated an interest in more systematic inquiry. One of the officers, for example, requested statistics on the relative prevalence of arrests for resisting arrest:

Of the list of calls we had, I think we should know almost percentage-wise what amount of 148s occur in family beefs, when they occur in car stops, walking stops. Do young-looking policemen have more? Do recruits just out of the academy have more? What type of policeman has the most 148s? And then, if we can put our finger right on a specific problem, maybe come up with some reason as to why they're happening, and maybe a solution.

Another officer called for more concern for reliability in the content analysis of street incidents:

When we went through a couple of incidents, we went immediately to an analysis; I would have preferred to have more incidents on the floor so you could draw them to-gether rather than trying to do an individual analysis. We didn't want to move to the analysis of the incidents as quickly as we did. We would have preferred to have the information out and then do the analysis so you have more possibilities to draw from.

One group member advanced a suggestion for a concrete research project; he suggested that volunteer officers tape their family disturbance calls, to permit a step-by-step review by the group:

Officer: You mentioned the actor-type thing where you go through these emotions of the typical family scene. Why couldn't we go to these things and have the officer tape it, rather than try to act the thing out?

Staff: That might be extremely useful.

Staff: Are you suggesting a hidden tape?

Officer: Hidden, naturally, from the people involved. And it would give us that point of view. I'll admit the officer will perhaps not present it in the same light he would without this. But by the same token, it would give you an idea of the things that do present themselves and develop a pattern.

Officer 2: We certainly would get the citizen's side of it.

Staff: We've got seven officers at this table some of whom will be responding to that kind of call.

Officer 3: We'd look kind of obvious carrying a tape . . .

Officer: No, just like small things. Just like your transceiver. It wouldn't make any difference, and then you could see how each different officer handles. . . .

This idea was not pursued during the session, but was revived, discussed, and implemented at a later date. This also held true of other ideas raised during the first sessions.

Trust problems did arise, but on a low key, and usually with overtones of humor. The following exchange is fairly typical:

Officer: Well, I'd like to be called Sam from now on. Because everytime he refers to Mills he's using my first name, and I'm the one that's going to get the ax.

Staff: May we have it for the record that Joe is Sam.

Officer: One thing that I heard several times tonight, and I'd like, of course, to express my opinion, was I think there's some doubt on the part of you gentlemen, not the officers, but the gentlemen who are conducting this program, as to our honesty, because of the trust we might place in whatever's going on. And I think that you're going to have as complete cooperation as possible. I don't think there's going to be any problems withholding information, not wanting to say something because you're afraid of what could happen. Going on to one of the points that Hiram made. . . .

Officer 2: The name is Genevieve.

A staff member who handled the first group summary paraphrased several spirited remarks made by the officers during the session. One of these quotes sparked the following interchange:

Officer: The summarizer mentioned, "if violence was to occur, hit first," which was kind of general. And I'll clarify that very briefly, because it doesn't sound good on the tape, first of all. Secondly, we were speaking of a specific incident at the time, and the general conversation, at this particular time in the conference, was that if you happen on an individual that was outwardly going to become violent, we were in fact in position where it would not behoove us to lose. And that if this were to occur, if in fact violence were to occur, and were to be leveled on us, that it would be much to our advantage to level it first in coping with the situation. So I'll leave that.

Officer 2: How are you going to put it, "the officer should be in the position to take appropriate action"?

Officer 3: I thought what you were saying was that the best defense is a good offense?

Group members did show some reserve in relation to other officers — often producing an illusion of harmony and unanimity. One of the men noted in the summary that

> I think there was some reticence on the part of the group to challenge each other. I saw people who obviously didn't agree with the other guy sort of let it go, and I don't think there's anything wrong with challenging each other. I mean, we're all trying to find areas here. I think if we test each other, we'll move a little bit forward and have a little better possibility of getting to these points . . . if somebody doesn't agree with somebody, that's fine.

In addition to the indirectly raised issue of trust, there was resistance on the part of one group member to the emphasis on officer violence. The argument raised by this man (which he renewed in several other sessions) contained two themes: (1) police officers tend to respond to civilian contacts in standard ways; and (2) civilians are responsible for any resulting violence:

> *Officer:* The officers here are all experienced; they've been on these calls. I think it behooves us to think about that we are all one nature, that even though there are certain small things that we would tend to differ with, that we are police officers, and we are of a state of mind as police officers. We should, perhaps, get into a different plane, perhaps interviewing people who are the victims of family disturbances.
>
> *Staff:* Participants?
>
> *Officer:* Participants of family disturbances to find out what is going through their mind, what response, what state of mind they were in when the officer arrived on the scene. At the point where they settled down and discontinued their

violent nature, what caused the discontinuation of their violent nature. And this is just scratching the surface of family disturbances here. There are many other conditions. We only discussed ten; I'm sure there are many others.

In connection with the tape recording idea, the same officer proposed that the tapes would demonstrate that

The officer goes in and uses all these ideal responses, and still gets the militant type response from the people; it may show that it's not entirely at the officer's discretion to prevent these things from happening.

Beyond this objection, the group voiced little concern or reluctance. They stipulated their mission, accepted the staff, and launched into their assigned subject. If they harbored resistances, these remained latent. Testimonials ranged from "I enjoyed the session. I feel like I'm much better for it," to "I'm going to learn a lot up here," and "a lot of what was said up here will keep coming back to me." The program had achieved — it seemed — qualified acceptance.

Evolving a Joint Frame of Reference

The second session continued and amplified the exercises that were initiated the previous evening. The group moved to a second category of violence-prone incidents, involving crowds of juveniles. Again, personal experiences were used as a basis for discussion, and there were some disagreements among group members about the handling of calls. The analysis proved systematic, compared to that of the first session. The group produced a detailed inventory of situational cues to violence, and discussed the consequences of behavioral options facing the responding officer. There was discussion of "games" played by officers and suspects, and of component "strategies" and "moves."

It had become obvious, late in the session, that the group had accepted a common language, which it used easily and comfortably. As a staff member put it:

I think when we speak of "games" from now on in, we all will be pretty much talking about the same thing. When we speak of "cues" and "moves," we'll be talking about the same thing. It isn't just a matter of anybody using this language just to do somebody else a favor.

Several members of the group voiced their surprise as they discovered systematic differences in police conduct, including their own. One officer stated that

I was under the impression that these are all the results of incidents, and everybody that's involved here, that is, all the policemen that are involved, have always been the same. I've had a tendency of not having any insight into how I did anything. It was revealing to me to lay it out and just to compare it with the rest of the fellows just to see where the differences were, in regard to what was suggested for me, and the differences in my attitude. Perhaps I'm all wet in my attitude, I don't know. But I never had given it any thought before, and it has been enlightening looking at myself.

The dissenting voice was that of the previous night's holdout, who reiterated that

We have a sameness of mind and a sameness of thought; it does exist, I believe. And I don't think that it should be forcefully changed to please the staff. Not that you're inferring this, but I just thought I would bring it out that we have the same sameness of mind and thought that you do.

These views were ventilated in the context of a "no holds barred" debate, featuring open but friendly disagreements. One officer noted proudly that "tonight we exposed our souls possibly a little more, and we're willing to talk about things and take variance with each other more than we did last night." Others concurred with this assessment of the evening's climate. As another officer put it:

I have something to say about last night, and that is that I'm very pleased with last night because it got us to where we are tonight, and I find myself somewhat disappointed that tomorrow night's not going to come until next Wednesday. The ball's rolling, and you just kind of hate to see it stop.

Coming after a sixteen-hour marathon, such tributes confirmed the existence of a surprisingly high level of group morale.

Facing the Larger Implications

During the third session, the group received a visit from their Chief, Charles Gain. The Chief endorsed the violence prevention program, and emphasized the uniqueness and importance of the group's work. He said, in part:

> I'd like to impress upon you the significance this project has to me and to the Oakland Police Department and policing in general. We find in policing today that so many things are occurring, and sometimes we don't know why, and too much the tendency is to do nothing about it. So that when we can identify that there are problems, and this is a problem area as you well know, to me it is absolutely essential that we explore and that we find out what is going on, why it's going on, and what can be done about it; hence the emphasis on this program in my judgment. It's highly important; it's not something I can do at all. And there are many areas, of course, where this is true. It's something where we have to have people who are involved in the nitty-gritty, gut level, if you will, of police work. So it's highly significant to me. I think it's going to be a landmark thing for policing if it turns out the way it should; and, of course, that's totally unknown now, I suppose, to any of us. But it will be a classic type study, one that will surely benefit this police department and individuals in an area where day by day we are finding there are problems on that street. And there will be a spin-off and a trade-off for policing throughout the country, so it would benefit officers as regards safety of their persons, and also citizens. I think most importantly, it's something that you have to do. Again to emphasize that I can't do it. It's something that no number of experts could do from the outside. It's something that individuals who are involved in the work process themselves have to engage in, and that is a highly important part of it.

Pleased with this endorsement, and bolstered by the Chief's expression of confidence, the group set to work. It proceeded to randomly review arrest reports of high-incidence officers. The result was an animated but unsystematic discussion, with little closure. One officer complained:

When we get down to going over these reports, which I thought was a waste of time — it's my opinion, of course, maybe everybody doesn't agree, and I want to hear about it. But I don't believe that we had any objective or purpose in mind when we started going through these things. We didn't know really what we were looking for. I'm speaking of myself; I should say "y" — I didn't know what I was looking for; I didn't know what to look for, and I think, in my opinion, we kind of went off on a tangent of nonrelevant analysis of the whole thing that didn't really . . . when I think about all the discussion about all these different reports, I don't think we came up with anything that was worth a damn as far as furthering our real objective in this thing. And it's because of the lack of objectivity, because of lack of purpose on my part, that I wasn't able to come up with anything. Had I known what the staff, who, I might add, has been very patient in letting us run on these things, . . . had I known what really to look for, it could have well been that I would have come up with something. But I didn't think that I had any cue at all as to what to look for, and so consequently I just ran through these things and listed things that really didn't move me at all. I don't think I've gotten anywhere with this report reading.

Another officer took issue with this negative assessment; he complained of a tendency among some group members to defend every action of the men who had filed the reports:

In going over the reports, I don't think it was a total loss for me, because there are a couple in this stack right here where I would not have done what the officers in this particular case had done. It wouldn't have been that important to me. I can't go against Joe's analysis that it wasn't good police work. I just don't think that the end result at this point in my career — I'll put it that way — would have made the damned thing worth while to me. Everybody looks at it differently, probably everybody in this room does — the officers anyway. I just feel that it isn't worth the hassle at this stage. Ten years ago it might have been different.

The same subject also brought a personal reaction by one of the staff:

I must confess that I have trouble with visualizing an officer standing there watching a person who is handcuffed being beaten up. I have trouble coping with this thing, and I have a hunch that here's an area for me to work through; I don't know which way I want to go. I just have an unresolved problem here which I find myself worrying about at this stage.

This statement elicited solicitous concern from several members of the group:

Officer: [You object] from a humanitarian point of view?

Staff: Yah, I guess so. The problem is I really want to be with you guys. On the other hand, I can't reconcile myself to that kind of business.

Officer 2: I could have a solution for you after it's all over.

Staff: O.K.

Officer 2: You've got 32 hours a week you can ride next to me in a patrol car.

Staff: All right, I will take you up on that.

This interchange produced an arrangement whereby one of the staff sometimes accompanied group members on patrol. This not only furnished feedback opportunities, but also helped cement rapport between staff and officers.

Third session morale was again high, and discussions uninhibited. A spectrum of views (with "right-wing" and "left-wing" advocates) had begun to appear. The group had also begun to form identity and in-group loyalty. In discussing possible interviews with high-incidence officers, for example, there was much concern about locker-room reaction:

When we talked about the possibility of bringing officers up here and possibly showing them some report and asking them what they thought about it, and hoping that they would give some idea as to some of their problems, there are going to be officers on this department, and probably some of those that we choose, that are going to be very resentful of the fact that we've picked them out to partake in this study, or whatever you want to call it. And I'm just wondering is there some way that we can protect this resentment and prevent it from going downstairs amongst the ranks to where it would be harmful to our program? All it takes is one officer to go downstairs and say "these guys are a group of finks," or "this study is no good," and it could spread around this department like wildfire, and we'd have a real problem.

The group had coalesced despite differences, and felt that it had a distinct function. In the weeks ahead, it was destined to struggle with the definition and scope of its aims.

The Inadequacies of the Academic Approach

There is a Russian story about the trans-Siberian railroad. A man gets on, and later a woman. Over weeks of travel they sit silently facing each other. At length, the man offers a slice of sausage; weeks later, the woman hands him some soup. After one more week, the man turns to the woman and bellows: "Now, enough of this talk! Let's make love!"

At its fourth meeting, our group had reached the juncture of discontent with talk. In the session summary, one of the staff diagnosed the condition as follows:

> I think if we don't (get to work through the details of our projects) the group is going to get an increasing feeling that we aren't getting anywhere, that this is too vague and sort of bull-sessionish, and it's going to be very hard to conquer this, because sort of saying that there is some vague sense of something that we are carrying away, which is knowledge, ain't going to satisfy us. There's just so long that we can say "Gee, I'm getting a new look at this," without this getting a little unconvincing in our own minds.

This statement provided the stimulus for a frank explosion among the officers. One group member, who had previously declined to comment on the session, proclaimed:

> *Officer:* I'm at a point of really wondering just what the hell we're up here talking about. I think a good example is our discussion with the sergeant in the lounge before we came up today. The only thing that we could relate to this man about what we're doing, the only thing I could say was, "well,

our purpose is to see if there was some way, through research, that assaults that occur on the street, directed against police officers, can be proportionately cut down. I realize they can't be completely obliterated; it's impossible. But our purpose is to find some way, if any, of how to proportionately cut them down." Now, great, you know!

Officer 2: The next question is "How?"

Officer: Well, honest to God, I just sit here right now; I'm tired, I was argumentative tonight . . . I'm almost at a point of frustration, because I don't think we're getting anywhere. I don't know what to say. I don't know what we're trying to do, still! . . . I think what the staff is doing is sitting back on their laurels, and waiting for us to come up with what they want us to come up with anyhow. Now, wouldn't it be a shortcut if you just tell us what the hell you want, so we can get into it and maybe find out something! That's all I have to say.

Despite feelings of this kind, which were shared by other officers, the group had made progress on several fronts. For one, they had experienced an opportunity to test and revise a formal hypothesis. In reviewing incidents volunteered by one of the group, the officers had guessed that one of the suspects was violence-prone. The "rap sheet" was secured, and the hunch confirmed. Later, in another incident, the civilian proved to have a record clear of assaults. This finding produced an interest among the group in further investigation of police assaulters.

The session had also yielded a volunteer among the group for a trial interview, who was furnished the opportunity to explore alternatives to his actions. The officer, who had struggled with the temptation to defend his behavior, commented:

I feel that one thing that's got to be destroyed in part of us — in all of us to a great extent — is our automatic attitude of defending the officer's action. We identify very quickly with the officer; and I think we're going to have a tendency, to a great extent, to try to find reasons why the guy was right. I really don't want this totally destroyed in me, but nevertheless, I'd like to be able to have enough of it broken down so I can at least look at the problem objectively and say "well, damn it, the guy did make a mistake."

The staff tried throughout the session to deflect the group from the habit of evaluating (and therefore, defending) officer actions. In context of this struggle to arrive at a non-evaluative level of discourse, the idea for a critical incident questionnaire was born:

> I'm not going to argue with Officer Mills there about everything is good police practice, but I think George and I can agree that it would be kind of nice to find out what other officers think about what's good police practice. And I think we can do this; I think we have the imagination here among us, the way we talk, to build the instrument, to put down the incidents and the questions that relate to the incidents, so that we can find out what people think.

The staff also dealt throughout the session with the group's feelings about lack of progress. Exhortations had proved inadequate; to present predesigned projects was unthinkable. The alternative was to formally review project-ideas that had emerged to date. This procedure was implemented at the next session.

Prelude to Action

The fifth meeting started with a member of the staff commenting on his experiences while on patrol with one of the officers. He described the handling of several violence-prone incidents, and observed:

> I think the main thing I learned was I had an opportunity to watch some very effective, and quite consistent ways of reducing violence; a very definite kind of pattern, sort of strategy which I saw working. I also felt, and this is something which, I suppose, I ought to elaborate some other time, that it was a substantial learning experience for me in the same way, in reverse, I guess, as the group might be a learning experience for the group. I find it very hard to put down in writing now how much more I know about what it feels like to be involved in these situations as a patrolman, but I know a lot more about what it feels like. I'm quite intent on doing more of this — as much more of it as possible.

Following this feedback, the staff presented a description of research possibilities that had originated with the group. The group set to work. It initiated four projects: (1) it collected all arrest reports by one officer, and studied these for patterns; (2) it discussed a trial run with live recordings on the street; (3) it resolved to administer a critical incident questionnaire on police interventions, and (4) it resolved to interview the civilians (Hell's Angels) involved in a recent conflict with police.

The group expressed satisfaction with its progress, and with the staff feedback that initiated it. Bill, the officer who had exploded in the previous session, asserted:

> We had a guide to follow tonight when we came to work, and I think as a result we got a few more things done, and we had a little more direction than we've had in the past.

> *Officer 2:* We can thank the staff for that.

> *Staff:* Excuse me, but I think we can thank Bill and the comments when we left off Thursday; we had a mandate to be well organized.

With regard to each project, the group took concrete steps. In relation to the interviewing of suspects, the staff summarizer noted that there was

> the decision to bring in the officers and the Hell's Angels involved in the whatever-it-was last Saturday. Then we discussed the approaches and all that we would make for these interviews, and the number of people to be at the interviews. With the idea that this might, in the future — if it works out — become the going thing.

The questionnaire survey and the taping did not invoke enthusiasm, but the group decided to proceed with them. In the case of the taping,

> we talked about the use of the tape recorders, and while we did have a strong difference of opinion as to how they should be utilized, I got the feeling that the question here was, we ought to try it a number of ways and see which way it works out best for the group without any attempt to stick to one particular system during this trial period. I would still view it as a trial procedure. Then the group has to make the de-

cision as to whether it's fruitful or not. And we'll have an opportunity to run this test sometime this week.

A number of practical difficulties were discussed. The group resolved to notify other officers involved in taped incidents beforehand, to obtain their consent. In the case of the critical incident survey, the group discussed implications of the findings. As noted by a staff member,

> I think we have laid what one could over-fancily call a conceptual base for this critical incident survey. I'm not quite sure that we are all convinced of this being terribly worthwhile, but I think we have enough concensus here so that we can proceed. And it will be our first really formal research effort, in that this will call for the development of items, for the design of some kind of sampling procedure, for formal analysis in which we will be engaged; those of us in the group that have not done formal research before will be engaged in the kind of thing that is usually reserved for Ph.D.s.

The pattern analysis of the officer's reports yielded a number of hypotheses, which the officers thought plausible. One of the group commented:

> I think that we got a lot out of the reports tonight, at least I did. In studying a lot of reports from one particular officer, I think that you can see a pattern as to why he might be having some of the trouble that he's having out on the street. I think that it was a much better way to go about it than studying a lot of different officers' reports, and trying to get something from that. Just sticking to one man you get a much better view of it.

For the first time the officers analyzed incidents in terms of patterns, as opposed to merits or demerits of action. One officer argued:

> Maybe we ought to be getting off the kick of justifying every action that a police officer makes just because he is a police officer. We seem to be heading in that direction an awful lot. We spend an awful lot of time justifying what is done,

rather than finding some of the reasons for it.

The group was pleased with progress, but the labor of the session had none of the "honeymoon" flavor of the first meetings. A staff member summarized the phenomenon and extrapolated it by telling the group:

> It seems to me, we worked pretty hard. This session was probably a little less fun than some. On the other hand, I think we are off the kind of note of unhappiness we were on at the end of last session. In order to get off it, we had to sacrifice some entertainment, and I had to sacrifice some correct procedure and do a lot of pushing that I don't like to see myself do. But from here on in, I think we are working, and next time we will be forced to immediately go into the business of working out our interview if we discover that we have people available. And from 8:00 on, this group is going to turn into a research group, in the sense that it will actually be out there asking questions, getting answers; then we can think about them. The next day, Thursday, we can revise our procedure and our thinking in terms of what we've found the previous day, and again we'll be busy getting information and thinking about it.

The Travails of Planning

The next session brought another stage in a cycle which repeated itself, with variations, throughout our project. The joys of untrammalled debate had been followed by a call for action which resulted in working sessions. The latter usually proved taxing. Restless interludes were followed (as we shall see) with elation over achievement; this led to doubt over impact.

The sixth session was one that required detailed planning, and the group showed apprehension and boredom. A staff member summarized the sequence of events:

> We started the session by going over the tape recorder and its use, and there was a lot of joking about erasing and the procedures for erasing, and a lot of reluctance to talk into the tape recorder. There was a reiteration of the doubts in reference to the recording of other officers and even of recording incidents which we got yesterday in the last session.

... From the tape recorder we moved into the instrument, into the design of the critical incident instrument. The group went right to work on it. They produced a whole series of incidents, although at one or two junctures they got off into collateral discussions. . . . During that discussion two of the members of the group went down to the patrol division to make their contacts, and upon their return they reported that there had been some joking about the unit's role as a fink group. . . . When that discussion of fink-type joking was initiated, the whole range of public relations problems for the unit was broached. Some members of the group made the very sensible suggestion that the members ought to make themselves available for questioning at line-ups about the function of the unit. They also expressed some anxiety and interest relating to an Information Bulletin about the unit which was to be released soon.

The staff member analyzed the situation, as he saw it, for the group:

By and large, I think we can regard today's session as being 90% a working session. It's about the first time we've actually sat down and worked — other than, say, what happened yesterday when we looked over these reports. I was a little afraid, because by and large I know how boring this can be. I warned you about this last time; I warned you about this when we started. It's, on the one hand, obviously a little frustrating to just sit around and have a bull session, because you get the feeling you aren't getting anywhere, and we had this out last week. On the other hand, when you really move to respond to this, and you start saying, "well, let's not talk at all, and let's start working," this brings in another set of frustrations, and you have to face those. It's going to pan out, because as soon as we go on to the next step, we'll get information back, and when you get information back and you look at it, and it makes sense, and you have questions that are answered, that's where all this frustration looks less frustrating. But at the moment, when we're just kind of sitting around, worrying about thinking up incidents and how to word them, and so on, there is no immediate payoff.

The "payoff," as it happened, was relatively close at hand. In fact, it emerged during the next session.

The Fruits of Labor

In its seventh session, the group conducted (and analyzed) an interview with officers involved in the incident with the Hell's Angels. The group also reviewed the first version of its critical incident questionnaire.

The group emerged from the evening with the feeling that their mission had integrity, and that they could easily defend it. As one officer put it:

> There is a closer support of the staff and confidence in this new experiment or process. (We feel) that we are in fact moving forward toward an end product that we, I think, find mutually agreeable. The enthusiasm we had tonight was comparable to the first couple of times we were here. I think this enthusiasm brought us back to the realization that we haven't severed ourselves from the other officers, a feeling that was kind of . . . allayed tonight.

The cooperativeness of interviewees left the officers with a feeling of potency. One group member commented:

> I don't know that my enthusiasm ever did reach a terrible low point in this project. I guess I always hoped that something was going to come out of it. But after tonight I find that, although I may not be able to express it, that somehow I've got a renewed enthusiasm that there can be some good come out of this group and that there probably will be. I'm beginning to understand more why the staff have been so cagey with us, in perhaps letting us see this for ourselves, rather than telling us maybe what we can accomplish. No question in my mind that they had a lot that they hoped we could accomplish up here, and that they could have told us what they hoped we could accomplish. If they wouldn't have an idea what could be accomplished out of this there would have been no need for the project. After talking with these guys up here tonight, I think that maybe we all saw in that one incident, the Hell's Angels incident, that there was perhaps a very big alternative. And it renews my enthusiasm that something meaningful can come out of this.

The session also produced a research idea that was to occupy much attention at a later date. This idea arose during discussion with one of the interviewees, Officer Beam. As noted by the summarizer:

> One thing that we thought about and Beam brought it out himself, was the influence that the older officer has on the new officer, the training officer on the rookie officer. And I think we should and will take a long look into this aspect. Do we need to be more select in placing new officers?

The group tried hard to "sell" itself to its guests. In this effort, it met with partial success. The interviewees did "buy" the group's credibility, but not its concern with violence. The group, in turn (to maintain credibility), showed no inclination to argue the violence case, once the interviewees forcefully made their point:

> During the interview, the group took the opportunity to try to sell the four officers on the merits of the Violence Prevention Unit. They tried to sell it on the basis of it being an avenue to reach the Chief — and incidentally, the interviewees voiced all kinds of strong feelings about the administration. So one of the ways the group justified its existence was by characterizing itself as an effective avenue for the expression of grievances. There was also some talk of reducing violence, but the interviewees seemed to cut this short by voicing very strongly their views that violence was a function of the situation, and that the only way to deal with violence was to have adequate weapons and physical force and competent physical specimens — and that furthermore, violence isn't really necessarily bad. I mean, "why all this concern," was the question, "with riots"? The implication being that maybe a good riot isn't so bad after all.

The informal leader of the visiting team, Officer Beam, availed himself of the group forum to make a strong pro-violence statement. According to the summarizer, he

> talked almost continuously, and very volubly, and not only related two incidents in response to questions about them, but expressed himself at great length about his own philosophy with regard to interpersonal interactions, police work,

and responses to violence. There was a strong pitch about the necessity to meet force with force, to instill respect, to show power, to set precedents by moving into situations forcibly — the merits of direct physical action, the merits of hardware, the need for some kind of tactical force, and so on.

Members of our group listened to this statement with seeming reverence. A staff member later confessed his trepidation, wondering whether

Beam's pitch was so convincing that it could set us a month back. And as I was sitting here watching everybody nod their heads and say, "Isn't that true. Shit, isn't that exactly what it's like! Isn't it really true that we gotta go out there and display force in order to get them to respect us? And isn't it true that we gotta mount a machine gun on the rear fender? Ain't it a fact that the only thing these guys understand is a show of force?" There was a kind of nagging doubt in my mind about, gee, you know, we lost everything!

Although in its analysis of the interview the group returned to previous form, the lesson remained. The pull of the locker room had been felt. In the months to come, we would experience it repeatedly. We could build a subculture, but we couldn't, with equal ease, insulate and defend it. Contagion runs both ways. Change agents are subject to change, and to impact.

Review of Aims

The principal activity in the eighth session was identical to that of the previous day: the group interviewed officers involved in the Hell's Angels incident. This time the question of interview objectives was raised and cast a pall of gloom over the group.

The issue was posed by a staff member, who embarked on a talk about interviewing procedure early in the session:

I picked precisely the wrong moment to feed in some technical information about interviewing. The reasoning behind it was, "well, we're now in the process of interviewing; this is the time it would make most sense — while we're doing it." In fact, it backfired because what it very plausibly sounded like was a kind of critique of what happened yesterday.

The technical information was lost on the group (in the words of one officer, "most of it went over my head"), but the discussion did pose the question of aims and accomplishments. The group had rushed to embark on research. The aim (comparing police and suspect versions of an incident) had receded in favor of divergent, unverbalized ends. One of these was to "sell" the group; another to explore the philosophy of special duty officers; a third, fact-finding, and a fourth, group-thinking. Once this became obvious, the success of the previous evening's venture was less evident. As the staff summarizer noted:

> We did emerge, by virtue of this ambiguity of our objectives, into a kind of unhappy state where we were shouting at each other about what went wrong when in effect that is a question you can't really answer because you can't talk about what went wrong when you don't know what's going right.

Group morale was low. Interview-participants felt attacked and deprived of credit. Others demanded structure. One officer stated:

> I think it's about time we start getting down to the nitty gritty of what we're doing, go back a little ways, bring up what we have done, and perhaps this will give us some sense of what direction we're going to go. Now we've been here two months, and we've rambled on and on and on, and we've brought up a lot of problems, and we've brought up a lot of different areas that possibly will be applicable to this survey, but it's been two months, and we need something solid and concise to go on. We've been here eight times; I'm sorry, one month, and I think now we need to get things set down in concise terms as to where we have been, and where we're going to go.

The interview again went smoothly. It was lively, with much give and take. The exploration centered on "special duty" philosophy, and stimulated considerable discussion among the group. One of the officers volunteered to prepare a summary of interview content and conclusions. Another group member brought up the critical incident survey, and the group spelled out sampling and distribution procedures.

Two Steps Forward

The next session saw a rebirth of morale. The group witnessed a significant victory in the form of a good tape. A cassette recorder had been borrowed for experimental use, and one of the officers, Bill, had produced a powerful, pointed incident. Bill supplied explanatory comments, and the group added to them. Several officers suggested that the discussion, added to the tape, could make a useful, self-contained training tool.

The group spent several hours with the commander of the special duty unit whose members had been the previous week's guests. The officer had requested the interview under the impression that the group was interested in his unit. Although the time was tangentially invested, it proved satisfying. The interview went well, and the group was flattered by the opportunity of talking with a supervising officer:

> There's no question that everybody was very much with it. Again the group gave a number of testimonials to a guest about their own conversion and insight, and so on. And even when he sort of misunderstood and sidetracked, they returned to it to make sure he got the point. I think the group was also reinforced in that they saw that they were perceived as powerful outside. The questioning today was nowhere near as irrelevant as it was last week, in the sense that most of the questions that were asked were fairly incisive and to the point, and there wasn't any of the spurious agreeing with. It could have been extremely inviting. After all, the man who was here was a lieutenant.

The group also discussed definitions of the police mission (a subject re-opened by the interviews) and the Chief's problems in implementing his definition. The officers resolved to take up this question with the Chief at an early date.

A Happening

The next session proved to be a high point in the group's development. In line with previous plans, the suspects' version of the Hell's Angels incident was obtained, together with information about the motorcyclists' view of police, life and each other.

The officers felt that the interview was eye-opening, and that their guests (in particular, the Oakland chieftain of the Angels) were impressive spokesmen for their camp. One officer exclaimed, in the wake of the experience:

> I'm really at kind of a loss of words, because I'm so damned impressed with that Sonny! I can see why those guys look up to him, because, it seems to me that whatever in hell he decided to do in life, he would have been "A-1" at it. The guy makes a lot of sense. I'm very impressed with him. I'm not saying that I'm so sympathetic with the Hell's Angels that I'm seeing their side, and not the police side; that's not the case at all. The guy put forward a very frank and forthright presentation; his answers were very concise, very clear. Undoubtedly the guy lives and believes what he represents. I was very impressed with it. You know the full impact of it, I really haven't had time to think about it, and I'm sure that I will be giving a lot of thought to exactly what took place in this exchange of words in this interview.

Another group member confessed:

> You know our orientation as to what the Hell's Angels are. Before coming on the police department I heard about their big rape raids across small towns in the United States. When you first come into the department, going through rookie school, you hear various officers talk about them; nothing good is ever said. I was so surprised that a guy could sit there who is an outcast as far as society is concerned, that the guy could sit there and just speak so frankly and in such a way that everything he said, you could just hang on the word; the guy's got a hell of a way of expressing himself, and I guess the reason it is, is because it's so damned simple.

Some members of the group proposed a Hell's Angels session with recruits in the academy. One suggested a video-taped discussion. Another officer argued that veteran officers, like himself, could most benefit from group contact:

> I think it's too bad that more people couldn't have heard it besides us seven. I'm wondering if maybe the fact that it was so spontaneous in such a unique situation, if maybe this

wasn't. . . . I'm wondering if they went before a class of recruits or something I think something would be lost in it. Maybe not, but that's my opinion. I think something might be lost, and right this minute I think the most important thing isn't impressing a class of recruits, it's impressing the officer that's working the street now, like I was impressed.

The interview had gone extremely well as a technical effort. The men had spent the afternoon with a non-police group, and had created an atmosphere of cordial openness, in which much information was obtained. A staff member characterized the session as an "impressive exercise in communication and seeing the other guy's point of view." He added:

> Except for one little tense moment involving a little notice on the board, which was not meant for our guests, depicting police officers confronting eight motorcyclists with a legend such as "It's pretty lonely out there —" except for that, which they took with pretty good humor, there was really very little tension about this. An extremely free exchange. And I mihht say I was extremely impressed with the way we were able to question these people without being patronizing, hypocritical, or hostile. There were some questions asked that were quite sharp; the answers were frank. What we told them seemed to me to be quite frank.

A point noted by the summarizer was that, viewed as a subculture, the Hell's Angels had orientations and problems similar to some police officers, and particularly to the "special duty" officers with whom they had clashed:

> One point that we certainly got out of this, most of us got out of this, is that there are some parallels between Hell's Angel problems and police problems. That came through quite striking with points such as young Hell's Angels, young police officers; the code of brotherhood. And also we sensed, I think, that in some of the things they were describing, they could have been talking about one of the units in this department very aptly.

One officer said that in managing group problems, the Hell's Angels might, in some ways, be better socializers than their police counterparts:

He mentioned something to me that impressed me, that is diametrically opposed to how we think, how we act, and what we, in fact, do on the street. And that's when he brought up the fact that "when we see a guy out of line, we stop him, man, and kind of let him know that he's out of line." This is diametrically opposed to anything I've learned in six years, and it's opposed to what Sam has learned in all the time he's been on the force. I'm wondering if it might not be a good idea. I think that it could be done in such a way, that Bill brought up plenty of times up here, or a few times up here, that he's maybe saved somebody's ass, or maybe saved some policeman from getting the grease by very tactfully and unnoticed grabbing some guy and getting him the hell away from there. We make mistakes; I've made mistakes; everybody here has. Just like Sonny Barger said, the whole Hell's Angels group has to suffer because of one man's mistake. We have to suffer because if I get in the shit, and Sam and Bill have to come in and bail me out, they're not going to be happy if I'm wrong; then they have to ride my heat too. We brought it up, but it's something to think about.

The success of the experiment did not blind the group to the need for planning further activity. They scheduled interviews to document their case for more systematic assignment of training officers. They discussed recruit training innovations to improve the sophistication of young officers in the human relations area. They also talked about questionnaires.

A Rebirth of Anxiety

In their next session, the group prepared itself to meet the Chief the following night. In the context of worry about the Chief's reaction, the group became concerned about its effectiveness to date. Once again, Bill was the catalyst of discontent. It was noted in the summary that

When we were talking about our discussion with the Chief tomorrow night, Bill made a statement that kind of kicked off a good deal of discussion and kind of brought us back to that third or fourth session when we started saying, "Where in the heck are we going?" It seems kind of surprising that it would pop up at this time, but Bill said that if the chief asked him what we've accomplished down here, he says he wouldn't know what to tell him, and I think it probably made us all start thinking, "well, what the heck would we tell him what we've accomplished down here?" Then it kind of gave us the idea and a little bit of worry that, "son of a gun, have we really accomplished anything?" I know I think it kind of affected me that way to a certain extent, and I find myself wanting to charge ahead and act on a lot of proposals that have been made, a lot of ideas that I thought were kind of held in the balance.

It seemed plausible that such worries were inspired by awe of the Chief, but they took the form of complaints about progress. The staff faced these complaints by reviewing the group's work and its plans:

With his (staff) summary of the things that we do have in the fire that have not really been pushed to the wayside, I think perhaps it kind of made us feel like, feel better about what we had accomplished up here, of what we may accomplish.

The men spent part of the session interviewing an officer who had a high incident of conflict experiences. The interview was a model of self-study. The interviewee — a young man with some graduate school — was articulate in thinking about himself. He produced a number of observations, one of which related to the impact of training on his own development. The officer's testimonial renewed the group's enthusiasm for its study of training officer assignments:

It seemed to be in Joe's mind that the training officer will cause many lasting impressions in the new officer's method of operation on the street. Joe can see a lot of merit in properly selected and properly trained training officers. He seemed to indicate to me that he changed after four years, or during the four-year span of time, kind of by the trial and error method.

Group morale was raised by the interview, and by the discussion it inspired. But the men remained concerned throughout by their impending talk with the Chief.

An Identity Crisis

The summer was at its mid-point, and the group had progressed far in its development. It had identified with program goals and had isolated relevant parameters. It had come to view its context in terms of critical junctures for impact and change. It had asked questions and obtained data.

Throughout, the group had struggled with its role. It felt itself powerful, but saw no impact; it viewed itself as productive, but saw no products. It felt itself needed, but had no praise. In the context of this crisis, the Chief's presence was propitious and ominous. Too much was at stake, and too little was possible. The hidden agenda of the session made demands that were unreasonable and doomed.

The Chief witnessed hunches rather than data; he faced crude ideas and hopes for change. He saw a group in search of a mission. His role was that of a creditor whose clients had prospects, but little collateral. Given this fact, the Chief did the best he could. He urged the group to proceed; he shared thoughts about the department and its fate; he testified to faith, and he expressed hope.

The group felt deflated, without knowing why. One of the staff observed that

> The Chief responded, it seemed to me, perfectly frankly, in terms of what went on in his mind, from the vantage point of his desk, to some general questions we raised. The fact that he was doing so here, and the fact that he was putting so much effort into it, could conceivably have been seen as a positive feature; instead I think it sort of made us increasingly depressed. I don't quite understand why.

The session was contaminated by the group's depression. The group interviewed the sergeant of a special duty unit, without knowing, or caring, why. While waiting for their guest, they listened to tapes which had been recorded under unsatisfactory acoustical conditions. One incident had been recorded over, and the rest was static. The experience was described as a "waste" or "minor tragedy".

The sergeant, who had requested the session, appeared in a friendly and expectant mood. The group had no questions, and the sergeant made a statement, throughout which the men sat preoccupied. There was a long silence, which one officer broke by inquiring about the Hell's Angels incident, which had been reviewed on four previous occasions. While the sergeant covered the ground once again, the men doodled. At length an officer inquired, pointedly, about the prevalence of violence among the sergeant's men. The interview ended and the sergeant left.

Bill, who had been one of the most obviously depressed members of the group, reviewed his role, and came close to an apology:

> *Bill:* I don't know if I've been a disruptive influence on this group for the last couple of days. I think I have, for some reason, fiddley-fucking around with a piece of paper while Jack's trying to summarize, which isn't really very cute for a grown man.
>
> *Jack:* It's all right — it's all right.
>
> *Bill:* No, but I'll tell you what. Maybe I've let a few personal problems I happen to have lately in to sort of push this thing out of my mind, and I've lost a hell of a lot of enthusiasm for some reason, I don't know why. I don't want to. But maybe like Waterman says, if we can get down and start producing something concrete, it'll come back. And that was a real boring, shitty night, as far as I'm concerned, and practically a complete waste of time. And like I say, I don't know why.

Other members of the group were equally puzzled, but saw some hope. They called for project-related work, and resolved once more to move ahead.

Task Force Activity

Officer Waterman, the group's conscience, had called for small task-related work groups. He had proposed that

> I'd like to spend some of this time instead of talking and interviewing, I'd like to go to smaller groups and sit down and get some of this stuff down on paper. I'm a paper man when it comes to projects. I would really like to pursue this training officer thing. . . . And we've all bitched about this radio room for as long as we've been on the street; we've told our sergeant about it, sometimes we've bitched about it

on the air; we've called him up on the telephone so mad
and told him, the dispatcher, off over the phone because
we couldn't do it over the air. Here's a chance maybe to do
something about it, and I'd like to get down to the nitty-
gritty. I really would.

In line with this proposal, the group divided into subgroups,
and worked on the training officer study, the idea of a radio room
survey, the technical problems of tape recording, and the analysis
of the questionnaire pretest.

Progress was made on each front. The critical incident group
diagnosed a communication gap within the department on the
basis of supervisor-subordinate differences. They discussed special
uses for the instrument, involving a number of target groups:

It was brought out that it could be sort of found where the
communication gap lies, if any, between the DC and the
Chief, the Deputy Chief to the Captain to the lieutenants
down to the sergeants and the patrolmen; whether or not
the patrolman was reacting in a way that the sergeant wanted
him to react, or in other words, differences of opinion; if
these differences between particular sergeants exist and
influence subordinates that work under them. And the patrolmen, just giving it to them in a straight way, and then giving
it to them and having it filled out on the premise of "What
do you think the Chief would want you to do?" to find out
if there's a lack of knowledge as far as the Chief's policies
are concerned. It sounds kind of garbled. Then we brought
out that it could be given to special groups, rookies that are
just on the street, and Sam came up with the idea, or somebody did, that it'd be kind of interesting to find out what
they'd put down on this thing. Then, of course, time on the
job would have something to do with it, and the high 148s,
guys that we've talked to, especially from — that do have
a high rate of 243 and 148, and to see if their answers are
a little different.

The live taping group explored ways of editing material, and
devised a "sound-on-sound" technique for the processing of incidents. Waterman, whose avocation is electronics, became director
of the project:

We talked a little bit about the ways of transcribing these tapes, and dubbing information into them to make the critical points in the incident more meaningful. We talked about whether to do this by a stop-and-go process; in other words, play a part of the incident, then when we reach a critical point in the incident, where maybe it turns to violence, or where violence was averted, stopping the incident tape and dubbing in by voice sort of an explanation of what occurred there from, say, from what we've learned up here about the way people react. This is one way we talked about it; another way that might be meaningful was discussed as to whether or not to try the sound on sound technique of bringing the incident in kind of full bore, so that the whole incident can be heard, not the whole incident, but the critical points of the incident, and then kind of fading the incident into the background and bringing the narrator's voice in till it's in the foreground; in other words, when the narrator's being heard, the listener will still have the psychological effect of hearing the incident going on in the background, much like these narrative shows in TV do. I feel personally that it wouldn't be too hard to do with sound-on-sound type equipment, and I brought up the point that I have some rather nice recorders at home where this type of thing can be carried out, and I'm perfectly willing to make a few experiments at home, not only by myself, but anybody else who wants to come over and kind of tinker around; we may try this technique. It may be more entertaining to the rookie sitting in the classroom listening to it in this manner.

The total group felt encouraged (with one caveat):

Officer: Well, I think overall for tonight, we've gotten more done just from the standpoint of deciding what we're going to do, and then getting right down to the nitty-gritty of planning it out. I saw a renewed enthusiasm from this standpoint, that we were getting down to doing something of what we're here for.

Sam: Well, I'd like to go on record as saying that I can't stand that word "NITTY-GRITTY"!

Officer: Strike "nitty-gritty."

Officer Waterman, the organizer of the subgroup procedure, predicted continued progress:

Seriously speaking, last Thursday I thought was a catastrophe. I think everybody here thought it was a catastrophe. Today I came in very sleepy, you know? I wasn't really looking forward to. . . . No, I feel we've got something that we're all going to be sinking into from here on out; at least for a couple days, the enthusiasm is going to be renewed.

But not all was auspicious. The Oakland police were facing strike possibilities, and several of the men were worried. The officers were also in an oddly humorous mood: Bill talked of mass resignations, and someone mentioned firing the staff. In a more serious vein, the issue of locker room reputation had again risen:

Joe brought in an incident which I think is worth mentioning. He was present in a situation in which an officer had become a little impatient with a suspect, and Joe found himself forced to exercise a little calming action. Then it developed that another officer present at the scene took it upon himself to misrepresent Joe's participation in a way which could conceivably partly reflect on Joe's membership here. Now I guess that we decided that there probably was no immediate connection between the repercussions of the incident and Joe's membership in this unit. We decided, I think, that this was probably the backwash of an interpersonal difficulty, a personality conflict. But on the other hand, it gave rise to a series of comments that have to do with the reason why Joe brought this up here, namely that there is a question of what does our role here imply in terms of how we are seen, and what does it imply in terms of the strategy we have to follow in order to be able to do what we feel we ought to do? But I think, at an even more significant level, what it implies is that some of us, at least — and I think many of us here feel that in some way — if we haven't changed our thinking, at least we have articulated it a little more, so that what we have to cope with is not what people think of us as members of this unit, but what we have to do in order to cope with what we feel is new and different about the way we think.

Despite these ambivalences, the next session (the fourteenth) went smoothly. Members of two subgroups embarked on individual research assignments. One officer interviewed the commanding official of the training division, while his subgroup drew up criteria for training officers. The radio room task force embarked on interviews with dispatchers, and on observations of the radio room (including the monitoring of calls). The group also began to prepare a flow chart of the dispatching process.

The questionnaire group, temporarily unemployed, spent its time reviewing the design of the entire project. In response to inquiry from one of the officers, a staff member shared the project proposal with the group, and delineated the men's role as trainers in the next stage of the study. The subgroup began to discuss the procedure for selecting trainees and control groups:

> One of the biggest things that we discussed in my opinion was how are we going to get these people up here, the second group which will be seventeen people that are violence prone? And then we have another group that we are going to watch, that we aren't going to do anything with that are also violence-prone, for comparison. We discussed how we are going to get them up.

The entire group met briefly for status reports, declared itself satisfied, and disbanded.

Diminishing Returns

The fifteenth session was reserved for subgroup reports to the total group. It went badly. The bulk of the discussion turned on the need to revise some of the questionnaire items. Several hours were invested in rewording four questions, and the task was boring. An effort to add one question to the instrument, which consumed thirty minutes, proved fruitless. Bill, a member of the questionnaire task force, felt particularly despondent, in part over the redundancy involved in the group's review of subgroup work:

> But then again I feel that when we sat in here for five hours and went over these things, that we were much more aware of what we were doing and what we wanted to do and that it was just as impossible for the others to come in here and to jump right in and understand the whole picture as it would have been impossible for us to jump right in and understand their study of the radio dispatcher or the training officer, because we just didn't spend that much time talking about it.

Staff expressed some worry about group morale:

> But I do think in general the fact of the matter is that we need to think of some way of enlivening the situation here with some variety. I mean, we have responded to the call for complete tasks. That gets us into a lot of routine. I think maybe it's about time we swung the pendulum back pretty soon and got into something which is a little more interesting, and then got back to our tasks.

The officers had not reached a complete "low," but made it obvious that they were bored. During the last hour, which called for the summary, the men abstained:

> The group was most blatant tonight in a growing tendency to shut off the shared discussing and summarizing during the last hour of the day's session. It reached a point tonight where it was made blatantly clear around the table that none of the officers were to contribute anything, and indeed that was almost 100% the way it worked out. The staff made the main statements that were made and only upon being called upon directly did Bill add anything to the discussion.

The session ended early, on a restless note.

The Feel of Success

The next session (the sixteenth) was a stormy one, but suffused with enthusiasm. Closure had been reached on several projects, and the men were happy with their achievements. The questionnaire group had a draft of their instrument, and a design for its administration. The tape group had produced an incident which inspired a stimulating analysis session. The dispatcher group presented an impressive draft report.

Controversy arose with respect to the training officer project. Several objections were raised to the criterion list, including a demand by staff for more emphasis on human relations skill. Waterman, as spokesman for the task force, replied very heatedly. Another officer (Bill) played a conciliatory role:

> I got kind of hot last night about somebody talking about or criticizing what we had done in here on this questionnaire

thing when we had spent four hours. I didn't think it was
right for anyone to come in here and in five minutes kind of
rip me apart. So I've got a lot of sympathy for Hank, because
you guys have really worked your tails off in there apparently and really thought this thing over. You've done a lot of
hard work on it and I'm appreciative of it. I think it'll work
out and we certainly don't expect you to come in here and
everyone to agree with everyone else.

Waterman, who had agreed to review the criterion list again,
stressed the group-product aspect of the projects:

I was somewhat offended by what occurred after I finished
reading these criteria. I don't feel I could — I guess I was in
a way. Like Bill said, this was my baby, but in a way this
whole thing is my baby, too, everything that's happening in
this unit. It was a response that I didn't expect. I by any
means didn't expect staff's response, and I don't think he
expected mine. Anyway, I just wanted to point out that this
whole field training officer thing is a group effort of the
whole subcommittee, both phases of it so far, as the additional phases will be.

Both the negative and positive reactions showed ego-involvement
of officers in the projects with which they had been concerned.
Each subgroup member became an advocate of his group's effort.
A staff member recalled that

When we started the tape-recorded incident today, there
was a lot of restlessness and a lot of kind of sighing and sitting back with a pained expression on their faces. But when
they heard the results, they became quite sold, and of course
it is significant that Young, whose incident it was and who
was the main participant, was especially sold. He was quite
anxious after the session to inquire how do we incorporate
this into group training and so on. The same thing happened
with these other projects. For instance, Bill, who is by no
means gullible, has become extremely sold in the critical
incident study to the point of seeing all kinds of applications
of it that are even vague to me. Both he and Sam have been
trying to sell this instrument to the rest of the group, where
at least Bill, before he became involved in tabulating the

responses, was asking questions like "what the hell good is this?"

The men were generally pleased, and looked forward with vociferous anticipation to early tangible products.

The Group Has a Guest

The seventeenth session was spent with a visiting expert, Chief Fred Ferguson of the Covina (California) police. The staff had invited the Chief because of his role as innovator, particularly as the originator of ingenious training techniques. The Chief's men had participated in role playing on the street, including a stint as jail inmates and a night as make-believe skidrow alcoholics. Chief Ferguson related these experiments, and the group listened with interest and enthusiasm. In turn, the men broached their own activities to the Chief.

The group's reaction to Chief Ferguson is illustrated by comments such as:

> Quite possibly we should have had Chief Ferguson in here when we first started, because he is quite dynamic. He does something new and different every day, or I get that idea. We started on a project here that's never been tried before and I think it would have been helpful to us to have gotten his views early in the game.

> I feel that this man has an awful lot to offer law enforcement. Apparently, I don't know how many people around here have even heard of him. I never had until he came here. That's probably my fault. It was really a pleasure to listen to him, and it was also a pleasure to be associated with somebody of his calibre, and I'd like to thank the staff again for bringing this man here. If you've got any more like him we'd sure like to see them.

The techniques discussed by Chief Ferguson proved of considerable interest. Bill — a natural mimic — became especially taken by role playing as a training technique:

> I can see a lot more use in this role playing as a training method now that I've talked to him and I really would like

to go and see it. I think it would be an asset to the group; and like I was telling Joe — he couldn't believe it — I'd go down there on my own time and pay my own way down. I really would. I'm that interested in it.

Chief Ferguson, in turn, was impressed with the group's work and with their enthusiasm. The officers talked about specific projects, each emphasizing the work with which he was most closely associated. One officer stated:

The interesting thing to me about this last hour, for instance, is that if we had this guy here two weeks ago, and if we had gone around the table and we had described the group to him, we would have said all kinds of things about what we were doing here, none of which was said. And it wasn't only that we have the most recent experiences in mind when we think about what we do here, but also that we seem to be very involved in the projects that we are associated with. And each one of us, I think, is most strongly attached to the project that he is immediately involved in.

Chief Ferguson had planned to stay for half the session, but was sufficiently impressed to spend seven hours with the men. He left with parting remarks concerning the "power" of the group.

An Unsuccessful Exercise

The next session began with a review by staff of the outline for the second phase of the project. The group was almost exclusively concerned with the manner in which they would introduce the project to the Stage-Two trainees:

Step one would be to introduce the program to these people, to put out a sales pitch to them, to let them know that violent experiences are an asset as well as a liability, I would suppose, and that we're neither condemning nor condoning these violent-type situations. Also, that we don't want anyone fired. It was kind of agreed that this would be a very good pitch, that we felt anyone who is having these problems, if he's a good officer, he's worth saving. He's worth helping him keep his job.

The staff emphasis in the outline was on the final stages, in which the participants were scheduled to review their own incidents and to work out new coping skills. One officer volunteered as a subject to help demonstrate the self-analysis process. He was cooperative, but the demonstration failed. The subject, Sam, short-circuited the analytic process and produced plausible, ready-made explanations for his past involvements:

> You can't win them all. I think one difficulty with working with Sam is that he has already thought about this stuff so effectively himself that there is no analysis to be done, really. We didn't need to go over a single incident, for that matter; and we didn't really, very effectively, because Sam already had the pattern all worked out . . . I would say we could all at this point enumerate various aspects of Sam's involvement which, with anybody else, it would have taken us a good long solid cross-examination to even start to suspect.

One interesting sidelight evolved as a residue of the previous session. Sam had declared himself incapable of role playing, and was goaded by Bill into a display of short but unplanned anger. He confessed that

> in what Bill was doing — this role playing on a small scale — he did raise me up. For a second there he got me going a little bit, which was spontaneous. He did a very good job of it. I think there's a lot of merit in what he did and the way he did it.

Another positive event in an otherwise dreary session emerged from a tape played by one of the officers. This tape provided an excellent recording of excerpts from a session in which the officer had dissuaded a motel guest from committing suicide:

> We played Joe Young's recording at the Thunderbird, where he helped this fellow with the solution to his money problems and turned a real sympathetic ear to the guy, perhaps helping him to work out his emotional problems as well. At one point staff stopped the recorder and asked Joe if this is police work. I think we all agreed that it is police work. My own thoughts on this is that we go out and catch a burglar for instance, and we take two or three

hours sometimes to write up the reports and tie up the loose ends and get the evidence. I think the possibility of a man losing his life, or the fact of possibly saving a man's life is possibly worth the two hours that Joe stated he spent on this particular call.

The remainder of the session was perceived as relatively unproductive, and was terminated early.

Intensive Work

The next two sessions were spent in project-related activity, partly in task forces. The group's concern in the first session was mainly the tape project, and in the second, the questionnaire results. The taping discussion was initiated by Officer Waterman, who had prepared an impressively edited incident:

I showed up a little late for work with some tapes that I'd been working on until about 4:30 — a tape I was working on. During the past couple of days I've been working on this sound-on-sound technique. Actually, what I wanted to do was to make a tape that would demonstrate the process of using sound-on-sound and keeping the incident phased down in the background so you could still hear the incident at the same time you were hearing the explanation. Much to my surprise, it came out better than I'd really expected. I came up with an almost finished product. Perhaps it needs a little bit of editing, but it turned out very well. What I did was I took two incidents that I recorded over the weekend from our little SONY portable recorder, and from that recording I made a tape in one track of one of my stereo recorders. I used the other stereo recorder; I jacked the incident from one recorder into the first track of the recorder that I was doing the composite tape on and hooked the microphone into the other track. As I went along recording the incident, at certain points I would just use the volume control on the track that had the recorded incident in it and phase it down to a low level and just speak into the microphone some explanations of what was going on at that time, some descriptive explanation.

The results were impressive. As Bill describes them,

Although it was quite some time after the incident happened, you still got the feeling that he's like a newsman standing out where Rome is burning or some goddam thing and he's telling you all about it.

The taping group discovered, as the evening wore on, that it had the beginning of a respectable library:

We spent the whole evening listening, first of all to this composite tape that I'd put together, and then after that we went through three cassettes that were recorded by Bill and our two Joes. We found that we had a good variety of incidents — much more than we expected from our previous experiences.

The subgroup made a determined effort to communicate its enthusiasm to the other officers, and to promote more tapes. Bill argued:

It's probably hard for the guys that are in the other room to get real enthused with this, because you haven't done anything with it. You've been working with training officers and radio room projects and you've been real involved in these things where we've been involved here, and it's hard in turn for us to get enthused about what you're doing. But we've really got something in these tape recordings, in these critical incidents that we're putting down on tape. It's going to be something that's going to really be a fantastic first. It's going to be a hell of a training tool. But we're going to have to have everybody's cooperation. Now I've been guilty of leaving that thing in the locker myself. But with this sound-on-sound we've got something that's really going to be good, it's really going to be worthwhile.

Bill also reasoned that the dramatic impact of the edited tapes should be a motivator among second-generation trainees:

Another thing that just crossed my mind is that it's not only a training tool, but if we can work these things up interestingly enough this is going to be a real good thing for involvement next summer, when we get these guys up here. Because if the tapes sound good enough and wild enough, and interesting enough, they're going to want to take that goddam recorder out and do the same thing. I would.

On a more low-key note, the subgroups concerned with the dispatchers and the training officer study reviewed outlines of their reports. They anticipated having completed drafts ready for editing at the next meeting.

During the next session the reports were written, despite the fact that some time was required for coding of the questionnaire. At the end of the session, the studies were ready for editing and presentation to the Chief. The critical incident data had been coded. The tabulations showing intra-departmental differences were summarized by the subgroup.

Stage Fright

The group began its penultimate session by scheduling task-force presentations for the next afternoon. According to the staff summarizer,

> We started off with going over our schedule with Chief Gain tomorrow and outlined a program that we'll present to him. Chronologically we'll begin at 2:30 in his conference room. The field training officer will be gone into. It's printed up in a nice form, I was really impressed with it and from what I've read of it, I think you did a real good job on it, for what that's worth. At three o'clock the training tapes will be presented to him. And at 3:30 we'll go into the questionnaire results. At four o'clock the dispatcher study will be presented. At four-thirty, the Chief will be down here and we're going to have a group discussion with him. We might even get into what we're going to do next summer with the Chief, if we can and if he's interested.

Planning was followed by a discussion, led by the staff, of eight principles of group dynamics, as summarized by Cartwright. The group considered each principle in relation to its own activities and those of prospective second-phase trainees. The discussion went well until dinner-time, but was then discontinued. Instead, the group wallowed in cynicism, pessimism and doubt. As one officer (Mills) put it:

> I can think of very little — nothing right now — that has

been acted upon that came out of the patrolman's line-up.
I will be very happy if anything comes out of this, but like I
say, I'm not going to jump into this thing 100% and bust my
ass on it and get all worked up about it until I see that there
is going to be some good that comes out of it. I really don't
understand how anybody could be that optimistic and how
they could throw themselves into a project 100% without
knowing that it was going to be acted upon. It's been very
hard for me to get with this program, as you probably know.

The men took turns making statements in which they emphasized
the need for the Chief to accept their recommendations:

Officer 1: Now when you ask these guys to change in the
streets and you just sit there and say "if you don't change
you're going to get punished," it just means that they'll figure
out another way to do it. That's all. But if you show them at
the same time you're asking them to make these changes that
Chief Gain is going to make some changes in the department
that are favorable to patrolmen, to make it nice, to make it
a little bit better, that he's coming around and he's going to
listen to patrolmen, this is going to be very important. And
I believe it's very relevant to what's going on here. You're
interested in violence; I'm interested in departmental change,
too. I think the two go hand in hand. If you have a department that's changing and it's because of patrolmen — like if
you bring these guys up here with the idea that they're here
because they are the reason for the necessary changes, it's
not going to work. If you bring them up here and you tell
them, "we're bringing you up here to help us make the
changes" it's going to work. . . . And then it's going to be
much easier next year to get these guys up here. Because
they're going to see it not only as a group that's studying violence. They're going to see us as a group that's doing something within the department. And they're going to see themselves when they walk in as being in a position of being able
to do something also, which is important, something constructive, something directly related to what they're doing
down there.

Officer 2: Now if we can show that we're successful in having some recommendations accepted by the Chief, that we

as a group are successful, then it will lead these other people to believe that they can be successful. If we fail they're
going to believe that they're going to fail. Therefore, they're
not going to work on these projects, and why should they
work on them? Now if they're not working on these projects,
what are they going to do up here? They're not going to work
on projects unless we show them that we're successful. If
we tell them about five projects that we worked on here and
we had a lot of fun and we documented a lot of stuff here . . .

The group was concerned about impact. The men had labored
hard, invested much, and were hopeful and afraid. They needed
acceptance, but could not risk assuming it. Unable to express hope,
they instead voiced their fears.

A Full Measure of Success

The subgroups met with the Chief all afternoon, and the Chief met
with the total group, briefly. The Chief's reaction throughout was
unambiguously positive, and the men were stunned.

One surprise stemmed from the fact that wherever written material had been available, the Chief had studied it. As one of the men
put it:

Jack and I met with the Chief on the field training officer
study. He had a copy of the study beforehand and as he indicated later, he read it in some detail. I don't know about
Jack, but I was totally surprised at his first reaction. He
indicated to us that he thought we had a heck of a good thing
here and that we'd researched it and we'd come up with
some real good ideas, which right off the bat gave us the impression that he'd bought the program in totality — and in
effect, at this point he has.

The men also discovered that the Chief was determined to give
them a role in implementing their proposals:

He threw the ball right back to us: "You guys have got it
started, now we're going to go into — you can follow it
through by doing the staff study routine". . . I think what
he's saying to us in effect, you know, "you've come up with

a good thing here, and you're familiar with what you want, and if we just hand this paper to somebody else and have them working on it, that a lot of your ideas are going to be lost. Since you are familiar with it, it's more or less your responsibility to go into the staff studies and to learn that these things are feasible or not feasible and keep as many of the points in your original proposal as possible, in the end product." Although he's thrown the ball to us to get this thing going, I think . . . we've impressed him with this thing to the point that he's willing to give us the responsibility of carrying this thing on through.

The Chief had thought of possible extensions of the project, and had proposed these as further group activities:

Another ball he kind of threw to us just in passing, which I don't really think I got the impact of until later, although I think I turned to Jack and thought "Oh my God, now what are we getting into," was the fact that he was talking about what the course content should be for this field training officer training class. There were some little words passed there to give me the impression that we may be involved in writing the program, what's going to be taught the field training officers.

The Chief's reaction to the data the officers showed him was similar to his thoughts about the proposals:

He thought of all these things that this could be used for, which I thought was very good. And he said he's very interested to see further analysis of this thing by putting out more of these. I did mention we were going to do it. In critiquing, for instance, feedback-wise in the recruit academy. He said he would be very interested to know just what point they were at in the academy when they fill out the questionnaire, and the study material that had been covered when this questionnaire was given to them, because there was an obvious ignorance of the particular laws that were involved in some of these incidents.

The Chief admitted that some of the material presented to him was new information:

> I feel that the Chief was very surprised at the results of the questionnarie. It was pointed out to him — I got in kind of late on this thing, but it was pointed out in the analysis that we had done and Carl presented to him that there was a very great difference in a lot of his thinking and policies and what was going on in the department. His indication was more or less amazement, I guess, that so many people had made arrests in some areas that he could see no legal basis for. We both pointed out to him that this was happening all the time and it was more or less accepted in some areas.

The Chief also appeared pleased with the competence demonstrated by the officers. A staff member who had observed the Chief's reaction commented:

> I think all of the studies, all of the presentations, did convince the Chief — something he may have thought of or not — but convinced the Chief of the ability of patrolmen given time and inclination to do staff studies and make recommendations within this department. And this came up very strongly and it sort of bubbled to the top in regard to his comments, in regard to "well, maybe I ought to detach all you people and put you to work on specific projects."

The group, following their meeting, expressed themselves relieved, stunned, and elated. The session had the air of a victory celebration. It had drawn the group closer and had made it aware of its mission and its responsibilities for the future. In the words of Bill:

> I don't know whether it's been a real pleasure or not. I think we said before, it's a hell of a lot easier to go out on the street for 16 hours and kind of do our thing on calls in a relaxed, nice atmosphere. Because this has been a lot of work. It's been a good experience for me, because I'm lacking in formal education and I probably got something here that I would never have gotten otherwise. And I am appreciative of everybody here, especially of the staff members. It's been

a good association. There's been a lot of name-calling and a lot of kidding, and I think most of it has really been in jest on my part. My sardonic, morose attitude isn't bad all of the time. Generally I feel very close to you assholes, and I'm looking forward to seeing you again next summer.

The Group's Summer Profile

FIGURE 1: Morale Level for 1969 Summer Session

Session	Level of Morale			
	Low	Medium	Medium High	Very High
1. In-depth analysis of police problems			■	
2.				■
3. Endorsement from the Chief				■
4. Unhappiness about lack of structure and purpose	■			
5.			■	
6. Boring clerical work		■		
7. Completed group interview				■
8. Doubts about objectives of interview	■			
9.			■	
10. Informative interview				■
11.		■		
12. Group identity crisis	■			
13.			■	
14.			■	
15. Boring clerical work		■		
16. Completed sub-group work				■
17. Stimulating consultant				■
18. Unsuccessful interview		■		
19.			■	
20.			■	
21. Anxiety about Chief's acceptance of proposals	■			
22. Completed projects presented to Chief				■

FIGURE 1A

| Name | Date |

SESSION RATING FORM

Check (✔) the appropriate box

	Very High	High	Average	Low	Very Low
Productivity					
Interest					
Group Participation					
My Own Participation					
Group Morale					
My Own Morale					

CIRCLE THE ADJECTIVES THAT DESCRIBE TODAYS SESSION:

Academic	Fun	Promising	Instructive
Enjoyable	Torture	Thought Provoking	Bland
Sick	Monotonous	Critical	Silly
Sensible	Relevant	Creative	Helpful
Beautiful	Wasteful	Phoney	Informative
Constructive	Pleasant	Puzzling	Frustrating
Challenging	Painful	Aimless	
Inconclusive	Unfair	Enlightening	Damaging
Slow	Immoral	Great	Confusing
Purposeful	Subversive	Nonsense	Encouraging
Uninformative	Strange	Weakening	Pointless
Valuable	Practical	Sane	
Hopeless	Sad	Weird	
Rambling	Honest		
Annoying	Exasperating		
Inspiring	Tense		
Irritating	Dry		

USE BACK OF PAGE FOR ANY ADDED COMMENTS:

We had attempted no formal measurement of group process and morale. To trace progress through the summer, we resorted to a rough content analysis of session summaries. Figure 1 depicts the profile resulting from this review and Figure 1A the form designed for systematic monitoring of subsequent sessions.

Figure 1 shows much variability. It shows a fever curve alternating between "high" and "low." We see a possible "Thursday Slump" syndrome: three of four "low" days fall on Thursdays, as do the majority of combined "very highs" and "highs." On the other hand, "very high" Thursdays outnumber "very high" Wednesdays.

More significant may be the nature of the task (or absence of task, or anticipated task) facing the group. High profile points seem to involve (1) substantial group efforts yielding immediate new information, and (2) products of long-term group activity. Group morale hinges on documented group achievement.

Conversely, low morale seemed related to (1) difficulties in seeing a purpose in group activities; (2) worry about the place of group products in a larger context; (3) unsuccessful effort and (4) work in which the product was not as yet available. Low morale seems tied to the unsatisfied need for documented achievement.

The cycle of group development appears to comprise (1) elation over learning from a new activity, (2) doubts over the significance of new learning, (3) evolution of re-defined new tasks, (4) involvement and contentment, (5) restlessness over the lack of tangible product, (6) elation over a product and (7) worry about the significance of product.

Several personal roles had evolved in the group. There was a "group barometer" (Bill) whose moods anticipated and stimulated feelings; there was a "group superego" (Waterman) whose responses to non-directionality catalyzed activity; there was an "agent of reassurance" (Sam) who promoted faith through optimism. The group also contained a "group skeptic" (Mills) and a "group amuser" (Young), although such functions were exercised by all group members. A final stabilizing element was the "group editor" (Jack) whose tolerance for paper work overrode the restlessness of his peers.

The officers had acted as a problem-oriented group, and progressed in logical sequence. They had indulged in problem-definition, formulated questions, obtained data, analyzed it, drawn inferences and initiated implementation. The change process was thus mobilized, and the stage set.

3 • Suspended Motivation

The training cycle for our officers ended September 1969. The next ten months provided a test of survival capacity for the group, as well as an opportunity to firm up projects and plan the second phase of the study.

The period was one of comparative inactivity. Some officers who were assigned to staff work went about their solitary business. Routine tasks, such as taping and tape-editing, were sporadically engaged in. The group met every two weeks for a summary and planning session. The rest of the time the men discharged their duties as working patrolmen.

One strategy we employed to keep the officers motivated was to arrange presentations for them at regional workshops and national meetings. Observers reported favorably on these talks, and the men enjoyed them. The talks themselves gave the officers a chance to conceptualize their experience, as well as to reaffirm its importance.

Two intensive work periods were scheduled during the interphase session. One covered four weeks in December and January, and was concerned primarily with planning for the summer. The second, in April, dealt with the mechanics of arrangement. This chapter will report primarily on the first of these sessions.

The Group Rediscovers Its Footing

The first planning meeting was the thirtieth official session — the first since the summer in which group and staff were reunited. Although the single agenda item was to plan the planning, there was also some pending business. One such item was a report on the training officer project. The officer responsible for staff work (Jack) reported that his assignment was nearing the implementation stage. The summarizer noted that

Jack has a rough draft completed. There are a few ideas to be worked out, some policies and procedures. But otherwise it's coming along very well and Jack is kind of outwardly proud, I think, of his progress, and he sure as hell has a right to be. If they put it into use, it's going to be a great thing. And I've talked to a lot of people down in the locker room as a side thought, and this is really a great thing for this police department. And he should be damn proud of what he's done.

There were several tapes prepared for group discussions, and the men approached these with verve. As Waterman (one of the tapers) pointed out, the commentary had a refreshing, open and pointed flavor:

We had kind of interesting things going on tonight. I guess if I was a psychologist or something, I might be able to explain it. The last time I remember being under the gun like tonight was when I came up with the qualifications for field training officer that staff loved so much. One former time that I recall very well was when I brought up a 148 incident that I had on the street for discussion. So this thing kind of goes in cycles . . . It's interesting that this group has developed over the months to the point where there's no holds barred anymore. Like open your mouth at the wrong time, baby, and you've had it! Handle a call in an offense-setting way and you're going to get a lot of controversy, and there's no question but what this is good. One of the things we haven't really done, we haven't exploited this thing in our taping incidents prior to these. There has been some discussion at the end of the tape, but it has never really been put on the person who made the tape hot and heavy as to whether or not the call could have been handled better. And these two tapes tonight — I don't know whether it was the two incidents on the tapes or whether it was the particular mood of the group, or if it shows just how far this group has developed as a unit. I think probably the latter is true. And I think probably more good is going to come out of these tapes as a result of really getting everything out in the open. One of the things — one of the really good, constructive things that came out of this open discussion of my incident was the idea that we could go back and get (the applicable) partic-

ular training bulletin and incorporate it into the tape. There
was some question about, you know, did I know what the hell
I was doing when I was out there? Or whether any of us know
what we're doing when we're out there. And I feel that this
is a good thing. And I can't say that I wasn't just a little bit
irritated when I was under the gun, and I think probably any
member would have been. We're going to all be defensive —
I don't think we've changed that much. But I can say that I
was kind of happy to see — and I don't mean this as any
form of revenge or anything — but I was kind of happy to
see one of the individuals who was putting it on me so hot
and heavy get it really stuck to him when his incident came
up!

The group's commitment and integrity were put to a test during
the session. One of the officers (Joe Young) complained about some
consequences he feared from his participation in the group. Young
maintained that his chances of promotion — which he viewed as
contingent upon his assignment — would be destroyed by re-
scheduling. The group was sympathetic, but urged Young to re-rank
his priorities. Young requested a poll of the group, with a call for
other members' reservations. The result was a full expression of
support for the project. Young remarked:

> I didn't intend to bring out my problem tonight. The course
> of action I was going to take, I was going to ride with the
> tide, down the river in the boat and not make any waves,
> and then when I found out I got screwed, I was going to say,
> "well, screw you." But I think it did one thing, in that it
> seemed to rekindle the fire under the asses of the rest of the
> members of the group, which is good. Because we did find out
> that — maybe everybody already knew it, I didn't — but
> there is a lot more enthusiasm about the group than I had
> expected, and maybe some others had expected.

Beside Young, Waterman discussed some of his private problems. He stressed that he viewed his difficulties as resolvable, but
that he felt that honesty called for shared doubts and worries:

> I figured, "well, Joe Young, he's telling it the way it is, the
> way he sees it. I might as well tell it like I see it too." There's
> no use harboring these things that bug us individually. I

think it says something for group development. I would
have been, early last summer, much more concerned about
my image in this group had I sounded off then. Well, the fact
of it is, early in the development of this Unit, I wouldn't
have sounded off, probably. But the group has come a long
way . . . And it's certainly a point that we had to reach — a
free feeling of being able to say what was on our mind. What
was said tonight was another point that had to be reached
in this group. It hasn't been particularly easy for me to look
at things objectively without — in changing the images that
I've had for a number of years, or to be pounced upon because of my views without hedging, backing off too much.
I sound like I'm rambling here, and I guess I am. What I'm
saying here is this: I feel I know this group well enough now
so that I can say what's on my mind, and I don't have to back
off, because what I say certainly may not be agreed with, and
I certainly didn't get too much sympathy with what I had to
say tonight. Sam and I yelling across the table to one another.
I think the only ally I had around this table was Joe Young
and he certainly didn't give a damn what happened to me—
he had his own bag to carry. But the point is that I said what
I had to say, I meant what I had to say and I'm not going to
go home and stay awake all night worrying about whether
you guys still like me or not. Or whether you ever did like
me or not.

Except for Young, the group argued for the subordination of
personal problems to project goals. A staff member pointed to the
importance of this stance in the history of the group's development:

I think the point of the matter is it helped us get into some
very real issues of our motives, in terms of career motives,
in terms of what about the project itself ought to involve us,
how much discomfort ought we be willing to suffer in order
to make this work, is it our long-range interests in terms of
making this a better department or our short-range interests
in terms of where we stand individually that ought to govern
us at any particular time? What motivates each one of us
in terms of what we see as keeping us here and simultaneously what lessons can we draw from this in terms of what
might motivate the other 17 guys in terms of keeping them
here? What about a sure thing versus a sort of innovative

experimental track we're on here, despite the fact that we have the Chief's obvious strong support? All of these and other issues were to some extent dramatized by this, and I think we went through them very constructively.

Clearly, the facing of personal and group goals can be a difficult point, and initially demoralizing. In a mature group, it seems that consensus around the primacy of group goals can be reinforcing. In general, the officers felt elated by the evening. One of them (Bill) commented:

> I really think a lot was done here tonight. And I feel good about this meeting. I'm not tired and I'm not in a hurry to get the hell out of here and go have a horn. Right now, I'm the least hung over I've ever been.

Another officer added:

> I felt during the past few months that we haven't had staff here, that we've grown a little lax, really, in the project. We did carry on Joe's and Jack's projects, because they were up there assigned to something to do and were active participants in this program. But, myself, I really didn't do anything, and tonight I felt real good. I feel like we're getting somewhere and we're really moving toward what we're going to try to do next summer.

The group's enthusiasm permeated the planning discussion. The officers not only outlined their priorities, but launched into specific topics. One member of the group suggested an idea (which was adopted) involving a schedule that included assignments on the street, as a break in routine. Another officer suggested a two-day workshop, in which all officers might get together for a combined program.

A third officer (Mills) discussed the nature of group projects. He stressed the need (manifest in the group's own experience) of planning for tasks that could be quickly and successfully completed:

> I think that we're probably going to need to bring out some maybe smaller and easier-to-attain successes for these guys to keep them interested, real early in the program next year. Give them a little hurdle to jump over and see that they

clear this one and then go on to something else. And I think every guy here at one time or another throughout this whole thing has kind of asked himself and everybody else "just where the hell are we? What have we done here?" And we can't really document too much. We get kind of a feeling at times that things are going in a direction. Maybe people from outside of this a little ways who have done it before know what's going on and they think that these are great successes, but the members in the group have to get a little bone once in a while and taste it, feel what success is like. And I think this will be very important to these people.

These ideas were the first of many that would engage the group for the next several sessions.

Straining the Group Mind

The next meeting was given over entirely to planning. Issues were explored, suggestions recorded and procedures broken down. The group participated in eight hours of talk, but showed signs of strain. There were expressions of discontent with the direction of the discussion, bursts of temper, and an air of impatience. The officers complained that the session was redundant, abstract, and concerned with contingencies. Officer Hill, the most disgruntled member of the group, remarked:

> I just get tired of listening to what sounds to me like the same thing over and over again . . . The problem at the time just didn't seem that damn important or complicated to me, that's all, and I just got pissed off! It's that simple, that I was listening to the same thing and nobody seemed to be deciding anything, so I just turned into my usual violent self. But my morale isn't low.

Despite growing restlessness, the meeting was comparatively productive. Considerable content originated with the men, and there was solid thinking. For instance, the group discussed the need for individual session-by-session morale measures:

> We discussed the morale graphs that staff drew on the board that was worked up back at the University. This was thrown out for discussion and consideration. Staff brought

up the point that this was haphazard and that a better method was needed, that there were too many inadequacies, although it is a supplement to accurate record keeping. Sam brought up the point, can a graph be made as you go rather than from the summaries . . . He discussed graph inadequacies from the point of you can't get personalities into a graph. In other words, we're talking about the morale of the group, when actually it may be one or two members of the group which gives the overall group the appearance of having a low or high or medium morale.

A second proposal was to institute a procedure for live recording of highlights of the group process:

I think we all agreed that when we reach a point where something seems like it's really going to be important to have an accurate record of, that we turn the tape recorder on. In other words, "does anyone have any objections to turning the tape recorder on?" I might say this for the purposes of getting a record quickly, that this should be a matter of the group deciding beforehand that it is permissible to turn that tape recorder on at any time that it looks like there's going to be an important interchange or an important development taking place.

The group also discussed the desirability of breaking up the training sessions with periods on the street. The group saw political advantages in this procedure, in that it reduced manpower drain. More importantly, there was the opportunity to make tapes and to experience family fights and other forms of violence. The "field trip" idea was one of several designed to cope with the dangers of boredom:

One thing we did decide, and I think we're all unanimous on this, that we do plan to use some variety here, no matter whether we go on the street or not. If we work with eight hour sessions, we have to make damn sure that one thing we do is have a lot of tasks available and that we rotate these tasks within sessions. So we don't spend eight hours like we did tonight here, simply agonizing over something. Or working on one project continuously, which may produce a lot of work, but which is an inhuman kind of enterprise.

The group then agreed on the merits of "quick and dirty" projects, attempted to think of some, and failed. The remainder of the time was occupied with planning the organization of summer teams.

The group set up leadership pairs for its three subgroups. The pairing was done systematically on the basis of recognized preferences and skills. For instance, one officer (Bill) argued for his pairing with another (Joe Mills), on the basis that

> My real interest in the group is that of changing people, or their behavior. I have a real interest in behavioral and attitude change, whereas Joe's interest has been with that of organization, structure, policy, and procedural changes. And he's done very well at it.

Another officer (Waterman) summarized his role in a second team by arguing that

> Something that I've realized for a certain amount of time is I am a pretty basically goal oriented type person who probably de-emphasizes . . . I understand that you're not supposed to analyze yourself, but still again you've got to take a good look at yourself sometime, and I think that I am to a great extent a goal-oriented person who probably de-emphasizes interpersonal relationships among my peer group. It doesn't necessarily mean that I'm not a warm person, or human being, it's just that I don't emphasize that point to any great extent. I think that because of this I am lacking one thing that I think Sam Hill can add to me, and that is a tremendous prestige factor. I think Sam has got a prestige that I personally am not going to have with that particular group, although I think maybe the goal oriented thing is going to be helpful to Sam.

The officers also decided to make the groups flexible, and to switch personnel (including leaders) as conditions required. Composition of the groups was left for the introductory session, in which leaders could observe trainees. It was agreed that the trainees could have a voice in selecting their groups.

In addition to the introductory session, a general "retreat" was planned for the third week of the summer:

> We expect . . . that we will be meeting a slump after about

a week or two of . . . a sort of surface cooperation. And then we will adjourn all of us to some setting like Asilomar, where we are going to hold a fairly intensive session, with a review of what we have done, with the asking of the questions "who are we" and "what are we" and "where are we." Hopefully we can answer these questions to everybody's satisfaction, with possibly the Chief coming in.

There was discussion of the advantages and disadvantages of the teams "going in three different directions". The conclusion (as summarized by staff) was that

By virtue of the fact that we have three groups, we do have the opportunity for systematic variations to be traced in terms of their effects, in addition to the common development that has to be available for all of these groups. We want this to be a systematic difference and we want to keep track of it, and I guess we have decided that leaving the difference to the people themselves doesn't destroy the possibility of this effect, because our role here is just keeping track of what the consequences are. Which does not require that we determine what shape the differences take between these groups.

These points — and others — represented results of hard work. On the other hand, the group's impatience signalled difficulties ahead. Planning was needed, and the men's task was to plan. Could they face this mission, and complete the structuring of their groups?

Rumblings of Discontent

The next week was spent on detailed preplanning of various procedures. During the first session the staff presented an outline of expected performance, dividing the process into stages for more convenient discussion. The proposed sequence progressed through:

(1) general analysis of problems of violence between police and citizens
(2) focus on the role of the officer in violence with citizens
(3) critical focus on the trainees' past conduct

(4) group discussion of constructive resolution of violence-
prone incidents.

With this outline in mind, the officers discussed appropriate
activities for each of the developmental phases. The discussion
did not proceed far. It started with the task of finding short-term
projects for initial weeks, and terminated with the discovery that
the group could not think of projects. One officer (Bill) voiced the
general frustration of the group:

> This short-term project thing I think we really got hung up
> on. And I'm the one that brought out well, you know, "how
> short is short and how quick is quick?" It's kind of hard to
> define. And it was a suggestion, in some things it would
> help the project sort of keep moving. I think we got hung
> up on it to the extent that it kind of wound up last night
> that if we don't figure out some short-term projects we're
> screwed. And it's not that imperative. It was just a sugges-
> tion that would help these 17 guys along. It's not, really in
> my opinion, that imperative. It's really hard for us to sit
> down and say "let's figure out a short-term project." It's
> damn near impossible and I think we've found that out.
> They're going to come up with a lot of things they're going
> to want to do and a lot of places they're going to want to
> go, with a lot of these research projects, just like we did. In
> a way I hope it's a closed subject, because I don't know how
> long we were on it last night, but we were on it a long time
> and I think that everybody said damn near all there is to
> be said about it.

The group also attempted to list resistances that could be expected
from trainees at each stage of the summer. Again the results were
meager, and it was decided to sub-divide at the next session into
more convenient task-forces.

There was also some objection among the officers to the pre-
definition of group development into stages. Officer Hill was the
first to register an objection, by predicting that the trainees would
advance more rapidly than anticipated. He expressed the view
that

> with us seven involved with these people, who are going
> to be pretty close to some of them, that we're going to get

out of Stage One in a very rapid period of time and
we're going to get out of Stage One as soon as we get involved. We're going to get into the other stages right away.
Now, we'll go back to One, and we'll go back to Two, but
it's not going to be in a chronological order. And we just
better get damn ready to take care of Two and Three right
from the start because they're going to pop right in your
face. And some of these people are damn sophisticated
that are coming up here, and they're going to try to eat you
alive. That's the only resistance I have to it.

At the following session the objection to the staff outline
became more serious. Waterman — heretofore the group's advocate
of planning — voiced a strong plea for spontaneity:

I'm speaking for myself now. I haven't really been that
wrapped up in this phase 1, 2, 3 and 4 thing. I can't get with
it. I'm sorry. I see it as an overcomplication. And maybe
that's because of my ignorance. The last 14 years of my
life's been in dealing with men in the military and para-
military type of outfits, and I don't understand the social
sciences at all. Maybe these are very necessary things that
the staff can see that's got to go in there that I can't see. But
in my dealings with men, I don't see it that way. I don't see
them as necessary. Damn it, I just feel like, you lay your
cards on the table and play it by ear. This is the way things
have always worked very well for me and you face each
step as you get to it. This has been the pattern of my professional life for the last few years. And it's just damn
hard to get with this type of detailed planning.

Joe Young (who had been preoccupied with his career problems)
objected even more strongly, and accused the staff of hopeless
obscurantism:

When we first started out I think it was an agreement on
behalf of the group, the officers here, that we were going
to keep this thing just as simple as possible, on A, B, C, D,
and E terms. And here we have it now, it's so goddamn
complicated I don't understand it. If I don't understand what
I'm doing, I'm not going to be interested and I'm not going
to participate. I don't see why we have to look at violence

in relation to all policemen, and then in relation to individual policemen, and then in groups of policemen and all this. We could have just put up problems and possible solutions and not gotten so damn technical with it. I don't understand it, either. I'll be truthful with you. 90% of the time you're talking right above my head. There's a reason for it, and you may understand it thoroughly, but you're not talking to your peers.

Despite such claims, the men showed that they had grasped the proposed outline. Subgroups had been assigned the task of anticipating resistances (and planning counter-moves) for each stage, and these produced relevant material. Sam Hill, reporting for the "Stage One" group, suggested the following listing:

One of them would be what is called good police work, which would be one area of resistance. Then the thin blue line and then the apathy of the public and educate the public. And then the numbers game, and the people on the street failing what we call the attitude test, gripe sessions and the argument that all officers are doing things alike. And then it was pointed out that we're going to have officers that are going through the motions out of persecution complexes they have about being in this Unit. They might develop a resistance and a negative attitude because they are here, against their free will. And then there's a resistance to the academic involvement. They feel that they want to be on the street and don't want to spend their time up here playing around with this when they're needed out there and they feel that their time would be better utilized out on the street. Under "activities," in Stage One, we're talking about starting out, perhaps, with types of violent incidents. Then we went to a review of critical incidents — the review of our critical incident survey. Then going into the 17 involved coming up with more critical incidents, to augment and discuss and maybe get a bigger critical incidents list going.

Joe Young, the "Stage Two" Group spokesman, reported:

For "resistance" we had listed most of the comments for the attitudes we felt these people would take. I'll just read

them as I've got them down. The first being no one wants to
go to jail. This should be an attitude that they're going to
take at first. Then there'll be the insistence that we're dealing with assholes and what do we expect out of them? Another will be you're not going to get cooperation no matter
what you do. I'm a policeman not a social worker. A reluctance to get involved in the Monday morning quarterbacking
of going over somebody else's activities or actions and then
deciding whether or not they're right. Not having the time to
sit down and take into consideration what a suspect might
feel or think, or to listen to him yell or scream. And then
again not knowing — an attitude of how do we know what
they're thinking, how do we know that maybe their wife just
got run over or something, and this is the reason they resisted. How are we expected to know what these people are
thinking? And one that I'm sure will prevail is you can't let
a guy back you down or he'll walk all over you. And then
there should be a reluctance to even get involved because of
the peer group acceptance, the fact that they're up here and
not down there.

In "development" we felt that if they acknowledged that
policemen do make poor arrests at times, that this is good,
or it's a change. To acknowledge that there are occasions
when policemen inadvertently contribute to violence, that
officers have been known to jack people up or to back them
into corners to make them resist. We feel that they have to go
a step further, that they have to agree that this is a questionable act. When they acknowledge that policemen do make
contacts when it's not necessary, such as in the "pig" situation, when they acknowledge that in some cases it's just in
order to get back or to exert authority, and when they realize
that it's baiting and it's not really worth your while and that
when you do allow yourself to be sucked into a position like
this, you're more or less playing their game and they're coming out ahead. And under "development" would be any suggestions they might have for further involvement in the
study.

Under "activity," I think our primary interest was the
discussion and survey of the 148 reports, at least for four
reasons. First to show that some officers do get a prepon-

derance or get the largest number of 148s. Secondly, these should show that some of the original causes for the arrests themselves were kind of questionable. Three, that procedures — the approaches used — are questionable with some. And then fourth, whether or not the police should have even been involved in the situation. And then, I think all we had were discussions, the first being on techniques used on handling crowds, like unruly juveniles walking down the street, things like this. And then a second set of discussions on the 415s and the car stops like we originally did when we first got started. And then I guess we should get into the discussion on alternatives and patterns, possibly using the 148s as a basis for consideration here.

Despite such ideas, the group left the fourth session convinced that it had been posed an impossible task and had wasted its time in a futile effort to carry it out.

Calm Before the Storm

The next session was an apparently smooth working session. It was occupied with the pre-selection of trainees. Each officer made a list of names that he expected (from personal contact) to find in the program. A similar list was prepared of candidates who qualified "by reputation." Two nominations were necessary for inclusion in the final list. The tabulations were transcribed, and the compiled lists sealed and filed away.

The schedule called for a selection session in April. At that time, a master-list of high-incident officers would be available from the computer. Inclusion in the project required two independent sources, one of which had to be the high incident list. The group saw the logic of this procedure and had no difficulty assigning reliable ranks. Nevertheless, there was unverbalized concern. What threatened was a polarized view of "social scientists" and "policemen," and resentment premised on the assumption that the role of the former was being imposed on the latter. This resentment was to take shape all too shortly.

Open Revolt

At the opening of the next session, one of the officers (Waterman) announced that he had a statement to read. He reported that he had

discussed the meetings with another group member (Bill) the previous evening. He had become increasingly disturbed, and had sat
down at 5 a.m. to record his feelings. Waterman's statement was a
strong objection to the planning activity. He said, in part:

> We've been planning, analyzing, projecting, debating and
> yelling and we've been talking about names and resistances
> and projects and personality classifications and we've at-
> tempted to follow and even indulge ourselves in social
> sciences principles. I wish I had an individual morale chart
> for each of us, because I think mine would be kind of an
> all-time low over the past two or three weeks. I'm ready to
> face reality. I'm not a social scientist. I'm a cop, and I'm a
> very concerned cop at that. . . . There are some sharp men in
> this room, but most would make pisspoor social scientists.
> It's just not our bag. Therefore let's exploit our greatest asset
> and that is — let us exploit our ability to cope with situa-
> tions spontaneously. This is what we're trained for — this is
> what we're best at. And we're extremely practiced at it. Just
> as the social scientists, or I should say the staff in this room
> are practiced at planning things long-range.

Waterman's fellow-plotter, Bill, endorsed the manifesto, and
added strong language of his own:

> What he's saying is that we go out on the street every day
> and we sometimes have seconds to make one hell of a big
> decision. And we make it, and somehow we come out on
> top all the time, because this is our job. Now, if I can't get 7
> policemen working under myself and the other two members
> of my subgroup and make decisions and overcome obstacles
> that are going to come up, I don't belong on the street,
> much less up here. And how in the hell can you talk about
> obstacles that aren't there? . . . And when you're under pres-
> sure and when you're under stress, a lot comes out of your
> brain that you just can't believe was there in the first place.
> And I just don't think that that type of complex, detailed
> structuring is necessary. . . . But we're to the point now
> where we're not going to learn anything. We're to the point
> now of complete, utter, total, devastating frustration. And
> we think now that maybe we're going to know what we're
> going to do. And I think that this being our last meeting,

we're going to be able to sit down and figure out what we think is necessary to structure from the point of view of a policeman, and give up this crapped-out idea of becoming post graduates in social science. We're not going to do it.

Both men had stressed the skill of police officers to effectively "play it by ear," with the corollary that planning activity (in addition to being the alien pastime of social scientists) was superfluous. In addition, Bill made the point that the group had sufficient charisma to insure against undesirable contingencies:

We've got peer group influence with these policemen. That's going to surmount tremendous obstacles, just the fact that we're cops like they are. And they're going to be asking the same things we asked — what's in it for me? And it's not going to take them long to find out that there's a hell of a lot in it for them. Just like we found out. We're pretty goddamn important people around here. Whether you feel it or not — and I know everyone here does if they cop out to it — we're pretty important on this police department. These 17 people that come up here and jump into this program, if and when they do — and I'm sure the majority of them will — are going to be important people on this police department. Now that's what we should be thinking about.

Waterman too stressed the role of peer power. He conceded that the engineering of peer influence — particularly in the opening interview with trainees — was a relevant subject for planning:

The old time principle that first impressions are lasting has a lot of merit, and we can make or break this project in the initial interview of these 17 candidates. Our planning had better center around what message each of us 7 can convey to and impress upon these 17 candidates in the interview session, which incidentally should in my opinion be strictly us 7 identifying with these individuals in this interview exchange. As far as I'm concerned, this is Phase I of this program. This is where we can sell it, this is where we can make or break it.

The staff replied in a positive vein. They commended the officers for their frankness, resonated to their frustration, and re-emphasized faith in peer influence. Staff also offered to refocus planning on the initial interview, as proposed by Waterman:

> The statement is not one that at this stage comes as a surprise. But what is awfully pleasantly surprising is the thoughtfulness that has gone into it, and I think some of the eloquence. It's quite obvious again, you know, that we have a lot of power here. I also think it's quite obvious that we have shared a lot of what to us are very obvious fundamentals. But they aren't to everybody else, and it's nice to know that they are to some of you, too. This peer influence idea, for instance, which I think many of us now seem to share, is one that to us is extremely important. And it sounds like it's awfully important to you; and of course, you're the guys that have the stake in it. You're the guys who can feel it beginning to work, who have seen it work in other ways, some of which have been less desirable than others. And to see what's going to happen here as a systematic exercise in peer influence makes us, I think, 100% in accord. . . . The second part of what Waterman said, which is that these past three weeks have been an awfully frustrating and agonizing exercise, and that although we have gotten a lot done, probably more than we think we have gotten done because there is a lot planned, the fact of the matter is that many of the questions that we have posed are really incredibly difficult types of questions to deal with. And it doesn't matter if you're a social scientist or a cop. And it doesn't really make any difference whether you're a social scientist or a cop, because it's a question of using one's head, and social scientists don't have any better or worse heads than cops do. They just use slightly different language . . . You prefer not to do it. My hunch is that on that level the response has to be to graciously back off. You do, on the other hand, say that you want to plan some things that you consider to require planning immediately. I take it that that would be the initial interview, and that you'd want to think about this some more. And I think we ought to put this on the agenda today together with some housekeeping matters that we have to resolve before we adjourn.

The dissidents declared themselves pleased by the staff rejoinder. Waterman declared:

I can appreciate what staff had to say and he kind of took me by surprise a little bit too. The tone was a little bit different from the response that I expected, and I really don't know what kind of response I did expect.

Waterman also reiterated his faith in the future of the project, given the sound instincts of officers:

What I'm saying is that we're taking people just like us who happen to get put in the wrong boxes perhaps when they first hit the street, and taking them out of this box and putting them into another box where they're comfortable talking about a different thing. And if they're comfortable exploiting something called anti-violence — which I think they want to do, because violence is really not a very comfortable thing, it takes a real wierdo to enjoy really beating some guy around — I don't think these people mainly are comfortable where they are. And I think that they'd like to have another road, they'd like to have other boxes to be in where they can feel comfortable.

Hill extended this note of optimism, and assured the staff that success would be easily attained:

I think one of the main things that we're going to have to try and do is point out some of the alternatives that these people haven't even thought about, that I've had 18 years to think about, and for some people it doesn't take that long. A lot of these people think this is the way to go and I think once it's pointed out that it isn't the way to go, that there are other ways to go, that we're going to make them more comfortable, that they'll fall into a niche. A lot of the people that were on this board, they're a hell of a lot sharper than I am as far as police work is concerned, but they just don't know how to handle themselves in some areas, that's all. It's just a question of what's important and what isn't. Give them a different set of values, that's all.

A staff member returned to the issue of planning, and suggested that objections were in fact directed at staff-defined planning, as opposed to planning per se. He addressed a non-involved officer, Mills, and requested his thoughts about the direction of planning.

Mills suggested starting with a definition of objectives:

> *Staff:* I was very pleased by your remarks, Bill, that of course we're going to plan and of course we need a structure, and we're ready to go and do it. Now, one of the things that's been coming out here is planning vs. no planning. I don't think that's the issue, really. I think it's more we put up our phases and our kind of structure and then ask you guys to play with that — that kind of planning. I think without calling names or getting excited, let's try to think now what kind of structure is there that's different from what we've put up, and let's not even think of it as different, just what is it? For instance, Joe, what do you see us doing next summer?

> *Mills:* Well, I can picture doing next summer what we have already done and to that degree I would say we do need planning, or we need a skeleton of a plan. This is what we'd hoped to do — state some kind of an objective which is dealing with these 17 people. We do have to have a plan. I think what went wrong here is that we went into such a detailed plan before we laid out the whole plan. We were detailing very minute parts of small sections rather than laying out the whole plan with an objective — a stated goal at the end. And it's very hard to see why you're going into all these little details if you've lost sight of this final objective. I think we've got to keep that in sight and relate everything we're doing to that objective. The only way we can do that is to lay out an outline of what were those objectives and then at a later date if we think that we need the details on them, then we go into the kind of things that we were dealing with yesterday. I think that we do have to have a plan — I don't think anybody really means that we just start. We do have to have a rough plan, but we are just getting so detailed right now that we're just bogging down.

> *Staff:* Are we ready to try to structure the nature of that outline — that plan?

> *Mills:* Yeah, I think so. I think you have to do it now. If you're going to have any plan at all, now that we're talking about a plan.

The group adjourned with the mandate to renew planning, starting with a specification of aims, and proceeding to the details of intake interviews. The revolt — it appeared — had been converted to constructive ends.

Selling the Program

Between the Christmas planning period and the selection and interview of program candidates, the group returned to a sporadic schedule. This period, however, was no longer concerned with pending tasks. It was a forward-looking time during which the men were preoccupied with setting the stage for their existence as a training unit the following summer.

The group became obsessed with the need to prepare their appearance vis-a-vis three types of audience. One was the group of 18 trainees with whom they must work. The necessity of outlining a "pitch" to the trainees did not arise until April, but the men found themselves discussing their general handling of trainee interviews at almost every meeting. They decided to conduct the interviews by means of a panel on which each of their three teams would be represented. They decided to place the premium on frankness and full disclosure. They decided to accumulate information to make a preliminary assessment of the men possible.

The second audience for the program was the department as a whole, and in particular the supervisors whose manpower had to be drained. The officers placed weight on the need to convince street sergeants, through personal contact, of the benefits of their project. The delicacy of the task was highlighted by the extent to which the group became concerned with anticipating resistances they would encounter and devising ways of countering these resistances:

> Bill: So we're taking a lot of the burden off (the sergeant), and I think that would be a good point to bring out. "You as a sergeant are responsible for the actions of your men on the street. You don't have time really with all the administrative pressure on you to write a letter for this or for that . . . you don't have time to nursemaid some of these men out on the street. And a lot of them do have a problem and they need some help. And we're going to take a lot of the heat off of you."

> Waterman: Right. And "they'll be more open with us as patrolmen than they will be with you as a sergeant."

Bill: Where do you think this would get us in a bind? Do you see any way it could?

Staff: Yeah. If some guy really felt that he was supposed to be able to do this and prided himself in it or something.

There was optimism about the chances of success. For example, as one officer put it:

Usually when you meet resistance when a guy comes on trying to put you in a corner for being up here, if you just turn it
around a little bit and ask him a few questions about are
there guys in the department that he'd just as soon not work
around because they stir people up, the guy's got to say yes
to that, and then the next is "wouldn't it be nice if you could
point out to some people that are causing all this trouble
that there might be some errors in their own ways." And then
he'll say "yeah, it would be nice to get this point across."
There's about ten different questions you could ask and the
next thing you know, he's got to be on your side. Just if there's
only one guy messing up on the police department, the sergeant has to be on your side if you ask these questions.

The third audience was comprised of the Chief and the top command personnel of the department.

The Two-Edged Sword of Salesmanship

Before we describe the group's efforts to establish their legitimacy
with the top leadership of the department, it is germane to consider
the consequences of the emphasis on public relations at this stage
of the group's development.

We mentioned that in the attempt to legitimize itself in the eyes
of others, the group had a vehicle for raising their own commitment.
The task of devising arguments to convince skeptics could contribute to combatting skepticism within the group; the need to
counter arguments and to defend against prejudices could cement
loyalty. The organization of presentations provided a vehicle for
inventory and review, giving each group member a more concrete
and structured concept of the group's task. One officer (Waterman)
appointed himself group historian, and pleaded with the others to
undertake a detailed chronological catalogue of their experience:

If you can really think back to the beginning, that first time we sat down here to this table and didn't know where the heck we were going, and Joe Mills saying "well, why don't you tell us where the hell we're going? We'll get there and we'll get it over with." And then we began to focus on something we could talk about and things began to develop from there. But what did happen? What did develop? How did we come to our conclusions on this field training officer study and how did we come up with the ideas on the tape recording and how did we get started talking about the dispatchers and the deficiencies up there? A hell of a lot of things happened, things that are significant as far as our own development is concerned. In our own development, this has a lot to do with the way we talked to the Chief today. We're not the same men we were at the beginning of the summer last year. I would just like to kind of put out a plea to everybody in this Unit — don't think of it as not having accomplished anything. Because, in my opinion, I'm not going to be able to put down on paper what we've accomplished. There's not going to be any way to describe it. Maybe this is kind of a plea for everybody to take kind of a self-analysis of himself and kind of an analysis of what's happened in this Unit. I think everybody will feel a little bit better about what's happened in this Unit.

A third element was that of building a set of future obligations: selling the group, committed its members to living up to the quality they claimed. One must make good on one's prescriptions because these are now public and verifiable. One has placed oneself on record where one is subject to evaluation by an audience that matters.

Another function of selling was to raise collective self-esteem. In making an impact, the officers began to conceive of themselves as of more general importance than they had anticipated. Even in their presentations to the Chief, the group began to see itself as significant and powerful:

We developed these programs and went up there and showed the Chief that little peon patrolmen sitting around a table can talk about a police department and make some real — I hate to use the word meaningful, that floats around too much — but make some meaningful analysis of what's wrong with the job, and come up with some real practical solutions. The point is that we produced something and I think he's probably got just a little different view of patrolmen and the impact they can have on a department. Now he's saying "follow up with what you've started. Go back to the patrolmen and let the patrolmen tell me what they want in terms of training." That's progress, anyway you look at it.

Lastly, the selling function cemented the group more closely to parties with whom they dealt in their presentations. Thus the officers had become non-alienated from the Chief and concerned with the Chief's motives and premises. They were troubled by the contrast between their empathy and the fashionable scapegoating and grousing of the locker room:

The last time when the Chief came up here, when he left I thought pretty highly of the guy. And when he left I had a pretty good feeling about him. I haven't had any contact with him up until today from that time. He hasn't made any decisions that I've disliked that have affected me or rubbed me the wrong way, and yet why is it today before he came in here I had negative feelings about the guy? And that I think is peer influence. You hear a guy say "the Chief is an asshole" often enough and he becomes an asshole in your mind until he works it off. He's got a real cross to bear, that guy does. He's an asshole today, he comes in and he makes you happy for a few minutes, and then he starts going down the road toward being an asshole again. And even though he isn't doing anything to you. He comes in two weeks later and builds himself up or impresses you in some way, and then now he'll probably be an asshole the next time I see him, even though there's nothing in between. And that's peer influence.

The men discovered that they were now beginning to represent the positive features of the Chief in their interactions with other officers:

A thought kind of flashed through my mind. When I hear somebody say "the Chief — that asshole" it might be good for us to look at the guy and say "why do you say that?" Because we're kind of committed to this project, and with-

out getting carried away with a spiel about how we should
be committed to the Chief because of his involvement in this
project, I think it gets down to sort of an old adage which I
don't remember verbatim, but it kind of goes "when you work
for a man you should be loyal to him." And when you quit
the job and you're not working for him, damn him to hell if
you want. But maybe we should say "why" to a few people.
You know, I've found some pretty negative attitudes when
somebody said something about Gain and I made the
statement "well, I'll defend him." And then they say
"he isn't that bad really." I think it's like you say, he's got
a cross to bear and I wasn't really aware of what he had to
do, what he had to face, the problems he had until we became involved in them and saw the problems as they really
were.

In addition to such consequences of salesmanship, there are
disadvantages and dangers. Too much emphasis on public image
can lead to an avoidance of controversial activities; it can lead to
investment of energy in public relations work to the detriment of
on-going activities. It can dilute integrity, impair self-perception,
and place excessive value on the views and judgments of others.

The Chief as Ally

The Chief of the Oakland Police Department was a critical ingredient in the project's operation. The Chief was a legitimizer
who could assure the men that they were engaged in an integral
function of the department and in a high priority activity. The Chief
was a consumer and expediter who could adopt and implement
group products. The Chief — as leader of the organization —
was a key factor in setting the climate within which the group performed its mission.

The Chief was also a friend of the cause. He smoothed troubled
waters, arranged for desirable administrative actions, and
bridged the gap between the group and powerful persons with
whom they interacted.

The Chief's role as a friend came to the fore shortly after the December meeting, when Joe Young, who had been preoccupied with
his chances of promotion, announced his resignation from the project. The other officers argued and cajoled to no avail. Young maintained that the project would destroy his chances of advancement,

and he could not grant that his continued group participation might prove an asset to his career. Young declared that his decision was irrevocable and final.

In despair, staff arranged for Young to see the Chief, for an "exit interview." Young returned proclaiming his intention to stay with the group. He did not describe his conversation with the Chief, but characterized it as follows:

> I talked to him for awhile, and you know that man should have been a salesman. And he wasn't trying to sell me, but he was very convincing and he really believes in this project. He really sincerely does, I think. And what he put forth was very convincing — that I was making a mistake, not only from my own standpoint, but from the standpoint of the entire department and the community; that this is a good project, it's a pilot project, and if it's successful, it will be one of its kind and probably will have impact on every police department in the United States possibly. I think the Chief was very, very sincere on what he was saying, and I really couldn't turn the man down so to speak, so I didn't.

The Chief's bridging function was also exercised on behalf of the officers. The Chief placed the group on the agenda of a meeting with command personnel. He arranged for the men to make a presentation to the meeting, introduced them, and entered the discussion on their behalf.

Three officers represented the group. The first to speak — Waterman — confessed his apprehensiveness. He described the atmosphere as follows:

> We went into the room. In fact things were quite silent in there and everybody's looking round like "what the hell are these guys doing here? They sure don't look like captains." So the Chief came in and the Chief made a short announcement, something to the effect that "you know there's been a Violence Prevention Unit in this Department since last summer, etc. We have representatives from the Unit here." The enthusiasm didn't pick up very much. So he introduced me — I was the one that was kicking it off.

Bill, an observer during the first few minutes of the presentation, relates:

> Harry was scared. The first ten minutes he talked his voice was shaking and quivering and he was breathing hard, but when he got caught up in his own rhetoric, he went on like a champ. His voice started to get even again, and he started talking with that sincerity of "goddamn it, you've got to believe what I'm saying, man, because that's it." He came across with a lot of enthusiasm and a lot of sincerity.

In the course of the presentation, the need arose to outline the training officer program, which raised sensitive issues. For one, it carried the implication that assignment policies were not conducive to effective training. There were problems in the fact that the Training Coordinator was to be a patrolman. As issues such as these began to surface, the Chief intervened:

> Chief Gain came galloping to the rescue after I got put on the spot by a couple of captains there. Chief Gain says "we're going to face the fact that there is no field training officer program in this department. We wanted a field training officer program for ten years. Not only do we not have a field training officer program but no police department in the country has an effective field training officer program. Now we've been talking about it for ten years. I think it's about time we acted on it. We are going to have a field training officer program; if we have to relinquish a certain amount of manpower and so forth to do it, we're going to do it. The general order has been written up and everything. It's going to be coming around for your comments and your suggestions. But we're going to do the program."

The Chief also contributed at various other junctures of the presentation. Bill reports:

> I said something about this program being impossible to implement without the understanding and the cooperation of the command officers, and that's when the Chief came in and started his little dissertation on how it was important that they should cooperate and since they now understood, blah, blah, blah, that there would be no real problem getting this VPU thing and having it catch fire and sort of spread throughout the department.

The command officers were to varying degrees receptive. With respect to the training officer program, one of the captains spontaneously remarked, "I think it's commendable that this type of thing is going on. And what I really think is commendable about it is the fact that it's going on at the patrol level." The same captain discussed the substance of the presentation at two of the patrol line-ups, and helped to increase receptivity to the expanded training program:

> I'd like to say that Kong brought up at the line-up the 17 that will be involved in this thing, the additional people, and that possibly somebody in the room would be involved in it, and he pointed out that it was a good thing to be involved in under the circumstances.

The captain's presentation in turn favorably impressed some of the officers at his line-ups. Members of our group were approached by several men with inquiries about membership in the Unit.

Bill's presentation contained a summary of the critical incident survey results. A sensitive issue was raised by discrepancies in the definition of police work implied by the questionnaires. The command officers' reaction, however, was unambiguously favorable:

> And I didn't know how I was going to get across the point that there was a big communications gap between the Chief and the command officers. I said, "well, we found out something very important," and I looked at the Chief and sort of smiled. "We either found out that it's been a long time since the Chief's been on the street, or the command officers don't really know what he wants done as far as policy and procedure goes." Well, it made them happy and it made him happy and I felt a little more comfortable about it. But it was really well taken, and there's no sense in going into what was said about the critical incidents study, except that they're really enthusiastic about it, and they're all gung ho about giving it to every man under their command. They don't see anything wrong with a guy putting his name on it, because I think they're kind of convinced that it is an innocuous thing, and nobody's going to be hurt by it. I impressed upon them the fact that there are no right or wrong answers to this thing. It's merely a criterion by which we can get a little bit of data or statistics on what people think should

or should not be done on the street, or how they get involved personally, or how they're inept legally in a lot of aspects of their work.

George: You might add that Capt. A. asked us to at least give that critical incidents study to the members of the radio room.

Bill: Right. And then Capt. B. mentioned, "I'd like to give that in the jail too, but it would have to be revised."

As the meeting began to seem successful, the officers experienced ego-enhancing impact. Bill, in reviewing the experience, declared:

I have a propensity for either sinking into the abyss of depression to the point where I don't even think that I piss right, to the height of enthusiastic elation. And I'm really enthusiastic about this. And I'll tell you why. I think that we're going to find out, those of us that survive this thing are going to find out that we're involved in something real big. And I mean big. Whether or not you want to buy it, whether or not you want to buy the responsibility, is up to you. But I mean it. It's proven by this deal in Sacramento, it's proven by these calls from Washington. It's proven by the fact that we're accepted by 15 division heads, by the fact that a captain gets up and sells it to his line-up when nobody asked him to do it. This thing is going to catch on. And when it does here, it's going to go like wild-fire. And I mean all over the country. And I believe it. I've got to kind of really think about that, and sort of resign myself to the responsibility or get the hell out, because I'd hate to hold something as good as this, and as big as this is going to be, back. I really mean that.

The Chief saw to it that the group received positive feedback:

The Chief said as we were going out the door— he was giving kind of a summary to the captains — and he said "I don't think they could have been quite as articulate a few months ago as they were today." That was just before we made our exit. When I finished my initial presentation leading up to the projects, he says "extremely impressive presentation," or something like that, you know. So he was right in there with us.

It is obvious that the Chief's role was not merely a supportive one. He was a key participant, without whose help the second phase of the study would have resulted in serious organizational shock.

Selection and Interview of Trainees

One juncture in the transition to the expanded project was the selection and interview (by the first generation officers) of prospective trainees.

This juncture had to occur late, to insure the relevance of performance records; it had to occur early, to permit necessary administrative arrangements. A reasonable compromise was mid-April, and the group convened then for a week of predictably intensive work.

Selection occurred in accord with our research design. The department's Planning and Research Division provided computer data about violent incidents from March 1, 1969 through March 15, 1970, broken down by individual officers. The names of all men with five or more incidents were taken from this printout. This list was compared with independently obtained nomination lists, and refined to include officers who qualified on the basis of two separate sources. Fifty-seven candidates were obtained in this fashion.

The pool was randomly assigned to the experimental group and to one of two control groups. (The procedure used — multiple-coin-tossing — occasioned predictable interest). Two control groups were used to check for the impact of selection and contact.

Officer Joe Mills had since the inception of the group defended the proposition that violence among the police could be cheaply reduced with a regime of fear. In line with this, Mills argued that our interviews with trainees (highlighting their violence) would themselves produce resocialization.

The availability of a sizable pool of candidates made it possible for Mills to test the deterrent impact of the interview. An "informed" control group was to be contacted in the same manner as the trainees. In each case the interviewees would be told that they might be members of the project or might be used for comparison purposes. A second (uninformed) control group would not be contacted at all.

After selecting trainees and controls the group set up a schedule and returned to consider the substance of the interview. A role-playing session took place in which Bill, who portrayed a militantly resistant interviewee, attempted to sidetrack and annoy the interviewers. Although the mock panel prevailed, Bill led it from its schedule into a defense of the project and a debate on quality of arrests. Bill explained, in retrospect:

> I really tried to kind of remember a lot of things I've heard some people say, the reactions they've had to particular statements or the reactions they have to particular incidents, and how I felt at one time. And it was hard to do. It was hard to get completely immersed in this thing. You can't block out what you know. I don't think it was that important that I led them off the structured form of presentation because I had a lot more ammunition to do it with. I think that's a fair and realistic statement. I did feel like I succeeded in screwing them up, though. And I did lead them astray purposefully. And I did get them involved in a debate purposefully about what's good police work.

The mock interview illustrated the need for sequence and structure. Mills declared:

> If we're going to have these things we better have them pretty well set up, pretty well structured and possibly, after a brief introduction to the guy and having him come in and sit down and get a little bit comfortable, run right through the formal part of this thing. It would have been a lot easier for me to defend my position and probably put on a stronger case for the project if I'd done my homework a little bit better and had a little more of a formal outline that I would follow, whether I was reading it or whether I was just giving it. And Bill, being Bill, took advantage of all this.

On the whole, the panel managed to conclude the interview on its own terms. To this end it relied on the prestige and status of its members:

> There were all kinds of indications that the fact that there were three patrolmen involved in interviewing in and of itself gave the thing an awful lot of power, because at a number of junctures one of the interviewers could turn to the others and point at them and say to the interviewee, "do you think that we would lend ourselves to such and such," or "as you look around the table is this the sort of line that you think we'd follow?" And Bill, despite the fact that he was

being very aggressive, would have to step back a little and say, "no, now that you mention it, I don't." And that came through.

The rehearsal made the group feel secure and prepared for the interview sessions.

Sugar-Coated Deterrence

The interviews proved pleasurable, harmonious and amicable. At an early stage Waterman, who was teamed with Bill, reported:

> Bill and I were shocked this morning when the first man right off the bat was just ready to jump over the table to get involved in this program. It's making us think well, you know, we'd like to tell the guy, "yeah, you're going to be here." We had to keep telling him "you may be, you may not."

Mills emerged from a second panel to retract his prediction that interviews could serve as behavior modifiers:

> I thought the interviews went real well and I think they accomplished what we had in mind — to orient these people. Not to sell them, just to tell them what we were doing up here. It was pretty good to see how enthusiastic everybody was. I think everybody we talked to wants to come up and be a part of this active group. I don't know how successful this warning shot is going to be to these guys, because I think there were either two or three out of our four that when they recognized that there's a problem — and they told us that there were problems on the street — they seemed to point out that the problems were with other policemen and not with themselves. So I suspect that just from this small amount of information that I gathered here today, that these guys are going to continue to behave just the way they have been out on the street, even though we consider this a warning to them by calling them up here.

Even sensitive information appeared to have little impact:

> They didn't even so much as flinch when we brought up the internal affairs card filing system, and that we had in fact

checked it and we had actual access to it. There was no objection, no mention, not even a change of expression, which shows either very good training or they don't give a damn. That was something we were very paranoid about.

The interviewers felt comfortable about their role. They saw themselves as prepared and informed and able to deal with any question or comment. They stressed the value of their informal approach:

It was kind of a "hi, Joe. How you doing? Sit down. We're going to turn up the microphone and get ready." And there was a lot of small talk at first, like "how's your new baby?" "I guess you know why you're up here." "Yeah." So it was all conducted in a very informal way.

One of the problems with the interview was the effort of our group to gain rapport, to mitigate the shock of assignment and to create a favorable impression. The difficulty lay in reconciling this objective with the task of placing violence (and its personal implications) in the foreground. Bill placed almost complete emphasis on rapport-building:

Bill: One thing that we did consistently, or that I seem to have done as I recall consistently, is this. "You're up here because we want to tell you about the Violence Prevention Unit, because we're expanding the unit by 18 men and we're interviewing a total of 36, one of which of course is you, and there is a 50-50 chance that you will be assigned to this group."

Staff: You told them that pretty early.

Bill: Right out front. It was laid on the table the first thing. Then I worked at alleviating their fear at being part of the group. I tried to sell it to them. I think we did.

Fortunately, Bill's co-interviewer, Waterman, perceived his mission to be that of balancing Bill's dedication to salesmanship:

One of the things that I wanted to do, was with Bill handling so well the fact that this was such a great thing for you, and you have so much input to give and it's really going to be great having you here if you come up here and what it can do for you. I kept getting these little nagging fears that since one of the reasons or one of the stages we expect these people to go through is after they say, "you know, there are problems in the department and problems with certain individuals," that somewhere along the line they're going to have to say, "I've got problems and I want to do something about them." So I wanted to try to get back off of Bill's pitch about "you're up here because you're a nice guy, because you've got so much to offer the group." I wanted to get the focus back somewhat to the fact that "you're not totally up here because you're nice. You're up here because you came off the 148 list. "That was the number one criterion, and you've got to give the impression that it's not a fact that you were pulled off the merit list to come up to the Violence Prevention Unit. I didn't think we should oversell that thing. . . . But that was kind of my m.o. throughout the interview. Bill is so great at giving the big sell that there's got to be some equilibrium reached when he's on that side, and somebody's got to take the other side. And that's why it worked quite well for us.

In general the emphasis on violence presented no problem. Interviewees seemed ready to stipulate the existence of a need in the area. Mills observed:

From the guys that we talked to, if I was an outsider, outside of police work, I'd be very interested and delighted to know that there's so many policemen so concerned about reducing violence out on the street. A guy outside of this field would probably be very surprised to learn that street policemen actually felt this way.

In fact, the "problem" for our interviewees always existed among other officers. In cases where their own violent incidents came up, the men discussed them as "war stories" rather than in a spirit of self-criticism. But the interview did not pose problems. It defined the area of inquiry, familiarized the trainees with the project, and created an atmosphere of receptivity.

Post Script

At the conclusion of the 16 interviews, the officers were ready to begin their new career as group leaders and trainers. The training project was slated to start with a general meeting in June, during which our officers would serve as chairmen and panelists. The sub-groups would form and would meet around the clock (two days a week) throughout the summer. Each group would be monitored by staff. Members of the groups would fill out self-rating forms at each session and participate (in rotation) in the summaries. Group leaders and staff would meet and critique sessions.

Such were the bones of the structure of the project. The flesh — the content — would be supplied by the officers in their new role as group leaders.

PART II

This section describes the second phase of the project. Chapters IV through VI summarize the meetings of the groups led by our seven trainees. Chapter VII deals with general sessions. Phase two of the project took place in the summer of 1971.

4 • Group one: Action Review

The design of the Oakland project envisaged a sequence of activities ranging from relatively general study through increasingly person-centered concerns. In the last stage of this sequence, members of our groups were slated to discuss their own activities. We anticipated that destructive patterns of conduct would be exposed and criticized, and that alternative modes of behavior would be explored.

It is fair to say that none of our groups progressed through the sequence as we outlined it in theory. The fact that groups departed from the hypothesized sequence does not mean that they did not experience what we had envisioned as the climactic stage of their development. All of the groups engaged in critical analysis of individual members at some juncture. In several instances such activity occurred relatively early in the life of the group. In one group — Group One — it remained a permanent concern.

The Catalytic Discussion

Although peer interviewing did not formally germinate in the group till its fifth session, the seed for the project was sown during the first night in which the group met. Generally speaking, the first meeting of each group can be described as a honeymoon experience. There was enthusiastic discussion embodying a variety of job-related concerns. Participation tended to be universal, and the atmosphere lively and spirited. Individual members seemed elated by the opportunity to find a forum in which to ventilate ideas which could not be appropriately broached elsewhere. Group participation and morale ratings averaged close to the ceiling — a high point to which they never returned.

Group One met from 11 p.m. to 7 a.m. At 6 a.m. during the first session, discussion was cut off for the taped summary by the group leader (who initiated the summary during the first session in each group). The leader reported that "I am pleased because . . . it doesn't seem like it should be 6 o'clock in the morning . . . the time went a lot faster than when I'm on the street . . . I think it was because we had 100% participation in the discussions." Another member added later: "I felt that (this session) went by real fast. I didn't expect it to go by like it did. I thought the night would really drag, considering the hours and so on. But we got into it and the thing got quite controversial."

During half the session the conversation dealt with undesirable dispositions brought by officers to interactions with citizens. There was talk of the possibility that unhappy experiences at home or during lineup could affect a man's equanimity on the street. There was mention of the dangers of being seduced into "mob psychology" in a crowd situation. There was talk of "threshholds" of explosiveness or emotionality. The bulk of discussion, however, focused on the likelihood that young officers or recruits would enter the arena of police work with undesirable psychological dispositions, insufficiently corrected by training and experience.

After its 3 a.m. lunch, the group returned, and found itself exposed to a tape that had been made the previous week by one of its members while out on a call. The tape had been produced in response to a plea for tapes issued by the seven officers during the general meeting held the preceding week. The production of the taped incident clearly was a gesture of goodwill and an expression of willingness to cooperate with the group. What was actually accomplished, however, was that the group was felicitously exposed, during its first meeting, to an exercise in systematic analysis of a behavior sequence. It is this analysis which culminated, several sessions later, in the peer interview project.

The Interview Experience

The incident taped by the officer was a violent encounter which started with an effort to examine a suspect's eyes with a flashlight. Our officer was the first person to have contacted the subject, but his subsequent role was that of supporting cast to the officer who arrived later.

The tape of the incident suffered from relatively poor fidelity. Our officer — whom we are calling Jones — was able to fill in from recent memory. He played the tape, supplemented it with narration, and answered questions that were posed by the group. The group leader (who had been a subject of systematic interviewing) began a more detailed reconstruction of the incident; a participating staff member involved himself in a further analytic reconstruction — which in turn led to a general discussion by the group.

As it happens, Jones had proposed that the discussion of his incident be taped. We thus have the discussion on record, and we can draw excerpts. These excerpts may show how our group witnessed, during its first session, the results of a diagnostic process on which they subsequently capitalized.

The reconstruction of the incident starts with Officer Jones arriving on the scene, where he encounters the suspect (in the vicinity of a reported burglary) working under the hood of his car. The analysis starts with this encounter:

> *Jones:* I arrived first, and I talked to him and got his driver's license. And he was trying to tell me about the car, but he wasn't making any sense at all.
>
> *An Officer:* Was he cooperative with you?
>
> *Jones:* Yeah.
>
> *Staff:* So he didn't seem to be alarmed at your presence at all at that point, huh? In fact, he was sort of viewing you as a source of help and advice with his mechanical difficulties?
>
> *Jones:* No, I don't think he was doing that. He appeared that he had this problem and he was going to do it himself.

Staff: But he was telling you about it. He wasn't viewing you as a menace?

Jones: I don't think so.

Staff: And you asked him for information and he at least gave you that.

Jones: Yeah.

Staff: And then what did he seem to be expecting?

Jones: He went right back to his car. He said he wasn't going to drive it, though. I got his license and he said the car had rolled down the hill and on the sidewalk. And he said "I don't care if I ever drive it again." And then he went back under the hood and started playing with these wires. He had a real concoction of thin electric wires rigged up under there for some reason.

An Officer: Maybe he was practicing putting a bomb in it.

Jones: He mentioned that. He said "there's a secret bomb under here."

Staff: So he was sort of joshing with you.

Jones: Well, maybe joshing at that point, but with everything else he seemed to be serious.

Staff: Did he seem to be scared of you at all? Did he seem to think that you'd do anything next?

Jones: No.

Staff: So as far as he was concerned the interview was over and he was going to go back to work on the car.

Jones: Yeah.

The degeneration of the incident is explained by Jones as resulting from the suspect's drug intoxication. Jones indicates that he had become apprehensive about the suspect almost at the point of meeting him. The group was intrigued by this fact, and probed further:

An Officer: And then what? Did he show any type of belligerence to you before your cover got there?

Jones: No.

An Officer: Well, then, why were you apprehensive? That's what I can't understand.

An Officer: Because of his physical condition? Was there any difference in your sizes?

Jones: Yeah, he was bigger than me. Everybody's bigger than me.

Staff: But when you say "high" now, that means he was nervous, incoherent, sort of happy. It does not necessarily mean that he's aggressive or nasty, does it?

Jones: No.

Jones explains his apprehensiveness on the basis of his "experience." His fear grows as the suspect drops a piece of tin-foil on the sidewalk (subsequently the foil proved empty) and the apprehension reaches its high point as Jones' partner, Dave, arrives on the scene. Jones tries to communicate his impressions to Dave, without success.

Dave meanwhile independently decides to verify the suspect's condition by shining a flashlight in his eyes. The man has no prior warning of this contingency. Jones, for his part, expects trouble:

An Officer: Did you or Dave, one of you guys, tell him what you were going to do with the flashlight, or did you just come out and put it in his face?

Jones: We just stuck it in his face. Dave said, "let me see your eyeballs."

An Officer: Nobody explained, "I want to see your eyeballs. I think you're under the influence and I want to give you a sobriety test," or something like that?

Jones: No.

Leader: You said that you anticipated him making a move, you expected that he might move. When did you first get the feeling that he was going to make a move against you? Did you have the feeling before the other guy got there?

Jones: I had the feeling from prior experience that if I tried to take him to my car, he would probably resist.

Leader: This is before the other guy got there.

Jones: Yeah.

Jones indicates that the suspect — up to this point — has given no indication of apprehensiveness or concern about the presence of two officers. As he is suddenly faced with the flashlight in his eyes, the man strikes out at Dave's arm; Jones at once grabs the suspect around the neck in a choke hold, and Dave uses his mace on the man's face:

> *Co-Leader:* What was his first resistance? You said something about shining the light in his eyes and he shoved it away, or something?
>
> *Jones:* Yeah, Dave said something like "Let's see your eyeballs." And he stuck the light up in his face. And he pushed the light away from Dave, and then I grabbed him around the neck and started choking him out. He wiggled out of that, and that's when Dave said "if you keep it up you're going to get hurt." And he poked the light in the guy's stomach a little — he didn't jab him, he just kind of pushed it. And he started coming back at Dave again, so I grabbed him again and Dave pulled his mace out and maced him and me.
>
> *Leader:* Were you close enough to see when Dave wanted to look at his eyes — apparently you were, because you grabbed him, right?
>
> *Jones:* Yeah, I was right next to him.
>
> *Leader:* How did he do it?
>
> *Jones:* You mean how did he push the light away?
>
> *Leader:* Yeah. Stand up. You're the suspect.—— is Dave. How did Dave shine the flashlight on the guy? Did Dave have ahold of him?
>
> *Jones:* No. He was standing right next to the car, his back was to the car, and we were standing in front of him.
>
> *Leader:* Show us how to get it. Now how did the suspect do it — he went like that? That easy?
>
> *Jones:* No, he hit it hard. He didn't have a chance to do anything, because I grabbed him around the neck then.
>
> *Leader:* Why did you grab him?
>
> *Jones:* To control him.

Leader: What were you thinking about then?

Jones: We were in such close proximity, he could have just taken a step and started in on Dave. Because we were just inches apart. So I grabbed him so that he wouldn't.

Leader: What did you think the guy was doing when he made his move?

Jones: Well, the first thing, getting the light out of his eyes?

Leader: Is that what he thought?

Jones: Yeah, because I had the feeling that he was high and he didn't want this light in his eyes, and I knew he was going to go to jail eventually.

Staff: But if all he wanted to accomplish was get the light out of his eyes, and he had gotten the light out of his eyes, what made you start assuming that he would then go and do other things?

Jones: Well, the way he did it, he hit, you know, hard at the flashlight. It wasn't just like a swatting away. It was a good hard jab at that light.

The group analyzed the sequence of events in several different ways. Their first concern was with breaking the incident down into steps, and exploring the assumptions of the officers at each juncture:

Leader: I think what we're interested in is the sequence of events and Joe was trying to sort of draw a diagram of what was happening between you and this guy when you were alone with him; of him ignoring you, a feeling that you would have that would control your next move which is, One, you're apprehensive about him because you've arrested people that have used drugs before, and they have always resisted. Or you've always had a problem with them. So, this guy is going to give you a problem. Two, you were expecting him to make a move toward you although we brought out that there were really no signs or cues that gave you that reason, merely because this has happened before. So these two cues that you have, rather unconsciously on your part, are going to govern what you do next. Officer Two drives up. You try and tell him the guy is high, but he doesn't

catch it. He doesn't talk to you, so there's no consultation.
You haven't gotten rid of your uptight feeling about this
thing, you know, in talking to the other guy about it. You
kind of feel like you might have to handle this whole thing
yourself, because the other guy isn't aware of how dangerous
this man is. This is probably what you were thinking.

Jones: Yeah.

Leader: When he shines the light to check his eyes and the
guy says "keep the light out of my eyes," maybe he moved
the flashlight away and all your expectations have at last
been fulfilled. This guy moved and showed that he's done
what you expected him to do. That would cover your maybe
hasty move in grabbing him around the neck . . .

Jones: Yeah.

The group proceeded, in a positive and sympathetic fashion, to
guess at Jones' motives and premises, and to illustrate their plausibility by citing experiences in which other officers had been involved:

Leader: Like this guy really wasn't playing your game until
you shined the light in his eyes, because you kind of anticipated all kinds of things to happen, and none of them were
happening. The fucking guy's cooperating, talking kind of
slow, fumbling around like he's high, sort of clumsy and
nonchalant about the whole thing, and that's not really what
you want to play right then. You've got a real dangerous
dope fiend on your hands, and you know he's going to make
a move at you, but the cocksucker won't do it.

An Officer: How many of you have gone to the door of a live
party? I hate that call more than anything else. I hear that
report on the radio and I'm ready to fucking quit, you know.
I worked six Saturday and Sunday nights and there was
always parties I'd have to take. You'd go to the door, and
there'd be 100 people inside this little apartment and they're
gassed and having a fucking ball. The stereo's blaring out,
and they're all dancing and drinking and having a great time,
and you go up and you bang on the fucking door, and usually
a couple of them saw you come in, and they go and say "he's
coming." A lot of times you're by yourself, and somebody

will swing the door open and say, "well, come on in" and they'll just leave you. They swing the door open and tell you to come in and then just go back to dancing and drinking and having a great time and just leave you standing there with your thumb up your ass. Nobody comes forward or nothing. Maybe you can latch on to someone and talk to him and then they'll shuffle off and ignore you and you're really frustrated as hell. And then once in a while you'll manage to get a hold of the host, and then somebody in the background will say "let's barbecue that motherfucker," or "let's throw his ass out the window . . ." I know when that feeling gets to me the most, where I'd love to get a bunch of goddamn guys and wipe the place out, just because I'd been treated so rude when I was there.

Leader: I haven't had that happen to me, but I find that when you try to stop a car for a traffic violation, a lot of times they just stop where they wanted to go in the first place. And they get out of the car and you get out, and they just sort of walk away, and there you are with your headlight going — like if you ignore the guy, he'll go away. He's not real. I say "where the fuck are you going? You know, I haven't got that light on for my health!" And they'll say, "oh, yeah, I didn't see you." But could that be what was happening? You've got the other guy's strategy all figured out in this game, and he wasn't doing that? . . . I guess if I was standing behind the guy and he made a swift, very forceful jab I'd lose control somewhat.

This "but-by-the-grace-of-god-it-could-have-been-me" approach to the officer's motives made it possible for Jones to seriously consider other possibilities, and to admit to them:

An Officer: . . . Is that the way you felt?

Jones: Well, I think the gun was maybe in the process of going off, but this might have been the situation. Or I thought it was going off and maybe it really wasn't.

The group not only attempted to reconstruct Jones' perceptions and concerns, but also those of the suspect. This type of analysis enabled the posing of questions about the interaction of motives, and about the transactional genesis of violence:

Leader: Maybe you wouldn't have to say he was scared so much as he's surprised. He's making what he thinks is an innocuous move — hitting the flashlight out of his eyes — when he's attacked from the rear. And he finds himself being choked. Trying to look at it from his point of view — he sees a light in his face and all he wants is to get it out. So he makes a move and then he's being choked. That's what he sees happening. I'll bet you ten to one if you talked to him, that's what he'd say. "Shit, I wasn't doing anything, and the next thing you know a light was in my eyes. It hurt my eyes and I wanted to get it out." He would probably add "I said please, and I didn't slap it — I just reached up to move it, when all of a sudden this fucking maniac is grabbing me around the neck and trying to choke me to death!" That's what he would say. And maybe that's how he really saw it. Because there were some things that he drummed up in his head about you maybe, because of a contact with another policeman.

Jones also became involved in the analysis of the suspect's motives, and began to see the other side to the interaction:

Staff: Now this guy is panicky because he has been grabbed about the neck, right?

Jones: I would say he was, yeah.

Staff: And the rest from there on in is more and more panic.

Jones: Yeah.

Staff: So he's really getting scareder and scareder and scareder until he's sitting in back of the car screaming.

Jones: Well, he's screaming because he hurts.

With the evolution of a group-shared frame of reference, it becomes possible to explore new courses of action, and to discuss these with Jones:

Co-leader: You don't think there was any way you could have talked to him, just talking, talking until he was in the car? I'm not talking about a "you're under arrest, you're going to get into the car one way or the other" approach. Don't you think you could have talked him over to your car? Like you could say, "well, we got a call about a burglar. I'm going to check into this. You want to come over and . . ." and you're walking while you're talking, and you open the door for him just like you might open the door for your wife, and the first thing you know you're sitting in the car talking.

Jones: It didn't even enter my mind, I don't think.

At this juncture, Jones can view his incident in terms of options, including some that were clearly destructive or represented errors in judgment:

An Officer: Do you think macing this guy was necessary?

Jones: I wouldn't have maced him, myself . . . I was surprised when Dave came out with it . . .

Staff: At that point he was really pretty effectively restrained?

Jones: I thought he was. I thought I was doing a pretty good job. He was starting to gag a little bit. He was just starting to feel the lost air, I think. In fact, after he was maced, I kept the hold.

Staff: What do you think gave your partner the impression that he required mace?

Jones: That's a good question. I didn't expect it.

Leader: Why do you think he thought he needed macing?

Jones: Well, like he said later, the guy didn't have his shirt on, so he didn't have any clothing to control him with. Or he thought that was the best way to control him at that point, to mace him and let him worry about himself.

Finally, Jones can consider contributing errors, including problems inherent in his customary mode of operations:

An Officer: If he was being cooperative, totally, when your cover arrived, how come you didn't, still observing this man, take time to relate the situation to Dave?

Jones: Because he's the senior man, and I usually let the senior man do what he's going to do.

Staff: Could he have assumed that you had already gone into all the explanations necessary, because he didn't know what conversation you had with the guy? So he might have thought the man had been briefed.

Leader: Could he have also assumed that you had already talked to a complainant and this in fact was the guy that she felt was a burglary suspect?

Jones: He could have, yeah.

Still missing at this point is the working out (in the group context) of alternative solutions. This last stage, however, was soon to be supplied.

Foundation-Building

The second eight-hour session of the group can be described as a period of exploration, leading to the building of trust and group purpose. The conversation ranged widely, as is illustrated by the following summary excerpt:

We discussed police states, crowds that gather at scenes of arrest and how sometimes it would be beneficial if you could get across to the people that gather why you have taken the action — why the guy's all bruised and sitting in the back of the police car and bleeding. Why it takes an ambulance so long to get to a scene. Why they can't talk to a prisoner in the back of a police car, or maybe that they can talk to him, maybe they can give him cigarettes, things like this. A. brought out an example of a call that he'd been on that was very touchy where he assisted a person that had been shot by a policeman and gained the sympathy of the crowd. And then we discussed the using of a person in the crowd to assist us in our work so that the people that gather can get some kind of identification with us, that we're there to help. That we have one of their group sold on whatever it is that we're doing, and therefore they should be sold on it. We discussed the locker room talk, the locker room atmosphere and how it could possibly influence new policemen in their actions out on the street. How locker room talk can be used by different officers in a kind of status-seeking thing. Then we got off on a discussion of marijuana, alcohol and the justifications for making it legal or illegal.

The officers uniformly described the session as "rambling;" several characterized the topics as "tangents," and called for the initiation of project-related work. On the other hand, the group noted with pride and pleasure that ideas were presented openly and freely. Several members stressed that the session was "honest". As the following statements illustrate, they became pleasantly aware of a developing propensity to speak without constraints:

> B. mentioned to me at a break that he felt that it was very good that we were getting down to talking to each other and being fairly honest about it, and that the ice is sort of being broken, and this is going to be very good for the unit. I think that the first four hours that we spent here, although it did seem rather rambling and blah blah blah, was very valuable for group development.

> People today opened up and said things, even though they may not be directly, right then, relevant to violence, they might not directly be relevant to a project that we could study, they are honest opinions that maybe we're a little surprised to hear. Things were justified, feelings were rationalized, other people opened up and admitted a few things that they probably wouldn't have said if this hadn't happened. So although we didn't get any work done, I think we reached a level of a high degree of honesty and openness with each other which will be beneficial in future discussions.

> On the whole the one thing that's come out of this that strikes me, that stands out very much in my mind, was that we found out tonight that although we're all policemen, we don't all think alike in any particular instances out on the street. And I think we'll see as time goes on in here that we'll all have a little bit different ideas of what our roles are out there on the street as police officers.

> I believe this is a beginning to break down our own feelings to each other and strip to the bare truth what our own feelings about issues are in the process of becoming honest with each other.

The lack of project-related effort led to the request by one group-member for guidance from staff. This request provided an opportunity to reiterate the rule that project-ideas had to originate in the group. A staff member indicated that

Part of the problem with this sort of a project, and one of the problems that came up very often last year was the questioning of "what do you want us to do?" And while you didn't say it quite that way, you were talking about what are the directions of the unit, and the aims and the objectives. And we can't answer that. We can say what we want to do generally. The title of the unit implies that. But in terms of telling you what to do, or what projects, that would destroy the intent of the project. It simply would, because if we tell you what to do, then it isn't a group of officers deciding what should be done. And while there are ground rules, we can't teach molotov cocktail making or anything like that I suppose, the ground rules are very limited in that regard. And that's my reply generally. Now, it's not a cop-out. It's really and actually true.

The group leader confirmed the point, and recalled that in the previous summer, "we went through that crap for hours and hours and weeks and weeks," until the group became convinced that it would not receive substantive guidance from staff. He concluded that

we're going to have to come up with it. And it's a son of a bitch when somebody says "we're all sitting down now. Think of something good." There's no harder task in the world than to think of an original idea. It's an utterly unbelievable frustrating, bastard experience. And it is. And this ain't all gravy. I hope I made the point strong enough that this is true.

Another trust-theme that emerged in the session related to the question of impact. Here, also, the group received reassurance, but the result was inconclusive:

It's a little hard to believe after four years of having people tell you "well, when you want to make a change, wait till you become a captain," it's hard to believe that anyone around here will say to 25 patrolmen "you come up with some ideas and we'll make the changes." It's still a hard thing to accept that whatever ideas we come up with, even if they're really good, it's still right now hard for me to believe that they would be implemented even if they meant saving the lives of five policemen next year. It's still hard for me to believe that these organizational changes would be implemented.

Staff: The only reply I would have to that is test it.

Officer: Well, I'm willing to give it a chance. It's just that right now I'm still skeptical.

Germination

During its second week the group participated in the general retreat in Asilomar (to be discussed elsewhere). The next session was the fifth project meeting and the third group session. It was during this meeting that our principal project — the Action Review Panel — was born.

The session started with Paul (later categorized as the "group filibusterer") bringing up a television show that had impressed him. The discussion quickly branched out, became increasingly germane, and grew quite spirited:

> Smith somehow brought up the fact that he saw two New York policemen on television, and they had long hair and long sideburns and is this a good thing? Do policemen have certain rights that are taken away from them, that might help them on the street to identify with certain groups of people? We got into talking about conformity to sets of rules, and do the police have to conform to a certain degree. And this of course led into the ideas of rules and regulations, general orders. Are we given too many general orders and rules and regulations, to the point where maybe the men on the line level don't even know what the rules and regulations that we have are? That we just sort of know that they're a vague set of laws in a Great Big Book. And that even if we know the rules, that a lot of times we will violate them to do the job out on the street. Knowing that possibly nothing's going to happen unless we get caught and unless the administration has a big thing about the rule that we do violate. This then led into the idea of the militarism of the police department, or is there militarism in the police department and are we a quasi-military organization, and is it in fact necessary to be this in order to accomplish the "police mission?" And then C. [asked whether] in the realm of rules and regulations, can line patrolmen come up with guidelines that would be followed by other members of the department?

At this point Officer Jones, who had been thinking about his experience in the first session, initiated the topic which led to the project idea:

> About this time Jones came up with the point that the attitude
> of a particular officer, if he's an old-timer, or if he's been on
> just a little while, greatly affects a new patrolman out on the
> street. And that maybe when he's been working with the
> old-timer and he gets out and he works with a little more
> agressive police officer, that he's suddenly finding himself
> in the midst of a large conflict in how to accomplish his
> police mission, because of the diversity between the two
> approaches.

It was this posing of the problem which set off Officer Kent — the author of the panel idea — in search of remedies. Officer Kent (not his real name) has remarkable facilities: he is not only equipped with a strong theoretical bent but has the capacity for working ideas out on paper, in detail, in the midst of noise, distraction and sometimes chaos. He himself summarized the birth of his idea, and describes it as follows:

> And about here I started scribbling ... And I started making
> little notes about maybe coming up with trying to work up
> some sort of system where we can have line patrolmen or the
> peer group meet in some sort of order review or some sort
> of review unit where you can analyze the problems that the
> specific officer might be having on the street when it becomes
> apparent. Recommendations from superior officers, numer-
> ous trips up to Internal Affairs, just numerous violent inci-
> dents on the street. This would not be a disciplinary unit or
> anything like this and it wouldn't really come up with any
> particular finding pro or con about the officer's actions.

The idea was immediately endorsed by a staff member, by the leader, and by Officer Jones:

> Jones mentioned that he certainly could have used (such a)
> unit and would have come up here willingly had a unit
> offering this type of service been available, because he did
> have a judgment problem. But that the problem wasn't pre-
> valent enough, although he was aware of it and felt it, he

didn't feel that it made sense to go to anybody else on the department. I would imagine for a number of reasons — that they would have thought him this incompetent guy, or he doesn't have self-confidence, or what the hell's the matter with him? Which is a problem all of us have — if we have something that doesn't go right on the street, it's very hard to go to someone and say "hey, Joe, I need a little help." Most of us just don't do that.

The group leader not only noted the importance of Kent's idea, but spelled out the need for the development of skills necessary to implement it. He pointed out that the acquisition of such skills involved continued experiences with systematic interviewing and pattern analysis:

> The idea Kent came up with about perhaps offering the VPU as a service to guys on the department kind of showed me that after 400 hours seven of us couldn't come up with everything, and it encourages the hell out of me, because this is only the fifth session and bango, we've got something that we can work on and look into. And as an offshoot of that suggestion we're going to have to be able to somehow learn to skillfully extract information from a particular officer who is in need of aid from the unit. We're going to have to get that information out before we can really get down to the crux of anybody's problem.

The group immediately implemented this advice by proceeding to interview Officer Graham, one of its members. The interview was mainly conducted by the leader, and proved incisive but inconclusive. Graham (a previous skeptic) participated in the summary by expressing surprise and satisfaction with his experience as a subject:

> The first time we brought out someone's reports I was very disappointed in it, in comparison to listening to the tapes, in comparison to some of the more interesting topics that we got into. But now after going after my reports, I think that I now feel that it can be good. But the person who gets the most good out of it is that one individual, not everyone in the group . . . I may have forgotten a lot of the incident, but I still remember well enough that I remember getting the call and most of the general appearance of everything, from the house

> to people who were there, emotional flare-ups, little things that I remember about these things but don't go into length to describe and that aren't reflected in the report. . . . I didn't think too much of going over reports before. But for the individual who is having his reports on the chopping block, it is beneficial and little things can be conceived as a possibility, that may be applicable to that case. And in the future I think maybe you'll be looking for maybe a couple of those little conclusions . . . whereas I didn't think much of this before, I do see a lot of benefit now, for the individual who's getting his report reviewed.

The leader disagreed with Graham's point about the restricted benefits of the interview, and pointed to the possibility that patterns might be generalizable:

> But I have to disagree that it's not profitable to everyone else . . . I'm sure that it will increase and pretty soon you'll kind of get to the point where you can have a lot of fun with these things, and sort of laugh at each other and laugh at yourself. And I know damn well that I saw myself a few years ago in every one of your incidents, as a matter of fact. In fact, I had a couple of little analogies here that matched mine so much that I'm not going to go into it now because every one of you will hate my guts.

Graham, however, was validated in one respect: although the group rated the session enjoyable and moderately productive, their participation ratings proved low. The group was beginning to see the point of Kent's scheme, but had not yet moved to share in its implementation.

A Side Trip

In the first half of the next session the group continued to explore the pattern analytic theme; in the second half, a new project idea took temporary precedence.

The men concentrated for a time on the premise that had inspired the panel idea — the fact that an officer who had developed destructive patterns could perpetuate these through contagion:

We discussed how training officers have an influence on an officer's behavior, and the things that an officer's told by his training officer and taught by him can carry over into his career. And this was discussed at some length and I think it was found to be very important. That an officer is taught many good and bad habits and many attitudes that he sees in his training officer that carry over into the long-range action of the trainee.

The group also conducted a short, relatively impromptu interview of one of its members. This interview developed in fairly circuitous fashion through exploration of tangential topics:

And then we discussed how members of the community would react to this incident, and how the police react. And then we discussed whether or not police should be more sensitive to cultures. Whether or not they should be aware of the individual culture of the people that live in the area in which they work. We stressed more positive ways to stop people on the street, and we got into Al Cole's approach to stopping people. And Al was more or less criticized by the other participants because he at least said that he was rather impatient and he didn't go to any length to tell the people exactly why he had stopped them and what the reason was, what the crime was in the area that may have precipitated that stop.

During the discussion following the interview, the group's co-leader stressed the generalizability of patterns, and the fact that interviewers could learn from the interview experience:

In reference to Al's walking stops and things that we discussed, it ought to be remembered that when we're bringing things out and discussing them that although you might be on the hot spot at one particular moment, everybody in the room is kind of listening to the discussion going back and forth. And sometimes an impression comes out that maybe you do this all the time: in your case I don't think this is true. But the rest of us as we're sitting here listening to the discussion going back and forth on your methods of stopping people on the street, we're taking all of this in. A lot of us do things at times that aren't correct also, and when you're discussing your case with someone else, all of us are learning something at the same time. Whether or not it's actually true that you do this, it's important this discussion did go on. A lot of us picked up tips on walking stops at the same time you two were discussing it.

The remainder of the day was spent in session with the sergeant of the internal affairs unit, exploring questions related to discipline. The group felt that this interview was "informative," but not suggestive. More positively, the willingness of an outsider to meet with the group was encouraging for the men, even though hasty planning and unclear objectives deprived the experience of more concrete benefit.

Defining the Mission

The fifth session was probably the most constructive and fateful in the life of the group. Paradoxically, the meeting started with a free-floating, rambling exploration of tangents. The summarizer notes that

> When this meeting started off, I actually thought nothing was going to get done tonight at all. It was the most rambling start — from Internal Affairs back to the shooting, the most idle conversation — that we've had so far. It went just on and on without even talking about anything at all.

Other men made similar observations. One member noted (on the back of his reaction form) that "the meeting started slow and rambling — not staying on the same topic, but going back and forth." As the group adjourned to an early (2 a.m.) lunch, prospects for constructive work appeared slim.

Directly after lunch Officer Kent pulled out a thick stack of notes, and began to expound the details of his panel idea. He proposed "some sort of review unit made up of patrolmen. When another patrolman gets into a behavioral pattern (such that) he is having violent incidents on the street — and it becomes apparent that he is . . . help him out, help find where he's going wrong, before he had to go up to Internal Affairs, before he gets hurt on the street."

Kent stressed the necessary informality of the procedure, the desirability of an "off the record" approach, the need for a positive, constructive emphasis. The sessions of the panel, he indicated,

Would be conducted more as an interview rather than an interrogation. And what you're going to try to do then is review the behavioral patterns of the person and analyze what he's doing and somehow make him, in this process, come up with some self-critique, like we do here. You know, after he reads the report somebody asks questions. "There's some questions in some of your reports that you'd probably want to go over" — "why did I do this this way?" And you'd have to stop and think, "do I do that very often?" I think this type of review is going to be helpful. In other words, just sort of as an assist unit for the individual patrolman.

The group quickly took up the discussion. One point it made was the desirability of having relevant insights originate with the officer being interviewed, rather than with the panel:

Officer 1: Wouldn't it be good if we could sort of switch it around that he bring out his own problem?

Officer 2: I think that's the only way.

Officer 3: You bring out his problem and you're another Internal Affairs.

Officer 2: That's why I said we've got to have a system or technique in order to bring it out. It would be a self-awareness on his part. In the interviewing and talking to him all of a sudden the bell would go off.

In connection with the need to have the interviewee arrive at his own inferences, two points were made: First, that pre-classification of the problem resembled traditional supervisory technique, and second, that this method could produce retreat into inactivity. A person who did not spell out his own difficulties in specific terms was apt to equate a diagnosis of poor quality with a mandate to lie low:

Officer: You're never going to get to the crux of the problem by pointing to the problem. Because this is the m.o. that this department has always used. When there was a big purge in patrol division, all these guys were called into the D.C.'s office and told if they have any more 148's they're going to be fired. That's what happened. "Killer" Baridon went to (a neighboring department) and "Killer" was a pretty sharp guy. He could have worked out a lot of his hangups on the street — he has. But my point is this. The m.o. has always been "look, Louie, you've got a problem. And you'd better stop whatever you're doing, although you don't know what it is, or you're going to be fired." And the guy walks out of the room saying "son of a bitch." I did when I was called in by a captain several years ago. I really thought that I was doing a good job. I'm a hell of a cop. I get involved, I get out there and I fight crime and I'm running into nothing but assholes — bad luck. You know, right, we all do good police work and it's the citizen's fault. Resistances. And I thought "fuck them. I'm not going to do nothing."

Probably in an effort to convince itself of its integrity, the group became concerned with the need to "sell" its panel to the interviewee, while remaining completely honest with him. Both the ethical implications and the pragmatic aspects of approaches to the interviewee were ventilated:

Officer 1: You could destroy a good tool by being completely honest. Why don't you tell your wife about all your extramarital love affairs and say "but, baby, I love you!" I did that, and it's going to cost me $4000 a year for the rest of my life. I was completely honest with her.

Officer 2: I think you were a dumb shit.

Officer 1: Right. That's exactly the point. Now, would we be dumb shits?

Officer 3: Are you going to tell that guy that's 6'9", 250 pounds as you walk up to him and you know he's a burglar and you walk up to him and your cover ain't there, "you're going to jail." I wouldn't do that. I'd walk up to him and say "what's your name" as I look over my shoulder, "where the fuck is that cover?"

Officer 4: Jack, what you say does make a lot of sense. I guess this is it — these could be some guidelines to think about. If the guy says "why am I up here?" We tell him, "your supervisor recommended that you come up." If he doesn't say "why am I up here" I guess you don't have to say it.

Kent: In your initial interview, state the purposes of the VPU as a whole. Very, very basically state it as a whole. "Lower the violent confrontations, fewer cops get hurt, and in order to do this, this program has to come up with new changes. In other words, this is a program of change." Get that across there somewhere. Then tell them. "You've been recommended by your supervisor. Now the reason you've been recommended is because apparently you've been getting involved in the street. So since you're getting involved in the street and you seem to be concerned with what's going on, two things can happen from it. One, you can help us and then we can help you."

There was general agreement that the panel had to be introduced to the interviewee by stressing its benefits to the police in general, and to endangered officers in particular:

Officer 1: Maybe we could say we don't want to emphasize that, because he's going to be aware of it, and I guess that would sort of be adding insult to injury, you know, to emphasize it. "You know why you're up here, Charley, you vicious bastard you!"

Kent: You've got to get across to them that the purpose is two-fold. One, to prevent the violent confrontation, and because you're doing this you're going to help policemen 1) not get fired, 2) not get hurt. Whichever order of preference you want to make it.

Officer 2: We could say we want you to help us to prevent people from getting fired, screwed up. Not you necessarily, but everybody.

Officer 3: What you are able to offer us may help some other guy coming up next.

A number of procedural alternatives were explored by the group, and their advantages and disadvantages were ventilated. One such alternative was that of "embedding" the interviewee in a discussion group, or involving him with other officers who also had demonstrated difficulties:

Officer 1: The one that has a problem may be included in that group so that the other people don't really know and just start going over this. As an example, or something like this. So you don't put one specific person on the hot seat . . .

Officer 2: There's just a slight hazard to doing it that way . . . Let's put it this way. If we had 3 people up here at one time who were recommended or were having problems and needed a little consultation, it wouldn't be too smart to give them even odds. You know what I mean? It's kind of hard to talk to a guy and bring out an incident when you have two other guys sitting there saying "bullshit, he did the right thing. I think we ought to kick the shit out of all of them sons a bitches, you know, mow them down." If you have too many guys.

Staff: Of course there is another complication to this which one ought to consider, and that is that unless you pick 3 guys awfully carefully — your problems are different enough from mine so that we can get awfully confused if we start trying to discuss them all at the same time and the same place.

Officer 3: You've got to break down to the fact that a lot of confidence is supposed to be here. If a man comes to a psychologist, he wants to tell him his problems. Say he's a businessman and he's got a lot of hangups. Well, he doesn't want two other businessmen sitting there listening.

A related possibility was that of involving the interviewee indirectly, by dissecting the patterns of other subjects with his participation:

Officer 1: Or we could do it this way. We're going to have to do the homework on the guy before he comes up here, right? . . . We all know who we are. If we see his reports and hit on some where we have that same type of pattern that got us into shit, start talking about that pattern as related to ourselves first — criticizing ourselves, and then as the discussion goes around the table to him. Maybe by that time he's reading his own report. He can more or less see that same pattern, but never referring directly to his reports. Do you see what I mean? In other words, if you're always having trouble with women, like the one guy did as an example, pick out our reports where we had trouble with the broads, and then maybe in the discussion while we're talking about "well, this is what I did" you say something like "son of a bitch, I have a lot of trouble with women." And maybe this guy will look at his report and say "so do I."

Officer 2: He's probably going to say "do you assholes really think I don't know what you're trying to do?"

The group moved from discussing procedural variations to the planning of sessions in which techniques and strategies of interviewing could be tried out. It proposed to start with members of the unit, and subsequently to branch out to volunteers secured elsewhere:

Kent: I think initially (we ought) to continue what we're doing now. From within our own group here. Within the three groups that we have. To see if we could work out some kind of interview system here, since we are as close-knit groups as we are now, the guy being interviewed would say "now look, you're beginning to piss me off" or "I'm beginning to feel in a corner. I don't like the way you're doing this. Let's forget that line of approach in questioning me regarding these particular incidents." Things like this. Because really, as you look through the three groups, it's a pretty good cross-section of patrol.

This discussion led to an unexpected testimonial from Officer Graham, who revealed that in a post-interview session in the cafeteria he had arrived at unexpected insights into his difficulties, and now saw a pattern in his involvements:

Kent: As an example and this struck me very much, what you and Graham went through the other day would have been a tremendous thing . . .

Graham: Can I say it, because I went over it? . . . I had a problem and didn't even know it — wasn't aware of it. Me and Bill (the leader) were really having a lot of laughs on my reports, and I walked out the door and still didn't have any awareness or conclusions. It was a lot of talk. But then we started bullshitting out there and he related a couple of incidents and then I remembered the Angels and I pointed out the one about the Angels and then Bill pointed out something. And I found that I was, without even being aware of it, anytime there were insurmountable odds against me I was tearing-ass into it. Three Angels in the —— and no cover. "Outside, all three of you, let's go. Take you on." No cover. I could have waited. Two men inside 647f already slammed the door in my face made a statement they're going to kill the motherfucking pig. I didn't care — I went right on through anyway. "Here comes supercop." Without even realizing it.

Staff: With a slingshot.

Graham: Yeah, that's what he said—David and Goliath. And I never realized I was doing that. I'm surprised I haven't got my back busted or my neck broken. I don't really know whether I was trying to prove anything, because I wasn't expecting anyone else really necessarily there.

Graham himself indicated his satisfaction with the interview as a procedure, and so did other group members. The session was universally characterized as "constructive"; it was rated extremely high in productivity and morale. The group leader summed up the spirit of the occasion by exclaiming that

I never cease to be amazed at how you people are getting through these eight hours as compared to how we did. It's unbelievable. Everything I've got on this session rating form tonight is very high. I can't think of anything bad about it. I think we've come a hell of a long ways in coming up with this idea. And it's going to take more work, but it's going to be worth it. And I just want to say that I feel real good about it.

The session ended with a collective determination to expend whatever time and energy it took to get the review panel idea firmed up, so that it could be proposed to the Chief as a strategy worthy of adoption.

Constructive Conflict

The sixth session represents a forced departure from group project development. The leader of the group had been scheduled to instruct the recruit academy in "violence prevention," and requested help in the preparation of his class outline. Collective drafting exercises somehow proved painful to our groups, and this one was no exception. The period was enlivened however, by spirited conflicts of views relating to training concepts and techniques.

One of these conflicts related to the word "game," which had become a staple in the working vocabulary of our first-generation officers. To them the term was synonymous with inter-personal interaction, and denoted moves and counter-moves with latent purposes and assumptions. The new group had by-passed the conceptual exercises leading to the development of vocabulary, and thus was unfamiliar with "in-group" language. One of the officers objected to references to violence-prone "games" — arguing that the word was unnecessarily flippant. A lively discussion — initiated by the group's co-leader — followed the objection. Interestingly enough the new members joined the "old-timers" in defending the word, and the dissenter declared himself eventually satisfied.

The second argument was not similarly resolved. Again, it stemmed from a prevalent first-generation assumption, relating to the value of role-playing as a training tool. One of the new officers (Graham) objected to the technique, classifying it as artificial and unconvincing. (The point was a carry-over from the "retreat" session, where the same officer had made it.) The group spent considerable time on the pros and cons of various forms of role playing, and even staged an impromptu demonstration. The debate terminated in a proposed sub-committee on role playing, which was never constituted.

Probably of more interest than the subjects of these conflicts was the form they took. A staff member noted in the summary that

> Part of what we ought to be looking at is what happens here other than the content of what we are talking about, just in terms of, for instance, how we get along. It would seem that from that point of view it was rather interesting that what we had after what Jim calls lunch was a complicated kind of thing. We had a lot of fun. We were all chuckling pretty well, but along the line we also did quite a little solid fighting which we wouldn't have done if we didn't trust each other enough to say all kinds of pretty forthright things; in the process I think we discovered how we really feel about a subject in terms of where we all stand with respect to it, and now we can all start working on it constructively.

The relaxed group atmosphere could be viewed as indicative of the development of trust. Another such index arose when two group members reported that they had been adversely received in the coffee room by three officers to whom they broached the subject of the unit. They discussed the incident as follows:

> *Officer 1:* There were two patrol officers and one from traffic and (we) were sitting there talking to them, and they were so entirely negative to the VPU idea period. If their thinking is contagious —
>
> *Officer 2:* Were they negative because of their lack of knowledge of it, or because of what they had heard by rumor, or what?
>
> *Officer 1:* We tried to talk to them a little about it, and it was like talking to the wall, wouldn't you say?
>
> *Officer 3:* Well, I said "I like you and everything, but I can't help it if you're not progressive and have a very narrow mind."
>
> *Officer 4:* That was a very forceful, diplomatic way of putting it.
>
> *Officer 1:* Well, if you had seen how negative he was!
>
> *Officer 4:* Did you feel like getting violent with him?
>
> *Officer 1:* Yeah, like reaching over and knocking his head in.

One of the officers who complained about this encounter suggested that the reaction might be more general and pervasive. He recalled that he had been previously subject to negative feedback:

> Well, you know what I think: A lot of them . . . really think that we are a peace and flowers organization, "turn the other cheek, run up and kiss them." You know what I mean?
>
> "Blazers with flowers on them" — what else did he mention? "Take your gun off." Those two points they both mentioned.
>
> And I think that a lot of them feel that way. Because I went all the way up around Clairmont or somewhere to cover somebody on 10 or 11 for two hippies who went up behind a building and ran up in a middle of a block of apartments

behind some stairs. One officer comes in this way and is blocked by a fence and yells "there he is" and another officer literally flew over a fence and came down on the guys, put them right down to the ground, a wrestling match out to the car. And one of them in his frustration, who is a good friend of mine, looks at me and says "how would you prevent that?" And I never even thought anything! You know, this was a guy who just splits and all they did was take him. And he looks up and he said "how would you prevent that?" And I said "I thought you did pretty good police work." But part of this was that we are supposed to be sitting here saying "oh, you pushed him down. Did you scratch his elbow?"

The group leader was reassuring. He characterized adverse views as unrepresentative expressions of uninformed envy:

I guess it's kind of like the guy who has a Cadillac. If you can't afford one or you can't get one, the normal thing to say is "I don't want one anyway, and I wouldn't have it." My conclusion is that that's about it. You know, there's kind of a fear of it — something new. You're a little envious in a lot of respects. For instance, I wouldn't take very seriously what either one of these two individuals said. I think we both know them.

He also, somewhat indirectly, counseled patience and forbearance:

Last summer we tried to ride with the punches and not create any more animosity than was necessary. But I also got to the point where I was bugged so bad one night, for instance at the Public House, by a guy who I went along with for about an hour, and I finally got him in a corner and said "look, Joe Blow, you've had an awful lot of fun at my expense. And I would suggest very strongly that you change your line of conversation, or I'm going to knock the shit out of you." But I rolled with him for a long time. I'm not suggesting that you'll have fist fights. I've never done that in my life, and I hope I never do. But I think we can play the game with them, talk to them about it, maybe sell it. But it ain't going to be easy.

On a more serious note, the leader suggested that sobering experiences were healthy, and that their absence would be alarming:

> Getting back to what Bob said about he was kind of dis-
> couraged, I'm glad. Because if you weren't discouraged a
> little bit I wouldn't feel too good, because I went through an
> awful lot of that and I guess maybe it's just because we've
> got a few hundred hours under our belt and a lot of digging
> remarks that you sort of get used to it after a while. It's sort
> of like being called dirty names on the street. If you weren't
> discouraged, I would be discouraged. You know, I mean, if
> you really didn't give a shit, I'd feel bad about it.

Despite this reassuring conclusion, the men felt that the session
was anti-climactic. There were many ratings of "average," and
words like "exasperating" and "inconclusive" cropped up among
the (largely favorable) characterization of the meeting.

Tooling Up

Much of the next session was taken up by the first effort of the group
to prepare itself systematically for a panel interview through analysis of background information.

The prospective interviewee (slated for the following evening) was
a member of the project consensually regarded as violence-prone
and impervious to influence. This characterization was not only
shared by the group, but was part of the officer's general reputation
in the locker room.

The group agreed on the point that "if we can make impact on
this guy, we can change anyone." However, they were not hopeful.
As one of the men put it:

> I'm a bit pessimistic insofar as he's concerned, because I
> don't really think he's the type of individual we're going to
> make much headway with. He obviously knows what the
> attitudes of his fellows are here and he's obviously unin-
> fluenced by this attitude; and I think he'll be similarly
> uninfluenced by our attitude toward him or by anything we
> say to him.

One officer noted that the interviewee's anticipated obduracy
made him an ideal "test case" for the interview procedure:

While we're all probably pretty pessimistic about this particular individual, especially those of us who have had an
occasion to work with him even if it's only one time, that if
this particular individual who had such strong convictions
can be made aware of the fact that he does in fact have a
problem — because I don't know that he's really aware of it
— there shouldn't really be anybody else that we would
have as much of a problem with as I think we're going to
have with this one.

The first approach to the background analysis was a qualitative
one. Members of the group read reports aloud, and hypotheses were
formulated about general themes. The group also solidified its impression of the magnitude of the interviewee's problems:

It was a bit thought-provoking to think that such an individual actually goes out there among the citizens. I'm a little
staggered by it. I'd heard all the stories, but it's another thing
to see the man put it in his own words and tell it the way he
sees it!

In digging deeper, a system was devised for tabulating salient
features of the report. This innovation again originated with Kent,
who recalls that

While we were all sitting here talking, everybody had a report
or a series of reports in front of him, and we were all just
generally making comments. And it began to hit me that
there were certain areas or patterns that were developing
just from the casual conversation that we were having before
we were even really going to analyze these reports. So I just
took a little piece of paper and drew a bunch of white squares
on it in order to pick out some of these things.

The group thoroughly enjoyed the classification exercise which
followed. Almost all session ratings were "high," and the adjectives
most frequently used in descriptions were "constructive," "relevant"
and "purposeful."

The Opening Night

The group arrived the following night full of anticipation and curiosity. The interviewee (whom we can call John Spark) appeared on time and reacted positively to the introduction. He spoke freely, although at times he showed apprehension or nervousness.

The group leader conducted the first portion of the interview, and did so incisively and with surprising success. Spark was taken through various reports step by step, and a pattern emerged, not only for the group but for Spark. The pattern showed a propensity for personal vendettas against citizens who had challenged Spark's supremacy on his beat. These vendettas invariably culminated in a relatively petty arrest, in which Spark used the municipal code to assert himself vis-a-vis his opponents. The following are excerpts in which the summarizer (Jones) details the manifestations of the pattern:

> When we discussed his first report, I noticed that he kept track of a witness and he stated "I didn't particularly like her." So he's been running a warrant check on her about every month and he finally came up with a $39 warrant which he is bent on serving. This brings up the personal involvement that he gets in these things, and I think this leads him to having difficulty. He also stated in that report that he can't stop doing the job because a suspect has a gun, which leads to an element of danger because he has the attitude that he's going to get the guy no matter what.

> In the second report . . . he was challenged on how much officers will take in the eyes of the public. . . . And then he reacts with arresting somebody for something. . . . They weren't using profanity so he couldn't use that for a crutch. So he used littering when somebody picked up some papers and threw them on the ground again. He also wrote the driver eight violations on this second stop, after he'd already cited him once for speeding.

> Going on to the next report, it was a high speed chase. The driver gave him a funny look; he explained that he thought that the driver was hoping that he wouldn't notice and wouldn't turn around and chase him. He almost begged for a high-speed chase — he turned the red light on two blocks behind him. And he stated that he hadn't been in a chase for a while and he was kind of hoping that the guy would run.

This sort of indicates to me that he appears to go looking for trouble.

Jones characterizes the pattern as he sees it. In doing so he includes concepts adopted by our first generation officers (eg., "playing in the opponent's ball park") which have spread to our new trainees:

> At this point it was appearing to me that he was being drawn into the other guy's ball park, and he was trying to win in his ball park when actually he wasn't, and he was looking very bad. He stated that the cop is the ultimate authority, and this is the way he works. That's his Territory and he's the guy who's going to run the show, although going over these reports, he's running the show rather badly. And he's not playing in his own ball park, although he thinks he is.

> Again, when he loses control in a situation, he reverts to an arrest. This seems to be the only out that he can use . . . These were personal challenges: the first one on the 415. This gal that he's running the warrant on called him a "mother-fucking pig" I believe it was. And he was challenged there. The funny look on the driver's face in the high speed chase challenged him. He takes all these things personally. He's using these personal challenges, and the way he wins them is by arresting these people on anything he can think of.

The process of elucidating Spark's conduct through interview, after study of his reports, proved to be especially instructive. Hypotheses based on the written material were helpful in directing the questioning, but had to be reformulated as new data emerged. One officer summarized the positive contribution of this experience by saying:

> We had a lot of material to work with, we had a good background study last night, and I personally felt good with myself because I began to pick out these traits of people that are being interviewed. And (with) some of the other people in the group (that) had been interviewed I had had a little bit of trouble finding the things that they did leading to the problem that they had. And of course Spark had some pretty glaring problems that weren't too hard to follow, and I think this has helped me find these traits and be able to follow them to a problem.

The discrepancy between the written and interview versions of the incident led to negative speculations about the function of the written report. Here the "official" version of the incident was seen as a rationalization of the private encounter — not only for the benefit of superiors, but also for the man's own use:

> *Officer:* There's a lot of things you wouldn't put in a report, like the kids. He declared war on them. He told them that they were fair game several days, months or weeks before. "I'll have you — I'll get you — I'll take care of you at a later date."

> *Staff:* I think part of his pattern is the real stuff never goes on his report. Because he uses the letter of the law to accomplish some other purpose, and that other purpose is only in his mind and it cannot go on the report. He cannot say "I got this guy for turning around this corner because I wanted to curb prostitution." He can't say that. He has to say "failure to signal." He has to say litter. He couldn't say "I was in a war against these kids and that's the first excuse they gave me." The report is the excuse he uses. What we got today was the reason why he's in this business, which is to get people. And it's to get people who have shamed him in public or who he disapproves of because they are making a mess of his turf there. Which he's in charge of. And there is no way you can put that in a report.

Another learning experience was related to the issue of insight and change. The first part of Spark's interview was insight-centered, with Spark responding like a textbook case. At the conclusion of this interaction — when Spark warmly thanked the group for helping him to understand his past conduct — the leader moved to terminate the interview. The group, however, continued it — focusing on Spark's current practices and his future plans. The leader — who retreated somewhat into the background — later complained:

> I thought, "goddamn. We won this battle — we really did. And now we're blowing it. Because we're giving him too much room for justification." Now that was my opinion. However, it was explained to me, and we talked about it quite a bit over lunch, that there had to be some way that we could go into future contacts that Spark would be having with people

on the street and somehow relate them to past contacts which have resulted in a whole pile of 148s. I didn't see that — I didn't see that.

Group members noted that while Spark was freely conceptualizing his past conduct, he showed little indication of willingness to extrapolate from these concepts. As a staff member put it, Spark

> was filling in a picture which was neatly detailed, made absolute sense, was completely coherent, and every additional piece of information he gave us tied into it. And it's quite understandable that when one has it all together, one should say, "well, thank you and goodbye." What happened, however, is that we kept on saying yesterday, as you'll remember, "if we can break this guy, we can break anybody." And we lost sight of a couple of little cues. Namely he kept on saying, for instance, "yeah, that's the way I used to be." And the clear implication was "that ain't the way I am now." Obviously if that's not the way I am now, then all of this is history and it doesn't have any relevance. Except you're giving me some pretty good insights into the way I was when I was young and inexperienced and green.

Indeed, as the interview progressed, Spark showed an exasperating propensity for justifying his escapades, and for refusing to acknowledge the contribution of psychological factors to his current problems. As the interview concluded, the group felt that they understood Spark, but that they had made no impact on his conduct. They felt elated at their success in securing data for analysis, and at their role as interviewers. The co-leader (generally predisposed to skepticism) asserted that

> The main thing that I could see tonight was that we did achieve the purpose that we set out to do. That is, that we had an interview with someone with regard to the 148's that he's been involved in. And after Bill's initial introduction, probing and discussion, everybody here did enter into it in some degree. And this is what the hell it's all about. It was real good. Then after it was over it was even better in that everybody had an awful lot to say about what went on — what they saw developing or happening. We had a real good discussion.

He stated the feeling of the group in noting that the information secured from Spark testified — among other things — to developing interviewing skills:

> And I think that if we had an interview with anybody now, that any three or four members in the group, regardless who they were, could conduct an interview and keep it moving . . . He threw out some real big stuff that wasn't in those reports. And that was after we started chipping away. And I think maybe we tonight were working on our own particular MO, our own interviewing MO, in that you get a guy talking and there's a hell of a lot not written in that report that he will tell you. Like I say, there were no elements in most of these reports, yet when we went back through them chipping away on some of the little stuff, picking through and going back through the hours and the location and were there other people around, what was the crowd situation. . . .

As for failure to produce impact on the interviewee, questions were raised about how much of this could be expected. A staff member noted that

> The element which may have been a little hidden by what happened today is that somehow, despite all the guff yesterday about this is the last man we expect to change, everybody came in here today deep down inside expecting a tremendous conversion to take place in this room. Now actually we got a long ways toward something happening. That is, we got some insight here. And we got the guy on the defensive here and there. And we just have a large question mark here as to what's going on in his mind.

He pointed out that

> We needn't castigate ourselves for not getting him to walk out of here a convert, and a changed man. I think we have given him some room for thought. I think he did say some things in this room that he has never said before. I think we have made a good start.

He added that

We'll have an opportunity, since (Spark is) going to be with us in the next month or so, to do a little more observing and see the results, if any, of our session with him. I suspect there are bound to be some. I think we shook him up. We'll also have an opportunity, if we like, to bring him in for a follow-up interview anytime that he feels he's ready.

In addition to discussing the possibility of re-interviewing Spark, the group considered candidates for further "practice" interviews. One such candidate, a notoriously troublesome officer, had been recruited as volunteer in a neighborhood tavern the previous evening. The group decided to invite him next. Other prospective candidates were also named and discussed. The profusion of subjects — and the feeling that the group knew what it was about — produced much self-congratulation. Officer Graham, who announced his departure for two weeks of military training, said in parting that

I can remember about a week ago Paul and I came in here with a stunned look on our face, like it's hopeless. Two officers just talked to us and condemned the hell out of us — it's hopeless, we'll never get anybody up here. But my last thought as I'm preparing to go out the door is, there are more people right now during this test time than we have time to prepare for. Volunteers. We've got more people right now that you want to hold a mock interview to learn how we're going to do this in effect than you have time to prepare for them. We're already talking about "no, you can't have him Monday. We don't have time to prepare for it." And you've got another one lined up who I'm totally surprised is coming up here no matter what game he thinks he's going to play . . . if you have him in here that's a hell of a start right there. So I'm totally encouraged once again with the idea of the VPU board.

The group's ratings of the session divided between "high" and "very high"; the leading adjectives were "promising" and "valuable." The group had developed a sense of purpose and an awareness of their potency.

The Man Who Came to Dinner

The next session put the group's self-confidence to a solid test. They

faced their first outside interviewee, and — as if this were insufficient — their subject was an officer whose record of activity (and
to some extent, of physical involvements) had made him a legend
in the department.

Officer Beam had volunteered for the interview, with some per-
suasion from Bill, the group leader. As one member put it (the
preceding evening):

> Last night at the Public House over his Ballantine Scotch that
> Bill bought him after losing a game of dice to an unnamed
> officer, he very skillfully directed this officer into coming
> up here. I was a little surprised that he thinks that he volun-
> teered to come up here.

The origin of the idea aside, Officer Beam expressed interest in
serving as a subject, and did so for his own ends. His ends included
clearing his reputation by demonstrating the objective necessity of
his physical encounters; pointing to changes in his conduct (but
maintaining that these had not sprung from changed attitudes);
rectifying false impressions about the nature of police work, and
being of help to others who might have problems.

Whichever the dominant motive, Beam's appearance was self-
defined as that of an expert witness, a man without problems who
had wisdom and information to impart. In the face of this fact, the
group set out to analyze Beam's pattern of conduct with a view to
arriving at some understanding of it. The result was a Mexican
standoff that left both parties satisfied. Whereas Beam departed with
the conviction that he had enlightened the group, the officers (in
their post-interview analysis) felt that they had arrived at meaningful diagnosis.

Descriptively, Beam's pattern involved a propensity for arresting
narcotics users and a tendency to physical interactions with some
of them at the point of arrest. In the words of the officer-summarizer:

> People that he has arrested, and has had problems with,
> have been people that he has known or knows to be using
> narcotics. And this appears to be a very important thing with
> him. All through his interview he repeatedly referred to
> people who used narcotics and the way that they will act,
> and the way that he handles narcotics when he is going to
> arrest them. He stated that he makes the first move on a hype

"if I think I'm going to have to fight them, because they're nervous, paranoid and overall dangerous." He also stated anyone who doesn't cuff a hype either is a fool or the bravest person on earth. "They're all fighters" — and he emphasized this over and over — all hypes are fighters. They're the most dangerous people. He says "I'm always prepared to fight, I'm careful and I've never been nailed" — meaning that he's never been hit by one.

In an extended lecture, Beam defended the proposition that narcotics users were unpredictably violent persons — dangerous to deal with — and that it became necessary, at times, to act to prevent injury. He admitted to being "specialized" in his interest in narcotics users. Bill, the group leader, classified this as a "crusade" or "war," and this characterization resulted in a brisk exchange, with Beam defending his activity as rational and objective. According to the summarizer:

> He said "Everybody's happy including me, because I put this person in jail and I've solved some burglaries and maybe some robberies and maybe some violence, plus I've also got this narcotic that no one else could catch but me."

The group inquired into the origin of Beam's interest, and he referred to two precipitating events:

> We got into why he developed this interest in narcotics. And he related an incident about when he first was on the street that he arrested a person that was high on narcotics and this person told him that if he would have arrested him 15 minutes earlier that the guy would have probably killed him. This made him think about people that are on narcotics, and he became concerned about the violence of these people, and also the narcotics problem . . . Again, in his background, he evidently went home to Boston and he was talking to his sister and some friends about drugs, and he found that his sister had been using drugs a little bit, and some of his friends were now in prison for serious crimes because of their narcotics use. And he has a feeling that he must protect them from their own actions.

During the analysis session, the group speculated about the role that fear — and its suppression — might play in producing Beam's pattern of conduct. As one officer (the group co-leader) put it:

> Maybe I'm all wet in this little analysis that I have here, but I think that he's operating out of fear. I think that he's so god-damn afraid that he probably came into police work to prove that he could overcome this, which he does — and I think that's one of the reasons I have so much respect for him. I think he's got the shit scared out of him, and that's the main reason he's chosen narcotics work and specialized in. But he's not a dummy, he's armed himself with all the laws on narcotics and a hell of a lot of information, a lot more than normal patrol procedure calls for out on the street. He's always talking about snatching people first and never losing control of the situation, and then going through with some physical thing to restrain a guy — getting the handcuffs on him, getting him out of circulation real quick. And I think the reason he does this is also based on fear.

Another officer (Bill) pointed out that Beam

> always is attacking individuals, or the problems of individuals who he has built up mentally to be sort of invulnerable creatures of strength, incomparable demons in narcotics. I really believe he believes that, although I don't buy his story about being scared to death by a hype in a men's room, and this is why he's on this personal vendetta. I think that's some sort of mental justification.

This analysis was elaborated, later in the session, by one of the staff members, who argued that

> In a way he's built up the drug addict here as the real fiend. And you can maybe find some cases, but drug users even on the more stimulant drugs don't have a history of being tremendous menaces to society, in terms of real violence. But he's obviously sold himself. To the extent he's conning, he's conning himself on that. It would fit, if you're trying to prove to yourself that you're real tough. And remember, as Bill said, he wasn't a tough guy back in his neighborhood — he was a con. A real crucial question is when he stopped being just a con. He obviously hasn't given it up. And this

image of being physically aggressive really took over. And Bill made some suggestion that it might have been with getting in the uniform. Anyhow, if you were trying to build a case of "how do I handle this feeling in myself, that I can't rise to challenges, that I've got to make up a challenge where I can really overprove to myself that I really can make it, that I really can do it" it would seem to me that he's done a rather beautiful job. And we all agree he's bright, and he's made up a bright rationale here of the evil of these guys who use drugs. And then for a safeguard he puts in this "I hit first."

You've certainly got a beautiful pattern here for actually getting a physical confrontation over and over again. We don't understand enough of it, but from what he's been telling us, giving himself reassurance that he can take on challenges and can meet them. And I would think of the drug addict as actually a relatively safe challenge. I don't know that I'd buy that he's really taking on anything that's rough.

Another staff member, in a fairly lengthy statement, produced a different version of Beam's hypothesized vulnerability. He reminded the group that

One thing we have already brought out — I think Bob brought it out — is the element of physical detection. That is, it's sort of like witch hunting. When people hunted witches they prided themselves in being able to locate witches by marks that were left under their crotch or under the armpit or by various little indications that they gave. Beam considers himself an expert at locating these bad guys with a physical indication. He's able to separate them from the rest of the world, and goes about this business very assiduously. And it's extremely important to him to separate them from the rest of the world, which means that he has the world sort of divided and the people who are drug users — the ones that he can locate as bad guys — represent something very intimate to him that upsets him terribly. And he has to control them, which means, I think, that he has to control whatever it is in himself that he somehow senses in them. Now, I guess it's Bob who somehow recanted, who said before Beam came up here, "it must have something to do with his neighborhood, and the people he grew up with." And then that proved to be an extremely well-confirmed hypothesis because it's one of the few things that Beam was quite willing to answer. That is, it's true that he pulled this incident in the basement men's room as sort of the turning point in his career, going from one type of evil person, namely the traffic violator, to another. But then he started talking about what it is that really was the occasion for this need to control hypes, as he calls them, and it had to do with two friends he had whom he was apparently close to who ended up in serious difficulties after they started using, or he thought they started using, and his sister. I don't know what to make of his sister, and we might think about that a little bit, but one can venture two possible guesses as to what it was about his friends. The first one was that he felt acutely disappointed by them. Now, that doesn't seem very plausible. The second one was that he said to himself, "there but for the grace of God go I." That is, "these are people that grew up with me and this is how they ended up, and whatever it is in them, I got to fight it in myself." And he fights it in himself by fighting it out there in the world.

He recalled that Beam had presented as a reason for his campaign the fact that narcotics users do harm to themselves. The staff member suggested that

Part of what that means is that they are extremely vulnerable, which means "I'm extremely vulnerable." Then the other part of the answer I think is related to that, in that they become very "irrational." Their mind gets tampered with. They lose control. They become aggressive. They become evil. They become stupid. They become irresponsible. Which means that I guess in part what he's saying is that "in order for me to keep control over my mind," and the fear element may enter in this, "I've got to fight like hell this tendency for people to have their minds tampered with, and to become irrational monsters, which I can become myself given half the chance."

The discussion later returned to this point, stimulated by an afterthought:

Staff: I just want to throw in one additional word that he uses here that gives me a feeling that sort of supports my hunch about him. And that is one of the key words in his talking about these hypes is the word "control." That is, he says that he's in the business of controlling them. Now I would suspect, Phil's discussion of the rehabilitation rate of addicts would have very little bearing on what he means by "control." I think he means "subdue." I think he means "suppress."

Kent: He said their personality changes when they use it, they resent authority and you can't tell them what to do.

Leader: He did in fact talk about suppression.

Staff: Which may kind of lend some support to the feeling that this is sort of a metaphor. That is, that he is really trying to control what he thinks of as the drug problem. which is the change in a person's mind from rational to irrational. And this is a very intimate, personal type thing.

Officer: That's where someone like Jim has an advantage. He has the answers.

Leader: Yeah, but you see he doesn't have the alternatives to his answers. And furthermore he doesn't believe they exist — that's the problem. I think he might think about it.

The group concluded that Beam might be relatively difficult to change — and that the interview would have made relatively little impact on him:

What he essentially wants to do is go out there and fight his private crusade, or as Bill put it his private war. And he would like as much approval as he can for this. He would like to convince as many people of the rightness of his cause. But if he can't, he'll do it irrespective. There's no amount of pressure today that has had much effect, simply because the sources of the pressure are irrelevant, because people he feels justifiably don't have any feeling for this crusade that he's on. And he's right. They don't.

The group also agreed, however, that if any officer was worth preservation and utilization, it was Beam. As one officer put the case:

> I have a hell of a lot of respect for him, because in each line
> of work somewhere along the line there's something out-
> standing in whatever he does. Most people just go along
> and they do a job. There are people who play violins and
> then there's people who are damn good violin players. And
> then there are guys who are policemen. There are some
> 700 policemen, and then there's Beam.

One staff member, who had never encountered Officer Beam before, urged:

> I sure hope that you people that know this guy can stay
> with him, because of all people, you hate to see him go
> down the tube when you get to know him. This is a very
> powerful guy . . . It seems to me besides talking, there ought
> to be some strategy developed to get him to be a real
> participant.

The group concluded that further interviews and other follow-up
activities involving Beam were well worth the effort, even if Beam
— like Spark — was admittedly a "tough nut to crack."

Ratings of the Beam interview testified to the feeling that the
time had been constructively invested. The "productivity" line
reached a peak unequalled except for the first session. Group
morale was rated unprecedentedly high. And members felt they
had participated fully. They also felt they had learned much, and
classified the experience as "instructive" and "informative," as
well as "constructive" and "valuable."

A Command Appearance

During the group's next meeting they found themselves faced — at
the initiative of another group — with the opportunity of a
"summit" meeting with the Chief. They arrived at this encounter
completely unprepared, and were unable to present their ideas.
As a result, the Chief occupied himself with other matters. He
responded to questions from members of a second group, and
(during a lapse in the questions) reported on his recent experiences
with a police department in another city. As Bill summarized the
situation later:

> With the Chief you can't give him 30 seconds of silence,

because the man is extremely intelligent, he manipulates group conversation. He dominates it because he's extremely brilliant and he's a very eloquent man. He is; there's no doubt about it. And that's what happened. He shot the whole thing. He carried the ball the whole time. He's never in a corner. Joe drew a beautiful picture of a Southern Pacific Railroad Roundhouse, and let me tell you something. He was in the middle and we were all revolving around him like the earth and the sun.

As a constructive by-product of the debacle, there was strong incentive to structure the review panel idea in proposal form. In response to Kent's vague description, the Chief replied that he'd like to know more. As Joe (the co-leader) pointed out:

He stated several times "that's a great idea — you guys work up the finished package and show it to me." And I think that's what we're going to have to do. I think before you get anything across it can't be a generality or any vague idea. It's got to be the specific facts, a finished product all ready for him to sign and send on or it's not going to get anyplace.

Kent, who felt personally responsible for the failure to inform the Chief, immediately set to work drafting his proposal. Amid much pleasantry and aimless conversation, he sat grimly formulating the document. As a staff member observed in the summary:

Kent has made a great deal of headway there — he is well on his way to writing this proposal. We can give it to the Chief as soon as it's done. So we may have in fact moved faster in this area than if Bill had been eloquent, although it's quite obvious that the Chief would have listened and from what several of us know about the way he thinks, he would have been extremely sympathetic and supportive and excited.

The group, however, was still largely discouraged. Their session ratings reached an all-time low, and hovered around "average." The two main rating terms were "fun" and "exasperating." Similar ambivalence was reflected in words such as "rambling," "irritating," "monotonous" and "enjoyable." The meeting had offered entertainment, but the group did not feel materially furthered in its mission, nor was it proud of its accomplishment.

A Study in Complexity

During its next session the group was back on course, with another volunteer interview. The subject, Officer Kennedy, advertised himself as a changed-but-unreformed practitioner of violence. Kennedy had had contact with our original group, in the context of research into a battle with Hell's Angels. At that time Officer Kennedy had impressed the group with his willingness and ability to conceptualize events. Thus, when he declared his interest in assisting in subsequent inquiries, the offer was welcomed.

Officer Kennedy is a brilliant young man, with a distinguished academic record (including a graduate degree). Despite his excellent mind, Kennedy had placed a premium on muscular prowess, with emphasis on boxing. He had also accumulated a reputation for explosiveness, which he was working (successfully) to overcome.

Kennedy is a self-styled Violent Man:

> He stated that violence is attractive to him. He liked the idea of street justice. He liked to draw people in to make them move so that he would have an excuse to hit them when he decided that they would have to go. He said that he must restrain himself in violent situations. He has an impulse to strike out when he is mad.

Kennedy's recipe for producing violence is to "come on soft" so as to give the impression that he is a "push-over." This encourages prospective opponents to assert themselves and provides occasion for attack. In confrontations like these, Kennedy asserts, he has never been beaten:

> He said "I will always fight to the end. I will never be beat. If I am beat that time I will remember the person and I will get him later. I can't lose." . . . [He recalled] some of his high school days when he was in a tough crowd and it was kind of a big thing and you got into a beef and won the fight. Also, when he was in the Marine Corps he evidently didn't lose too many fights.

In his early associations — Kennedy recalled — his physical confrontations had brought status with his peers:

He said that he fought for status, and he mentioned the codes. The code that he had in the Marine Corps, and the code he had here dictated that he must fight for his status, that he had to demonstrate his fighting ability, to acquire his status here or in high school or in the service. And this status was what his peers expected, or this is what he feels is expected. He feels that in order to be worthy of their expectations, he'd have to be a competent fighter.

He asserted that the same circumstance obtains in the police:

> He thinks there is a code among police officers, probably gathered from the locker room, that you are cool because you got into a beef and you beat the crap out of somebody. This makes you feel good and you talk about it and everybody looks up to you.

Simultaneously, he felt that the police organization— particularly at the command level — kept the level of violence in line and suppressed it:

> And were it not for this pressure, the pressure of command and the pressure of Internal Affairs, he would conduct himself as he sees the police, and that is as commandoes. I guess that's kind of the bit where you swing from the ropes and kick down the doors and go in there with machine guns blazing, and you leave the bodies there for the Graves and Registrations Crew to come through and pick them up.

The same characterization of unnaturally suppressed violence ran through Kennedy's discussion of individual motivation, and particularly, of his own. He indicated that when a status issue arises — when he is challenged — this liberates "anger" or impulses and permits him to fight:

> His violent encounters start when someone is running away to avoid arrest or when someone is degrading the uniform and he becomes upset. He says that "I hit people when it is necessary and I lose my cool." When "I've lost my cool or when I'm angry, I'm letting that person know who is the boss."

The model Kennedy sketched of himself was that of a suppressed volcano, with a propensity for occasional eruptions. The result of eruptions, in addition to satisfying violent impulses, is the consolidation of status or dominance:

> Another quote here — "these violent urges." He seems to equate these violent urges also, I notice constantly, with the adrenalin flowing. With the flow of the adrenalin comes the violent desire. And he used words—for instance "challenge," "dominate," "conquer," "beat into the ground," "John Wayne has got to win," "it's to win."

The problem becomes compounded when Kennedy claims that he reacts against the eruptions of others, but — as one of our group members notes — the paradox is resolved if one considers the suppression of others as indirect self-control. (This explanation — as may be recalled — had come up in connection with the previous interview):

> He said things like "control these impulses in me," "anger gives way to violence." He constantly mentions when you act in a violent way, this is giving way to some animalistic tendency. Real animals doing vicious things are violent themselves. All men are animals down inside. And he says when he sees somebody acting in this animalistic nature, it gets on his nerves, and he tries to stop it. And maybe it's because he has the fear of the same thing in himself. And by doing so, he comes to fight the fire with fire, fight the animal on his own terms of being an animal, and yet feeling bad maybe that he has to do it that way.

Lastly, Officer Kennedy made a strong point to the group of his assumption that the department had checked his violent propensities, and that he could expect no further physical involvements on the street. "I go out of my way to avoid fights," he maintained. "I don't want brutal cops on the street." With respect to this stance, one of our officers (Kent) speculated:

> I think he came up here to tell us that he had changed. And to give us some sort of reasoning for his sort of joining the Establishment. I think he was looking for approval from us. I think maybe one reason for this is that he wasn't finding

— because he had changed, he had already decided that he had to change in order to advance — that maybe he wasn't finding the peer group approval from the locker room. So he had to find it somewhere. And even more so, I don't know — like I said, the guy is no dummy — maybe in the back of his mind he felt that this information would get passed on somewhere else, the fact that he's changed his approach. I think the reason that we saw so many of the contradictory statements was that he's still got to maintain a partial identity of the tough guy with the peer group that he finds down in the locker room. And this is where we find our contradictions.

Given this explanation, there were other complexities and inconsistencies in Kennedy's self-portrait. Bill, the group leader, categorized some of the themes in Kennedy's interview, three of which he labelled "the idealistic tough guy," "the introspective marshmallow," and "the justifier." There was some speculation that at least some of these roles were being played for the benefit of our group:

Here's a guy saying "I enjoy violence," and some of us get upset. And we say to him "don't you see all these alternatives? And how can you enjoy violence, and isn't this terribly shocking?" And I think at that juncture what was happening to us is we had a game of honesty played on us, where the fellow says "I'm going to be completely honest with you" and then proceeds to say all kinds of really deep dark things about himself and at times you almost want to stop him and say "look, I've got to protect you because you're really exposing all kinds of terrible things." And he says "well, you know, I'm making sort of a monster out of myself," with a little snicker. And sure enough, you take a look and the guy is making a monster out of himself — there he is, "I'm enjoying violence, I've got all these deep dark urges. When I repress them I sit there clenching my teeth and have my hands in my pockets and I've got to go to a sex orgy to let all this energy out, because that's the kind of guy I am." You start having the feeling that you're being tested, that you're being goaded just like these people out in the street. You're being goaded this way because you're the Violence Prevention Unit and this is the way that you can be goaded, by my saying "I am the Violent Man — I'm what you're fighting" . . . But then you also have this business where he is trying to suck us in. He says "I enjoy violence, we all enjoy violence." Meaning, "you guys enjoy violence." And "what nerve do you have having me up here for being a guy who joins the police force to get a little action when it's quite obvious we all do. Let's all cop out to how we are all really violent and the only thing that's keeping us from being violent is Internal Affairs."

Role-playing aside, the picture presented to the group was clearly paradoxical, and considerably more complex than the patterns emerging from previous interviews. The group considered various ways of reconciling disparate elements. One of these was summarized by a staff member:

Now this commando or Green Beret model of policing that he has is a little odd, because he gets something here that says each of us is sort of an uncontrollable force and it's the job of the police department to squelch us. And it sounds like if that happens you can be proud both of being potentially violent and also of being squelched, so that you can't really lose. Because essentially Kennedy can say "look, I am still capable of winning fights, and the only reason why I don't win them is because the police department is not permitting me to fight. And I don't mind in one sense the police department not permitting me to fight because I am also in this police game. That is, I don't like people out there stirring up trouble. But at the same time I myself am still capable of doing the things that I have been doing. And it's only the system that keeps me from doing them." Which I think is sort of in miniature the feeling he has about himself. That is, that he is sort of controlling himself, although he's capable of exploding at any minute. There's all that adrenalin there that is flowing. But still, there is the mind over matter bit, and he emphasized this very early in the game. He says "I don't lose my cool — I choose to lose my cool. And now I don't choose to lose my cool as much as I chose to lose my cool before." So he has to feel that he's in control, but he also has to feel that he can get out of control and can have these highs and can have this fun and can be this monster, whenever he can get away with it. That is, he does not like the self-image of being a guy who had the controlling forces in command. It's got to be sort of a precarious balance at all times. A constant battle, where the only time you can be nonviolent is when you can give yourself some pretty solid reasons for being nonviolent. Then you can stand there saying "there but for the grace of God goes another corpse. And it's only the system, or these things that I choose to give way to, that keeps this guy from being a corpse." And that way, save face. I must say he has me convinced when he comes in and says "I am a violent man, I am a monster." I think he is. I think, however, that's just one part of the picture. I also think he's a guy who's very capable to coping with this, but in a situation in which he doesn't get any excuses for coping with it, he isn't going to. I think that's part of what he was trying to tell us.

The group decided that some of Kennedy's self-description was more revealing than he suspected. Thus one of the officers observed:

Whenever Kennedy gets into any kind of a confrontation like he was here tonight, you'll notice that right around his collar-line it starts a brilliant red color, and it creeps right up. I was watching it as he started taking us on here tonight. It finally covered his whole face. Evidently there's some physiological change that goes here and maybe this is this apprehension that we're talking about.

Except for "group participation" ratings, the session brought the quantitative indices back into the "high" category, with the group feeling that it was developing its procedure and learning much. The most frequently checked adjective was "valuable," followed by "thought provoking" and "constructive"; other recurrent rating terms were "challenging," "promising" and "informative."

Back to the Drawing Board

The next meeting was a two-part working session. During the first half, the group met with a captain who had requested that one of his men be interviewed. The purpose of this session was to brief the group on the interviewee's problem, as assessed by the captain.

The group was pleased by this session on two counts. First, there was pride in having been perceived as a resource — particularly by a member of management:

I think we can be flattered somewhat that a command officer

sat down and told us that he has exhausted just about every means that he has available to him in an attempt to help this officer, and now finds himself (working with) patrolmen who have come up with a proposal that might do the job better than he himself can do it. And, I think that is something to be damn proud of. I really think that it is something that we can kind of wallow in for a while.

The second source of satisfaction was the fact that a commanding officer might become sufficiently concerned with helping a patrolman to take the trouble to explore available resources. Simultaneously, the group felt that the department might face a general problem in not having supervisors equipped with information or skills relevant to the diagnosis of problems. The group discussed the possibility that the supervisor's role might make if difficult to exercise constructive influence:

Like he was aware of several danger signs, he went through the standard procedure of calling a man in and talking to him, not really having any plan or pattern or any idea what was bugging the guy, what the man's individual problems were. And it's an indication to me that something's lacking around here in all ranks. That possibly a training program could remedy.

In the second half of the session the group broke up into subgroups to work on the details of projects. One of these subgroups, chaired by Kent, worked on the review panel idea. The other group dealt with a questionnaire exploring possibilities for using lineup time for short-term remedial training. The line-up survey group reported progress, but added that "everybody subverted each other all night long." The action review group characterized their session as "an agonizing exercise" from which they "emerged a bit torn up mentally."

Session ratings ranged widely, with some men classifying the evening as productive and pleasant and others declaring themselves exhausted. The most frequently used adjectives were "thought provoking," "challenging," and "inconclusive."

Running out of Steam

At the next meeting the group was faced with the prospect of more planning and collective thought. No activity was scheduled, nor was there a consuming pending task. One concrete assignment was the planning session relating to an interview the following night. The remainder of the time was occupied with drafting and discussion. This portion of the meeting was somewhat slow. Its most negative assessment came from one group member, who said that

> After lunch I felt that we all fell apart. As I looked around the room, I found everyone . . . doing something other than the work that was going on or should have been. We spent an unproductive second period of joking, doodling, and making obscene gestures at one another.

The group leader viewed the session somewhat more favorably. He observed:

> There comes a time when you kind of think you run out of things to do and rather than think about something and rather than really push yourself on it, you have a tendency to want to not do anything. And I think we were damn near at that point tonight, because that's how I felt. I seem to relate everything to how I feel. And I wrote down that the group seemed to move tonight simply because it wanted to. I really didn't think I'd be able to get on board tonight, but I found it really easy when things started moving. And it was merely because you guys started participating and producing something.

A staff member's assessment fell somewhere in between:

> I think Bill put it very accurately — it was a tough session, we had a lot of thinking to do today; we didn't have anything entertaining to do, like interviewing somebody. And we sat around for eight hours, and we did some solid talking and thinking and looking at information and reading, and we got through it and we survived it and we got some ideas to take with us that we didn't have when we arrived.

The interview planning session did capture the interest of the group. It produced some observations, but no conclusion:

> We sensed that there was a person here who has a tendency

to put himself in a situation where some people have given him some warnings that they're going to be unfriendly if he orders them to do things that they're not going to do. And then he jumps on them when they predictably respond, or fail to respond. There is still a certain amount of mystery about this which is healthy — because it kind of shows the point to which one can proceed with these preliminary reviews and the gaps that are left, which is a lesson that we have to learn. And we will learn it filling in tomorrow.

The group also decided to adopt a new member, Officer Spark. Spark belonged to another group, where he had become the focus of tensions. Adopting Spark was a calculated risk, and the group took it freely and lightly. Several members observed that as things stood they need not fear potentially destructive influences. The group felt that it could proudly regard itself as a regenerating environment.

Except for morale ratings (which were high) the officers were disinclined to boast about their accomplishments. Nor did they despair. Almost all rated the meeting as "constructive," and some thought it was "creative" and "valuable." However, there were complaints about occasional "rambling."

Accomplishment

In a sense, the interview of Officer Fels represented movement from the sandbox into the battle field. Whereas previous subjects had presented themselves as volunteers, and as participants in the design of the project, Fels was neither. Here was a man who had been ordered up for an interview, with reason to be wary and resentful. The order had emanated from a superior who had previously voiced strong reservations about Fels' conduct — who had remonstrated with him, ordered, cajoled, sermonized and threatened. Officer Fels suspected that his conduct was the issue, and assumed that the proceeding was adverse. He knew nothing about the group, nor had he more than superficial past contact with any of its members.

Not surprisingly, Fels entered into the situation coldly, sullenly, and determined to remain silent. He started by refusing to read his reports, and responded "I don't recall" to every one of Bill's questions. According to an outline-chronology by Kent, the first hour and a quarter of the interview transpired as follows:

My first entry on this little conglomeration of notes that I keep, says "he's extremely defensive, stern." At 8:05, this is 5 minutes after he sat down, I wrote "his responses will be like testimony." At 8:12 I made a notation "things are going bad." At 8:20 I made a notation, "Bill sounds like a cross-examination." Also, I put down the first report in this case that we thought was a good report was bad actually, I think. Because it put him way on the defensive. We picked up a few things. At 8:45 I made a notation that we were belaboring that first report. Then we go to the second report; then we jumped right to the third one. This is 9:15.

Fels' initial reluctance to respond had adverse impact on the questioning. The issue began to revolve around a concerted effort to wring a concession or acknowledgement from Fels. In one report, for instance, the group worried about Fels' reluctance to permit an intoxicated woman to be taken to her nearby home. As one officer (Graham) summarized this incident:

In an attempt to get him to open up, everyone kind of got on a bad bag. Whether they couldn't find another one or not, or what it was, but you wanted to try to make him open up and think about alternatives. So you're trying to come up with an alternative in this drunk case. And you couldn't get him to come up with one, so you suggested one, and then everybody took it on and you wanted him to admit something which he didn't believe. And everyone kept bringing up the aspect of possibly letting the suspect go, which may have been an alternative. But nothing else was mentioned, and then it went on with "haven't you ever done this before?" "let her go, let her go, let her go." I kept hearing this cry from the group. And he kept sitting over there saying "well, I don't see why I'd have to let her go — isn't there any other alternatives? Is that all you've come up with?" And I felt that possibly at that time, that he might, since he's new and hasn't heard all this, be thinking along the lines of "is that their alternative, period?" No 's' on the end. "Do you have to make these arrests just because she's a little drunk?"

Eventually, after an indigestible Mexican lunch which produced innumerable complaints from the group, the atmosphere began gradually to relax and Fels talked. He started "remembering" details, including those not entered in the report. He began to speculate about motives and to discuss his premises. He became — ultimately — voluble. It became clear, as Bill later noted, that Fels "was ready to talk to somebody . . . really wanted to talk to somebody."

Fels speculated that at some juncture he had developed a pattern of reacting personally to suspects and bystanders. He indicated that he had permitted people to "get under his skin"; "respect" had been an emotion-laden issue. He confessed to feeling "challenged" by lack of respect and to creating confrontations: "He was out there thinking of himself as having to uphold the whole legal structure when anybody defied it by saying something to him or by not responding to him."

The group was not surprised by this analysis because it corresponded to hypotheses formulated the previous evening in the review of Fels' reports:

> We did a very good job confirming all the hunches that we built up during the agonizing four to eight hours that we looked over this stuff. That is, almost everything that he told us about himself we had thought through, and in a sense this was a kind of confirming session . . . Which meant we did some solid thinking. It was right to the point.

Like Kennedy, Fels presented a picture of having been suppressed and controlled. He produced two versions of this sequence. His first model was that of a "pendulum" movement which he thought was fairly general with policemen:

> He definitely thought when he was coming on and he first came on he was very susceptible and quite liberal, and open-minded. And then some training officers in the peer group and some of the observations got to him, and also his personality, as he puts it, got molded to the point where he was taking these things personally . . . And then he was able to get out of this into another period in which now he can view things more dispassionately.

In this model, Fels attributed his transition to education:

> He said he had been taking college courses and reading black literature. His view had broadened. He can see why Blacks act the way they do, and how they view the police. And this

affects the way he acts.

He described the result as a set of insights, and indicated that he had found them to be valid assumptions, confirmed through experience:

> He used to utilize the law to enforce respect for the law. "Now I know it won't change them, it doesn't change me and it doesn't work. You can't force respect on people . . ." Fels has realized recently that he approaches people different. He talks and listens, he smiles more, he can get their view as to their actions and get their side of the story. And he can relate to them better. His first words made a difference. He tries to give the person an out . . . He has gotten over some of these premises . . . like for instance this business of "it used to be my attitude if I am saying it, you better do it. Now I feel I ought to explain." He said "how can somebody call you an MF if you walk up smiling?"

Fels' second version of change represents a strict compliance model, in which the new pattern results completely from administrative pressure:

> He's changed not really because of any changing in his mind, but he's changed because of administrative pressure here, which he thinks is unfair. He realizes that this is the environment that he's living in. If he wants to stay here he's going to have to do certain things.

In elaborating this model, Fels characterized himself as apathetic, and asserted that he was working less hard, and enjoying it less:

> He says, "I enjoy the job less. I don't go after crime like I used to. I don't know how to be aggressive and keep out of 148s." . . . He said he hadn't thought about any alternatives to being aggressive and being effective and staying out of 148s. He says now he doesn't have any initiative . . . "The department is telling me I'm bad because I have a lot of 148s. Yet I don't think the department has the facts."

According to Fels, the reason for his low productivity consisted of the blanket nature of the censure to which he was subjected. By

subjecting his street conduct to criticism, the department had failed
to distinguish between his constructive activity, and his corollary
problem behavior:

> He definitely feels like he's in a strait jacket when he's going
> out there . . . The point he made several times (is) that just
> telling him that he has a lot of 148s without any explanation
> made him very angry, especially because when somebody
> tells you that you have a great many 148s they also say you're
> a bad police officer. They don't distinguish that 148s and the
> quality of police work are definitely tied together.

In the course of the interview, the group discussed the differentiation between low quality (violence-prone) productivity, and general
activity. They pointed out to Fels that his supervisor was concerned
with his problem, as witnessed by his high opinion of Fels and his
desire to "save" him. Fels acknowledged that these arguments were
reasonable, and indicated that the discussion had been helpful. In
general, he reacted to the group very positively and appreciatively.
As he left the session, he said that he was prepared to support the
review panel project, which he viewed as necessary and constructive.

The group, in turn, was elated. Bill, the leader, introduced his
summary by indicating that he had been "trying to think of how I
can talk into the tape . . . without sounding like a kid who just woke
up on Christmas morning." Jones, on his reaction form, waxed
lyrical ("it's been shown that a rough road can end at a beautiful
meadow.") Officer Spark, the new group member, characterized the
review unit as "great," and expressed the hope that he could be
used on future panels.

Productivity ratings averaged "very high", as in the first session
of the summer. Almost everyone rated the session as both "tense"
and "constructive." Other adjectives (in order) were "enjoyable"
and "purposeful"; "valuable," "relevant" and "promising"; "instructive," "inspiring" and "beautiful." The summer had reached
its climax.

An Interlude of Alienation

Joe, the co-leader, introduced his contribution to the next session's
summary by saying:

> We really didn't have anything going that anybody wanted to

bring out right off the bat. There are a lot of things that are on policemen's minds today and we brought some of them out . . .

As another officer put it (on his reaction form):

The before lunch session *screamed* many frustrating things felt by policemen today.

The "frustrating things" had to do with recent snipings at police officers in various major cities. Once this subject came up, it branched into increasingly remote areas. At first, there was concern about the sufficiency of protection — was there enough "backing"? Then there were issues of priorities, strictures, arbitrariness of rules, lack of appreciation. At one acrimonious juncture Joe advanced the proposition that

It's going to be a hell of a thing to sell a violence reduction program in police work when you're getting policemen snuffed out left and right all over the country,

Bill, who had tried (unsuccessfully) to curb the discussion, "dropped out" of it, and became a low participant. Eventually, the group returned to business, and turned to reviewing the records of its next prospective interviewee.

In the summary the evening was penitently reviewed, with the only positive note injected by a staff member, who indicated that the evening's discussion might have some bearing on the concerns of several interviewees:

The idea is "well, they . . . are trying to make me stop doing work." Which then gets to the issues of is this police department, or is the Chief, really serious about doing police work? Or is he in the community relations business? And although the discussion itself may not have been terribly relevant, the more I think about it, the more it's obvious that there are some indications in this kind of discussion that are relevant. They have to do with the issue of good people like Fels for one, and maybe even possibly at some juncture Spark, saying "I feel like I'm being forced into a position of not being able to do my job. And I'm going to be unhappy and I'm going to be inactive and I'm going to view this department as in a sense not designed to get the job done." And on another level it relates to the feeling of maybe they aren't serious about protecting me from snipers. Or maybe the Chief isn't really on our side, maybe he's just a politician as opposed to a guy who's out there trying to facilitate our work. So in a sense the theme is related.

But the group was unconvinced. The session was rated relatively low, and the adjectives reflected considerable ambivalence of feeling. The top four rating terms, for instance, were "enjoyable," "constructive," "inconclusive" and "rambling"; these were followed by "valuable," "frustrating" and "subversive." The group had permitted itself a cathartic experience, and was now determined to return to business.

The Interviewer as Theorist

The next session was that of September 1, the last group session of the summer and the penultimate meeting of the project.

This evening started off somewhat disappointingly, with the scheduled interviewee, for whom preparations had been made, not appearing. Fortunately, Officer Chico Bond, a member of Group Two, had stayed in the building and volunteered for an interview. The group spent an hour getting ready for Bond and then subjected him to a review session. In the final portion of the meeting the conclusions reached about Bond were compared to those obtained with other subjects, and some general assumptions of a theoretical nature were advanced and discussed.

Chico Bond is a relatively young, slight officer, whose physical encounters had taken place almost exclusively with suspects of Mexican-American extraction — most of them youths. Officer Bond admitted that he sometimes felt personally challenged by these persons, and that he felt compelled to respond:

He said. . . . "The suspects failed to comply." "The suspect appeared hostile — looked like he was mad at being stopped."

He felt that he was being challenged at the time. This young man was a threat to him. He says "I played his game and I met his challenge. I put myself in a position to lose face if the suspect didn't leave." And also the suspect would lose face if he did leave, so they had kind of a standoff here.

At the simplest level, the hypothesis about Bond was that he sensed a similarity between himself and his Mexican-American suspects, which he than set out to disprove:

> With all the problems he has with Mexican-Americans it was perfectly plausible to me that there's a great deal of similarity between some of these Mexican-American teenagers and Chico Bond. He isn't in some respects an imposing, muscular physical specimen. And it's entirely possible to speculate that he's also out there occasionally trying to make a case for his being an imposing figure. And he runs into other people who have the same case to make. You get a collision there, on account of there's only one imposing physical figure at any given altercation of this kind. And there is not room for both unless there is some kind of compromise possible. And you don't get the feeling that there was much compromise.

A more sophisticated (and more general) formulation was advanced by Officer Kent, who summarized it as follows:

> What I've noticed here, and I don't know if it's going to come out with the rest of the people we're dealing with, but the word I've got here again . . . is fear. Here you have fear of Mexican-Americans just like earlier we saw fear of hypes, fear of Negroes, fear of the crowd inciter and now we have fear of a Latin American. It seems to follow a pattern. And I'm wondering if when he has this particular fear when he approaches a person on the street, a person tends to get tense, and when he's tense because he has this fear that he's trying to control, if this causes a breakdown in his ability to verbally communicate with somebody. And when you have the breakdown of this verbal communication — this willingness to get out and talk to the person on a police officer-citizen contact, it almost seems like it's going to be a corollary that you will have physical contact, because you have this mutual misunderstanding. Because the citizen's going to be afraid of the policeman too at a particular point. And consequently, if you have just orders coming out and he doesn't want to comply, you have both people that are nervous, tense, tight and sooner or later somebody's going to take some sort of action. Because obviously the verbal communication is broken down.

The application of this view was elaborated by one of the staff members:

> I do think there may be something to this fear bit . . . That when Chico gets afraid he becomes a different person. That he isn't the mild, sweet gentle Chico we all love. And you kind of have the feeling that maybe the one game that is going on with these Mexican-Americans is that he is in effect challenging them. That is, he isn't so much being challenged as he is challenging them, and there is communication going on here, and they are getting the message. I'm impressed, by the way, by the fact that we are putting some life on this bone of people refusing to comply with orders, which is in fact how eight out of ten 148s start out according to the statistical analysis. The statistics just give you that fact. One thing you get from Chico is that very often the order that is given or the instruction that isn't being complied with is really impossible for the person to comply with, not physically but in terms of the way he has already pointed out in some way or other to the officer he's going to to be able to act. And it seems to me that one thing that you get with Chico is he does present difficulties to the civilians that they can't resolve. And it isn't so much that he gets mad with people who don't follow his orders, like another guy we had up here, but he has a tendency to give people orders that are boxing them in and then he gets into trouble. It's interesting that in many of the instances, that is at least those instances that we've looked at, you've got a 148 where there's no real grounds for arrest in the first place.

This formulation led to a long and spirited discussion among the group. Joe, the co-leader, demanded a dictionary definition of "fear;" Graham worried about the implication of manifest fear among police.

There followed a discussion in which officers who had been interviewed speculated about the role of fear in their incidents. Jones maintained that he could detect fear in his own encounters; Graham (in response to arguments from other officers) began to see a possible involvement of fear in some of his own incidents:

> Jones: This reminds me of this incident that we've got on tape that I went over. Remember when I snatched the guy when he swung? This is probably the same type of thing

that we're talking about here. I reacted so fast because of apprehension, fear of what might happen.

Graham: Do I really need to prove myself when I go through the door, or is it because — well, I find that hard to believe about me . . .

Officer: You know, in your character, in your ideas about fear, you've rationalized in your own mind that you've corralled fear and you're able to rationalize any incident that comes about where fear should be a part of it . . .

Graham: Well, there were two incidents like that . . . I mean I was already ready to pick myself up from the sidewalk and fly through the window.

Graham: Why don't you expound on this fear thing? The group mentioned this as an observation about Beam. And then I just took it like an explanation. And now Kent is actually making a kind of theory out of it. And I don't know how you're bringing in fear, but I'm having a hard time imagining policemen out in the street afraid.

Bill: You've never been afraid?

Graham: Not as a running emotion, as constant a factor as this theory suggests.

Officer: Everytime I get in the car I've got it.

Graham: Well, on a particular incident, yes, but I find the theory being presented as a constant.

Bill: Could the fact that an officer could or could not act out of fear be because he's in a position where he can't make an exit? I would say that if a person was in fear or afraid other than a policeman it's obviously possible for him to get the hell away. A cop can't do that; he's got to stay there, although he feels that fear. Which makes him act out of that fear. You can't leave the scene like a truck driver or a banker or an insurance salesman or anybody else. You've got to stay there; that's your job. It makes it pretty goddamn awesome at times.

Graham: At times, but no one answered this question about the fear as a constant.

In response to Graham's request, a staff member elaborated on the possibility of behavioral patterns based on habitually suppressed fear:

> All right, lets say it's a constant in some respect but not in others. For instance, forgetting for the moment about the fear but thinking about what would happen if it were there at some level, and at some level meaning, you can't leave the scene, like Bill says . . . One thing is you can run in there without cover just to show you're not afraid. Another is you can go out there and be a man of steel and exaggerate the danger of all these people, and the more danger the better. That's another thing you can do. Another thing you can do is pick the first little guy you come across and beat him up, which is as a matter of fact the most terrible way of all. That's the way bullies do it. That is, you make other people afraid and the more afraid they are the more you feel you're an inspirer of fear rather than a feeler of fear. Another thing you can do is brave it out, and this is where you get the Chico Bond type of thing. That is, you come on more harshly than you would if you weren't afraid. The point being that all of these maneuvers and some others are designed for two purposes. One is to fool yourself, in the sense of making it hard to view yourself as a guy who's capable of fear, and the other one is fooling the other people involved, or the spectators or the opposition . . . It's possible that one of the main problems in the police business is how to make yourself accept fear as a perfectly decent, respectable emotion to have if it doesn't run away with you, obviously. Not panic — fear. Admitting it. You know, the locker room doesn't compensate you if you go in there and say "you know, I was scared out of my pants today."

The staff member argued that the suppression of fear could be a reaction to a self-image which labels fear as a symptom of vulnerability or weakness:

> I think one thing we've got to understand is that when you say "fear" you're dealing with something that is sort of like the middle of a sandwich. That is, in these situations that the guy feels afraid . . . what he is feeling and what he is doing is fighting off fear. But on the other hand, that isn't the answer either, because then you can go on and say, "why is

that such a big issue?" And then you start getting some other answers. Like, for instance, if you can admit that you're afraid, you admit that you're *weak*. And you may have a big problem about feeling weak. So you can get the Man of Steel type thing, which really says, two steps removed . . . "I'm really not much of a guy, I'm really pretty vulnerable," and then you end up making yourself invulnerable. But in between is this feeling that you've got to fight off because it would make you admit what you don't want to admit . . . But on top of everything else, this is a dangerous job. We've got fear running through this whole business, and then we've got some guys who seem to have more of a thing here than others.

The group also returned to the fact that several interviewees (including Officer Bond) had reported that their conduct had changed. This led to a discussion of the review panel as a context in which constructive movement (whether real or fictitious) could be positively discussed and rehearsed:

> They wouldn't go around the locker room saying "I have changed." They say it here. And I think the exercise of saying "I have changed" and documenting it, is healthy. That is, one of the purposes of this interview might in fact be to give an opportunity to a guy of emphasizing those things about him that are positive, which otherwise might be submerged again by talking about inactivity, which is quite popular. It's quite respectable. Even Joe would regard it as respectable for a guy to say "well, this department has gotten me down and so I'm not doing any work." No one in the locker room would look down on you for this. But if they are talking more, "and I used not to tell people much and now I talk to them," that doesn't strike me as something that would get you many pats on the back in the locker room.

The session had thus provided an opportunity to conceptualize further the role of the panel, to begin generalizing about the dynamics of problem officers, and to discuss concepts meaningful to the analysis of patterns.

Despite the fact that some of the discussion had involved personal conflict, and despite the abstract nature of the ideas, the group felt good about the session. The ratings were high. The only negative adjective was "puzzling." Other terms used to described the session were "academic" (a positive attribute), "enjoyable," "sensible," "constructive," "relevant," "promising," and "thought provoking."

The Activity Profile

FIGURE 2: Group One—High Points and Low Points of Profile

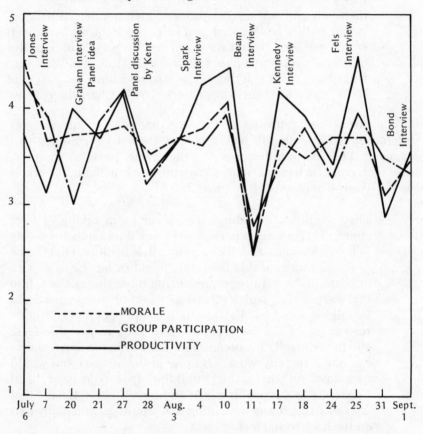

Figure 2 presents the profile of quantitative ratings for Group One. The high points of the productivity graph are identified, and all relate to the review panel. Interviews and interview analyses produced favorable ratings, and interviews with "outsiders" ranked higher than the less worrisome "in-group" exercises.

The group morale rankings proved relatively stable, except for three "low productivity" sessions (in which morale dropped) and the first group session, in which morale was uniquely high. Participation was often closely tied to productivity, but occasionally proved independent.

A General Comment

In a later section we shall attempt to evaluate the Action Review Unit as a contribution to the police and as an experiment in planned change. It now remains to discuss the brief life of Group One as a functioning group.

The first impression that strikes an observer is this group's high degree of task orientation. It may be noted that almost every session has some relation to the main project. On the first day the stage is set and a preliminary rehearsal takes place; the discussion of the second meeting is germaine; the idea is formalized in the third meeting. In almost every subsequent session a task is performed or concepts explored that feed directly into the review panel.

Several other projects were stillborn during this period. Their life consisted of explorations of rationale, discussion of practical problems and — in one instance — the design of an instrument. In no case did a side project occupy more than a fragment of meeting time and a few members.

The success of the group (if we use summaries and rating forms as criteria) can be attributed to three factors: (1) Time was taken up with consuming practical tasks which were related to an objective that the group identified with. These tasks (the interviews) were intellectually stimulating, controversial and challenging, and productive of generalizable information. As the officers developed as interviewers, they attained insight into the conduct of their peers and into their own behavior, as well as becoming informed about their jobs. They increasingly saw the value of interviews; even the subjects saw the experience as useful for themselves and for others. (2) The group enjoyed sophisticated leadership. Not only were the sessions conducted with sensitivity to group and individual dynamics, but group leaders had acquired substantive background which was deployed at critical junctures. Both leaders (especially the main leader), had perfected pattern-analytic and interview techniques before the project was born; both had become familiar with concepts that provided a framework for discussion; both had group experience that helped them deal with victories and defeats to which they were subjected. (3) The group contained key members who were stimulating and self-stimulating, and who were able to originate ideas for the group and conceptualize them in detail. It is obvious that Kent would be a figure of power in any group. Somewhat less obviously, other permanent members (particularly Jones) and even some of the guests made critical theoretical contributions.

The role of staff members in the group was not that of non-directive observers. Typically, staff made two contributions: (1) they
added to the analysis following interviews, by building on concepts
advanced by group members; (2) they produced observations about
group process, especially in the summary. Staff members also
participated in interviews, especially at first. In this connection,
one important factor is the complete trust between staff and first-
generation officers. This trust spread to the group, so that staff were
considered full fellow members.

Group One enjoyed a happy, harmonious, and productive life.
Its single-minded and effective dedication to its self-assigned task
made this group a model problem-solving enterprise.

FIGURE 3: Group Two—High Points and Low Points of Profile

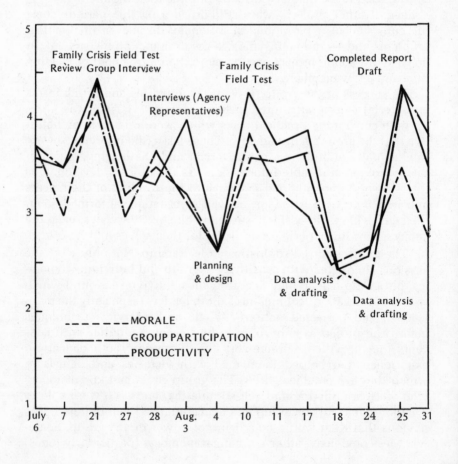

5 • Group Two: Family Crisis Teams

The second of our groups defined its mission differently from the first. Like the first group, it took an interest in police responses to street situations; but it evolved projects which invoked largely organizational solutions to police ineffectiveness.

One of the projects originated by the group was not directly related to violence. We shall touch on this project briefly, and trace its relationship to group process and productivity.

The second activity of the group — which we shall discuss in detail — is unique in several respects. For one, it represents an effort to adapt an experiment originating elsewhere The adaptation is one which (in line with the concerns of our project) isolates violence as a theme, emphasizes systematic data gathering and analysis and invokes peer influence as a training tool. The project also carried the group from the conference table to the field, where it conducted live tests of project feasibility. In addition, the group used help and information sources from outside the department, involving agencies and groups in the Oakland community.

The quantitative profile of the group is available in Figure 3, where the high and low points are identified. The high-ranked experiences were those relating to field experiments, to encounters with outside professionals, to project planning and project impletion. The low points include sessions in which data were tabulated and analyzed and reports were drafted. We shall return to this pattern at a later point in our discussion.

Preliminary Explorations

Group Two did not embark on its career with a spurt of enthusiasm. Instead, the first session ranged casually over several areas. This included an exchange of ideas relating to violence, a general "gripe" session, and a firmly formulated project proposal.

The discussion relating to violence was initiated by a group member (Officer House) who questioned the rationale of the unit. His manner of posing the problem is reflected in the summary:

> The issue that we did get hot and heavy on right before lunch was the question of "why keep talking with a suspect when you have wasted two minutes on him already and he has failed the attitude test?" And we had a wide range of issues here and I think we still are fairly sharply divided on these issues, and it's going to take us several weeks I'm sure before we can get House on our side . . . I might say, at last count House was holding forth in a kind of eulogy to the John Birch Society, so we have not really made what you would regard as a substantial dent in him.

A more positive outcome was achieved with a related discussion, in which the group addressed the problems of an officer faced with other officers bent on "street justice." This discussion was stimulated by Spark, who recalled an incident in which some angry colleagues had apparently beaten a suspect. The group stipulated that "street justice" was undesirable, and worried about its causes and consequences. They showed particular concern for the "witnessing" officer, who stood between the frying pan of his conscience (and departmental orders) and the fire of peer pressure:

> We went off on a second subject which engaged us quite actively, and it came from an experience which one of us had very recently, in which at the tail end of a very exciting high-speed chase, a number of officers who had arrived on the scene fairly late took it upon themselves to very forcibly restrain the suspect. And there was some question as to whether all this forcible restraining was really absolutely necessary. And this took us on a fairly intensive discussion on when does one and does one not have the right to lose one's cool, what about the officer who engages in street justice, some subdivisions of street justice (such as those that leave lumps and those that don't), what are the repercussions for the rest of the department of somebody having dispensed street justice at some stage . . . And again we didn't resolve these questions completely, but we had the issues quite nicely posed and we were beginning to talk about, if we did take the position that at least some type of punishing on the street after a person has been restrained is

not good police work, how do we go about making this clear to people who have been doing this or might be tempted to do this . . .

We did also, I think, worry a little bit about the officer in whose presence that type of thing is committed. Who obviously, in terms of what's right, has some kind of obligation here to intercede or try to prevent this kind of thing from happening again, but who on the other hand is under fairly strong pressure from the peer group — and speaking of pressure from the peer group, we talked some about the locker room and its emulation of officers who have good war stories to tell.

The ventilation of complaints occurred late in the session, and ranged from the macroscopic to immediate, "housekeeping" gripes:

We also talked some about the criminal justice system and the prevalence of negotiated pleas and light sentences and so on, and we had a number of standard gripes in this area . . . We ended up with the number of chairs in the report writing room, and then it suddenly occurred to us that maybe we were off the subject.

The proposal that came before the group originated with Caspar White, a trade-union-oriented officer. White harbored a long-standing concern with the problems presented by reserve officers — a category of part-time police volunteer who functions in restricted capacities, mainly on weekends. White's feelings about reserve officers — mainly negative ones — were couched in the form of questions about their training, qualifications, performance, and level of integration into the department. The other officers agreed to pursue these questions, since these involved research and could lead to constructive change. The group resolved to interview some reserves, as well as the sergeant in charge of the reserve unit.

The ratings for the first session represented average rankings for the summer ("high minus"); the adjective most often invoked was "honest." This was followed by "enjoyable," "constructive," "creative," "inconclusive" and "rambling."

Tooling Up

Except for a brief, abortive effort to continue the previous day's griping, the second meeting was task-oriented.

Part of the time was invested in the reserve study and in the design of a questionnaire dealing with reserves. A portion was taken up with a projected four-hour field exercise in which the group intended to respond to family crisis calls in order to collect tapes. The rest of the session was occupied with a review and discussion of street incidents.

Officer White was the key figure in planning for the reserve study. He presented the substance of a report he had prepared about the program. This report contained background information supplemented with personal observations. Although these were tendentious, White advocated an objective inquiry with meticulous concern for methodological safeguards. The group invested considerable effort in drafting items for a questionnaire. Each member wrote several items, and the pool went to a staff member for editing and collation. The officers also designed a sample of respondents, stratified by assignment and time on the force. White proposed that the critical incident questionnaire (put together by our original group) be administered to the reserve force:

> White: If we're concerned with reserves, why not a questionnaire for the reserves, to get their feelings on this thing? Did any of the reserves fill out this critical incident report?
>
> Staff: No.
>
> White: That might be worthwhile, to have them do that.
>
> Leader: Boy, this guy does a hell of a job! . . .
>
> Staff: It ought to be very interesting to see how they stack up against experienced officers, recruits. Joe's guess would be, I gather, that they'd talk very glibly about moving into all kinds of situations in which an experienced officer does not. Although we have the other hypothesis now that they do just the opposite.

The exercise in methodology contrasts with the group's casual approach to other projects. The officers decided to spend four hours on the street, in specialized cars that would respond to family crisis calls. This outing was partially motivated by a desire for variety and was not viewed as a prelude to further effort. The group's verbal concern was with mechanical matters and administrative detail.

Similarly, the spontaneous "interviews" involving members of the group were not designed to feed project-related follow-up activity. They did lead to discussions of substantive issues and to critical comments. Officer Spark, for instance, was attacked for indiscriminate car-stops and for failure to call cover. Another officer (George Gross) expanded on youthful errors in judgment. The discussion of his incident included concern for the suspect's perceptions and for distortions in a recruit's view of his job:

> Later on we took one of George's reports and read it and broke it down and talked about it. . . . This was a report that George had — or a situation that George had when he first came on the police department — about his second day on the street alone. And it was a situation where at the time, he thought he had a felony arrest. It turned out that it wasn't a felony arrest. But being new and everything, and in the excitement, and without having the proper background on what you can and can't do, he told us that he had been prepared to use deadly force if the guy had spun on him, and it was quite interesting in that a lot of us probably have the same kinds of feelings when we get out there. You know, you're a little hot-doggish in the beginning anyway, and when confronted with this type of situation, you're just liable to take some action that you wouldn't take after being on the police department for a while, when you run into a few of these types of calls. Another thing that was brought out was the feeling of the individual involved, in that in this case it was a mental case, but on the other hand we can certainly sympathize with the feelings that a normal citizen could have had under these circumstances, in that he may have seen a policeman coming at him with a gun drawn and he hadn't done anything that warranted even a police contact, and he boarded a bus. And the next thing you know he's on a bus with a policeman trying to get him off it. And it could be quite a traumatic experience for somebody, not knowing what the policeman had on his mind.

In general, incidents brought before the group elicited little more than cursory exegesis, with no closure. The group was disappointed with the session, and morale ratings in particular dropped. The descriptive adjectives included "slow" and "inconclusive," as well as "critical" and "constructive."

Shaping a Group Mission

When the group reconvened two weeks later, it had two key experiences to digest. One was the retreat in Asilomar, which included a discussion by Dr. Bard of the family crisis experiment in the New York police. The second was an evening spent answering family crisis calls. The group also — as part of its session — interviewed three members of the reserve unit.

In reviewing the activities of the previous day, the group listened to two tapes of situations the officers had encountered. Both tapes evoked questions relating to outcome of the call. The men decided to answer these questions empirically, by contacting the complainants. In both cases, telephone interviews yielded testimonials about the handling of the incidents.

One call had begun alarmingly with a report of a man who presumably had attacked two persons with a knife. The officers discovered that injuries were negligible and that the suspect has suffered a share of damage. The incident had featured a three-way altercation between husband, wife, and wife's son. The wife had been scraped on the forehead with an ice-pick, the son had been menaced with a knife, and the husband had secured a black eye. The wife at first demanded that her husband be arrested and jailed:

> *Woman:* My head is bleeding. See, icepicks bleed inside.
>
> *Officer:* Yeah, well, if it penetrates at all it will bleed inside. Well, this is a serious accusation you're making. Would you be willing to go through with a formal complaint?
>
> *Woman:* I sure will!
>
> *Officer:* Even if it has Edward doing about 5 to 20 years in the penitentiary?
>
> *Woman:* I don't care! I do not care. You see that icepick — he threw that.

At length, the lady declared her willingness to entertain permanent separation from her husband, and indicated that she would subsequently file charges against him:

> *Officer:* You wouldn't be satisfied just to have Conrad leave for the night, huh?
>
> *Woman:* I'd be satisfied if you'd have Conrad leave for good.

Officer: Well, are you starting any legal proceedings against him?

Woman: Yes I am, because he threw a knife on my teenage son.

The husband, in turn, agreed to leave, but he insisted on an impromtu property settlement, including the right to remove household furnishings:

Officer: Your wife says if you take off out of here and don't come back for the night . . .

Husband: Well, I can't do it on five minutes. I've got to call people. I've got more furniture in here than she's got.

Officer: Well, you're not going to take your furniture tonight. You don't have any place to put it tonight . . . If you're not out of here in two minutes, I'm going to let your wife press the charges.

Man: Well, I can't go anywhere in two minutes!

Officer: That doesn't mean gathering your goods. That means gathering your clothes and get ready to go. Tomorrow or some other time you can arrange to pick these things up.

The wife watched her husband depart without regret, and with the expressed determination never to renew their relationship:

Officer: If he should come back tonight after we leave, you give us a call and he'll go to jail.

Woman: He can go to jail now.

Officer: You'd be in love with him again tomorrow.

Woman: I bet you I won't. You wouldn't be in love with your wife if she did what he did to me.

Officer: Your son tells me this happens all the time, ever since you've been married.

Officer: Where's he going to stay tonight?

Woman: I could care less.

Officer: Does he have some friends around the area?

Woman: I could care less.

As a symbolic gesture of irreversibility and finality, the husband was enjoined to deliver the keys to the house and to the family car:

> *Officer:* You're about all ready, huh?
>
> *Man:* Yeah, I'm ready.
>
> *Officer:* Well, let's start downstairs right now, O.K.?
>
> *Woman:* I'm pressing charges.
>
> *Officer:* Well, you think it over tonight, and if you decide to go through with it, you go down to the second floor tomorrow.
>
> *Woman:* I will.

In discussing this incident, the group divided on its probable aftermath. Some officers took taped verbalizations at face value and predicted a separation. The men who had handled the call argued for a probable reconciliation. The group's leader (who had been a responding officer) telephoned the wife, who indicated that she had re-joined her husband, with whom she declared herself in love. The police end of the conversation reads as follows:

> *Officer:* You remember I talked to you last night? I just wanted to call up and see how everything's going. Good! You didn't sign a complaint then? Yeah. You and Conrad got back together? You talked to the police this morning? Good! Did — how do you think the officers did last night when they were there? You think so? O.K. Do you think that they should have arrested Conrad when they were there? O.K. And you thought they handled themselves pretty well, then! Do you think that they should have done anything differently? O.K.
>
> I wanted to ask you one more thing: Had the police ever been there before? He's called them on you before, but there's never been any problems? It never lasts too long, anyway? I just wanted to make sure the two of you were back together and that you weren't having any more problems. You shouldn't have any problems anymore, then, right? Real good, Mrs. Jones, thank you very much!

The second incident involved a minor disturbance between neighbors, with the complainant claiming trespass on her property.

The matter was handled by gathering both sides of the story, and by relaying information about the complaint to its subject. The call-back revealed that false rumors had circulated about the actions by the officers, and suggested that the complainant had endeavored to invoke police aid in a vendetta against "undesirables" in her neighborhood.

Both callback experiences left the group with the feelings (1) that they had successfully handled their calls, (2) that they had discovered a means for monitoring the solution of police problems, and (3) that much relevant information about the nature of crisis calls could be secured after the incident was resolved. The callback procedure was thus considered a constructive innovation, illustrating heretofore unexplored possibilities that the group could explore.

The group discussed the way incidents had been handled the previous day, including such matters as time spent, the desirability of separating the parties, and the merits of making an arrest. The idea arose of introducing systematic variations in street experiments, with the provision that such variations would not include unnecessary arrests:

> *Officer 1;* I would just like to make a suggestion on what we could do the next time we went out to make tapes. What I was thinking about was actually make an arrest where it was feasible and then call the complainant back and see what she thought about that. This was fine on kiss-offs, I mean on kiss-off assignments it seemed to work out pretty well, everyone was satisfied. I'm kind of interested to see what the complainant would think if we actually locked her hubby up, to see what she would think about the police department the very next day and to see if she followed up on it . . .

> *Officer 2:* Well, I think there is a reason why we can't, and that is I think our main objective is to go out there and resolve these without an arrest. Now we're being kind of unfair if we go out there and say "well, tonight's the night we're going to arrest when we can."

> *Officer 1:* What I'm saying is if the situation merits an arrest, why not make an arrest just to see what's going to happen, just to follow up on it?

> *Officer 3:* By "merit an arrest" — I don't want us to get into

the bag of if a guy commits an offense, an automatic arrest type thing.

Officer 1: It would appear to me that if you give these recruits nothing but kiss-off assignments, assignments where no arrests are made, the situations are adjusted without an arrest, they're going to form the opinion that you never make an arrest on a 415 situation.

Officer 4: I think there's an ethical question here. You get into the bag where you make an arrest just for the sake of making an arrest. I think if we just kind of cool this thing, eventually if we do enough of them we're going to come up with one where we're going to have to make an arrest anyway.

Officer 2: Even as you're making the decision, if you're in the call and you say "o.k., I can make an arrest because she's got a lump on the side of her head. On the other hand, I could probably settle it by putting him out of the house, and she'd be just as happy with me," then I should put the guy out of the house and let her be happy, rather than to resolve it by arrest just to find out what the follow-up will bring.

Officer 4: If we do make an arrest on any of these 415s, why not follow up with a phone call like we did on the others?
One other thing on this Family Crisis Intervention Unit. I agree if we are going to have one, we might as well have as much to say about it as we can, rather than having somebody from the outside who doesn't really understand the problems of Oakland come in here and set up a pre-patterned method of having a unit like this.

As the group discussed its experiences in handling family disturbances, it began to think in terms of a family crisis team project. No formal decision was made about adopting this task, nor was there a plan for pursuing it. The group simply stipulated that they were engaged in working on the problem of police response to family crises; previous to this juncture, they had viewed themselves as collecting tapes for training use.

The group discussed the fact that a university representative had approached their department about duplicating the Bard experiment. The officers expressed reservations about this approach:

They agreed that their use of tapes would insure a more sophisticated type of unit, and they anticipated the need for other innovations and modifications. They began to talk about the prospect of a formal proposal.

With regard to the reserve study, a group interview took place which explored the views and problems of reserve officers. The atmosphere was cordial, and questions (which had started as implied criticisms) became increasingly sympathetic.

Officer White — who had begun his inquiry as an anti-reserve campaign — initiated suggestions to improve the lot of reserves. He was especially impressed by the reserve sergeant (a black officer), and invited him to join him on patrol. (Previously, White had proclaimed that he would refuse to ride with reserves.) Officer White commented in the summary that

> These reserves are outstanding people, I think — especially Connelly. And I don't see why perhaps something couldn't be arranged to send Connelly to patrol to talk to the lineups, like was suggested. Just having him come up here and talk has opened my mind, somewhat.

There was discussion of the benefits of personal communications especially when misunderstandings could arise based on incomplete data:

> *Co-leader:* Last year when we had the Hell's Angels up here and we had CPU, the same thing happened. We had them up here purely for an interview. And it seems to me the greatest value this served was it opened up an avenue of communication, something we don't have in this department. And today, just like last year, I think it's regrettable that the only guys who get to experience it are us. And it's too bad that we couldn't figure out a way to afford a larger body of patrolmen to get involved in this.
>
> *Staff:* Why can't we?
>
> *Co-leader:* Well, we have. We've made a start. Now, if this reserve officer goes down to the line-up and he gives a little talk, this is a way around the chain of command, the letters, and all these inter-departmental things that confuse and hinder all these attempts for interdepartmental communication. And it would seem to me that this is one kind of thing

that we're missing here — that is, a line of communication, direct communications. And if we could figure out a way to get it to the rest of the people, it would be invaluable.

In general the meeting had been lively, busy and characterized by full participation. Even Officer House (who had shown a tendency to slumber, or to leave the room for private excursions) entered into the discussion constructively. The group felt appropriately elated; ratings were the second-highest of the summer, after the session in which proposals were presented. The most-used adjective was "valuable"; this was followed by "constructive" and "purposeful." Other adjectives invoked were "relevant," "thought provoking" and "promising."

A Data Processing Session

The officers entered the next meeting eager to begin work. They concluded within five minutes that they needed data to justify their family crisis proposal. Bard had suggested at the retreat that family fights, if unresolved, produced assaults and homicides. The group undertook to verify this trend.

Officer House, who confessed to experience in data processing, rushed off to obtain offense printouts and geographically distributed incident records. The men began to go over the information and to tabulate relationships. Part of this is described in the summary:

> The information obtained from the IBM data sheets that House returned with is very complex. We passed around several IBM sheets — they contained dates, time, nature of complaints, arrest numbers, OPD numbers, addresses and types of places at which the event had taken place. House understood — had a working understanding of the information given to him and attempted to explain to us exactly what the information was on each sheet.
>
> We then sent an officer down to homicide to pick up a report on a recent 187 because we decided to research it. We then decided to check the assignment card to see how many times the police were dispatched in a family disturbance or other types of assignments. This is prior to the 187 itself. In choosing the report, we wanted to establish some kind of relationship between the deceased and the suspect.

At the conclusion of the operation, an officer reported that We have learned some valuable things this morning. We spent several hours doing some preliminary research on just one small facet of a specialization project, and I think it shows the value of a teamwork approach. We went through an awful lot of data and we have come up with some very rough ideas of what we might run into in dealing with family trouble calls. We haven't had any particular correlations between police interventions and homicides, but we can see some trends in addresses, where in a one-month period there would be a number of calls for what would call for social services. And so we can get a very rough idea that in certain addresses, in certain places they are calling upon the police on a regular basis for handling family problems.

In addition to the work on a data base for the family crisis unit, the group also discussed arguments for the creation of specialized teams. The co-leader drafted a document in which he argued for advantages in terms of "better community relations, free the beat man for other work, lighten the work load with referrals to other agencies and lessen the likelihood of injuries among the officers."

There was disagreement on other issues. Officer Young, the group leader, advocated a training function for family crisis units, including the cycling of recruits through the program. The group divided sharply on the merits of this procedure.

While the officers participated in this (and other) discussions, their interest lapsed during data inspection periods. A staff member observed that "there's been a lot of this running in and out of the room," and suggested:

If just two or three people are necessary for a given task, the others ought to be working on something else, not exchanging war stories or glancing at the ceiling over there on the other side of the table. That makes for a very boring session. I think in general we had a lesson today about how we've got to get more carefully organized.

The group seemed to concur. The session was rated "average," and adjectives such as "rambling," "slow" and "dry" crept into the descriptions.

Foundation Building

The next meeting was spent in additional data gathering and analysis; both projects gained shape and focus in relatively modest ways. The reserve project benefited from a discussion with the sergeant in charge of the unit, who discouraged the inquiry, but added facts of interest. In particular he added fuel to the group's concern with lines of communication by describing a feeling of isolation among the reserves.

In relation to family crisis management, the group discussed the distribution of calls and designed a radio room survey to provide exact information on concentrations of assignments. They then took up the matter of training needed by family crisis specialists. Unlike the New York model, their version had no provision for civilian professionals; patrolmen would handle the training and clinical tasks would be assumed by referral agencies.

Arrangements were then made to secure information about available referral agencies, and to establish links with key personnel:

> We set up for Monday morning an interview with a person from the Legal Aid Society who will enlighten us as to what the actual function of the Legal Aid Society is, and he's going to be raked over the coals for a couple of hours. On the afternoon of Monday, we're going to get a couple of people from Welfare to tell us about the different agencies in Welfare, what they do, what they will handle and won't handle.

The meeting was generally viewed as an improvement over the previous one, in terms of participation and morale. Since the bulk of time was invested in discussion, the "productivity" rating was low. The session was characterized "relevant," "informative" and "promising."

Forging Links with Other Agencies

The following session was spent in interviews. The first part of the meeting dealt with the Legal Aid Society. The attorney who met with the group was obviously surprised at the client-centered nature of the group's concerns:

> We wanted to find out how we could open a channel of discussion, how we could open up a means of getting informa-

tion back and forth. And we also wanted to find out what we could expect the Legal Aid Society to do for us, and what their limits were, so we wouldn't make bad referrals. And also so that Legal Aid would know what we do. We wanted to find out where we could get some information from the Legal Aid Society. We found out that they have a confidentiality which was already known about. Then we had a discussion on landlord vs. tenants disputes, and we went into quite a bit of depth; we returned to this topic many times. We then talked about civil disturbances, and we wanted to find out where the policeman could go to get information on what he could do to change a particular abnormal situation such as a house that was completely unfit in relation to landlord-tenants. Then we talked about the debts, the problems with people that are receiving aid of some type, getting involved, even if they're not receiving aid, but people with a limited background — educational background — getting themselves over their head in debts due to unjust business practices, etc. and what could be handled from there.

After three hours of constructive information exchange, the group found itself side-tracked in a conversation about police image, black-white relations, and police brutality. This topic led to a short confrontation between the more militant members of the group and the attorney. With no hope of resolving the issue, the interview ended amicably.

After lunch the group's guest was an official of the welfare agency who gave the officers a frank and detailed picture of problems and prospects in welfare management. The group asked many questions, and the interviewee, in turn, was fascinated by the prospect of collaboration in family crisis management. At one point during the interview, an offer was extended by the welfare representative of having volunteer service workers ride with the officers on their next field experiment:

> We were then advised that if we would like we could have, as a group, on some of our street problems that we will be going out on next week, a social worker in the car with us. This would be quite helpful to get immediate feedback, and also help us to find out where we can make some referrals that are proper referrals.

The officers accepted this proposal, and were excited by it. They were also delighted at the mass of information collected during the interviews. Session ratings were very high. Most frequently used adjectives were "constructive," "valuable," "practical," "informative" and "encouraging."

Loveless Labor

No major business had been scheduled for the next session, and the group divided into task forces charged with detailed planning of projects. The task force involved in the reserve study worked on their questionnaire and readied it for administration. The family crisis subgroup wrote a section of their proposal, and otherwise became enmeshed in minor details, such as the choice of card size for recording forms:

> *Officer:* That's a 3x5 card; do you think maybe you could go to a 6x10 or something? I don't see how you could possibly get all the information you want to know on a 3x5.

> *Officer 2:* Why don't we use a 3x5 card in the car for the officers responding to the call, and then we can have a more complete form in a separate file in the office for collecting data?

> *Officer 3:* Oh, no, you want this information for when someone goes back the next time.

> *Officer:* It seems what you're doing is just making an improved assignment card. You're going to put in writing what you already know now.

> *Officer 4:* There's no reason for putting down all this other little stuff, like being an alcoholic. It's up to you, being the man on the unit, to put it down. You would know this. It's got to be discussed, but there's no reason for putting all that on the card.

> *Officer:* Well, you'd have a summary, of course. I'm talking in terms of a checkoff list, like marital status, sex, age — well, not the same questions, of course, but source of the case, employment, nature of the case. But it seems like there's a whole batch of things. You could have a bunch of things you could just check off rather than have to write it all in.

Officer 4: It would be an awful big piece of paper.

Officer: Well, you know a 6x10 isn't that much bigger — just need a wider box to keep it in.

The men not directly involved in these activities spent much of their time in idle conversation, or in extended expeditions out of the room. As the co-leader characterized the situation:

> We lost it today. We didn't get a damn thing done except at the very end. In the beginning we didn't do very much. I don't know, but I was kind of pissed off about the whole thing today. And I think the best way to do it is the way we did it that last Tuesday. And if we're going to work on our project, four can have this room and four can have the other. Because all we did today was bullshit and screw around. We didn't get a damn thing done. All this stuff here written up about our proposal was written up in the last hour. So that's seven hours wasted and one hour of work. It's a waste if that's the best we can do.

The session ratings were low. The adjective list showed substantial variation. Highest-ranking terms were "slow," "wasteful," "frustrating" and "puposeful."

Fertilization and Cross-Fertilization

The following session consisted of another family crisis field test. This time, the group viewed their experience in terms of implications for a family crisis unit. They were concerned with possible follow-ups and referrals; they were intent on reviewing the quality of their performance. The observers who rode with the officers had been instructed to be critical, and to provide critiques in a post-ride seminar.

Each of the social workers reported that he had learned a great deal, and several commented on the volume of calls during hours when conventional social services are unavailable:

> Everything does actually happen at night. . . . I couldn't believe it tonight. I said. "I've never seen so many children in all my life. The way they acted!"

The welfare workers declared themselves uniformly pleased

by the way in which the officers handled assignments:

> *Observer 1:* I was just favorably impressed with the way the officers handled themselves tonight. Very clear about their roles with the people. They did their best, I think, to be very supportive to them, particularly on the first case with the drunken father and the family situation. The case where the man, I think, was unemployed and felt some loss of manhood at that point. Officers were very supportive, gave them every break, offered them a referral which he kind of refused. It was slow, but all in all, I had a very enjoyable time and I'd like to do it again.

> *Observer 2:* It sounds like we had quite a few 415's. It was one right after another. And after seeing what was going on, I definitely feel that it would help if you had a follow-up, of some sort. I was very impressed with the way it was handled.

The official who had met with the group the previous week, and who served as an observer, discussed liaison possibilities. He indicated that his department — as well as the officers — could benefit from future working relationships:

> I think if you can test this thing a little bit, you certainly can make the pitch to our department to work out some kind of liaison. After our meeting last Monday, I wrote a memo to our Assistant Director, and he passed it on to the Director who called me today, and I just briefly indicated in the memo what had transpired in our meeting and what we were planning on doing this evening. And the Director said this sounds great and he's interested in knowing what the follow-up was going to be, and he made the statement that he would like to incorporate something like this into our training program. What he means by this I don't know, whether it involved taking some of the more experienced social workers and utilizing them in a field placement kind of capacity so that the social worker would have a better awareness of what the police role is in the community, so that we would have better relations between social workers and policemen, or whether he's thinking in terms of bringing neophyte social workers and eligibility workers into the program just to see this particular aspect of what's going on in the community.

One of the things I see as a possibility would be making a request of our department to use some of our professional social workers, some of our people with master's degrees who have some specialized education and quite a bit of experience, and perhaps utilizing them as resource people.

The officers were justifiably encouraged by these reactions, and pleased by their own performance. They rated the session very highly, and classified it as "enjoyable," "constructive," "instructive," and "valuable."

A Spontaneous Review Panel

One of the officers who had participated in the street exercise was Officer Spark. Spark had been teamed up with Officer Young, and with a staff member as observer. Young (as well as the observer) returned visibly shaken, complaining about Spark's violence-proneness. The next day, Young initiated a discussion of Spark's conduct, which developed into a group interview.

In the summary of the day's session, Young noted that

Today we didn't get too far with projects or anything, because we spent all day interviewing Officer Spark. In any event, we discussed with Officer Spark some of the incidents that he's been involved with in the street. . . . I think we maybe made the point to him that if the opinion of many is that some of the things that he's doing are wrong, I think that maybe he should take that opinion, and maybe he will. I hope he will. I think he's going to get himself in trouble or get himself killed or somebody else killed if he doesn't analyze what he's doing out there and maybe find some different ways of doing it. That's basically what we talked about today.

Spark (who had defended himself vigorously all afternoon) ventured the view that "this was a pretty constructive session." He even expressed the feeling that "I got a lot more out of it than anybody would even think I did."

The fact remained that the Spark interview occupied the entire session. The officers met briefly with the Chief, but at this meeting a hypothetical question referred critically to Spark's pattern of conduct. Some group members, who had been anxious to continue work on the family crisis project, complained about the preempted use of session time, and questioned the relevance of the exercise:

> I don't know if spending eight hours in a session like this
> — I shouldn't say it's not worth it. It just seems like it's a
> hell of a lot of time to try to get a point across, and I'm not
> sure we ever got it across, although Spark said we did. I think
> it would do if a few more of us would discuss some of our
> incidents. Instead of giving Spark all the pressure, I think
> we should spread it around as much as we can. But not at
> the eight hour cost. That's too much time. We didn't do any
> project work today and we had some that we'd planned on
> doing. I think next Monday we're going to have to break up
> into groups almost immediately just to do some of the things
> that I know our group was planning on doing this morning.

The session rating was neither high nor low. The content of the
meeting was described as "thought provoking" and "constructive,"
although there were individual ratings of "hopeless," "weird,"
"sad," "frustrating" and "exasperating."

Process and Product

At their next session the group became very output-oriented. They
divided into two task-forces which in turn sub-divided. Each team
had its assigned chores, all related to the production of reports. In
one corner, two officers chewed on pencils as they bent over paper;
elsewhere, a typewriter clattered, and a dispute raged over the use
of a second (borrowed) machine. Two men raided the computer
for fresh data on the distribution of family fights.

The reserve officer subgroup (consisting of three men) had received some returns of their questionnaire to the troops, and had
tabulated them. They had also interviewed a deputy chief, who had
commended them for their work. They spent their time writing up
findings and drafting recommendations, and concluded with this
task at the end of the session. They then read their material into the
tape, and expressed themselves satisfied.

The family crisis group, by contrast, had little to show for their
labor. The computer data confirmed previous findings; the drafting
subgroup was stalemated over the wording of several sentences in
the preamble to their proposal. They had outlined their entire
document, but reported that they then "started with the introduction and got bogged down considerably on the role of the police
officer and how to (describe) it."

The combined group ratings for the session were relatively high, but this fact disguises differences between the task-forces. The reserve officer ratings were "high" and "very high," with adjectives such as "constructive," "purposeful," "valuable," "enjoyable," "practical," "pleasant" and "relevant." The family crisis ratings tended toward "average"; the adjective list contained such terms as "frustrating," "irritating," "slow," "bland" and "monotonous." Whereas one group reviewed their work with pride (with the product in sight) the others were enmeshed in unfamiliar, strenuous work, and they could see little light at the end of their tunnel.

Paradoxically, the first group had reached precipitous closure, but the second group was beginning to lay groundwork for an innovative, high quality product, although another week would pass before this product would strikingly emerge.

A Tortuous Interlude (1)

The next two sessions can be described as essentially a sixteen-hour marathon of clerical effort, with uneven participation.

The first of these sessions was again split. The reserve group had received more questionnaires, which they tabulated and summarized. They redrafted their introduction and improved its wording. But the group spent much time going over the same ground, or wondering what to do with itself.

The family crisis group made considerable progress on its report. The officers had pin-pointed time and place of assignment, and had collected all necessary base-line statistics for the evaluation of the unit's effectiveness. They had spelled out the organization of the unit, and listed the categories of data to be monitored for effective evaluation:

> In the organization of this unit we've decided that first of all the cars should be two-man cars, with their responsibility being primarily the handling of 415fs. But they can be used in handling other 415s and as a cover unit, in order to keep the relationship with patrol division in a good frame of mind. The men should be picked for their expertise in handling 415s. The selection should be made by the peer group. Possibly the manner of selection would be a ballot election, and it should be a voluntary thing. They will be assigned to the Violence Prevention Unit, as we understand. Also in the organization would be the coordinator who, as we under-

stand it, would also be assigned to the Violence Prevention
Unit. Some of his responsibilities would be to appropriately
coordinate the program as a whole. But in addition to that
he'll have to coordinate the referral training on an on-going
basis to keep up a liaison with the referral agencies. He would
have to maintain statistics under the number, location, etc. of
415f assignments. He would have to set up and preside over
periodic meetings with the units for purposes of discussing
roles, changes in the program, etc. He would have the responsibility for compiling and providing training materials and
he would have the responsibility for making call-backs on
415f assignments, and to check on the outcome of any referrals made to whatever agencies they were made to. Some of
the research we think is necessary for an ongoing program
would be; a) the number of 415fs over the year, including
415s, 242s, 245s or the result of 415fs but dispatched otherwise. Some of the information we'll need will be the beat,
the address, the name, the date, the time of day; b) We would
like to keep track of any injuries sustained by officers on
415fs to be broken down into three groups — those officers
in the field crisis intervention unit, those officers arriving in
normal patrol units, and those officers involved in crime
prevention units, the wagon or otherwise; c) would be our
callbacks. We'd want to know what the complainants' impressions were of the services rendered. We'd want to know
also what the outcome of the disturbance was after the
officers had left; d) would be the dispositions on 415fs. We'd
want to know what arrests, if any, were made, misdemeanor
citations issued, what happened as far as referrals go, and
we want copies of all reports made.

These ideas were largely the work of Officer Johnson, the co-
leader of the group. Johnson had also drafted the preamble to the
proposal, the wording of which was now satisfactory to the group.
This preamble read:

Police departments have traditionally assumed the responsibility for handling family disturbances. The officer's role in
such a disturbance has been one of preserving the peace
while acting as an advisor, mediator or counselor. The
primary concern is to prevent violence and settle the obvious

problem at that given time. Family disturbances are of such
a complexity that they demand more time and consideration,
yet the police officer's role remains the same — that of a law
enforcer and as a buffer between the parties involved. It
appears that the responsibility for handling the social need
will remain that of the police department and that in order
to deal with it realistically the role of the police officers need
change. The emphasis should be less on law enforcement
and more on solving the immediate as well as the underlying
needs experienced by the parties involved. This can be made
possible by having only those officers who exhibit a great
degree of expertise in handling family disturbances handle
all family disturbances, and by developing means of bringing
the parties involved into contact with whatever agencies
could aid in the solving of their problems.

Despite the superlative performance, there were problems. Officer Johnson had worked with one team-mate, and two other
officers (Young and Spark) were left out in the cold; the ratings
reflected this condition. Johnson and his partner (Officer Bond)
rated the session highly, and regarded it as "constructive," "purposeful," "relevant," "creative" and "encouraging" (Johnson also
checked "weakening" and "annoying," though the latter word may
have referred to the rest of the group). White — the leader of the
reserve group — was also fairly satisfied. He declared the meeting
"constructive," "practical," and "critical." (House's ratings were
also high, but House had spent most of the meeting away on
private business.)
The rest of the group characterized the session as a disaster.
White's team-mates produced ratings of "very low"; one of the two
invoked a write-in four-letter word. Spark and Young also expressed
unhappiness. Spark used bottom-ranks, and described the meeting
as "monotonous" and "aimless"; Young wrote that

> I do not feel that four policemen, with very little interest
> in statistics and justification of projects can produce what
> is expected. I feel staff personnel should do the research,
> make the proposals, and receive advice from the officer
> involved.

The session generally was ranked lower than any other in the series.

A Tortuous Interlude (2)

The next session witnessed a miscalculated intervention in the self-charted course of the group. But this move had no immediate impact on either the high productivity of high producers, or on the unhappiness and alienation of the others.

The principal step consisted of Young (the nominal leader of the group) entering the session with the announcement that proposal-drafting was boring, and that more active projects were called for. Young describes his effort and its results in the following terms:

> I went in and told them that we're not that concerned about the deadline or having a finalized proposal, and this kind of really put a shot right in the ass of the project. "Here all this time we've been working on this thing we've been making an effort to get done, and now they say we don't care if we get it done." And I think that was the main thing. Maybe they felt that "well, these bastards are trying to have us work just to work and they don't care what we're doing, whether we're chopping wood or we're working on a violence-reducing proposal. They just want us in there doing something, keeping occupied. Here they stressed the importance of some of these proposals and now they're saying we don't give a shit about those proposals."

The second error was committed by a staff member, who took the opportunity (in mid-meeting) of sharing with the group his ideas about an alternative organization for the family crisis activity. Young later described the group's reaction to this announcement:

> What happened there is that I think they had thought about something of that nature, or thought about what was best in their proposal, had written up what they thought should be done, and somebody came in the room and said "we're not going to do it" — or maybe implied, or maybe they drew an inference, or maybe they felt as a result of what they said, you know, "we can't do it your way anyway" type of thing. And I think that, although it didn't have that much impact.

The group continued working on their proposal through the rest of the session, though they were increasingly alarmed at the possibility of having their ideas rejected. Again, productivity was not uniform. The reserve officer group was relatively inactive except as spectators. One member of the group participated in the analysis of one of his tapes, and the others worked briefly on their proposal. The family crisis group was more active, including Young, who drafted a new section of the proposal. Officer Spark alone was unoccupied, and House (as usual) unavailable.

The session, again, was rated low. Spark pronounced the meeting a failure. White was absent at rating-time, and his two cohorts ranked the session low. Johnson and Bond declared themselves satisfied with their own productivity, but not with the session. The staff member made a plea for efficiency. The group's rating terms included "frustrating," "weakening," "strange," "sad," "annoying," "tense," "irritating," "monotonous," "slow," "aimless" and "confusing."

The End of the Tunnel

The next day the group had undergone a transformation. The day was spent in an atmosphere suffused with constructive activity, and everyone (with the possible exception of House) appeared happy and productive. Johnson, in the summary, described the session as follows:

> Today we began right away working on the different projects that we were working on. . . . After a couple of hours of finishing up on some minor tasks that we had to do, we formulated or put together our proposal as best we could by putting them in the proper order and so forth. And I think we've got a fairly good package together. I don't know how an administrator or somebody who knows what they're doing would think about it. But it looks pretty good. . . . It's now at the point where you can look at it and tell what we're trying to say in the proposal. Next week we're having a meeting with the coordinator of social services in the area, and at that time we'll be able to gather data in regards to the agencies and services available to us and to families in need. And at that time we'll make a final insert for our proposal, and then it'll be just about at the final stages.

The reserve subgroup reported that "all we do now is type the proposal up, make a few corrections in punctuation and so on and so forth, and we should be ready to roll with it next week."

Young, who in previous sessions had abdicated his leadership role, took a guiding position, and helped organize the sequence of topics. He indicates that "I became more enthused, because I played a big part in helping to finally write (the proposal) up." Young explained the general change in atmosphere by observing that

> We're at a point now where everything we do is going to be an improvement rather than a wheel-spinner. We take that last draft that we've drawn up, we're going to improve on it, I'm sure. And we're going to be able to recognize the improvements. But if you take just one little area of that thing and improve on it, it doesn't look like the whole thing's improving. You're just kind of doing something that's worthless that's going to go in a whole package. But when you've got a package and you say "we add this to it and it makes it better," fine. But when you've only got part of the package and you say "we add this to it," it doesn't seem meaningful at all. . . . Monday we can sit down and take a long look at that draft. I know of a hundred different ways we can improve that — retyping, thinking about it. But now we've got it in a final stage. We can improve on a page and retype it. We can improve on the next page and retype it.

In retrospect, Young reconstructed the sequence of the last several sessions as a pattern, intrinsic to the development of any task:

> I think, in a task like that, when you're trying to gather information and come up with something, you will run into low morale and high morale days. In the very beginning I would imagine the trend would be to be high. "Here we are, we're going to create a proposal, we're going to start gathering all sorts of information to do something good." Then all of a sudden you have all of this information and you don't know what to do with it. So bang, you're down and you're flat on your back. "What can I do with this? Do I have enough? Is the Chief going to buy this?" We don't have any idea what the Chief is going to like or dislike. So you're down there, and then all of a sudden you say "fuck it, I'm going to commit it anyway." So you finalize it, and we're

up again, because even though the Chief may not like it, we've done our share.

In fact, the group did feel a sense of accomplishment and pride. Ratings were the highest of the summer. Most frequently used adjectives were "constructive," "purposeful," "practical, "informative" and "creative." Other comments followed suit. The group generally concurred with Bond, who exclaimed at the end of the summary, "we made it, finally!"

A Loose End

During its last session the group met with a representative of the local social planning council, who gave it an overview of referral agencies. The lady, a sophisticated social worker, was also helpful with hints on referral management:

> Social Worker: If one person doesn't step out and take the initiative and really con the other departments into working with him, you can't get action. And this really amounts to getting on first name terms with people in other departments, like sorting out who's the fellow that you can get to know as a real buddy over in welfare. And you call this fellow and say "John, old boy, I've got a real problem going here now. I know you're the only fellow who can give me the right kind of help on this. How about it, old buddy, tell me what should I do about this?" You get it down to those terms, with a couple of pals in health and a couple of pals in housing inspectors, and a couple in welfare, you can sort out these family things in a much better way. You really can.

> Young: Are there any specific individuals you can think of that we might want to talk to?

> Social Worker: No, I'd start out by calling and trying to make a buddy with the first person I meet. And if that doesn't work I'd say "well, you must know somebody in your department who'd be interested in this. Now, who would you recommend that I talk to?" And then on the next one, I'd try to get him to have lunch with me. Then I'd get a real chance to brainwash him. I think that that is the most effective way. If you're going to work with ——, for example, phone him and ask him to come down and talk to you about

family problems. Tell him you want to work with him. Tell him these things bug you and you don't have the tools to cope, and how's the best way to make referrals to him. And what are his suggestions? And keep him long enough so that you get to know him.

The interviewee predicted that the family crisis officers would find a limited number of agencies (which she specified) helpful, each in a major problem area:

Social Worker: I'm suggesting to you that you really don't need a complete list of services. You need four or five hot numbers.

Young: And get a real good coordination between the unit and these four or five.

Social Worker: Yeah, make a real good relationship between you and the three or four places that you're going to make the main bulk of your referrals. And for the rest of the referrals, use ——— and get her to tell you what to do, and who to talk to. And that sort of simplifies it to the place where any officer who's personally good at separating warring couples can remember it in his head. He doesn't have to have a whole list to go looking up and down. Because that's not practical if you're trying to stop a beef. You can't say "wait till I look on page 31 and see which of these things I ought to send you to." I mean, that's for the birds. They're going to think you're nuts.

The group was receptive to these suggestions and incorporated them in their draft proposal. They rated the interview and the session high. Leading adjectives were "enjoyable," "constructive," "relevant" and "practical." Except for the anti-climactic nature of the experience, it marked a positive end to a partially frustrating summer.

Final Comment

Group Two was manifestly less successful than Group One, for several reasons. Probably its chief handicap was its division of functions. The early introduction of the reserve proposal split energy and personnel, weakened group purpose, and introduced organizational problems. Subgroup development made the introduction of key experiences difficult, and loosened the hold of leadership.

The sequence of tasks was also less than felicitous. There were sporadic sessions in which the group actively invoked concrete data sources which it found enjoyable and profitable. At other times, self-generated statistical exercises provided hours of taxing effort with little obvious pay-off. Premature drafting tasks similarly involved painful, unfamiliar detail-work with no obvious results. Moreover, the division of clerical tasks necessarily excluded some members, with no incentive for their reintegration into the group.

Group leadership was less than optimal. The principal leader became dispirited when he lost control, and refused to plan for activities that would have restored structure. The second leader refused to take up the slack, in part because he had found a consuming (more or less solitary) task in which he performed supremely well.

· Group membership was another handicap. Three members were permitted to remain disinterested in violence as a problem area. A fourth member was an advocate of violence, but after the issue had been joined he was permitted to "drop out." A fifth member was subjected to strong group pressure, and then excluded by default.

If, despite these factors, the group produced a superlative proposal (and another, partially based on solid empirical data), this gives testimony to the resources available — and partially exploited — in the group. Most of the officers remained dedicated to project goals, insisted on a meaningful end product, and carried out the difficult steps to their self-assigned goals.

6 • Group Three: Five Men in Search of A Project

On the basis of its final product, Group Three can be labeled the "recruit-training" group. The interest in training, however, developed late in the summer. During most of its life the group experimented and explored, touching on various topics but completing no projects.

FIGURE 4: Group Three—High Points and Low Points of Profile

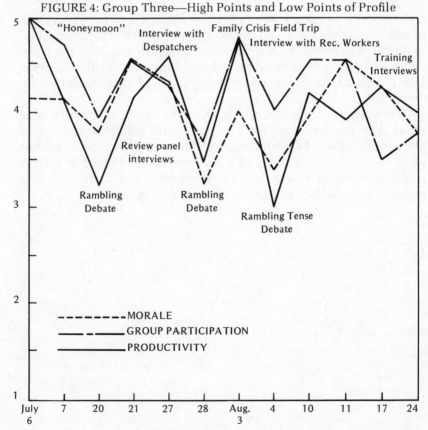

The group was comparatively small. One of its members, who had been on vacation, was slated to join in mid-session. He expressed reservations and was permitted to resign.

The leadership of the group was directive. The leader was much admired, a veteran officer who exercised charismatic influence and led the group with a firm, opinionated hand. The coleader, also a strong figure, provided a more non-directive atmosphere.

Figure 4 depicts the profile of the group. In general, the summer's ratings tend to be high: low points correspond to "average" ones for the other groups, and peaks are close to the ceiling. The patterning appears familiar. Session 1 shows a "honeymoon" high; other highs correspond to field and interview experiences; low points relate to sessions in which free-floating discussions took place.

Telling It Like It Is

In its opening meeting the group broached several subjects: procedures of the radio room, requests from special units, the exercise of police discretion, and problems of violence. In each case, the officers explained all problems as due to deficient information. In each case, the group proposed an information campaign as the solution.

In relation to the radio room, the group reviewed specific grievances against dispatchers. They proposed two steps to ameliorate the situation. The first of these was to send radio personnel to patrol lineups with information designed to dispel tensions and rumors:

> We also brought up that perhaps the dispatchers . . . could go to the lineups and discuss these problems that they have. Even if the 18 or 24 of us are aware of this thing, it might be beneficial for other people to hear of it. I think even just the fact that they are down there and discussing the thing and trying to present their side of the story — not that they have to or that there is that big a case against them — I think it would alleviate a lot of tensions, a lot of feelings that people have in patrol about some of the problems that they have, or mutual problems. I feel even if they're just down there, for Christ's sake, and don't say a hell of a lot, the fact that they are interested enough to be down there, it would alleviate some of the pressure.

The group also proposed to meet with dispatchers, primarily to relay gripes to them:

> When we get together with these individuals from dispatch to bring up the realization that good dispatching can mean safety and the difference between attitudes of the patrolmen and complainants at the time the patrolman arrives at the scene of the crime or disturbance call. By doing so through courtesy over the phone and complete facts to the officer on the beat. And also to discuss with the dispatchers ways in which patrolmen can create less work and prevent confusion for the dispatchers themselves. Because certainly it's not a one-way street, it's two-ways.

The group talked of sending other segments of the department to explain their problems to the rest of the force:

> I think it would make the whole job a little bit easier and more understandable for all of us, instead of those "prima donnas" in Juvenile, or the "assholes" on the bikes, or those "idiots" on patrol; it would give everybody perhaps a little better idea of what the other person is up against in his job and make it easier and safer for all of us involved.

The same solution was presented for the image of the group itself. In general, the men felt they had a good product to sell, and that they could sell it:

> *Officer 1:* When I first approached my watch commander and one of the lieutenants on our watch, I explained after the first (general) session that it was quite enlightening and it had a lot of possibilities to help policemen in general. And that it was not a fink squad, etc. They made several jokes to this respect. And they both immediately took a lot more interest in it when I personally talked to them. And they asked me if at a later date, when I had more facts and everything, I'd be willing to run this down to the lineup itself. . . .

> *Officer 2:* This is another thing. Don and I at lunch time talked to Lt. Smith on this, and he didn't have the slightest idea what we were doing. Being a command officer, and having six of his men out of his lineup out here, he really

didn't know. He was real interested. He wanted to talk all night about it.

The proposed course of action involved the formal dissemination of facts:

> Maybe we should write some type of memo on this and let the other divisions know what exactly this unit is doing . . . I've talked to several other officers and they think this is more like a brainwashing thing, and actually they have a total misconception. I think we should let it be known, write out a memo and let the other divisions know what we're doing.

Session ratings were favorable. Four participants labelled the meeting "constructive," and three of the four called it "honest," "promising," "thought provoking," and "encouraging." (In Groups One and Two the leaders completed the rating forms, but Group Three confined ratings to members: one member left early, and didn't rate the sessions).

Faith and Exploration

In its next session the group ranged widely once again. It discussed in-service training, problems of supervision, special duty units, information programs, and the radio room. The radio room discussion occupied most of the time and energy, and included some review of data. One officer brought up forms used by dispatchers and the group perused them briefly. The sergeant in charge of the radio room made an appearance and discussed his assignment with the group. Otherwise, the session remained discursive. Efforts by the leader (Hill) to stimulate project design proved largely fruitless. A staff member noted in the summary:

> It is obviously easier to talk than it is to get tied down to specific tasks. I noticed Hill about three times tried to call us around as to who was going to do what and what we were going to do, and then it seems that we pretty quickly went off on three or four more pretty good trips, what kind of incidents we knew and whatnot.

A round of self-congratulation occurred toward the end of the session. The men concluded that the average Oakland police officer was a dedicated, change-oriented individual, unlikely to engage in reprehensible conduct as he might have in the past:

> *Officer 1:* When I first came into law enforcement, from where I was in ——, the way they taught you in the Academy was "don't cop out to nothing and if the guy says you're a fucker, he goes to the hospital." This was the law and that's the way they taught you and that's the way you learned. Now of course it's changed, and probably that's what's happened in Oakland. And that's the way I first came on. I went out on a beat and the thing was you saw a punk on the street you jacked him up. This was the way it was. I didn't know any better . . .

> *Officer 2:* My whole life's attitude toward law enforcement is that if you gave me something that would pay me twice as much I wouldn't leave. I am interested in it, I like police work and I like policemen and I like people. And I think you've got to like people. The thing is, I remember guys being worked over, and we talked them through. Things like this happened, but I would not do those things today. I did do them myself, and thought nothing of it. You know, I did think something of it, and that's why I've changed around in a lot of places. But this is the best department that I have ever been in, that's for damn sure. We have more going here with groups like this and other things this department's got. And I've heard this from the chiefs from other parts of the country. It certainly is a good department.

The group itself was discussed as a constructive experiment, and the officers all indicated that they were proud to be a part of a change-oriented venture. Simultaneously, evidence cited for the benefit of group-membership tended to center around the person of the leader:

> *Officer 1:* I think it's safe to say that if Sam Hill is up there the program must be worth something, because if he walked out the door, you'd have to move fast because I would be right behind him.

> *Officer 2:* It shows we have a lot of confidence in Sam.

> *Officer 3:* I never pictured Sam in this kind of program.

Staff: Did you picture yourself in this kind of program?

Officer 3: No.

Officer 2: At first I didn't. Now I do. When I saw Sam in it and the way it was running — both Jim and Sam. Because I respected both of them and I worked with the both of them.

The honeymoon atmosphere persisted through the session, with much enthusiasm for the group. Simultaneously, the image of the group remained vague and amorphous, and independent of task-involvement. Even "productivity" ratings were high, despite the lack of output. The session was described as "constructive," "informative," "relevant" and "purposeful."

An Abortive Planning Session

Some of the discussion at the next meeting was inspired by the retreat. Dr. Bard's presentation about the New York family crisis experiment gave rise to suggestions relating to record-keeping and statistics. Statistics were viewed primarily as a tool for "selling" family crisis teams to the Oakland department:

> We got back into this family crisis thing. One thing that we talked about but didn't really act upon was the possibility of having a card file system, such as Dr. Bard's officers have in New York, showing family crisis information, so that the beat man when he gets a call for a particular address or a particular complainant, however it happens to be filed, might be able to go into the card file and find out when the last time the beat unit was at that particular address . . .

> We'd like to draw some correlations between the number of homicides where there has been previous interventions by police for, say, disturbance of the peace or family or neighborhood fights in order to see whether or not some of the homicides could have been prevented as a result of effective previous police interventions. And then also in that same respect, how many of the 148s that we may have had over the past two years — that is, over the same period as we're talking about for the homicides — would stem from 415 families, 415 neighborhoods, in which perhaps more

effective police handling of the call could have maybe lowered the number and maybe the number of resulting injuries and the loss of man days, and the loss of money which are all factors in trying to sell this type of program to the Oakland Police Department. To talk about manhours and money would be perhaps our biggest selling point.

Another project-idea related to promotion of a family crisis unit was a pre-implementation survey designed to demonstrate rank-and-file receptivity to the innovation:

> I'd like to go one step further than Jack on this questionnaire being handed out to the command officers on whether or not they feel that the family crisis unit would be worthwhile. Have it go out to the individual members in the divisions, so that when and if the program is ever initiated that the men will feel that they've had some kind of voice in it, and it'll be more readily accepted than something that's being shoved down their throat. Speaking for myself and I'm sure for a lot of others, things that do come out from the administration without any explanation or "do you think it will work?" Is sort of like the old story of "you just do what you're told and don't think about it." I think if the survey questionnaire went out to the members, I think they would accept it, and I think that they would probably more readily accept it knowing that they had a voice in its implementation.

There was also discussion of the training applications of experience accumulated in the handling of family crises.

These ideas were presented as hypothetical projects, with no sense of immediacy or urgency. As one officer summarized the brainstorming: "I think it's really a good project — something that quite obviously can be developed with this group later on as the summer progresses."

The usual miscellanea came up in the rest of the discussion. Political and promotion problems were discussed. One officer reviewed an incident he had experienced, and the group concluded that it would be interesting to listen to the radio tape. (No arrangements were made). An encounter brought up by another member drew a round of uncritical acclaim. There was the usual discussion of dispatching, and additional reflections on the need for an information bulletin about the unit.

This time, productivity ratings were low. Positive adjectives ("thought provoking," "purposeful") were joined by negative ones. Terms used to describe the session included "slow," "inconclusive," "dry" and "annoying." The honeymoon was over.

A One-Man Review Panel

The group spent its next meeting reviewing past involvements of various group members. In each case the leader (Sam Hill) pointed to violence-prone actions by the officer, and the culprit concurred. Sometimes an officer would engage in spontaneous self-criticism. The first discussion is described as follows by the officer involved:

> I talked about an incident — this particular incident was a stabbing, and the suspect refused to be taken into custody. He resisted violently. There were no injuries to us; however, the suspect was maced. The point was discussed that a policeman should always attempt to use talk, perhaps reason with the man and attempt to convince the suspect to go with him . . .
>
> I think it was Sam Hill who asked in this particular type of situation we discussed whether the search was valid, the action that was taken, the particular steps. Sam Hill brought up the point that, was it worth it in some cases to actually pursue the matter and cause some type of disturbance?

A comparable discussion occurred with another volunteered incident:

> I talked about another incident involving an obstruction case. A warrant suspect was apparently protected by another person. I didn't arrest, but submitted an offense report. Sam Hill pointed out that perhaps experience would teach us not to be too overreactive in cases such as this where we're going to serve a warrant with two people in the house. The warrant suspect was in the house and he apparently informed us that the suspect that we were looking for wasn't in the house, when all this time in fact he was in there. But I think the point that was brought up here was rather than cause some type of disturbance at that particular time,

> I have a minor type of warrant and sometimes it is
> better to overall look at things differently and perhaps again
> talk to the person involved here and try not to take any-
> one into custody, I suppose.

The group, spear-headed by Sam Hill, agreed that violence
could often be prevented through tempering experience, by more
talk and by less precipitous action. They also endorsed the need for
more legal and technical information:

> Sam Hill brought up the point that perhaps we should be
> instructed a little more, or know a little more as far as the
> law goes for the crime reports — complete more details.
> That is — on situations that have to do with labor and
> management strikes.

> Apparently a pat search of the possible suspect was neces-
> sary and the suspect resisted. Brown himself pointed out
> that the case was dropped and apparently the pat search
> was illegal. It was formed at a later time, that's after he
> went to court, I would assume. The pat search was dis-
> cussed, and I had it here that perhaps we should all get
> better informed pertaining to the latest cases involving
> searches and seizures, especially when it comes to pat
> searches in the street.

The co-leader (Henry Waterman) extended this point by arguing
that officers need to be better informed about their impact on the
rest of the criminal justice system:

> He mentioned that he had attended a meeting where there
> were several judges present, and Waterman pointed out
> that from this conference with several judges that they
> agreed that police officers should be more involved in the
> follow-up of cases, such as perhaps, I would assume that
> when they arrest a person they should inquire to see what
> actually happens — if the cases are dropped, instead of
> complaining about it, perhaps just be a little more informed
> about it. Find out what they did wrong. And perhaps learn
> the feelings of the judges, and how they feel about different
> cases. In other words, police officers should follow these
> cases up a little closer than they have — further than
> just the arrests.

According to the ratings for the session, the group felt itself benefitted and considered itself better informed about violence and its prevention. Rankings were high, and the meeting was characterized as "thought provoking," "informative," "constructive" and "critical."

A Conversion Experience

At its next session the group went into action. The decision was made to proceed with an exhaustive radio room "survey," including observations and interviews.

At the start of the session individual assignments were allocated. Several officers set out to observe particular phases of radio room operation. A "gripe list" was collected from the dispatchers. The radio room sergeant and a group of his personnel were interviewed.

A content analysis of the reaction form revealed that dispatchers had serious recurrent grievances. These impressed the group, as did equivalent interview content. In the interview, radio room personnel

> discussed several of these gripes and beefs that these people had put down on paper, and I think it was a very rewarding session with these personnel, and certainly the majority of us I'm sure gathered a lot of valuable information and a much deeper understanding of the problems that come about due to officers on the beat not using proper procedures or handling the radio properly.

The plausibility and apparent legitimacy of dispatcher complaints restructured the communication problem in the mind of the group. The problem, as they saw it, had evolved from reform of the radio room into a need to help radio personnel. As Sam Hill presented the new challenge:

> I feel that they had a hell of a lot more to criticize us about than we did about them, the way it worked out. Some of the things they do up there are a lot of human things, just like some of the things the policemen do. But as far as procedures are concerned, I feel that the man on the street has violated procedure a hell of a lot more than they have violated their procedure. What we're going to do with it, as has been pointed out, is going to take some time and some effort, but I'd certainly like to see something done about it

and some more people made aware of exactly what's going on.

As at other junctures in our project, an initially critical inquiry had become more objective through an interview experience. Jaundiced preconceptions, after personal contact, had become sympathetic concerns. The object of study had been humanized and had evoked fellow-feeling and empathy. The experience was eye-opening. One officer noted on his reaction form that "this program is giving a new view." Adjectives such as "beautiful," "inspiring," "promising" and "creative" appeared on the descriptive inventory. Session ratings were extremely high. The group had discovered (at least hypothetically) a mission.

No Hand at the Helm

The next day Sam Hill was absent and Waterman took charge. He opened the floor for discussion; conversation soon rambled disconnectedly from subject to subject. One project suggestion was brought up from the floor. This was — characteristically — an information-disseminating idea. The officer argued for the need to have a weekly "information letter" originate in the Chief's office, with the latest "inside" news.

At length, a staff member impatiently argued for a continuation of the radio room project. He

> brought up the suggestion, which I think we've adopted more or less, to go to the patrolmen and ask them to submit problems that they have or suggestions that they might have that might include the radio room situation. We want them to come up with their own first-hand incidents, on what has happened to them, or what they might want to suggest. And to pass out these 3x5 cards, and each man write one comment per card, so that it will be easier for filing and following up. Also, he brought up the fact that we could have supervisors also make these cards out — sergeants and lieutenants. He also brought up the suggestion that we take these cards and sort them out and pick out the ones that we think are right, and take three or four of these different situations or comments and discuss each one of them in lineups, for say 15 minute periods over a period of two or three months and talk these things over with the different patrolmen in the lineup. Then when this thing is completed and we've got all

our cards in, it was suggested that each member of Violence
Prevention take four patrolmen and two dispatchers and
have a two or maybe three hour discussion between them.
And have the Violence Prevention member more or less coordinate the discussion.

The group listened with respect, but did no project planning.
They responded with similar apathy to several other suggestions
by the staff member. The conversation continued as an informal
exchange, largely of gossip. At length the staff member — in a
desperate effort to raise the level of generalization — delivered a
lecture on trends in American policing. The group listened politely,
except for one officer, who later indicated that the staff member

> was getting on my nerves. He was getting highly critical
> of the administration and the police department, and I kind
> of felt, you know, "who is this guy to sit there and talk about
> everybody else." I mean, that's the way I feel. Well, this
> particular session here just got me irritated, that's all.

The staff member characterized his intervention as a case of
"panic leadership." He indicated that as a result of panic "I inter-
jected myself way more than I would normally." He added that his
explanation was "not offered as an excuse; it's offered as a statement
of fact. Because we have to document what happened."

Waterman, in turn, attributed the group's rambling to the possibility that

> We kind of reached the point where we had just about beat
> old things to death. I'm not saying that nothing was accom-
> plished in terms of our old projects, but to the point where
> we pretty much had to get on some new things, because we're
> pretty well sold on the problems in the radio room — that
> there needs to be some kind of communication between the
> people on the street and the people in the radio room. In
> order to solve these problems, the first part of our session
> was just sort of tying up the loose ends on how we wanted
> to get the information from both ends of that problem and
> get them consolidated into some kind of form whereby we
> could take some meaningful content to both people on the
> street and those who work in the radio room. But what I'm
> saying is we had just about reached the point where this
> was finalized and there was need to get into something new.

With regard to his own non-directive approach to leadership, Waterman commented that

> I'm a big believer in spontaneity. I came on strong for this thing last summer. I think police officers have got to be the most spontaneous reacting people born. Because that's our function. We walk into situations with no information and we respond based on the initial cues and we keep responding spontaneously. And I feel like I've had a good deal of success in this regard on the street and I know that everybody in here has. You can't get along on this job without this spontaneous response. When things start bogging down, in terms of this group, there's ways to pick it up. And I think it can be done. Social scientists, college professors and so forth need to be just a little more structured in the way they put things together. In our line, most of the time we don't have time to be structured. I guess it's nice to have structure, but I think we have this type of skill — this spontaneous response — to fall back on.

As for the results of spontaneity, Waterman estimated that "by and large the session tonight came out very well." The group did not concur. Ratings on all three dimensions were relatively low. The adjectives showed divided assessment. Although three of the officers characterized the session as "constructive" and "thought provoking," two of the four termed it "irritating."

Action

At their next meeting, the men embarked on a tape-gathering mission. They spent a busy evening on the street responding to a variety of family crisis assignments and other disturbance calls. As Hill characterized the session:

> Several of us went out — four separate units, eight men in two man cars, and handled the 415s that were available from 11 o'clock to 3 o'clock in the morning. It was quite interesting. We've all handled these things time after time after time, but last night it was kind of a fun thing. It was something that most officers don't like doing — when you're regularly working you don't like to do it. But for some unknown reason last night there didn't seem to be any

other outside pressures and they were just running from one call to the other very enthusiastically.

The atmosphere was lively, and the officers — as they returned from their assignment — seemed uniformly elated. Hill confessed that "I don't think I've ever had so much fun on this goddamn job since I left the (vice) squad." The officers approvingly reviewed their tapes, and separated the ones suitable for editing. One innovation they suggested was the use of two tape recorders on one call, to obtain two versions of the incident from the contending parties:

> It's a good possibility of sending, say, one unit out with two recorders to be able to use the technique of separating the participants in a family beef and being able to record both sides and then consolidate them on a sound-on-sound tape as we bring it in.

The officers then proceeded to fill out reaction forms, in which they described their experience in favorable terms. Participation and productivity ratings were the second-highest of the summer; recurrent adjectives were "constructive," "valuable," "fun," and "promising."

A Controversial Proposal

The group spent some of the time at its next meeting discussing its fact-gathering and fact-dissemination ventures. No substantial progress was made, and the group attributed this to middle-management obstruction. Hill complained that

> This has been a kind of slow night all around as far as everything is concerned. We've got a few things going that are in the process of being done and we're in a natural bog-down period here.

The "slow" evening was enlivened by Officer Filberg Long, who reported on a long week-end he had spent in the woods with a group of slum children and two black professionals from the recreation department:

> He came back from his trip last week-end where he was

engaged with two dozen black children he had taken into
the woods, and he said "you know, I learned something
about violence. And much of it has to do with fear." It
seems that they had put on some performance involving a
mythical Indian ghost who came out of the grave. Fairly
elaborately staged. Long played the ghost and he had been
covered with a small layer of earth and he came up and
whooped, or whatever Indian ghosts do, and 2/3 of the
children ran away, and the other 1/3 started beating up on
him. And he said, "you know in that slum, maybe there
is a lot of relationship between violence and fear." And
stuff like that.

Long also proposed that the group meet with the two recreation
workers, to obtain their insights into predelinquent psychology.
This suggestion met with sharp opposition from some members
of the group, and equally enthusiastic backing by others:

> We kind of broke off into two armed camps and were going
> at it pretty heavily for a while. I kind of got the impression
> that there were frayed nerves at one point or so . . . A couple
> of snide remarks were made back and forth . . . We pretty
> well had to go the route of having the group, or at least the
> majority of the group, describing whether or not we wanted
> to go in a particular direction. We're beginning to run into
> limited time and it would seem that this is a critical point
> about choosing types of things we would like to go on.

The group did decide — over vehement protests by several
members — to authorize Long to invite the recreation workers.
The episode ended on a sour note. Only three officers turned in
ratings, and these were low; adjectives included negative characterizations, such as "slow," "irritating" and "frustrating."

Another Conversion Experience

At the next session the group met with the recreation workers
who had been the occasion for acrimony and the objects of controversy. Officer Smith, the chief opponent of the interview,
summed up the reaction by saying:

> I was one of the ones that didn't want them up here. I didn't

think that there would be any value in it. I can now say that
I am 180 degrees the other way, and would certainly recommend that we have meetings like this as often as possible
because of the information that we have received tonight.
I think that everything was quite open and aboveboard.
Nobody was afraid to say anything. It was a good atmosphere
for finding things out.

Smith recommended that in subsequent encounters the recreation workers be encouraged to take more of a role:

> We generally asked them all sorts of questions on what
> was happening on their side of the fence. But they didn't
> ask us what's happening on our side of the fence. And I
> think maybe they've walked away feeling that they've opened
> their minds to us but that we haven't opened ours to them.
> I hope they don't feel as though all we did was pick brains
> up here tonight and not give anything back in return. And
> I would hope that the next time they come up they would
> ask us things that really bug them, what are attitudes in
> policemen and what kind of training do we actually have.
> Things that I am sure they are probably interested in but
> just didn't get around to asking tonight. This is what I
> would suggest on the next trip, that they be allowed to
> ask us the questions that just aren't asked because they
> are sensitive questions. And if they are sensitive, well,
> tough! We've asked them some sensitive questions.

In general, the officers concluded that liaison among personnel
in "street-oriented" professions was uniquely valuable, providing
the opportunity to exchange insights and experiences about shared
clients:

> It boils down to this. They have a whole bunch of people
> in the rec department on the top and we have a bunch of
> administrators in the police department on the top, and with
> the exception of the people that can do anything about it, it
> boils down to all the peons getting together and working
> out something in a workable way.

> I think the example tonight is, why don't they have people
> who know something about what is going on on the street
> at their level, come in and talk to these people in the recruit

school, and not just the administrator who comes in and
tells you there are six districts or something like this?

The group also felt reinforced in their premise that patrolmen
could do useful public relations work — and, especially, that
police could increase positive contact with juveniles:

> You can't tell me that there isn't a fucking man on this street
> that isn't involved in community relations. It's 90% of your
> job, whether you know it or not, whether you enjoy it or
> not. Or whether you're involved in it or not. All we're
> talking about is a little extra effort somewhere along the
> line by 99% of the people that are involved in it. Their
> whole job is community relations. Every goddamn call we
> take.

> We've got to get out of that shield that we ride around in
> eight hours a day and meet these people. And these people,
> in turn, will become our eyes and ears like they should be,
> like they used to be many years ago in this field. I think just
> by a beat man getting out of his car and just watching the
> kids play ball. You don't even have to talk to them: walk
> in and say "hi" and toss the ball a few times, 10 or 15
> minutes, and then leave.

In general, the group was impressed with the empathy the recreation workers showed with their clients:

> This guy sat over here beside me, cracked me up the way
> he talked. He talks about these kids in the way he really
> feels about what the heck is going on. He really feels like
> what is going on inside of them. He's a fascinating guy to
> listen to. I think that we all got some impressions about
> particularly these West Oakland kids that never even oc-
> curred to us.

One insight into the psychology of juveniles that particularly
struck the officers was that of concern with status, embodied in
symbols such as clothes:

> If they have to go through all this hassle to put on that
> front, when you have a confrontation with these people
> the same front is going to apply, the same status symbols are

going to apply. They are either going to play their games with you or put on more of a show because of this need for recognition. If a guy would go through the hassle of running downstairs and changing his fucking clothes before he left the house and changing them before he got back every night, this status symbol has got to be an extremely important thing to him, where he can get into that kind of a bag. So it is just something where you can get into a little better relationship with them.

Another point that impressed the officers was the importance assigned to reputation in the peer group. They concurred that a young man's reputation could be tarnished if he was observed to associate with the police:

> Talking about junior high school, 5 or 6 kids are pretty well running the school and they're all kind of set up as heroes, as long as they're not running around punishing the kids themselves. As long as they have a running battle with the police all the time they can be just like Robin Hood.

> When you walk into these schools, don't be familiar with these kids, otherwise the rest of the group is going to cut him out thinking he's the local fink or something. That had never even occurred to me, that you can isolate a kid in a school by putting him out on a limb or pushing him away from his own peer group. It makes a lot of sense what these guys talk about.

The men felt that the experience of meeting visiting experts had been interesting and profitable. Session ratings were high. Officer Long (the sponsor of the event) checked every favorable adjective available, and others concurred with "constructive," "thought provoking," and "informative."

Tooling Up to Project Work

In the summary of the next meeting, a group member noted that

> We've met quite a few times and it's time we get a little more organized and get something done besides just an eight-hour bullshit session. We've come up with a lot of good ideas, but

we need a little action on them. A lot of hard action to get done.

The session, however, had the traditional "smorgasbord" flavor of previous meetings. In the first "course" the group discussed an impending meeting with the Chief. They planned questions, most of them related to project topics ventilated along the line. The outline included recruit training, in-service courses for supervisors, community relations work by patrolmen, information campaigns, and the handling of "problem" officers. The men also planned to urge the Chief to continue the Violence Prevention Unit beyond the tenure of the project.

The group then divided to engage in various activities. Several members drafted working papers on the radio room, the proposed information letter from the Chief's Office, and a release about the unit. Taping occupied a major portion of the time. The group processed a tape obtained the previous week, with a discussion that largely endorsed the officer's actions. Waterman announced that

> A lot of our time, in fact practically all of my time now for the rest of the summer will be spent processing these sound-on-sound tapes with different individuals, different ones of you. It's a matter of reviewing tapes and finding out which ones of the ones you people made should be processed, that have some sort of content that would be good for training purposes. And we'll just have to sit down for the night or however long it takes and work out this sound-on-sound.

Waterman also added a note of urgency to the injunction that future meetings be more task-oriented:

> We've had a lot of trouble getting started the nights when we've worked on our projects. I guess we can all kind of take it on the chin for that, because we sat around here tonight and b.s.'d for an hour or two, and we wasted a lot of time. And it would be my pitch, to myself as well as to the rest of you, that we'd be very much aware of how much we've got to do and how much time we've got to do it in, and we more or less come in goal-oriented. I'll kind of psych myself up for that kind of thing if everyone else can kind of feel that that's the way it's going to have to go.

Only two rating forms were turned in at the end of the session. Ratings were moderately high, and adjectives mixed. The two raters agreed that the meeting had been "challenging" but "irritating."

Mandate from the Top

The officers had a meeting with the Chief between sessions, and were elated with the results. The Chief had reacted favorably to the ideas presented by the group. The group, in turn, was amazed at the candor and directness of the Chief's replies. As one of the officers put it:

> I was very impressed with the answers we got. It was the shortest 2 and ¼ hours I have ever spent, the time just went by so fast. The questions were going right and left. I really enjoyed it.

The Chief was particularly taken by the possibility of exploring the quality of recruit training in the department, with a view to improving human relations skills:

> We did some talking about the recruit school. Somebody asked what was wrong with the recruit school. But he said, "Everything is wrong with the recruit school." This again, was a very straight-faced, very candid remark. We also informed him that we were considering doing some reviewing of the curriculum for the recruit school and the chief's reply was "good"!

The Chief went further. He suggested that the group could profitably spend its time in a thorough-going review of the quality of instruction in the recruit academy:

> He said that "I would appreciate it if you would take that training program apart." An appeal from the chief: "Take it apart!" He is talking about, "look, let's scuttle it and start from scratch." This would be the way that you would kind of take his remark in that respect. He is thinking about new ideas and new ways of bringing in content that is not being utilized now. Instead of having black people coming into class and saying this is what the NAACP is all about and what it is like to be black. We would like to see rookies

going up there and spending a lot of time visiting in the
community. Then we started talking about the recreation
department. He thought that was a good idea, to get rookies
and recruits staried on going there, having something to do
with these kids.

The group felt that it had received marching orders, and was
eager to proceed. The officers assumed that the results of their efforts
would be favorably reviewed and would have impact. Sam Hill
said that

I feel more than ever that the monkey is on our back and he
is going to go along with it as much as possible, but it has
got to be up to us to come up with something that he thinks
is reasonable or workable, that we can sell not only to him
but to the rest of the department.

The group was also inspired by the Chief's assurance that the
project would not end with the summer:

We asked the Chief what our future role will be. He said it is
essential to continue this type of program in the police
department. He said he can visualize a sergeant with the
program and several patrolmen. Like he was saying "in the
order of 10 or 12." which surprised me because I hadn't anticipated that large a unit, particularly on a full time basis.
And I still don't visualize that large a unit, at this particular
time, anyway. But one of the pitches he was getting across was
the fact that this group should make the proposal about where
this goes in the future. He is not going to tell us where to go.

Cheered by their encounter with the Chief (reviewed at the beginning of the next session) the officers went to work on the research
into recruit training. They concluded that

We have to knuckle down and get together and get our ass
moving. It is going to require a great deal of time, and we are
going to have — we have about 16-20 hours, to put in about
double that time on our own to . . . keep these sessions as a
full time thing. We are going to have something on paper to
prove that we are doing something constructive.

The group then worked out an interview time-table for each member, covering the following two weeks. The men would be coming at all hours to interview a random sample of graduates from three academies. They also resolved to review reaction forms about each class, and to spend time with the administrators of the academy.

The rating blanks were completed as the officers moved out to their individually assigned tasks. Ratings were relatively high. Recurrent adjectives were "informative" and "constructive."

A Review of Data

For the next two weeks the officers scurried around the building at all times of the day and night, securing interviews and recording their impressions. At the end of this period they adjourned to exchange observations. They also turned their notes over to staff for collation and editing in report form.

In general, the interviews had uncovered much dissatisfaction with the recruit training experience:

> In summarizing the interviews from the recruits out of the five classes, I think tonight we finally realized just how much evaluation and reorganization this recruit academy needs. Not only the courses presented, but the scheduling of the courses, the qualifications of the instructors and the methods of presentation the instructors are now using.

The group also concluded that the main problems with the academy rested not so much with its curriculum, as with its day-to-day operation:

> It looks good on paper when you read, as an example, the 55th recruit school and what's going on. But in talking to these people, "well, that guy didn't show up and we changed this," and "that instructor wasn't there," and "this didn't work out," and it gives the opinion that something was really screwed up.

The academy was deficient, as the men saw it, in innovative instructional technique:

> It seems like most of our beefs were the constant lecture-type courses that were given. There was a lot of objection to this,

out of boredom, or whatever. Even from people who had spent a lot of time in school.

And the "human relations" bloc — the Chief's principal concern — seemed especially in need of imaginative reform:

> Again, we talked about the police-community relations bloc that was 26-41 hours in these different classes. And it's an absolute flop. It's turning people off at a rate that's just unbelievable. And it's a very important subject, it's a subject that the chief is probably very conscious of and relates to, and possibly many of these instructors in classes were put in at his suggestion. I don't know how much input he put in with the suggestion, and how much of it was followed or wasn't followed. But whatever the answer is, it's not what we have. The course, as I related in the notes that I made, is I think one of the most important we have. And I think it's one that they've really dropped the ball, one that could be implemented in a lot of ways where it would be very beneficial.

The group documented training deficits with detailed survey results. Suggested remedies were more vague and less adequately documented. The main concern of the officers was implementation, through training, of a unified ideology. The Chief's appearance in the academy was considered essential:

> If he could bring up at the start of the school and let these people know exactly what he expects of them, that it would clear some things up. Because from looking at the instructors, they're going to get a lot of instructional cross-purpose that is going to confuse a lot of people.

The group also discussed various non-lecture training options, particularly experiences that could provide the flavor of life on the beat. The interviewees themselves brought up the possibility of early street assignments, and of academy-sponsored "bull sessions":

> Several of them did state definitely that they would like the chance to get together as a group discussion with street officers. Not necessarily command officers or anything, but with street officers at a time maybe when they've come back

from this two weeks or a week on the street between training periods. And have group discussion critiques of problem areas where they themselves personally were having problems. Maybe in penal code or report writing or something, where they could get together with the group and hash these things out. And the group discussion type of class seemed to be something all of them wanted and would be more interested in.

Despite the relative non-specificity of recommendations, the men felt proud of their work. It had been a hard pull (rating forms filled out the previous week had been luke-warm) and it was unfamiliar activity. But the data were now collected and tabulated, and a coherent picture emerged. The staff member who had accompanied the officers remarked:

It is difficult for a group of people who are nonexpert in the training area but are expert in the patrol area just to walk in and do this sort of study. I think generally speaking the sort of comments that we've gotten back from interviews, etc. are very very good. I think we have succeeded. But it has been something of a trial, not in the sense of let's say hard work in the physical sense, but in the sense of it's an intellectual strain, it's a different sort of exercise than most of us have been engaged in.

The officers reported themselves pleasantly exhausted. They adjourned, having completed — as they saw it — their belated assignment. There was no product, but the men had worked fast and furiously, and — for once — in systematic furtherance of concrete ends.

A General Comment

It is hard to assess this group. It took on more than the other groups, and it accomplished less. Without the Chief's intervention, the group would have remained dilettantish to the last, hopping and skipping over quasi-projects with no hope of closure. Even with its late-discovered mission, the group confused results with raw data, and left processing in limbo.

Why discursiveness? Why the contentment with false starts and preambles? Why high morale with low productivity?

A partial answer lies in over-confidence, and a sense of omnipotence. Especially early in the summer, the men assumed that they could complete many tasks, simply by parcelling these out. With faith bordering on magic, the men equated assignment of a project with its execution. Time passed, and progress was tallied in the form of small, obviously inadequate steps. There was a need, clear to all, for emphasis and specialization. On the other hand, there was omnivorous interest and a reluctance to abandon free exploration of multifarious options.

This omnivorousness is a by-product of group atmosphere. From the first, the men enjoyed the "no holds barred" form of the proceedings, the chance to speculate on subjects that mattered in a context that mattered. The stress on speaking one's mind, on experience and insight, on diagnosis and hope, produced the feeling that change had, necessarily, to emerge. And faith in information, in the truth as a liberating tool, reified discussions into change vehicles.

Moreover, the men felt they were learning. The group's stance was passive, in part because its leadership was charismatic. The leader taught ideas and filled prescriptions. Each session gave the men the feeling of a trend into the future. They viewed these trends as spectators, but felt privileged and fulfilled.

At times the peripatetic ambling proved irritating. Several of the men demurred — two to the end. But the group's discontent was self-generated. On three occasions a project was about to germinate; in each case the men retreated into vagueness. The object, it seems, was to reserve options.

The men had embarked on a free-floating exploration of their professional lives. They abstracted, out of the gestalt of their job, meaningful — bothersome — problem areas. They asked questions about these areas, and saw the possibility of solutions. This process paid off to the extent that it brought a feeling of autonomy, a sense of direction, and a faith in progress. It served, at minimum, to reduce alienation.

> If you've got anything to say, if you've got anything to ask, say it or ask it. Because that's what this is about this morning. And I know if you have any feelings like we did when we came up here a year ago, you're a little apprehensive — you kind of wonder what it's all about.

With these emphatic comments, Chairman Bill had opened the first meeting with our twenty-four trainees. The group's anticipated stance was one of guarded non-communicativeness. We had countered this by stressing (and illustrating) a tradition of open and frank communication:

> I guess there's a few guidelines here that we've thought about for a long time . . . There's nothing that can't be said when we're meeting. The two days we're going to meet each week, there's absolutely nothing that can't be said by you. And regardless of what it is, come out with it, whether it's an idea or a pitch or a gripe. Don't worry about saying "motherfucker" because we don't give a shit about that. If that's the way you express yourself.

To forestall another danger — that of unlicensed griping — the introduction laid stress on the constructive thrust of past discussions:

> I would say we've spent around 400 hours in pretty intensive discussion, pretty intensive digging processes, and all of it relating to problems that we might have on the police department or job-related problems that could lead or did lead or might possibly lead or inevitably leads to violence.

There was emphasis on the opportunity to make impact on the department, and the chance to develop personal skills. Group achievements were listed in support of promised claims. The summarizer (Waterman) noted:

> It was pointed out rather strongly that the possibility of the development of the self — each individual who is now involved in this program, there is a chance to do some research, some program writing, some presentations, talks, numbers of other things which kind of helps us to get a better light about what the administration of a modern, large municipal police department is all about. That there is a good deal of insight that can be had about the department as a result of going about the department talking to people, collecting research information, putting this information together into a concrete proposal for change.

Despite this rosy vista, the reaction of the men was still guarded and cautious:

> There were some questions right after the break on Wednesday morning. One of them had to do with why there were no black officers in the Unit and another had to do with "why me instead of some others who are having more problems than I am out there?" And there was a question about where the tapes go.

The afternoon was taken up with the playing and discussion of tapes. The exercise was introduced by Waterman, who announced:

> Somebody brought up the idea of taping at our discussions. This is sort of the pattern, the way we move in this unit. If somebody brings up a good idea and we recognize it, then we begin to try to work out the details and see what we can gain. It turns out that we believe there's considerable value in this thing. We'd like to open it up for discussions. How do you, yourself, feel about it? If you have any negative feelings about it, by all means kick them out. It's your show.

The tapes proved ice-breakers. The men listened, and their reactions became concrete and animated. The first taped incident included commentary, to which the officers added their points.

Other incidents occasioned detailed arguments, touching upon specific and general issues.

The tape which most interested the group featured Joe Young answering a juvenile disturbance call. Young had deputized one of the youngsters to take charge of quieting the disturbance— a gambit which had worked. The group endorsed the procedure, but discussed the temptation to respond differentially when faced with more affluent youths. The group agreed that efforts should be made to achieve uniformity in approach. Disagreement developed when Young was heard to announce that he suspected all sorts of chemicals were being ingested on the premises, but that his only interest was in the noise level. The men concerned themselves — heatedly — with the desirability (or necessity) of tolerating violations of law.

The third tape featured a family disturbance which had degenerated — in part because our man had lost control. The incident stimulated a discussion of family crisis management. As the debate proceeded, it highlighted dilemmas which none of the men was prepared to solve:

> With respect to 415's in general the picture seemed to be that some officers in the group felt that you had to get in and out as fast as possible and these calls were a nuisance, whereas other officers felt that useful things could be done, although they agreed that the calls were a nuisance. The former group could not really present a very effective formula for getting in and out quickly. The latter group didn't seem to be terribly confident in their techniques for resolving such situations, nor did they seem to have their objectives clear.

An argument ensued when it was proposed that family disturbances be handled by other agencies. The position that family fights should be dealt with by social workers was followed with cynical comments about social work. The men argued that social workers were ineffective, and tended to make situations degenerate when they happened to find themselves involved.

A member of the group suggested that a police family crisis unit was a possible solution, and there was no voiced objection. The suggestion was followed with "war stories" of resolved family arguments, featuring a variety of approaches.

With respect to the benefits of tapes, there was concensus. It proved hard for the group to resist the enthusiasm of Hill's advocacy, especially when Bill specified fairly remote target populations:

> I remember when I went to rookie school — a 415 family
> fight. How do you sit up there and tell a 22 year old kid like
> I was when I was in rookie school how to handle a 415 fight?
> A lot of the guys we are getting now are not married and
> never have been. This is beginning to sound like Psychology
> 1A, like I'm trying to analyze this or something, which ain't
> that bad really. It is tough for cops who have been around to
> listen to this stuff, to be truthful with you. It's kind of corny
> to me — I got a little tired of it. But it won't be that way for
> them. There are a lot of ways that you can use it. We have
> gotten responses in L.A., Denver, and Washington D.C. In
> all the places we have gone, they have blown their minds
> over these tapes.

The men found the appeal convincing — or at least, overwhelming. While stipulating the need for tapes, they demurred on
questions of emphasis. The stress on circumspection in police
approach offended some of the men, and they appealed for more
diverse presentations. The implication that one should not "come
on strong" — they argued — would have to be neutralized with
incidents in which softness proved self-defeating.

Session leaders responded to such comments with sympathy and
at face value. The discussion about a multi-tape approach proceeded
as follows:

> *Officer:* I think in your presentation to the classes, I think
> you ought to make them realize also that everybody has a
> little different manner of handling a 415. Nothing is exactly
> right or is exactly wrong.

> *Bill:* That is a good point. That's the idea. It opens up a real
> broad area of discussion. For instance, you made the com-
> ment that everybody has a different way of acting or handling
> a 415. That's true, and the one that works is the one to use.
> I guess what we really want to get across is that if yours isn't
> working, why not try mine, which is an alternative method?

> *Officer:* It should be noted that some of the bad points in this
> tape may be some of the good points in another case. If some-
> thing is real bad it should be pointed out how 99 times
> before, if you made a mistake you got kicked in the ass.

Sam: This is why we need a variety of tapes. Things can be brought out. It's not perfect by a long shot, but if I was sitting in a rookie school I'd want somebody to tell me.

The officers became concerned because the tapes did not accentuate physical safety. Again, leaders translated comments into endorsements and elaborations of their own theme:

Officer: Another thing, when you are talking about safety on these 415s. I think in a case like that, you talk about having a narrator there, have him mention the safety factor. When you say you're going out to a four-fifteen call, you might add there might be a guy in the closet or whatever.

Officer: This could have been brought out on this tape there. I felt you let that guy get too close to you before you even realized he was there.

Officer: Perhaps you could make it known that there is a safety factor involved.

Bill: Well, the critiquing in this thing didn't cover those points, which as it turns out might be a good pattern to adopt. That's the idea. I guess if we kind of play the tape and let them talk about things like you're talking about them now. And maybe if they're not brought up, bring them out.

The opening sessions covered two days. On the morning of the second day the officers were introduced to various concepts that had been incorporated into the vocabulary of our groups. The summarizer noted:

We kind of began by Joe Mills, who was the chairman, giving an introduction about what we mean when we talk about cues and games, and the fact that it kind of means the moves that we make when we're interacting with citizens and the moves that citizens make. Also, that we get cues from the very beginning when we start out on a call.

The second topic was the issue of the radio room, which interested the men more and stimulated an extended discussion. One of the officers made a suggestion which met with universal approval:

> There was a proposal made by Long that perhaps getting together with the dispatchers and talking in a group setting may help to iron out some of the problems that we have between the policeman and the radio room, that we may be able to get across to the dispatchers themselves the need for more information out there.

Much time was occupied with analysis of information obtained through the critical incident questionnaire. The analysis stressed communication gaps in the department and the need for more relevant training.

The day ended on a hortatory note with a statement from Sam Hill:

> I've been around here a long time and when I told a certain captain when I was having a drink with him that I was on the Violence Prevention Unit he went hysterical — I thought I was going to have to call an ambulance. But I've heard people bitch in the locker room for 19 years and you've never been able to do a fucking thing about it, and I don't know whether this is going to work or not, but it's a fucking chance for us to change what we've been bitching about for a long time. It might be the last chance we have. If we've got constructive things that are our problems that we're concerned with and we present them properly, I think the 24 of us can make changes. Like I say, it's the only chance I've seen in 19 years. And it might be the last chance. And I think you guys are doing a hell of a job up here, and I couldn't be more pleased. Especially since I was the one who said it wouldn't work.

The men filled their Rating Forms before they left. Their responses revealed a high level of interest (scores were evenly divided between "very high" and "high"); morale achieved a mean rating of 4.25 on a 5 point scale. Participation and productivity ratings clustered around "high" (3.8 and 3.7 respectively). These latter dimensions did not reach the scale value of interest and morale, but this may not be surprising in view of the size of the group and the fact that 16 hours had been taken up with formal presentations.

The officers' reaction to the meeting proved equally positive in the adjective check list. Every favorable adjective on the form was employed. In rank order, the most frequent designations were "enjoyable," "thought-provoking," "valuable," "honest," "relevant," "promising," and "informative." Far down the list a few negative characterizations appeared. "Inconclusive" was checked four times, and "weird" twice. The word "academic" appeared on several forms, but its use by the officers did not necessarily carry negative connotations.

Informal reactions supported the questionnaire. One officer, who had requested exemption from the groups, withdrew his request and characterized the project as valuable and worthwhile. Several men spontaneously commented to colleagues and supervisors that they looked forward to their participation.

If the project later did not prove an unambiguous success, the blame could not attach to the seductiveness of the induction process. We had clearly started off with our best foot forward — possibly too much so.

Fertilization from Without

After one week of group meetings a retreat was organized to crystallize the direction of activity and to discuss themes of common concern.

Two speakers were invoked as catalysts to the discussion. One was Dr. Morton Bard, the originator of the family crisis experiment in the New York Police Department. The second was a former police officer who had completed a questionnaire study to define attributes of the police role.

The first day featured presentations by the guest speakers, and questions and discussions stimulated by this information. The bulk of the exchange focussed on Bard's presentation. Comments became heated because of the discrepant views among our group about the legitimacy of family crisis management by police.

Dr. Bard discussed consequences of poor crisis management in the shape of violence and injuries to officers. He stressed personal interaction as a dimension of sophistication and professionalism. Some of the men concurred and others asserted (with decreasing vehemence) that family fights were not police business; others expressed their personal disinterest in this aspect of enforcement.

Two topics implicit in Dr. Bard's presentation stimulated much thought. One was the idea of police "generalist-specialists," implying that an officer could become proficient in some aspect of police work, and that he could be permitted to concentrate in this one area while continuing to discharge all other (general patrol) obligations.

The second theme was that of training. Dr. Bard emphasized the success of role-playing in his indoctrination of family crisis teams. The group sharply divided on the merits of role playing but agreed that innovative educational experiments — and reorientations in the emphasis of recruit training — were urgent priorities. The following is an excerpt from this discussion:

> *Hill:* The whole training program is strict enforcement oriented. Everybody you talk to — you listen to those rookies up there in the academy and all they're talking about is how they can change the law around to fuck somebody. You know, "if they do this, can I do that?"

> *Officer:* One thing I always thought would be great, if you could have a guy going through the academy training, take him and put him in jail and let him spend the night, put him on that bus and import him out to —— for a couple of days. Let him stew out there for a day or two —

> *Officer 2:* Didn't somebody do that here on the coast?

> *Officer 3:* The chief from Covena. We had him here as a consultant.

> *Officer 1:* This would give a guy, like a recruit particularly — I know how I felt when I came out of that academy. I was going to stuff as many people through that back door as I could possibly get through there. And I think if a few of us knew what occurred after they get through that back door —

Although the talk about police roles did not attract the same interest as Dr. Bard's presentation, it did stimulate a variety of interchanges more or less germane to the presentation. The following is representative of this discussion:

> *Speaker:* Growing out of this isolation is the implication of secrecy. You're self-protective, you're covering up, you're sticking together, you guys always defend one another. All these charges.

> *Officer:* We really discount the fact that today policemen are completely alienated from the mainstream of society. It's really true. For instance, you go to a party and there aren't a lot of police there and somebody lights up a joint. What in

the fuck do you do?

Officer 2: Ask for another one.

Officer 1: The whole point is this. You're taking a chance staying there, you're taking a chance not saying anything, whether or not you partake. Of course I've never done it! But what I'm saying is, is that you're kind of safe with cops. You know, you ain't really the nicest guy to have around.

Speaker: That's right. You know, again, this thing in Washington recently jarred the hell out of me because it brought back all of the discomforts that I used to have in going to parties. I remember one case where I finally said "bullshit, I'm never going to admit that I'm a police officer in any social situation." And I did say the next party that I went to that I was a shoe salesman. And there was a guy there from Turkey who was a real high official in their equivalent of the FBI. And later I learned that he was the real policeman type and I wanted to talk to him. I was originally introduced to him as a shoe salesman, and I couldn't convince him that no, I wasn't really a shoe salesman, I was a police officer.

Officer 3: You look like a shoe salesman, that's why.

Throughout the discussions at the conference, our group of seven (with Sam Hill in the lead) took consistently "liberal" positions. The newer members were ideologically divided, and some at times joined the original team in assailing a man who advanced the conventional, alienated "party line" position. One officer found himself attacked when he expressed the feeling (popular among the police) that judges work at cross purposes with enforcement. He told the group that he had been invited to exchange views with a judge, but had rejected the opportunity as a useless exercise:

Officer 1: I could have gone. And you want to know why I didn't go? Because I could sit there and talk to that judge all day long, and that's not going to make a three time 211 man go to the ——. I don't think my talking to that judge is going to make any difference. I honestly don't think anything I'm going to say is going to influence him.

Hill: Do you think something he might say might let you know why he didn't go?

Officer 2: Do you know the reason? Have you ever talked to a judge or found out what the thinking is?

Officer 1: All I'm saying is I didn't go talk to the judge because I didn't think —

Hill: I would feel the same way. There's nothing that I could say that would make him put this guy down in the —. But I would like to know his reasons why he doesn't. This would be important to me. I'd like to know why he doesn't do this. Not that it's going to change anything, but I think it would give me a better understanding of why these people aren't going to jail. Maybe you wouldn't go for what he's talking about, but don't you think it's worth a shot to find out why he isn't going? Maybe you would agree, maybe you wouldn't.

Similar alliances between older and newer group members occurred during the social portion of the weekend. When one of the newer men began to create a disturbance under the influence of alcohol, a mixed delegation unobtrusively neutralized him.

Reactions to the weekend were unenthusiastic but positive. Ratings averaged high over all dimensions (3.75 for productivity; 3.69 for participation, and 3.62 on morale). The most frequently checked adjective was "thought provoking," followed by "constructive," "informative"; "inconclusive" came next — then "challenging" and "academic"; "enjoyable," "relevant" and "creative."

The most concrete benefit of the exercise was probably that of initiating project design. The family crisis idea originated at the sessions, and training concerns were reinforced by it. Beyond this, there was the function of consolidating commitment beyond the small groups, to the project as a whole.

The Final Session

On the last day of the summer, the men assembled in the room in which they had started ten weeks previously. The agenda called for (1) a review of accomplishments and proposals, (2) delineation of the Violence Prevention Unit to be established in the department, and (3) trainee reactions to their experience.

Young and members of his group led the discussion of family crisis management. They outlined their proposal, stressing peer nomination in the selection of team members, liaison with agencies, and continued documentation of team effectiveness. The peer nomination procedure (which promised to produce a first-rate cadre if implemented) was described as follows:

> So what we're going to have them do is recommend 4 guys, and they have to be capable of calming a disturbance immediately and maintaining control throughout the call with minimal friction between themselves and those involved. The outcome of the assignment must satisfy both parties to the extent possible. Also, he's going to have to describe, or he's going to have to say "I recommend Officer Murphy and the reason I recommend Officer Murphy is because I observed him handle a 415 in such and such a manner." And we're going to try to have them limit it to 4 recommendations. They can recommend up to four; they can only recommend one if they've only had one such experience. We should be able to come up with a list through the repeat recommendations of other officers watching the same guy work, and end up with maybe a list of 10 or 15 or 20 people, and from there through interviews and so forth we'll be able to come up with a final list of ten people who are willing to cooperate, and who would like to and also have the talent.

Referrals were discussed in terms of beneficial experiences with agency representatives, and in terms of the latter's positive reactions to the group:

> *Young:* I couldn't begin to go into some of the services that are available to people that I had no goddamn idea that there was such a thing . . .

> *Officer:* And they were quite receptive that something like this is happening in the police department, to actively take an interest in the community. Instead of the image that we do have. I really anticipate that we'll have quite a bit of cooperation with these people in these different agencies, where there's animosity now. I think we're going to find a little more rapport. And they admit there is animosity. The only time they see a policeman is when he's busting somebody.

Young stressed the fact that FCIU members, through selective

use of referrals, could begin to provide services to civilians in areas
of need:

> What would probably be the typical handling of a call, the
> Family Crisis Intervention Unit, one of the teams would go
> to a call and they'd find out that they've got a problem with
> the old man drinking. The officer would probably refer the
> wife to the Family Services Bureau, and they in turn would
> work out an arrangement where the old man could come in
> and maybe go into another agency to get some services for
> his alcoholic problem. And then part of Art's job and proba-
> bly part of the job of the field coordinator would be to follow
> this up to see if the people went and got these services, may-
> be even schedule appointments for these people. Maybe the
> field coordinator or Art as the project coordinator would
> call up the Family Services Bureau and say "hey, we've got
> a family in Brookfield Village that's having a problem. We
> would like to arrange for you to meet with the wife and the
> husband, can you do it, and when?" And then turn around
> and we contact the people and say "are you still interested?
> We'll send you out to where you can get some help."

The case for documentation was presented as "selling the program
to the department," as a means of maintaining the unit "on target,"
and as a monitoring device to insure and demonstrate effectiveness.
Bill stressed the importance of these aims, and their applicability to
all of the unit's projected activities:

> I think something that applies to every one of the projects up
> there is the fact that documentation is going to be an ex-
> tremely important part of the unit's future. This FCIU thing
> documented, followups on the families as a whole, follow-
> ups on the Jones family, the Smith family, telephone follow-
> ups, agency followups that they've referred to. Because
> everything up there has got to be justified. Not only is this
> FCIU thing an experiment, this whole unit's an experiment.
> Without some pretty good documentation that it's being
> successful, progressive and coming up with something
> valuable, it ain't going to be around long. So I would think
> that documentation is an absolute necessity.

Two possible extensions of the family crisis program came in for extended discussion. One was the use of family crisis teams for recruit training:

> *Young:* We discussed taking the recruits and running them through this, and having every recruit spend two days on it. That's a hell of an idea. I mean you wouldn't take away from the unit two guys who are experts. This guy would be just an observer. And normally people don't give a shit who the guy is in plain clothes. We've had Hans with us thousands of times and I don't think anybody's ever asked until Bill told them.

> *Officer:* The main objection I have to something like that is two-man groups who are working together every day, they know how each other thinks and operates. And you throw a young, rookie policeman in there, the chances of violence is going to go up, 59%. Because he doesn't know what the fuck he's doing. If he goes along as an observer like everyone else does.

> *Officer:* You can throw him in the water and say "sink or swim." That's what's happened to us.

> *Bill:* Of course, the training wouldn't end, Jim, would it, right after the call? I would imagine that between that call and another one there would be a lot of dialogue exchanged, a lot of information and ideas exchanged, a lot of explanations.

> *Waterman:* It seems like also this would come at a point in the recruit training after they had spent some time with our instructors from our unit doing some talking about these 415s and so forth. It's kind of a followup, saying "you've heard what goes on, now you're going to get a chance to see it."

As a second extension, the men discussed a "ride in" program (partly for training purposes) for representatives of the referral agencies:

> *Officer:* I think if we got someone like — over here at Welfare, let's say you've got three people who get all the cases that come in on one particular thing and they start feeding them out to other people. If you took those three people out

with the unit and showed them how you do it. . . . So they know you've done everything you can, so they're not going to say it's a kiss off. In that respect I think it might be good.

Young: Yeah, but the same holds true for all the agencies, because I was thinking that the agencies that would be receiving or treating these people would think everytime somebody comes in that door, "here comes another one of those fucking referrals."

Officer: Yeah, if they see that you bend over backwards to try and settle it and you just don't have any other place to go, you're banging your head up against the wall after maybe 25 minutes, so you write out the card and refer them, and the person is standing there and this is the guy who's going to get the card the next day.

Bill: . . . How many of these people have made appointments to go out to homes and found conditions existing that don't normally exist? This social welfare guy is going to walk into the scene just like you, and they're going to see this guy or woman in a complete rage breaking a lamp or slamming an ashtray down or yelling "motherfucker," and they would never see it otherwise. I think they'd get kind of a truer picture of the problem if they're there firsthand. Just like the officer.

Young: Some of them have complained that they don't know what our job is like, and it's a hell of a way to find out.

Officer: It can't help but break down some of the walls that were built up between the police and these other agencies.

Kent introduced his own proposal, the review panel. He stressed the notion that the panel could anticipate behavioral problems, and thus prevent the need for disciplinary sanctions:

By going over various reports of different people both within the unit and outside the unit, we began to see how certain people had developed some sort of patterns, where they had some particular thing on the street that had a greater probability of developing into a 148 or 243. So what we did is we structured the thing with the idea that line patrolmen would come up to talk to these guys on an equal basis, just bypassing internal affairs. In fact, the whole idea of the unit is to get ahold of these people before internal affairs does. When we see a pattern developing, maybe through this type of peer group interview, we can point out to these fellows that they have a certain problem on the street, make them realize it before they're told by the 8th floor.

Another advantage of the panel, which Kent did not mention, was raised in subsequent discussion. One of the men pointed out that officers are alienated through confrontation, and that productivity suffers. He noted that the panels could reinstill commitment and motivation for work:

> *Officer:* Fels was saying that he was losing interest. He was losing faith probably because of the lack of something like this — peers talking about whatever it is.

> *Bill:* He said it in fact in his interview. I was impressed. See, this has been the outcome, the only means of controlling, if I can use that word in a broad sense, an aggressive officer who seems to be overaggressive to command. The only way to control him is to say "hey, you're in the shit all the time. Knock it off. Slow down." This has been the outcome of that kind of approach, and it's been the only approach the department's had with that. You call the guy into the Deputy Chief's office and point out to him that he's had X number of 148s and 243s and it's too many. The outcome of that has been that the officers say "goddamn it, I was doing a good job. In my eyes I was doing a hell of a job, I was one of the best cops going. They don't want me to do that. So consequently, I will not be responsible, do as little as possible. Then they'll be happy." I think a lot of guys who have had what the department feels is too many 148s and 243s have felt that way. Lou made the statement quite pointedly that it really is possible for him to be as active as he was in the past and not become involved in as many incidents. Point blank. With that "I get mad at people, I get impatient, disgusted with them," and so on.

> *Kent:* See, our whole point is we don't want these guys to slow down. If we can show that, which nobody else has done, just in taking all their reports in an 11 month period and getting down there and saying "look, it might not be a

bad idea instead of just getting out of your car and putting your hand in the guy's pocket, maybe if you approached it just a little bit differently."

During the discussion, Kent mentioned that the panel would aid in communication between officers and their supervisors:

Kent: When Captain Smith came up there he was really quite concerned about Fels' problem. Their relationship is sort of strained and very, very formal. And yet Smith considered him one of the best patrolmen he had in his division. And then when Fels came up there he was under the assumption that Smith thought he was one of the worst patrolmen. And somehow there was no communication between the two of them . . .

Bill: Didn't Smith say in fact when he was up here that one of the big problems in talking to Fels was that it was so strictly formal? It's extremely difficult for a captain of police, a command officer, to talk to a subordinate or a guy working for him on an informal basis. Because the formality is written into the whole scene. "He's a captain and I'm a patrolman, and I damn well better be formal with the guy." It's hard to break that ice.

A final comment defined the panel as a natural extension of informal contacts — analogously to the way in which the Violence Prevention Program represented such an extension:

Kent: Basically, really, all this is, is the unit miniaturized. That's all it is. And set up on a permanent basis. This is why — I don't know if it happened in your particular groups, but in our group we had a very high degree of honesty real quick.

Hill: I've always had the attitude around here that somebody's trying to fuck me, and I've usually been right. But if you break this down, then fine. It's the same thing we all do. We all talk among ourselves in the locker room or over at the Public House or somewhere else and there isn't that feeling.

The panel notion was favorably received by the total group. The only reservation — relating to confidentiality — was easily countered:

> *Officer:* Does anyone else have access to the information you get from the interviews?

> *Kent:* No — absolutely not. The whole idea is that the information that is gathered is for the person himself who is being interviewed. This is the only purpose it is really for, in a sense. We'll have to keep some sort of records. But none of this is ever going to Internal Affairs. Because we want to make quite clear that there will be absolutely no disciplinary action or any records kept from the interview. But the primary purpose of the interview, the information gathered, isn't even for the review panel — it's for the person being interviewed.

Initiation Rites, Revisited

The next speaker was Sam Hill, who reported on his group's evaluation of the recruit training academy. Sam provided a singularly personal and forceful presentation of interview results. He summarized his findings as suggesting (1) that the academy makes its impact in reinforcing a hard-core enforcement orientation; (2) that community relations content produces "boomerang" effects; and (3) that transfer from the classroom to the street is minimal.

Hill pointed out that evaluation of recruit training can only occur through a survey in which officers are contacted after they have applied (or tried to apply) classroom material on the street:

> The evaluations that we're getting now from the people that we talk to, I think, would be altogether different than the evaluations that they gave while they were a recruit here. Because they've got something to relate to now. In looking back on it they say "it's the shits, it's worthless, it's not meaningful, we can't use it." They couldn't say it then because they didn't know. Get a hold of these people two months later and say "what did you use, what can you use?"

Sam reported that the retrospections of academy graduates were uniformly tarnished in the human relations area:

As I say, the whole community relations bloc, I don't think
there was one person there — if there was I don't recall —
that had anything to say that was good about it. They didn't
give a shit about suicide prevention or mental illness or anything else. They didn't feel that there was any room for it.
None of it, they felt, has applied in that area since they've
been on the street.

Among despised features of the human relations cycle, confrontation sessions with community leaders stood out as particularly
disliked:

They felt that all it was is giving these people a platform to
vent their spleen about what they thought about policemen.
They were very upset about it. They didn't have any rebuttal
time or anything else.

Hill argued for more realistic methods, and challenged our own
group to contribute its expertise and experience:

I think it's up to us, or that we can do a hell of a lot for it.
We can make it more interesting to recruits. And I think this
group here could come up with a lot of innovations, like the
role playing we're talking about, the tapes and everything
else, that would make their training more meaningful and
would make them relate more to the job before they got out
in the street, and it would make them adjust a lot easier. And
it would save them and us a whole hell of a lot of problems.

Hill also emphasized the unintended consequences of having
enforcement-oriented veterans present technical subjects, with
side-remarks and comments that impressed their students:

They related best to some of the instructors that came out
with that "screw them into the ground, boy" and "nobody fucks with an Oakland cop" type thing. This is what
they were really impressed with. This is what they liked,
this is what they listened to. And most of their ratings
on the subject matter was in that area. They thought these
guys were real great. It kind of reminds me of when I got out
of jump school. They tell you you can whip five men. It just
ain't that way. And this is the impression that these people
are given up here by some of the instructors.

In a more positive vein, the survey — according to Hill — revealed benefit in field training or apprenticeship experiences. Hill suggested that this finding argued for more life-like classroom experiments (such as role playing) and earlier use of street expeditions:

> A lot of them felt they would like to spend a couple of weeks on the street in the middle of their training course and then go back to the academy so that they had something to relate to. It was interesting that some of these kids had no way in the world to relate to the penal code or anything else that they're talking about. They just have absolutely no idea of what the hell it's all about. All it was is a lot of numbers and it's just not meaningful to them. It's not meaningful at all. And they sit there and listen to this stuff for 18 weeks and it still doesn't mean anything to them because they can't associate anything with it.

The alleged discontinuity between classroom and field inspired protracted dialogue, mainly between Hill and Young. Hill argued that discontinuity engenders alienation:

> *Hill:* They think everytime they turn around they may be running into somebody who's threatening suicide. On the street, that ain't the way it happens. What they talked about mainly was the biggest letdown they had — they're all geared up, Adam 12 shit and they get out there and they're bored. They've got nothing to do. Somebody's giving them the wrong impression.
>
> *Young:* That they're going to be gangbusters, you mean.
>
> *Hill:* That's the impression they've got.

Discontinuity, according to Hill, also produces fundamentalist interpretations of rules and instructions:

> *Young:* If they tell you this is the way you should make the car stop, and the first thing you should do is have your motor running, that that's the way it should be — you're going to have to have your motor running in order to make a car stop. Then you're going to have to pull your car over to the curbing, so if they say "pull your car over to the curbing" you don't smash into a car that's parked at the fucking curbing because

you have to get to the curbing.

Hill: But what I'm saying is that a lot of people have the attitude that if that's what the fucking book says, that's the way you do it.

Young: I think this type of thing should be brought out in the field training.

Hill and Young engaged in a debate about the relative influence of the academy and the locker room. Young argued that recruits must be segregated. Hill deplored the academy's inability to neutralize peer socialization:

Young: How about this? Suppose nobody says the word "nigger" in the recruit school, but you go down in the locker room and you sit on a bench next to somebody who's got 20 years on and he says "I dumped that fucking nigger tonight." Is that good influence? If it is, maybe I'm in the wrong bag.

Hill: I'm not saying it is a good influence. What you're saying is that you've got qualified people teaching these people something that they're supposed to be receptive to, and they're going to go down and listen to some 20 year guy on the police department and that's going to impress them more than what you're teaching him. Is that what you're telling me?

Young: Sam, you were in every one of those goddamn sessions when we talked about the locker room syndrome.

Hill: I agree there's a locker room syndrome.

Young: Do you agree with it or not?

Hill: I think in some respects it's bad. But what I'm saying is there's something wrong if that can influence the people when you've got an 8 hour a day whack at them. This I don't understand . . .

Young: The only thing I'm saying, and this is the last fucking time I'll say it, is that if there's something wrong with what influence they get in the locker room, a way to get around it is not to have them go to the locker room.

There was consensus when Young suggested that field training officers could best counter locker room values. Jack, who had been appointed field training coordinator, amplified this suggestion. After outlining his proposal, he stressed that the new program would permit better assessment of training and its impact:

> All we have now on the probationary officer — I shouldn't say all, it's quite a bit — is going to be the evaluations. Now there'll be evaluations during the school, there'll be evaluations by myself, there'll be evaluations by the field training officer, either his personal evaluations or the evaluations that result because of the way he's going to have to check off the checklist on his book, and there'll be evaluations of the supervisors. Now we're going to try to figure out a way to evaluate the field training officer, too. I think the first way to do this would be the same way they're doing it here in the school, and that's to have the probationary officer rate the field training officer. And he'll also have evaluations coming in by his sergeants. And all these evaluations will be part of the bookkeeping, I suppose.

Testimonials and Caveats

A panel on the permanent Violence Prevention Unit (complete with poster-size organizational charts) followed the project discussions. This presentation proved short and concise, since discussion was precluded by time limits.

During the final hour, the Phase Two Officers were encouraged to summarize their impressions of the project; they all complied. Several started with a confession of initial skepticism:

> I remember one of the first meetings I had up on the 8th floor in the conference room (a staff member) asked me my opinion. And I told him I was very skeptical. And he asked why and I said, "well, I can remember when I got out of the academy sitting in the lineup and hearing a patrolman making a suggestion to a lieutenant, and the lieutenant looking at him and saying 'when you become a lieutenant, you can make the changes. Until then, you do what I tell you.' " And I told (the staff member) that I was very skeptical, and this is the way I thought things were going. Obviously, the thing back here that's on the board shows that maybe I shouldn't have had as much skepticism as I did at the time.

When we came up here in June I didn't actually have that open a mind about the project. I think it took me about two or three meetings before I was willing to speak freely. I think this is probably one of the greatest opportunities for policemen, and I'm grateful that I got in on it. To actually have some input into the system, as we know it.

This view, although a majority position, was not unanimously endorsed. Three officers expressed disappointment with the group's impact, and one of them said:

I came up here pretty enthused about the program. Unfortunately one of the questions I asked at that time "show me something that's been accomplished," still hasn't been answered. I still do not see anything accomplished. I see two months, I see a thing here. I don't see a piece of paper anywhere with the Chief's name on it or any program in existence. I don't think I've gotten too much out of the unit.

The assertion "I don't think I've gotten too much out of the unit" represented a clearly dissenting view. Most of the officers spontaneously testified to personal change, which they traced to participation in the project:

It's been a great value to my own personal self in pointing out ways that I can do things differently and better, and it's helped me to even consider alternatives where I didn't before, in the way that I work.

I think it changed my working ideas on the street fantastically. I think I'm a hell of a lot better policeman since I got through this. I go about so many things so many different ways — before it was just a set pattern that you used. Now you can sit back and do it the way that you see, other than the way that you were taught. And what you can learn from watching — even rookies.

I think the last couple of weeks or month or so really were the most valuable weeks to me, because a lot of the bad points of police work that I was putting forth in a lot of my contacts with the citizens were brought up to me at these meetings, and I just find that I conduct myself a lot better out on the street as far as dealing with the people.

Well, a couple of people have told me that I've slowed down, that I treat them like people now instead of like animals. One officer in particular who works on an adjoining beat with me. And I seem to be taking more time with them and actually trying to solve the problems, rather than kissing it off like I have in the past.

Only one strong objection was ventilated. Although it was presented under the guise of humor, the message was seriously intended:

My ideas are just as strong and my feelings are just as solid that I was doing things right previously. And that this is one of the problems that is facing this group here, is the fact that it is an outside influence that is another front for soft-soaping and kissing ass with these idiots out here. And the only thing that's ever going to sway peace, or whatever you want to call it, is by, as I say up here, "choke them out."

Claimed benefits were at times related to projects in which the men had been involved. Family crisis group members, for instance, reported changed perspectives about family disturbances:

I've really noticed when I go to a 415f now. Before this I said "what a bunch of shit this is — what am I doing here?" and kiss it off. I go in there now with the idea that these are real people, and what the hell, I'm paid $1000 a month to see what I can do. I think I'm a better person for having been in it. I think there's a hell of a lot of potential here, and if we let it go, then every one of us is missing the boat.

Family Crisis Intervention Unit — I wasn't too enthused about that down at Asilomar, but the more I've been associated with it and going out and taping on the street, and actually volunteering for 415f's which is something I thought I'd never do — I found it quite enjoyable to be able to go in there with the idea that you were going in there to actually help them with a problem. Instead of going in there and kissing it off in an assignment card to get back on the street and maybe do something else.

Similar changes were traced to experiences with review panels:

I realized that I was making a few mistakes out on the street. And like the old saying is, I'm going to correct them. But I realize that these guys that come in here also, the ones that we had up in this action review unit, we talked to them, they all had unique problems that I never realized that these guys had. I don't think anybody realized them. I don't think they realized them themselves. . . . . And what I got out of it is I'd like to help these guys.

Almost all the officers expressed satisfaction with their studies and proposals; they voiced confidence in the Violence Prevention Unit, with the proviso that departmental backing could not be stipulated. Several men volunteered for participation, in whatever roles were needed. The few voices of dissent, though there, had no echo. In the words of the Oklahoma chorus, it had been "a real good clam-bake." Group morale, at least, ended high.

PART III

Parts I and II of this book have described (with some effort at flavor) the stages of our training process. In this portion of the report, we turn to the products of change. We do not aim at an exhaustive inventory. Rather, we shall sample one or two products in depth, and then summarize our findings and impressions.

8 • Action Review Panels: The Application of Positive Peer Influence

In chapter 2 we traced the evolution of the peer review panel idea. We summarized rehearsals of the procedure that helped the panel take shape.

These shaping experiences provided both positive and negative lessons. On the positive side we discovered that even suspicious subjects could become cooperative. We discovered that the panel could be seen by supervisors as an adjunct to effective management. We discovered that novice panelists could become skilled interviewers. We discovered that the paper record could yield hypotheses which could channel questioning, without impeding discovery. We discovered that after half a dozen interviews, psychological denominators emerged that could expedite interview analysis. We discovered that patrolmen could act as scientists in evaluating data and as clinicians in reviewing clues to personality dynamics.

On the negative side, we faced the fact that single interviews may be more productive of insight than of changed conduct. True, some of our subjects showed improvement after their experience with the panel. But in these cases, the panel was one of several concurrent experiences; we can, at best, hope that it played a contributing role. With other subjects the prognosis following their one interview was guarded, particularly when the interviewee continued to defend his *modus operandi* after making concessions about his past. Such experiences led to the suggestion that the original procedure must undergo modifications to strengthen its impact. I shall try to illustrate the manner in which such modifications were introduced; I shall try also to document their results.

In its original form, the review panel consisted of the following stages:

(1) *The necessity for the panel is documented.* Typically, the process would be initiated when an officer reaches a threshold number of incidents on an up-to-date inventory of violent involvements. The number used would not be the number of raw incidents, but a refined index in which the active role of the subject had been established. It would exclude situations in which unwilling participation had been secured. It would include instances in which another officer had filed a report despite the subject's active role in bringing violence about.

Other ways of mobilizing the review panel would include requests by supervisors or by the subjects themselves. In such cases, however, the record would have to bear out the man's eligibility by showing a substantial number of recent involvements.

(2) *A preparatory investigation for the interview is conducted.* Data relating to the subject's performance on the street is obtained from available secondary sources. This includes interviews with supervisors, reports by peers and all information on record. The investigation culminates in a "study group" where panelists formulate hypotheses and draft questions that streamline the panel session.

(3) Then comes the interview itself, which can be subdivided into three stages:

(a) *Key incidents are chronologically explored,* including not only actions taken by all persons involved in the incident, but also their perceptions, assumptions, feelings and motives.

(b) *The summation of these data in the form of common denominators and patterns* is undertaken primarily by the subject, with participation by the panelists. An effort is made to test the plausibility and relevance of the hypothesized patterns by extrapolating them into other involvements.

(c) *The discussion of the pattern* occurs last, and includes tracing its contribution to violence. This stage features the exploration of alternative approaches that might be conducive to more constructive solutions.

The Walls of Jericho

In chapter 2 we saw panels rehearsed with two officers whose conduct was strongly motivated and well-established — men who showed little inclination to change their approach to police work. One of these officers was John Spark, a member of our project. Here was a bright, dedicated officer who detests unnecessary violence, perceives undesirable personal involvement in his past conduct, but considers his current activities as a necessary, objectively motivated strategy. His reaction, both to the interview and to other pressures for change, was to acknowledge the validity of criticisms without compromising his stance.

Officer Beam's case was even more discouraging. Here was a "super-cop": tall, stately, calm, cool, self-possessed, serious, dedicated to the point of fanaticism, and extremely bright. Beam had volunteered for the interview as an exercise designed to educate panelists and to document the case for his one-man police force. Beam's interview yielded hypotheses. Beam, however, showed no inclination to consider these nor to abandon his self-image of privileged insight and superior performance.

Our group had no intention of giving up efforts to redirect Spark and Beam so to insure the unimpeded availability of the talents of these men. Repeat interviews seemed as doomed as the original effort. Other strategies had to be evolved. In the remainder of this chapter, we'll review the efforts of the group to achieve impact on Officers Beam and Spark. These explorations will illustrate variations on the original review panel idea that can tailor-make a change-campaign to even the most difficult, challenging and obdurate subject.

Kill and Overkill

After the expiration of our project, the Violence Prevention Unit began to monitor high-incident officers in the department, including those of our "graduates" who had returned to the street. Among their subjects, one of the most prominent was Officer Spark. The number of his involvements reached pre-project proportions, and exceeded them. Moreover, the quality of his interactions was horrifying, even on the face of their description in official reports.

In one incident, Officer Spark had encountered a group of black juveniles, and had stopped them for identification. He became physically involved after arresting one of the young men for not carrying his draft card. In another episode, Spark slammed his car door on the leg of a man who showed reluctance about entering his vehicle. Faced with obvious errors in judgment such as these (and several slightly less blatant ones), the panel coordinator resolved to attack Spark's case.

The strategy was to expand the review panel through the addition of prestigious outsiders. One of these (as we shall see later) was Officer Beam. Another was an investigating officer familiar with follow-up problems in Spark's arrests. A third addition was a supervising sergeant. The panel was instructed to ask sharp, cross-examining questions to create "stress" in Spark. And they resolved (after preliminary discussion) to maintain emphasis on quality (as opposed to quantity) production.

A second procedure employed with Spark was to use him as a panel member shortly after his experience as subject. This procedure, in part, served to ameliorate the negative aspects of the previous step.

The results of the strategy were immediate and striking. Spark returned to the street and began an incident-less career. After several months his record was "clean"; reports arrived from fellow officers of a change in Spark's reputation. Persons who had refused to work with the man now indicated that he was an asset. Others voiced incredulity at the constructive work they witnessed in responding to Spark's calls.

The New Man

Four months after the last intervention, we asked Spark about the review panel and its impact on him. Whereas the "old" Spark had been tense and impatient, these qualities were no longer detectable. The interviewer was sufficiently impressed with Spark's demeanor to raise the subject of "how much change?" Spark, in turn, confirmed the fact that he now felt different:

Staff: You know, I sort of get the feeling that you're awfully relaxed now compared to what you used to be.

Spark: Well, yeah, I used to have something more to be nervous about. I'd really have to defend myself on going over some of those sloppy reports and some of those bad arrests that were made, and stuff. And you'd see reasons to have to defend yourself.

Staff: You mean deep down inside you were uneasy about it?

Spark: Not deep down inside. Just plain uneasy about it. You know, a feeling of guilt. Whether it was right or wrong, just a feeling of guilt. And at least now when I go out there everytime I make an arrest, it's an arrest. I don't have to feel guilty about anything. I think about it later, you know, "did I do it right, should I have done anything different?" But still, at the time I know that I've tried 100% and if I've got to take the guy to jail, the guy's only going because of himself and not because of me. So I just feel more relaxed when I have to talk about it, because I know they're on the up and up.

Was the impression of a change related to the interview? Did Spark feel generally different? He commented:

As a matter of fact, it seems kind of crazy — you probably won't believe this, I go home and I don't feel as tired. The pressure seems like it's off. I'm out there and I'm doing my job and I'm coasting along. I'm not picking up the free check for nothing. I mean I'm still out there doing my job but I feel good about it. And when I go home it just seems like I'm half as tired as I used to be.

Spark added, "my wife would vouch for (the change). I mean, I do more things around the house." He felt himself changed, not only as a police officer, but as a functioning person.

The Change-Sequence: A Retrospective View

Spark's initiation into a change-relevant atmosphere was not overly auspicious:

Staff: Let's go back to the summer. By and large, you'd say the summer was a fairly unpleasant time, wasn't it?

Spark: Yeah, yeah.

Staff: Can you sort of describe the summer quickly in terms of what happened? You know, you come up here. . . .

Spark: I guess my first reaction during the summer was when you enter a group like Violence Prevention Unit, just by the name you think everybody's going to be down on you. And then when you get in on it, you find out everybody is. I think I had a hard time in the group because I didn't get along with a lot of the guys and stuff, but I think a lot of the guys had legitimate reasons why they didn't get along with me.

According to Spark, the experience was an unsettling one. Even while Spark's street conduct remained the same, he had new second thoughts and disturbing doubts. His activity, while similar to previous conduct, was carried out with a divided mind:

Staff: Are you saying that even while you might have been getting into some difficulties, like for instance to take a hypothetical example, you arrest a guy for not carrying a draft card, after it's over you think about it, that is, you thought about it in ways you wouldn't have before?

Spark: Yeah, I don't know whether you'd say that was hypothetical or not. I arrested some guys for not carrying draft cards. But in a particular case like that, it was something where you feel pleasure for about 5 minutes while you're telling this Black Panther he's under arrest for not having a draft card, while Roosevelt Hilliard and the rest of the gang watch with blood in their eyes, and you feel real great. But then you think afterwards of the rest of the people that were around watching you, and you think all these guys have to do is say "see the harassment we're getting" and maybe they have some meat they can stick their teeth into when they can point that you're taking this guy for no draft card, and yet half the guys in Oakland don't carry them.

Staff: And you're saying that after the summer now you were at the juncture where you were thinking like this, after the 5 minutes of pleasure, whereas before the summer you would not have?

Spark: Yeah, that's probably right.

Staff: But you were doing it anyway.

Why had Spark's experiences with the panel been of limited impact? He comments:

> Well, probably overall on every panel I've sat with is the —
> except maybe after the last one — is thinking that they're
> out here trying to restrict me from really doing my job, really
> doing what you're paid for and stuff, and then it just dawns
> on you that that's not — they're not trying to restrict you but
> just trying to help you a little bit and lighten your load a
> little in dealing with people and dealing with the job.
> Another negative thing would be, of course, nobody likes to
> be criticized, especially on your reports, when you go over
> your reports. To you it seems like that's the thing to do at
> the time and stuff.

Elsewhere, Spark describes himself as moving from (1) feeling his productivity attacked, to (2) admitting to differences in kind between his productivity and that of others, to (3) entertaining hypotheses about the reasons for his involvements, to (4) controlling his motives through variations in conduct:

> Well, my first thought was, when I was interviewed on all
> the violent capers that I've been involved in, my first thought
> was that it was only probably because I've encountered more
> crimes and maybe a few more calls than the average officer,
> that I had a high incident of 148s and other violent crimes
> committed upon myself. And this is what I thought even
> after the first couple of meetings, the first couple of times
> that we've discussed. And then the more I talked with some
> of the other officers on the committee there and found that
> even percentage-wise, they had had a lot fewer than I had,
> I figured that maybe I wasn't all right, which was kind of
> hard to take. And finally I thought the main reason I've been
> involved in so many of them, and which apparently turned
> out to be the reason because I haven't had any recently, was
> a sort of a fear of the situation getting out of hand, whenever
> you're handling something, whenever you're talking to some-
> body. And it's sort of — I guess you could call it self-con-

fidence, when you're trying to make an arrest on somebody or when you're handling a family disturbance or anything. It's a lack of self-confidence in yourself being able to handle the situation, and your main objective is to get the guy under control, whether it be placing in the police car or police wagon. And once you get them in control you feel relieved. And so I've tried to sort of avoid getting into that fearful state where you have to have the guy under complete control, and now I try to keep them under control by just talking with them and seeing if that doesn't work. And I've had terrific success, and I seem to enjoy the job more.

According to Spark, the final, crucial panel drove home the point of his atypicality by broadening the range of questioners and critics:

Staff: Do you think being as uncomfortable as you must have been at that particular panel made the difference — the fact that they had you squirming? And I assume that they did. Did they?

Spark: Yes. But I was squirming at every one of my panels. I would say it did, it had an effect, because here I had been in front of a panel at least three times or so and different members all the time usually — at least a couple of different members, and you keep getting that feeling that even when they're bringing in outsiders like the last panel, these fellows feel the same way as the rest of the panel members. So you know it's not just the panel members you've got against you. You've got two new fresh faces that you've hardly ever talked with before, and they say the same thing. So it's sort of like majority rules.

The panel had also invoked arguments about the impact of Spark's arrests that he found hard to evade:

Spark: I think Lt. —— brought it out the best at the last meeting, where he said "when you make an arrest, just don't think of the immediate arrest. To you, all you have to do is you grab that body, you make out the arrest tag, you make out the report, and maybe at the most there's an hour shot. But then that report's got to be reviewed by an inspector or a sergeant who's got to spend a couple of more hours on it, who's got to get a complaint, meaning that the D. A.'s got to spend a couple hours on it. Then the judge has to rule on the case, which means you're going to have to spend a couple of hours on that."

Staff: And some of this is high-powered help.

Spark: Yeah. Well, I consider myself high-powered help, but why waste everybody's time? Why get everybody to the extent where— on one thing where you could have hesitated for just a second before you jumped in, why waste maybe 10 or maybe even 50 hours of a lot of time? Especially the way the courts are tied up nowadays and the way our investigators are overloaded.

Spark also claims to have benefitted from "field trips" with other members of the unit, in which he had observed "model" resolution of problems that he might have mishandled. And there was membership in someone else's panel, which sharpened Spark's perspective on his own motives:

Spark: Like you bring me up on a panel, like last week, and I look at this fellow's reports and you read them over and you say "oh, my God, what's this guy doing?" And then you just remember back to some of your own capers and you say "I would have done the same thing." But you can see on this fellow's report how he really fouled up, whereas looking at your own you try to avoid self-criticism and you don't see it so much.

Lastly, Spark had rehearsed alternative modes of conduct on the street, and discovered their advantage:

I don't know if it's good or not, but I can remember one 415, one of the first ones I went on after getting out of this pan. Over the gal who threw the lamp at the husband and the husband who threw the ashtray at the gal and we just stood there and talked, and we went away and about an hour later they were hand in hand and my God, that impressed me no end. And there was a case where six months — not even six months, probably two months prior to that I would have jumped on the guy and grabbed him and wrestled him, probably hurt my arm or something, and had him out in the car. Probably would have had to take her too, or something.

If you see things that can be avoided, why add to the hassle?

Spark deliberately initiated his experimentation in one area (that of family disturbances), and then generalized the experience to other — more sensitive — situations:

> *Spark:* The reason why I said the 415 family hassles, that seems to be the one that you can really take yourself out of being personally involved.
>
> *Staff:* I see.

> *Spark:* And when you take yourself out of being personally involved in one thing, then why get personally involved in anything else, to the extent where it's going to tire you out, and run you down, and that's all you look for is to arrest this prostitute because she's peddling her butt on your beat, and it's a personal thing because it's your beat? But you start sort of losing that, it starts going away from you, and it's good.
>
> *Staff:* It's easier to see in 415s because you're less initially involved, huh?
>
> *Spark:* Yeah, right.

The positive feedback, according to Spark, not only consists of results, but of newly discovered satisfactions. Special motives (such as Spark's fear of victimization) are replaced by pleasure derived from constructive interactions:

> *Spark:* I think the whole matter is just a liking of the people, and by feeling that you sort of express it to them.
>
> *Staff:* That's great. You mean you actually find yourself liking them — I mean, after the ashtrays and the lamps.
>
> *Spark:* Oh, yeah. I mean anybody that you talk to for an hour, you sort of get to know.
>
> *Staff:* So another factor of what's happening now is you get to know a lot more people.
>
> *Spark:* Yeah.
>
> *Officer:* You're looking at them now more as people, rather than annoyances, as a call?

Spark: Yeah, that's right. It would always probably be the annoying that would get me, because why waste your time in a petty thing like that when you can be out doing something big. You know? And what's bigger — you leave these people and he kills her or she kills him, and then that's big, and you've got to take on that messy paperwork. It's just more enjoyable to me. You get to relate to the people's problems and stuff. I can't even remember making a 415 arrest in the last six months or so. And there's been plenty of cases where I know other officers would have made the arrest. So now it's sort of a challenge to me when I go in on a call, I'm going to see how I can get out of making this arrest, unless the gal's so bruised up or battered that you've got to take her. I figure I'm 100% success if I go in on a call and the gal's screaming "he's been trying to hit me, and he's been doing this and that," they'll both be sitting there watching T.V., or both of them will just be in there. And then I consider it a halfway success if one of them just leaves, and I consider it no success if the fellow or the gal keeps complaining and wanting the other one arrested, or "why are you calling the pigs" and stuff. But I find in most of mine now, that most people stay.

From Changes to Changer

Spark's perspective on his own role has changed. He had previously seen himself as a dedicated officer, engaged in a solitary pursuit of criminal elements. He now sees himself (1) as part of an organization, with responsibilities to it; (2) as a member of a team, with concern for the conduct of team-mates; (3) as a person who can exercise constructive influence on his team-mates; and (4) as a positive problem-solver on the street.

Having discovered both interest and skill in human relations, Spark views this as his principal asset, whose exercise gives him satisfaction:

Staff: Well, where are you going now? What's your perception of your job and your future in it and what you can do for the department? As of here on in. In terms of what you now enjoy.

Spark: I would say community services — I hate to even use those two words, but where you get out there and you're just the mediator, you know, you're not involved. You're the mediator in everything, since most of the things we handle aren't criminal— we handle a lot of 415s out in District One, even though the F troops don't know about that. Just to try and be a little more relaxed, to try and talk to people more, not be so apprehensive whenever you're talking to one person or a group of people, not thinking to yourself "this guy wants to jump me and take my gun" and all this stuff. And being prepared, however, to take action if that does happen, but not having the fear of just getting out there and talking with the people.

Having experienced the positive impact and rewards of his attributes, Spark senses their absence in others. He has become, in a sense, a missionary for constructive human relations:

Spark: The only thing that worries me the most out there and that I really never looked into before is that whenever you go on a family fight or something, and a lot of times it's brought up to me, usually the fellow will say it: "why aren't you like the last officer that was here? The last officer was choking me and taking me out to the car and stuff and you're different." You get to the point where . . . one officer might go there and foul it up and you go there and straighten it out and the guy does a complete reverse in thinking of the department, and yet the third guy goes out and fouls it up again. If you could somehow develop some consistency with just all the officers.

Staff: So you'd like to exert some influence, the question is how.

Spark: Yeah.

Spark finds himself on occasion sufficiently disturbed by the conduct of others to intervene and to spread the benefit of new insights:

It would bother me when I would see them do something that maybe I would have done six months ago, you know, but I'd be looking at it from a different viewpoint and it would look bad. And I'd even straighten out my beat partner sometimes when he'd do something that I don't think is right . . .

Spark is willing and anxious to formalize this concern through panel membership and through participation in training and re-training efforts. Having experienced the transition from "before" to "after," Spark has become conscious of the process and cognizant of its benefit. As a corollary of insight-centered change, the change-object is a change-expert. Ultimately, this role converts him into a sophisticated change-agent.

The Importance of Being Perfect

Whereas Spark's battle against change had been a rear-guard en-gagement, Beam's was a counter-offensive. Beam began by billing himself as an Enlightening Influence; three transmutations later, he advertised this same role. He started by asserting his unimprova-bility; after numerous changes, he proclaimed vehemently that he was (and had always been) an ideal officer.

In Beam's case, the panel took the following steps: (1) after the first interview, the coordinator showed Beam a copy of the analysis by the panel; (2) the panel offered Beam the opportunity of a second interview, with stress on alternatives to violence; (3) Beam was used as a panelist in two other interviews; (4) Beam was recom-mended to the Chief as a participant in a seven-week institute on community relations; (5) Beam was appointed to the Violence Prevention Unit, where he took responsibility for a study of police problem-solving; (6) Beam was given an assignment heading a neighborhood police team. Between the second interview and Beam's departure for the institute, his record was "clean." Again, informal word corroborated statistics. The sergeant of the Violence Prevention Unit reports:

> A fellow officer, presently the above interviewee's partner, asks in casual conversation, "What the hell did you guys do with him? He's different!" When asked about arrests and activity; "He still makes arrests, but he operates in a different way. He doesn't have much trouble."

At the institute Beam became conspicuous by advocating com-munity action; after his return he worked feverishly on projects designed to cement contact with neighborhood groups. He was involved in landlord-tenant cases in which underprivileged tenants were molested. The prosecutor's office, which had experienced Beam's enthusiasm for jailing addicts, now witnessed with surprise

Beam's new role as Defender of the Poor.

In a retrospective discussion, Beam belabored the assertion that he had experienced no movement so far. "From the time of the first interview," he proclaimed, "I felt one way, which hasn't changed. I still feel the same way." He recollects his panels as follows:

> *Beam:* The first meeting up here was a lot of fun, that was amusing. Let's see, I was up here twice. Which was the lecture— when did I lecture you, the first or the second?
>
> *Staff:* The first one.
>
> *Beam:* The second one I don't recall. What were the circumstances of the second meeting? It gives you an idea how much it impressed me, I guess. I don't remember the second one.
>
> *Officer:* Why do you remember the first one so vividly and not the second?
>
> *Beam:* Well, that was amusing . . .
>
> *Officer:* This is the first interview, the first action review panel?
>
> *Beam:* Yeah. The first one was the lecture, I think. The second one was where you were trying to find out why I had had this substantial decrease in violent encounters. Why had I changed? Right? And the second one was amusing again, because I hadn't changed.
>
> *Officer:* You said you were amused. I'm just curious as to how you were amused.
>
> *Beam:* I got a kick out of it, because to me it was an exercise in frustration on your part. And it was probably perceived as me giving you a hard time or playing the dozens or just giving you a game, and I really wasn't. I was answering you honestly. Both times I was honest. It came right from the shoulder. The second time I was probably not indifferent; I would say I was apathetic, a little bit aggravated that I had to have changed, because I hadn't. And I walked out of that meeting hoping maybe that there would be some concessions made to the fact that if you make a lot of narcotics arrests, then there is the opportunity for more violent encounters. The percentages go up. I hoped that I had gotten

that point across. I also hoped that I had gotten the point across that I really hadn't changed, that maybe the fact that I was working a different area might have had something to do with it.

Beam recalls that he was "pissed off" by the analysis of his first panel, which he interpreted as a manifestation of skepticism. He consented to the second interview, with the intent of again providing advice and counsel:

> That's why I came up a second time. I figured that I can help, anyway. Of course I had a different idea of helping. You people are trying to help me and I'm trying to help you. And a guy will believe a so-called good patrolman before he will a sergeant or his general orders or a training manual, because when you get street savvy that's a hell of a lot more important than book learning. And so for that reason I'd always take an interest in something like this. Even if it's to keep the people involved in it in the proper perspective.

On the second occasion the panel was more forceful than in the first interview. Beam recalls that "I was accused of giving them the run-around and was told that I was full of shit." He adds, as a concession, "if I do give you the run-around, then it's unconsciously. Because things just aren't as literate or as linear as I'd like them to be."

Beam's feelings about the panel were not unambiguously negative. He continued informal contacts, including discussions of interview content. And he responded readily when invited to become a panel member. He recalls that he viewed his participation as an imprimatur, which would validate the panel in everyone's eyes. Beam's first step, he remembers, was to make sure that the panel merited his support:

> *Officer:* Yeah. How did you feel about that, being a panel member? I remember you came up and reviewed the reports, and went over them to get patterning and classifying behavioral patterns. And your recommendation to us before the interview was "maybe we should recommend this guy be fired." You said that outright. And I remember telling you "we're kind of in the game of getting the guys down in this setting with patrolmen and talking about —"

Beam: I had reasons for saying that.

Officer: Sure, it was your initial reaction, "this guy was dangerous." There's no goddamn doubt about it.

Beam: No, that wasn't my reaction at all. You were dangerous. I just wanted to see where you were going.

Officer: Yeah, that's good, sure, talk about that. You said that to test me?

Beam: Well, to test the panel, yeah. I won't be a part of firing a policeman.

Officer: O.K., good. How did you feel when you said that? What were your motives? This is what we want.

Beam: What were my motives? Well, because I would have sunk you if that's what you would have done. I would have just gone down to patrol and just told them what's happening, "when you go up there you're going to Internal Affairs, pal, only they're going to grease you out of here a lot faster than Internal Affairs would." I would tell them that the first time I thought it was true. I would tell them that now.

Officer: So you said "I think this guy ought to be fired."

Beam: I said "this son of a bitch is crazy, we ought to can him right now."

Officer: O.K. And you were waiting for what response?

Beam: I was waiting for a response. And I was very concerned with what response. The response was favorable. "No, that's not what we want to do. That's why you're up here, we want to save him. We don't want to see him get fired." I could identify with that . . .

Beam found his first experience as panelist enjoyable and constructive. He says, "I felt it was good. And I felt that interview went real well . . . and I was glad to be a part of it, and optimistic of its success." The "part" that Beam assigns himself is (characteristically) the leading one:

Staff: What were you doing during that interview? You participated fairly actively, didn't you?

Beam: Well, I think I sold him on it, because I was sold on it myself. He knew me and knew of me, I think, rather than knowing me personally. And I was able to tell him to relax, that he could trust everybody there, and that I wouldn't be a part of it if he couldn't trust it. And he ought to know that, and I think he bought it. So I felt strongly enough about it to sell it.

Staff: Did you feel that he was getting any help out of this?

Beam: Yeah.

Staff: In what way did you feel that you in particular were helping him? You know, after you had gotten him to work with them?

Beam: Well, I don't know if this is conceit or not, but I think probably he can go back to the patrol division, and a lot of people trust me, and they say, "well, if Jim Beam said that, then maybe you ought to listen to him."

Staff: But in terms of giving advice, or in terms of understanding a little better what he's been doing — what in particular do you think he got out of this session?

Beam: Well, I think he got a lot out of it, for a number of different reasons. There were a lot of things said that we didn't agree with, and then to his surprise that I didn't either. Where I would say "you just can't do that" and all that. And I think he trusted us. I think it was successful. I think he believed what we were telling him. He realized, as he went through the sequential breakdown, that he was having problems.

Staff: He did?

Beam: Yeah, I'm sure he was aware of this. At the end of the interview he admitted it. He said "yeah, I've changed a little bit and I realize I have to change a little more." And I think he felt good because, I don't know if it was me or somebody else told him, "well, that's a beginning."

Beam's reaction to the review panel has become one of enthusiasm. He takes it upon himself — again, with a sense of his own potency — to "sell" the idea to others:

Beam: Oh, the review panel I'm behind 100%. In fact, I'm selling it to the command officers finally. "You know, gee, this is good, and it should have been started years ago." I'm 100% behind it. I've got every goddamn patrolman I ever talked to behind it.

Officer: How do you do that? How do you get them on?

Beam: I can talk to them a little bit differently than you can. But I have the advantage, I guess, of being a supercop. A lot of guys will feel that they can trust me, that's all. I've fought a few raps for a couple of guys. I've got a couple going now that I've fought the rap for.

Beam not only assigns himself the key role as panel "salesman," but recalls having informally used a type of "panel" approach himself:

About two years ago I started really thinking — maybe even longer ago than that. It was probably two and a half years ago . . . that's when there were a lot of violent encounters. But they were a different kind of encounter. When I started thinking, when I started using my head and realized that I had to be smarter than people. I can recognize certain patterns developing, that I seem to get in the shit the same way everytime. It's a breakdown, bang! When I see this happening, if I'm over to the Public House or I'm talking to some guy or something like this, at that point then I can see it a hell of a lot sooner now because I am convinced that patterns do arise, for one reason or another. And then at that point I will talk to them usually. And maybe very casual, not quite as obvious as it would be up here. Because it's not a stress situation. Bullshit is the word, with them. And pretty soon we'll just get down to the nitty-gritty of why.

Staff: When did you start doing that?

Beam: Well, let me see, maybe March of 1969.

Staff: So you did really have a headstart on us, didn't you?

Beam: Yeah, kind of. Now I would say that two things then are possible now, at this point. I don't know if this is defensive or not. That I have an inability to apply this to myself, or else it doesn't apply to me.

In any event, Beam has become an advocate of the review concept, and a strong and positive participant. His street conduct has improved.

At one point Beam was advised of the Chief's decision to send him to the institute. This development was one for which Officer Beam had no ready explanation:

> *Beam:* I was surprised. I was really surprised. I was skeptical. And just wondering. I walked in here wondering, walked out wondering what was going on.

> *Staff:* You must admit that getting you wondering was a little victory for us, wasn't it? I mean we had you asking questions.

> *Beam:* Oh, well, there was a real diversity in how I was thinking. I was wondering, "well, something's up and they're going to get me out of town." Or like "what are they doing, why do I have to be out of Oakland for two months?"

> *Staff:* So, "they're trying to get me out of town . . ."?

> *Beam:* I don't know, I was concerned, I guess, curious, concerned, amazed, shocked is better. I felt a lot of things. And standing I guess in the forefront would be "why?" Which I still don't know, why.

Pressed for a reason, Beam speculates that his reputation would make him a unique asset to the program. No one could possibly see him as a "sell-out," he argues: "Everybody says, nope, we trust you, you're the first one that went up there that we could trust." Beam concedes, however, (as an after-thought) that his own development might have been an issue, "that I wasn't useful right off the street, that I had to have a little bit more awareness so that I could kind of fit into the thing."

In discussing his institute experience, Beam places the emphasis on his own interventions, and on their impact on other participants. In response to probes, Beam admits to having carried away from the experience a number of new premises, which he describes with considerable eloquence:

> *Officer:* They bought your ideas, how about some ideas that were down there that you didn't have before that you were able to buy?

Beam: I can think of some ideas that I projected down there that they were saying "right on. I didn't understand that before."

Officer: Well, yeah, I'm saying what about — we all have good ideas. I might have some that you don't and I'm sure you have some that I don't and that's why we talk, right? Now what ideas did you get down there that you thought were applicable here, that you didn't have before? If any?

Beam: Trying to organize the community, that silent majority, black or white. I can see, say, the police departments and the silent majority as having a common fate, which from different types of charts and schematics and everything else, leads me to believe that there are then avenues of communication available to us that we should exploit. I think a lot of the tensions in the community, for reasons real or imagined, can be dealt with. But I see the necessity — one thing I did buy down there that I can identify with is that police departments are going to have to become more personal. I got a different perception of professionalism down there, a new definition.

Officer: What?

Beam: Well, that it isn't necessary to spit polish — of course a hell of a lot more than that. That we took an oath, that there's a good deal more to do than throwing people in jail. That that isn't all we can do. Which is all I thought we ever could do. You know, just throw them in jail. Like a hype, throw them in jail, and who knows, maybe they'll get 90 days in Martinez to dry up. O.K., fine. But I got an idea down there that there are people in this community who are stagnated by the system, that if we could plug into the police department and use them as a resource, that maybe we don't always have to arrest people. And this gets back to narcotics again. Because I see the narcotics addict as a nonentity in society, because there's no room for him. And the only other recourse is jail. But we can go into the community. And if I ever get a chance I can contact these people in L.A. and they can come up and sell the Chief on it — so all of a sudden we're walking into places that were forbidden before. Because we're not only there to arrest people, but let's find out why they're there. Because they need help. They want to help somebody. I realized and became optimistic about doing a little more than changing substances of image. I then became aware of the necessity of and also the need for changing the image itself, rather than the substance of the image, because that's artificial, that's phony . . .

It is interesting that despite the argument against arresting "hypes" (Beam's previous principal occupation) he asserts that there is nothing new here. He admits, however, that he has now become a change-advocate, despite a past (well-publicized) stand against the possibility of reform:

> *Staff:* Now before we had anything to do with you, I would guess you would have been fairly pessimistic about the possibility of inducing this department or anything else to change. Wouldn't you have been? You went along your own way feeling that sooner or later they might dump you but weren't offering very much hope of affecting anything.
>
> *Beam:* That would be a more than accurate statement, yeah.
>
> *Staff:* Do you still feel that way?
>
> *Beam:* No, I think it can be changed. I think I'm optimistic now. I'm optimistic that I, as a patrolman, and as only a patrolman, which is all I ever said down there, I realize I'm only a patrolman but — well, let's just say that I have reinforced something that I was beginning to lose as a police officer, and that's the power of oneness.

Beam has come to see himself, primarily and saliently, as a change source. As he puts it, "I can see myself coming up from the bowels of the earth, so to speak, to be reckoned with."

His views with respect to the change role are an amalgamation of alienation and liberalism, of struggle by the Little People (including the police) against a common enemy. Partly, Beam has not changed. He sees his role — as he always has — as that of the "supercop" overcoming institutional efforts to stymie and suppress. But the target of the suppression has shifted. In the forefront now is not crime-fighting (and the arrest of addicts) but social-problem-fighting with emphasis on self-help:

> *Beam:* I think we're going to have to be the conscience of the community, the spokesmen for the community. Because

the community's been left out of the system too, so to speak. We happen to be — since we're being killed as the representatives of the system, then maybe we're going to have to actually play that role. But be the people's representatives. Rather than being the victims. Because most police officers will say "hey, listen, you're right. We're all being manipulated by the system, by the politicians."

Staff: You mean "we have a lot in common."

Beam: Yeah, we have a hell of a lot in common . . . I say that the community perceives us as very, very significant change agents, because we do change their lives when we make arrests and stuff like that. The community has a very valid frustration with the police department because all they ever do is hurt you. They never help you. Unfortunately, they perceive it as an apathy, an indifference — you don't want to help them. This is also the frustration of a police officer, because you can't help them . . . But I can see it number one, as a significant community relations effort. I can see it as a very, very necessary image change. And I can also see it as a vehicle for eliminating the impotence.

Beam's own role is still that of a one-man vanguard for others. He sees himself functioning in the change-agent role at considerable personal sacrifice, but with a sense of unavoidable mission:

Staff: Do you miss the street?

Beam: Shit. yes. Being up here is a chore. Coming up here every morning is not what I want to do, so I have to do it. See?

Staff: But do you see enough in it to make up for not being out there?

Beam: There's a job to be done up here, and it's a job that somebody's got to do. And I think that I would be dishonest with myself and a discredit to them, the patrol officers, if I didn't do something.

Constancy and Flux

Has Beam changed? In many ways he really hasn't. He is now (as he was earlier) a dedicated man who feels sure of his role and of his ability to discharge it. He sees himself (as he did then) as a pioneer whose efforts must be emulated by others. And he is probably correct on both counts.

Whether Beam was once an Appeaser of Fear, or his conduct was otherwise over-determined, is a moot question. He has not acknowledged such dynamics and is not impressed by them. But Beam has embarked on a new career with constructive consequences. If new activities satisfy private needs, the issue is academic.

Beam has changed, in the sense that he is currently engaged in constructive work. He would argue that this is all a consequence of new opportunities — of the lifting of pressures. If Beam is right, the panel (and the Chief) have controlled the environment and have placed the actor on a new stage, with a new cast and script. This answer sounds over-simple.

It is more probable that the panels provided the occasion for Beam to confirm the fact that he was embarked on a self-defeating road. More than that, they provided a perspective of functionally equivalent alternatives.

Beam's first interviews forced him into self-definitions compatible with the panel's view of policing. Experiences as panel member and institute participant gave Beam concrete (and satisfying) illustrations of alternatives to past role-definitions. The view that he felt nothing new testifies to Beam's bridging skills, and facilitate the adoption of new beliefs.

Beam became a change-agent because he could be nothing less. He had always seen his role as central and autonomous. By using responsible functions as change-inducing ones, the panel affected Beam by harnessing his alienation: giving him the key to his own fate, and that of others.

The Belated Rehabilitation of Officer White

Officer White had been a member of our second group. One of the projects of this group was the investigation initiated by White into the problems of reserve officers. White's dedication to this activity reduced the time available for violence-related concerns. He himself tells us that he was not interested in family crisis management, nor motivated in areas other than the reserve program. On the other hand, he feels that he might have incurred some benefit from witnessing group discussions:

We just went a little deep into things that you normally wouldn't give a second thought to, such as this family crisis unit and what your mission was there. It did have some impact on me there, I think. Because of these, I think I've handled that type of assignment a little differently than I used to, take a little more time than I did. In fact I take a little more time about everything, rather than trying to rush through it. Trying to do the job rather than just trying to kiss it off.

Ultimately — for White — the group had to stand or fall with the reserve study. And on this basis, the group failed. As White put it:

(The reserve study) was the big thing to me, and it didn't go through, so to me the summer was a total waste almost. That's what I was working on. I put the effort in and nothing was coming back.

In retrospect, White's view of the summer is neither unhappy nor bitter. White is cynical, assesses the police department with misgivings and expects nothing positive to originate with it:

I fully expected what happened to happen. Because I have my own feelings about the way things go around here, and these type of things just reinforce it. I knew nothing was going to happen, in this particular regard anyways. Nothing was going to change.

It is surprising, given these facts, that a year after the end of our study, White requested that he be subjected to a review panel. The request came opportunely, because the record showed many violent encounters featuring White and his partner, and some intervention seemed necessary.

White tells us that he requested a panel because the summer had made him see some remote chance of salvation. He tells us:

I requested to come to this panel. I remembered vaguely one of the other groups during the summer was working on this panel and it sounded like a fairly good idea at the time to me. I was a little suspicious of it, but I had reached the point, up to about a month ago, I think, where I was just on the verge of blowing my cool, get myself fired or kill somebody or something. And I figured, "what the hell, I might as well come up and give it a try."

White anticipated the panel experience with a mixture of despair (based on a feeling that he had reached a dead-end point) and of trust. He was determined to share his concerns, and to cooperate fully:

> When I asked for this thing, I figured "what the hell, I'm going to just throw caution to the wind and tell it like it is and trust that everything will be all right." I figured there wasn't much that could happen because of it, from anything I might say up there, because what I was in fact doing was looking for help . . . I went up there with a basic understanding of what the whole thing was about, but I was just going to pour my guts out, so to speak, and let these guys do whatever was needed, whether it was to wring me out, or sympathize, or whatever.

In response to White's request, a panel was immediately constituted. This group reviewed White's reports and concluded that these clustered in clear-cut ways. The group summarized its findings and listed its hypotheses:

> 1. It appeared that the officer would take immediate action (often physical in nature) when a subject would fail to comply immediately with his verbal directions.
>
> 2. The panel felt that the above was of extreme concern because the officer probably felt that his authority as an officer was being challenged by citizens when they failed to "immediately" comply with his verbal instructions.
>
> 3. The officer had numerous incidents degenerate into violent confrontations when crowd situations developed. Action was taken by the officer "to prevent a person from agitating or inciting the crowd." This occurred in areas where the appearance of a "crowd" should not have been a startling event.
>
> 4. In a large number of incidents, violent encounters erupted after the officer had made a car stop. In all of these incidents there was more than one person in the vehicle.

5. A disproportionate number of women were involved as suspects.

6. Contrary to the trend of most active officers, this interviewee had all types of arrest situations degenerate into violent confrontations. (The normal pattern being that there are more violent incidents related to misdemeanor arrests than in felony arrests.)

White viewed the panel as an unqualified success. According to White, he now had a clear and accurate picture of his problems. He was pleased and surprised that the panel did not lecture or expostulate:

> They didn't tell me anything. It was just a — just all got together for a bullshit session, but nobody was trying to con anybody, and we all knew what the story was. And I realized with a few facts and figures and what have you, that I could identify what my biggest problem was.

White claims that he now feels "cooled off":

> But I think the biggest thing was I was just getting a bad attitude problem, with one thing building on top of another, which was getting to me, but I think I've cooled off considerably since then, once I realized I did have a problem and some of the things that were causing it.

He specifically says that he has curbed the propensity to react emotionally when suspects don't heed commands, or when they don't show respect:

> I know what my emotions are but I tend to control them. I don't know whether it's a don't-give-a-shit attitude, "do your eight hours and get out," or things are going to change or what. I don't know what it is, but at any rate I don't get that excited anymore. I detach myself a little more, I think. The name-calling, what have you, doesn't get to me anymore like it did. I think what happened was everything just blew up to a point, and maybe it was the panel that blew the top off. But at least I got it all out. I think I've got it pretty well out of my system now. I don't get too excited about it anymore.

There is no transcript of panel discussions, but a summary of key points is available. The following is an excerpt from the White panel summary. It suggests that the main dimensions of White's problem (as hypothesized by the panel) were covered during the discussion:

> . . . the interviewee stated that he was "sick and tired of taking things from the 'animals and social misfits' " he found on the street. He further stated that he now just does not have any tolerance when dealing with "these people." He further stated that he actually looks forward to when a person makes that error that is serious enough for him to effect an arrest.

> With further discussion along these lines, the officer stated that he was just tired of people not doing as he said or appreciating him. "After all, the policeman is supposed to be the 'good guy.' "

> It was then pointed out to the interviewee that on numerous reports that it appeared he took action that was probably not appropriate or necessary for that particular incident.

> There were several reports that appeared to have no crime committed until the citizen decided to disregard a simple direction of the interviewee.

> Several of the incidents involved pat searches, and the officer appears to have little patience with citizens who do not either immediately comply with his orders in these situations or understand the reason for a search and who question his authority to do so.

> It would appear that the officer's dealings with the citizenry is often blunt, overly direct, humorless, too quick, and unsympathetic.

> The interviewee became aware of some of the negative patterns that he had developed (specifically his over-reaction to citizens when they failed to immediately comply with instructions or wishes).

Only time can tell whether Officer White, in response to this new, intensive, personalized contact with him, has overcome his destructive patterns. White feels he has insight into his difficulties and conceives of himself as regenerated. Routinely, White will be invoked as a panelist. He is willing to play the role even with his friends:

I'd love to do it. I think maybe one thing of value — in my case the guys on the panel, I'd worked with several of them . . . And there's no bullshit there. You know when a guy's giving it to you straight. I think that's something you ought to bear in mind. I'd love to do it, wouldn't mind at all. But I think that'd be an important fact. I don't know if you've already thought of this or not, but having somebody there that knows the guy and works with him, and understands the unit. I do think it has definite value, I really do. I'm sold on it.

White has become a panel-advocate and has offered help in approaching subjects of future panels. White has interest in the reserve officer study and this raises the possibility of resuscitating the project. Beyond this, White may be subjected to panels, with variations if necessary.

In general, we can conceive of the sequence as cumulative. Each step increases trust in change agents, involvement in change and commitment to a need for change. White has seen himself as the carrier of a problem, has stipulated the effectiveness of peer-review, considers himself a partner with a stake in the enterprise. With each step the probability of White's regeneration is increased. Also with each step, White becomes part of change as it addresses the problems of his fellows.

The reports prepared by Group Two inspired the creation of an "experimental projects" function in the department (see final chapter). More directly, the recommendations led to one concrete "experimental project": the initiation, monitoring and evaluation of a family crisis intervention program.

We have said (in chapter 3) that family crisis management in Oakland differs from the New York model. There was to be no professional involvement; the men were to be selected for their past expertise, and were to be trained "on the job." The program was also to be research-oriented from the start. Base-line data for experimental and control beats were available; periodic review of key indices would document impact. The indices include need for callback, need for arrest, assault and homicide rates, and incidence of officer injury. There was also to be a cost analysis, covering amount of time and effort consumed, and time and effort saved.

The third difference pertained to participation of outside agencies in the solution of family crisis problems. Whereas New York had supplied referral rosters to its officers, it had done little else. As a result, agencies showed little inclination to cooperate even when clients appeared. In Oakland, the officers were scheduled to make their own referrals, to schedule appointments, to recontact agencies (and clients), and to keep a record of outcome. The Oakland concept is one that stressed (1) exploring avenues of active collaboration toward joint problem solving, and (2) systematically evaluating the impact of new linking arrangements.

As a first step, an organizational meeting was called in the police building. This meeting was initiated by two officers, the sergeant of the Violence Prevention Unit and the coordinator of "experimental projects" (Officer Bond). The participants were representatives sent by six key agencies.

A review of this organizational meeting may help to define the problems and prospects of the "outreach" phase of police problem solving.

Caveats and Rejoinders

Early in the meeting with agency personnel, problems appeared in the discussion. A supervisor representing one social agency announced:

> I'd like to raise a few questions that I have, and one of the reasons I'm here is I'd like to hear more from the officers about this. I wonder how treatable many of the people that you are going to be sending to us — how amenable they are going to be to the casework approach. I think you're probably coming in contact with really quite chronic kinds of situations, that people have acted out in this kind of a way over a period of years. I mean, this is the way they handle their problems, and when you make a referral to a family agency or to any other agency and some determination is made by the agency regarding the fact that these people are not amenable to treatment and are not seeking any kind of alleviation of the problem, what will the police do about this?

The sergeant (Bill, the ex-leader of Group One) responded by tracing the implications of a pessimistic stance. A residual option would be to give up the ship, and arrest people wholesale. As an alternative, one could tailor-make change approaches to clients, excluding those agencies who failed, and selecting "winning combinations" among the remaining resources:

> The other alternative is to arrest him, and nobody is "amenable" to arrest. So what we're saying is that I'm sure we're going to get some people that don't like the case approach, that are not amenable to change and they may enjoy it — some people do — they don't want to get as personal as would be necessary with you, at least discussing their personal problems. But I don't really think that's the end of it. I think when you find a family, for instance, who can be referred to your agency and you don't seem to be filling the bill, we're talking about utilization of all of us. You know, us. Not the police department and the Catholic Service and the

Jewish Family Service, and Wage Earner and Welfare and Health. We are us.

A representative of the welfare department (who had participated in one of our field experiments) rose in defense of case work as a solution:

> Now, I had the experience of going out with the Violence Prevention Unit one night — myself and two other social workers went out with them. And I have to disagree with you. The people that I met were in need of some kind of counseling . . . And what myself and the other social workers pushed after we were out on the calls was exactly what we're getting right now. It's a liaison thing, because these people are in great need and the police officers are in great need of what we have to offer him.

The original dissenter, however, once more raised doubts about the amenability of police clients to her agency's services:

> But I do think we get the kind of situation — that's what I don't know — this is my assumption — I've had no contact with the police in the past. I'm assuming that you get a lot of the kinds of cases that are going to come into our family agency, that are going to be the real sado-masochistic relationships that no one is going to intervene and break up. The community is going to be up in arms, but nobody is going to be able to put a stop to it.

The sergeant argued against precategorization, while conceding that some clients might ultimately prove difficult:

> One thing we're trying to get across to policemen departmentally is that you kind of have to get rid of predetermined ideas that have emanated from your past experiences. For instance, there may be some "sado-masochistic" people and "sadists" that are referred to you for counseling. That's not to say that they can't be counseled. . . . There are some which the police must confront that are not amenable to anything and have to be taken into custody and locked up behind bars, which unfortunately sometimes is the only alternative the officer has.

The dissenter demurred:

But I just want to raise that I think we're going to deal with some people that in the past social agencies have tried working with and have not worked with very successfully, and this can make for complications.

At this juncture, two agency representatives defended the program. They pointed to "crisis management" objectives and to the need to depart from a traditional view of available services:

Representative 1: I will at the risk of being a little naive, however, look at this in terms of the title of this program which is family crisis intervention. To me, I see possibilities not so much in terms of curing people of a long term mental problem but rather in reducing the number of assaults within families and upon policemen. And perhaps the greatest benefit, as I see it, might come in lengthening the period that occurs in the repetitive offender and perhaps reducing the overall number of offenses through the use of these policemen who are specially appointed to this kind of work, and whatever help then the referral agencies can give. I see this as more the ultimate goal, rather than an attempt to give long-term therapy or something like that to people.

Representative 2: I do see it as a way of perhaps doing just this to alleviate a crisis, an immediate crisis. This is what I think it might be all about.

Representative 1: First of all I'd like to say that I'm really impressed with the fact that the police department is taking a step in this direction, and I think in all of us being here that it does throw a responsibility on us of questioning what we are doing. You know we are going to, if we accept referrals from this type of situation, see people that we don't typically see. Particularly certain types of agencies. In Psych Emergency at Highland you probably see a good percent of this type of person to begin with, but we'll probably be seeing more and different types. And I think rather than moving to "they may be untreatable," we need to look back at ourselves and say "yeah, we're going to be getting a new type of person that traditionally we haven't seen," and question how can we, what are new ways of intervening. Now we all kind of point the finger at police, that they should be more service oriented, and here they're doing that and calling us in as a team to come and work together. And I think that's great, and I think we should look at our own agencies and when we say yes or no, we're willing to take that referral, say it with the fact in mind that yeah, you may have to be doing something different than you did before. And maybe certain types of methods don't work, but to decide beforehand that it's going to be untreatable, I think we fall into a bad bag when we do that. And we throw certain people by the wayside when we do it.

A strong endorsement also came from the head of the legal aid society, who had participated in Group Two discussions:

Let me say that I've talked to the officers here, I think this is the third time or fourth time, and I'm 1000% behind the program and I'd like to assist them in any way possible. I do dislike the attitude of pessimism that I've picked up, because I know that if you look at the police report for the city of Oakland last year you'll find that 15,000 arrests were on alcoholism. That's almost a third of their arrests. I know that if you count assault and batteries, etc., as many times as I've had fights with my wife and I know about my neighbors and I know about a lot of people who have had disagreements, etc., that there is a problem. And I also know that there is probably a need for this type of service. So I'm 1000% behind the program.

The pessimism voiced by one person had mobilized others in the group to voice and to define support. It had furnished the occasion for a more detailed presentation of project objectives. Finally, it had demonstrated that previous contact (including riding in our field tests) had resulted in two-way conversions: whereas our officers had arrived at more sophisticated thinking about referral agencies, agency representatives had come to better see the need for the unit, and the potential in working with it.

Group Problem Solving

In the course of the meeting, the legal aid expert raised a hypothetical example. His incident involved an argument between husband and wife: "she wants me out of the house; and I say I'm broke, I don't have anywhere to go."

One problem raised at once was that of transportation. The sergeant recalled that police cars could not carry civilians, except when arrested; he wondered about flexibility in this rule. He also raised a question about the availability of public transport tokens.

The central question in the example revolved around lodging:

> *Legal Aid Representative:* See, I'm thinking about the situation where maybe he does want to leave, or she wants to leave. They have nowhere to go. No money.

> *Officer:* Well, I think we could arrange somewhere to get him or her lodged.

> *L. A. Rep.:* O.K., that's the point I'm trying to make.

> *Sergeant:* Well, is there an agent here that could do it?

> *L. A. Rep.:* That's the question I'm asking.

> *Sergeant:* Sure, yeah, we have something that's very nice, and would make anyone feel comfortable. It's called an accommodation booking and you sleep in jail. I don't want to do that. Now let's face it, those are our resources now. Of course there's homes for wayward men. And a guy walks in with a $95 sports coat and $50 shoes and they're going to say "wayward, hell. See you around." You're right. Now if anybody has any feedback to us, or any alternatives that we could use, I guess that's why we're here, to kind of talk about it. It sure as hell is a pointed question, and it's very relevant, because that's not an unusual circumstance.

One participant raised the issue that mediation efforts might be stimulated by the dilemma, and could reduce the number of persons ultimately in need of lodging:

> It seems to me, if I can inject here, that the best solution at that particular point and no looking any further, are in terms of these officers. In other words, crisis intervention is always a time-buying thing in the beginning. You can't stay uptight in an assaultive way forever. And if these men can talk, just as you would with a suicide, or a would-be suicide, the natural process of adrenalin and so on begins to drop and the crisis begins to ease and I think that you're overlooking the effectiveness that these officers probably will provide at that point.

The problem pointed to the need to involve other agencies, which were not represented. The officers noted the omission, and resolved to remedy it:

> *Representative:* I see you didn't invite anybody from the Salvation Army.
>
> *Sergeant:* You're right, and that just hit me because I see the big sign here on 7th Street. Why didn't we invite the Salvation Army?
>
> *Officer:* I overlooked it myself.
>
> *Sergeant:* Chico coordinates this project. We will contact the Salvation Army.
>
> *Rep.:* That might be the answer.
>
> *Sergeant:* It might very well be.
>
> *Rep.:* Especially if the family is willing to repay the Salvation Army afterwards.

Another question concerned the availability of social services during peak problem periods. Again, the question originated among participants who had accompanied officers on their field tests:

> *Representative 1:* When I went on this excursion with the police officers it just dawned on me that nothing happens during the day. Everything happens at night. And if you have a client that tells you "my husband beat me and broke my leg and my rib," which recently did happen to me, and you say "when did this happen" they'll say "two weeks ago." I've never had a case — I've only been in social work for four years — where somebody told me "last night he beat me." So wait a couple of weeks or a couple of months and they tell you in passing "my husband beat me." I think a lot of help can be had if at the time of the beating there's somebody they can talk to, about "why did you beat your wife?"
>
> *Representative 2:* If you looked into it, I think you'll find that the social service requirements actually require somewhere along the line that we do have 24 hours service.

The outcome of the discussion was once more to raise a problem-solving possibility which had not been previously explored:

Representative: Yeah, I saw a very interesting program on television, last week I think it was. And it was showing a scene on the other side of the Bay, one of the counties, I've forgotten where, where a Protestant church had actually opened its doors to house people. Now I bring this out because I think that as a group we'd have to put all of our inputs into this thing and if we do not have resources to help us, we've got to see what we can do to make new resources available to us. Maybe an approach to this is our individual contact with the people we know in the field, maybe another approach with the police department is their contacts with the Council of Churches, to see whether or not they would be available to intervene.

In addition to the suggestion about exploring churches, the dilemma inspired a plea for the bringing of services to the client, conjointly with police:

Representative 1: We've got quite a few representatives from the agencies and some of the agencies aren't here. But I say it to the agencies that are here. Are there any people in your agencies willing to volunteer at night with police officers and sign a release, because that's the first thing I was hit with, relieving the police department of anything that happens to you. Be with the police department and throw your professional jargon at these people. Because I'd be glad to do it. You know we throw this professional jargon around like this. But this is two people trying to kill each other. And we just don't have the time to sit down and say "you've got a sado-masochistic relationship."

This same suggestion also appeared in another context. Our group skeptic had argued that clients were apt not to appear for their appointments. How could this situation be remedied?

Representative: Do you literally mean that you're going to make the appointment, or are you going to ask these people to call the agency you're referring them to?

Officer Bond: I would call and make the appointment for them, and call them. They would have the card.

Representative: My experience is that when an appointment

is made by the referring source, the likelihood is that the appointment is not kept. You have many more cancellations than when the client calls directly and makes his own appointment at the request of the referring source.

The sergeant mentioned reminders, but the questioner remained unsatisfied. This stimulated the hunch that police badges would deter absenteeism. It also brought a plea for agency participation "on the scene":

Representative 1: How are you going to get them to the office?

Representative 2: Why do they have to go to the office? Why can't we go to them? This is what I'm saying. The last time I met with them I threw this idea on, I don't know whether they accepted it or not. But I suggested possibly giving volunteers from the different agencies, from the graduate programs to be present at the welfare department with their own transportation. If something does happen that they do have radios in the cars and to make a call in and say "any of those professionals down there volunteering that can help us, then come up right now." I mean, they'd have to clear it, but you're talking about coming to our office. Why can't we go to them?

Representative 3: The health department does. Our field staff makes home calls and our service is an out-reach service rather than asking the client to see us. That's point number one. Point number two, I'm beginning to feel angry. I'm beginning to feel angry, I think, over this business of a client will not come to an agency, or how we're going to handle this thing. I would like to see the police department experiment. I see the police department as an authority, and I don't think the clients that the health department serves see the health department as an authority. And many times the health department has offered services and they have not come to us. They will lapse appointments. We have closed down our well-baby clinics because of this. They don't come in to us. But we are not an authority figure to them. And I think many of the clients that my nurses see in the health department feel as if the police department, at least, has some authority. And I think the response to you may be because the client sees you in this light. But I think you have to prove this to us, as a group. And I think it's worth a trial.

The prevailing mood, at the end of the meeting, was one of excitement and optimism. The group had dealt with doubts and resistances, and had explored the solution of limiting cases. It had joined to consider options, and had evolved program extensions. It now showed itself ready to explore and eager to learn. As one member put it, "we're just going to have to try this project. We call it an experimental project. Well then, let us experiment!"

Organization of Family Crisis Teams

Originally, the Family Crisis Intervention Program had two reference points in the organizational structure: the Experimental Projects Unit of the Conflict Management Section (formerly the Violence Prevention Unit), and the Patrol Division. The two unmarked motorized units technically operated under the supervision of the Patrol Division, but the nature of their experimental duties and the hours of their assignment, which cut across the normal watch periods, mitigated against Patrol Division control. (The hours and location of family crisis car assignment had been selected on the basis of the frequency of family crisis calls for service.)

Operationally, the unit's primary responsibility was to respond to family disturbance assignments. Secondarily, the teams responded to other disturbances of the peace, and to dispatched emergencies and preventive patrol.

Due to the experimental nature of the project there was constant close contact between the officers working the units and the Experimental Projects Section. The inter-play involved training and strategy contacts, liaison between the units and community social service agencies, and the data collection for evaluative purposes. An officer assigned to the Experimental Projects Section handled these responsibilities.

At the close of the experimental period, the administration of the police department expressed concern about the relatively low amount of activity performed by the FCI units. As a result, changes were made in the units' hours to improve field supervision. The unit members were assigned to work a regular shift, and were obliged to attend Patrol Division line-ups.

The units were also assigned to calls in three rather than two patrol districts. In addition, they were to be dispatched to calls of an emergency nature and to all felonies in progress. In the event beat units were not available, the Family Crisis Units were also to be dispatched to non-emergency situations.

Later, the units were given an even broader charge. While their primary responsibility remained the same, they were expected to initiate quality police action whenever appropriate.

The basic responsibility for the field operation of the units was reaffirmed to be the Patrol Division's.

Peace Keepers as a Happy Breed

Officers are prone to insist that "the police are not social workers." They like to boast about law enforcement escapades, and tend to downgrade human services as "not really police work." In our own groups (especially at first) several of the men had deplored calls that demanded peace-keeping functions; they had characterized these as a waste of their time.

Our family crisis team members had been cognizant of the fact that they would invest much effort in responses to peace keeping calls. They were flattered by their selection, and intrigued by the chance for innovating and contributing to professional development. They were curious and expectant. The officers were not at first "sold" on the concept of their unit, nor on the definition of police work that it implied.

After six months, we discussed the teams with three of the men. They all recalled that previous to their membership in the FCI unit they had viewed family calls with a jaundiced eye. One officer points out:

> When you get certain family fights and arguments that you feel that's strictly in the realm of the civil, you get the feeling that you don't belong there anyway. You say, "wow, something's going to happen down the street here," and you want to be there to try to prevent it or to arrest somebody; or you might have a team of burglars working on your beat, and the sergeant is coming down on you saying "where are you at when all this stuff is going down?"

A second officer concurs, and describes his past and present views:

Staff: Did you, before you came to this unit, feel that a 415 was a fairly unimportant piece of police business?

Officer: In terms of the other things that I had out there, I hated 415s. I wanted to get out there and arrest people, make felony arrests and lock up burglars.

Staff: How do you feel about this now?

Officer: Well, I don't particularly like to lock up burglars and kill a lot of suspects and things like that. As far as I'm concerned, the 415f, now that I look into it and see all the deeper ramifications that it has, I realize how serious a 415f is, in the broad spectrum. And I'm much more concerned about it now than I was three or four years ago.

Each of the team members now view family crisis intervention as a core function in police work:

Sergeant: Do you feel now in this unit, that you're accomplishing as much towards the police function or the police role — are you getting the kind of feeling of accomplishment out of this that you think you got before the unit came along?

Officer 1: You know, I really feel that we're accomplishing more, on the whole, than the average beat man. Stan and I were just talking about this last night. . . .

Staff: Now you two were nodding when he said that he felt that he was accomplishing more toward the police function now than before.

Officer 2: Yeah.

Officer 3: Yeah, I feel that way. I'll give you an example. Last week there was a 415f and the family, the father was drunk. He chased one of his sons out of the house. Approximately an hour or an hour and a half later, the son was arrested with a 10851, stolen car. Now I think that the father's responsible for the son stealing the car. He was frustrated, he was only 12 years old. And he went out and stole a car, he and his brother. His brother was 10, he was 12. Now I think that was directly related to what happened at home.

Staff: So your feeling is that by intervening in these family difficulties you are actually addressing yourself to a number of crime problems.

The men recall how previously they had developed techniques for "kissing off" family crisis assignments as rapidly as possible. One officer lists two such techniques:

Well, there's two types of things that I did, and I thought that I met with a pretty good amount of success. One was, I would go in and I would get the side of the story from the woman, because usually it's the woman who calls. Then I would explain to her, as briefly as I could, just what was going to happen by us arresting her husband.

Staff: Giving a little lecture on the law.

Officer: Right, that this wasn't going to get him out of her hair permanently. . . . And then when he comes back he might really be angry and might pound on her a little bit harder the next time. And then I also, in some instances, would take the man aside, and I would explain to him what was going to happen to him. And I think I would more or less appeal to his pride. And I would just let him know that he's heading right down the road to Jefferson Park or someplace. He's going to be out on his ear, he's going to lose his house, he's going to lose everything. He's going to be away from his family. If he keeps pounding on his wife, eventually she's going to get a restraining order against him, he won't even be able to come in to see his kids when he wants to. Any number of things. And I also emphasized the civil aspect of a family argument.

Staff: The limits on your authority.

Officer: Yeah. And then also we would more or less tell both of them "look, both of you might be going to jail. When we come here, don't just expect for us to haul one or the other off to jail. Because we may decide to take both of you."

A second team member describes a similar strategy, and testifies that he finds it now rarely invoked:

Officer: Well, if they're married and it's happened before, you can suggest that the husband take a cool-off walk. Or you could suggest that she take a cool-off walk, go over to a friend's house, something like this. And if that doesn't work, as a last resort you can ask her, "did he hit you?" And if she says yes, "do you want him arrested?"

Staff: Do you still occasionally now tell people to go take walks?

Officer: No, I can't remember telling anybody to go take a walk. I say, "let's sit down and talk about it."

Staff: You mean it's relatively infrequent that the person is asked by members of this unit to pack their bag and leave for the night?

Officer: Yes, as far as I'm concerned.

The third officer stresses that "listening" to family contenders was previously an excluded option, whereas team members make it a practice to lend a sympathetic ear to all parties:

Officer: Before we didn't have time to listen to that. You know, sooner or later we had to cut them off. And the minute you cut somebody off, it raises them up. It makes them seem like you're not interested in their problems. But we now have the time to listen to all this, and it's boring as hell, I'll tell you. Sometimes you want to cut them off. And sometimes we have to, anyway. But it isn't nearly as frequent as it used to be.

Staff: So you do a lot more listening now.

Officer: Absolutely, that's the most important thing, is listening. And letting them know that you're interested in what they're saying. Even if you're not really. Making them think you're interested.

It is fair to add that much of the credit (and blame) for the change is placed on pressures, compensations, and accounting procedures. The men feel that their short-circuiting of human relations methods was mainly prompted by the department's priorities. They feel that the average beat officer is under *external* constraint to rush such calls:

Officer: Before this unit, we were limited time-wise, and we had other duties to do.

Staff: So you would feel pressure to get out.

Officer: Yeah, just try to handle it and get back on the street.

The men contend that the officer's anxiety about terminating contact is communicated to the client, who reacts adversely. The men attribute some of their client satisfaction to the department's sanction of a more leisurely approach:

> *Officer 1:* I think they would sense also, when a police officer goes in and "let's kind of hurry up and settle the beef and get out." And it's kind of a rush atmosphere and they kind of get against it. And all of a sudden two officers completely snow them, they walk in and they sit down and, "let's talk this thing out". . . .
>
> *Officer 2:* Yeah, I was just going to say I agree with Sam on the time that we have to spend on these calls . . . they're all uptight and when we get there one of the first things we try to do is to listen calmly to both sides, and in that way they both come to realize that we're not there to make some kind of snap judgment and just more or less act prejudicially against one party or the other, and usually just snatch the man up and take him to jail. And once the woman gets this notion also, she appears to calm down and she's more willing to tell us about what the real problem is, rather than the fact that she just wants her husband or boyfriend to go to jail.

Despite the primacy of the time element in the officers' minds, there are clearly some other tangible and important differences in the substance of the unit's approach. For one, the men have relegated arrest to the status of an undesirable, low priority option:

> *Officer 1:* I would say one of the differences is that now we can more or less say that we rely on arrest as a final resort type thing. But before it wasn't a final resort.
>
> *Staff:* What was it before?
>
> *Officer 1:* Well, it was kind of high up on the priorities.

Officer 2: Number two.

Staff: Right after kiss it off?

Officer 2: Yeah, if you can't kiss it off, lock somebody up.

In contrast to the premium on arrest, the officers view themselves as rendering positive services. They see themselves evaluated, and appreciated, in terms of this contrast:

> They say, "wow, here's two policemen. I always thought these guys were mean, sadistic, and they were going to bang me over the head and take me to jail" — in the case of the man. Or in the case of the woman, that "the only thing this guy's really good for is to beat my husband and to take him to jail. And here they're trying to offer us some kind of help, something that's going to help us get along better with one another, or to help save our marriage, or if they feel that there is some mental problem somewhere in the family, to see that the family member gets the proper help." And I think this gives them a warm feeling itself.

In a strange twist on the usual police theme of the "solid blue line" the team members have come to value their role as professional specialists, in the sense of emphasizing the difference between their own actions and those of non-specialized officers:

> *Staff:* When you walk out of those situations, by and large do you feel you've done a pretty good job?
>
> *Officer:* Yeah. Sometimes when we walk out they say "you guys are different from the normal policeman."
>
> *Staff:* Oh, they do say that?
>
> *Officer:* For example, we had one last night who said "you guys really know what you're doing. We've had four different sets of policemen here within the last two weeks. And you guys are really different."
>
> *Staff:* Now, do they elaborate this in any way, do they say in some detail just what about —
>
> *Officer:* Well, some said it seems like we understand the problem more, and take more time. They are impressed

with the time that we can spend with them. And we aren't taking any sides, or anything like this — we just seem like we understand the general problem, from a third person standpoint.

The men have also developed a strong "we-feeling" and commitment, partly based on their recognized differentiation from the larger group:

> *Staff:* Do you gentlemen feel there is any kind of an *esprit de corps* about this outfit, in terms of pride in the little flag that we four are carrying and stuff like that?
>
> *Officer:* "Four against the world!"
>
> *Staff:* Yeah, is there any of this?
>
> *Officer:* I think so. Yeah, we occasionally get together socially and that sort of thing. I think there's a certain amount of pride in the unit. Especially, you know, when we're called "those damned social workers," or something like that. It kind of brings you together by force if for no other reason.

In this connection the men are helped by the fact that although they may be sometimes condemned by other officers, they are also valued for their service:

> I think there's a tendency on the part of most policemen to look at anything we're doing as just what they call it, social workers rather than policemen. But I can see that quite a few guys out there really appreciate what we're doing.
>
> *Staff:* And do they sometimes say things to that effect or —
>
> *Officer:* Not only do they say things, but a lot of times they'll call us in to handle a particular situation, where they couldn't.
>
> *Staff:* And just stand by until you get there.
>
> *Officer:* Yeah, right.

The men are also aided by the fact that they have faith in their own effectiveness as specialists:

You said "confident," and that's exactly how I feel. I feel more confident. I know many times before when I went in, I felt that I really didn't belong there, especially if nobody wanted to make a formal complaint.

Staff: You felt that you were sort of interfering into something that was none of your business.

Officer: Yes. And then many times I felt that my feelings were sort of out front as a police officer. Because many times if you're there, and you don't have the elements for an actual arrest yourself, and maybe the husband or the wife or somebody in the family is very resentful of you being there in the home, and they're constantly telling you to get the hell out of here. "What are you doing in my home? You don't belong here." And they're constantly giving you this all the time, and they're threatening you. And they're talking about your brother officers and everything, you know, about "you pigs are all alike." And you just feel like "why am I here?"

Staff: But they're still talking like that now, aren't they?

Officer: Well, I notice many times when we first get on the scene, they start this. But somehow or another we are able to change their views.

The officers trace their confidence in their accumulated experience of success with its residual benefits in the form of cues to effective action:

Officer 1: Once I get in and I get a chance to say something to the people, I feel that I have this positive feeling that I'm going to be able to get a certain point across —

Staff: Where does that positive feeling come from — from having gotten that point across quite often before, or because you have a list of referral agencies, or what is it that makes you feel, after you've said one or two sentences, "this is going to be smooth?" They seem to be responding and you recognize it, or what's the deal?

Officer 1: Well, I would say yes, in that area, maybe we are becoming psychologists to a certain extent. We can seem to read certain cues. You can tell when a person is more receptive to a certain line or phrase or suggestion than you would be at another time. . . .

Officer 2: I think that, naturally, the greater number of these calls that you handle, the more capable you're going to feel of being able to handle them. And especially when you handle them successfully, you're going to feel that you're capable. And I have found that since coming into the unit I feel much more self-confident on the calls.

The officers feel that they can analyze and break down their experience, and share it among themselves. "A guy relates how he handled a particular call," one of the men recalls, "and in the back of my mind I say, 'hey, that's one hell of an approach. Maybe I'll try that next time.' "

By contrast, the men seem disinclined to grant that their skill could be disseminated among the rest of the force. They have a strong feeling about the benefits of specialization:

Officer 1: I feel that the unit should be continued and expanded; I don't feel that it should be given to everybody in patrol because I don't think it would work.

Officer 2: The reason I don't think it's going to work is because I don't think most of the men on the street, or at least some of the men on the street are inclined to put the personal effort into it that we do.

The men are serious about their role as specialists. They want to do anything possible to enhance their impact. They have discussed the liability of approaching clients in police cars and uniforms. They know that civilian clothing would estrange them from other officers, but their primary concern is with client response. The same stance permeates their view of social agencies. They are grateful for cooperation, but would like more immediate — crisis — referral sources:

Staff: What would give us confidence that we aren't going to get callbacks?

Officer: An immediate source. Someone that you could refer them to immediately, and they wouldn't have time to equivocate, think about it overnight, and then be able to say "well, to hell with it, we've got our problems solved without going to this agency."

Staff: I see, so what we actually need is somebody for immediate follow-up.

Officer: Right. Maybe a family services bureau available on a 24 hour basis, or some sort of marriage counseling service available on a 24 hour basis.

The officers take their work very much to heart. Off the job, they worry about some of their clients' problems:

I'm a little depressed about several of them. . . . Because sometimes they tell us that there is a severe alcoholic problem. This is the crux of the matter. Or they say "I really think my husband or wife needs a little mental help." But they're not going to go in voluntarily, but yet they're functioning, the guy's working every day, whatever. "But he just comes home and beats me every night." Something like that. I feel depressed about situations like that.

In cases where they leave with residual concerns, the officers are apt to make unsolicited call-backs:

Staff: How much of this call-back type thing do you gentlemen actually do? In terms of calling back sometime later?

Officer: We go back strictly as interested parties, just to see how successful we were in quelling the problem.

Staff: Do you select particular types of situations to go back to ?

Officer: Not types so much as people. We see a situation where the people were about to kill each other and we go back a couple of days later to see if there are any bodies lying around.

Staff: Are those largely the people about whom you have a little doubt in your mind? You know, "did we really handle it right?"

Officer: Yeah, right.

As far as the men are concerned, they are performing a vital function, and performing it uniquely and well. They have become advocates of their own role, and of its expansion. In this sense, they, too, are change-agents.

Consumer Reaction

Our experiment must be evaluated, first and foremost, through impact measures. Did the team's response reduce the probability of assaults? Did it prevent injury to police? Did it resolve crises without conflict or expensive arrests? Did it have lasting ameliorative effects on family problems?

Such indexes concern us in our inventory of data, in chapter 11. Our current questions are more immediate and practical. Is the family crisis function one that can be discharged without adverse impact on police morale? Does it provide job satisfaction and skills?

The team members' testimonials suggest that it can and does. What about impact on the police image, on the clients' view of services? The officers feel that they are favorably received and positively reacted to. But they have pride at stake. Would independent inquiry confirm their assessment?

With the cooperation of the Wright Institute in Berkeley, a survey was run of a random sample of unit clients. The poll was a modest one, designed to furnish team members with some feedback. One student — a young black ex-offender who had grown up in Oakland — called on the families in the sample. As many call-backs were made as were necessary to make contact. Out of 26 persons contacted, 25 participated in the survey. This fact was encouraging, and seemed related to the questions being posed. We asked our interviewer whether he could have recorded similar cooperation with other subject matter. Would respondents have talked to him? He replied:

> No, they wouldn't. I know that for a fact. A lot of times I would say I'm taking a survey — from the Wright Institute — just a survey. People would say "I don't have the time."

The interviewer's approach was weighted in the direction of eliciting criticism and reservations. He quotes his opening remarks (and the typical reaction to them) as follows:

I told them I was doing a research project from the Wright Institute with the Family Crisis Unit and from their report they had been involved with this unit. And "I'm here to question you about the performance of the officers in their jobs." And they would say "great."

The interviewer's set was a stabilizing force. He undertook his task with an explicit anti-police bias, pessimistic expectations, and no familiarity with the unit. In a post-survey interview, he confessed:

Interviewer: I was awful shocked to get the answers I did, to be truthful. I wasn't familiar with the family crisis unit, and I didn't think I would get as many positive responses as I did.

Staff: You mean pleasantly shocked?

Interviewer: Right. Especially when I would say something like, "you know in order for an officer to perform his job we take this interview, and your answers can help correct the mistakes the officer made with you." And I still didn't get too many negative answers.

The interviewer reports that he not only received cooperation, but personal gratitude for his role. He recalls:

When I would be ready to leave after the questioning was completed, they would tell me that they think it's great that I was doing this here, on my part. They said that it should have been done long ago. This is the kind of thing I would get from just about everyone after the questionnaire was over with. They would say "it's really nice that you are doing it."

In the survey, twenty-three out of twenty-five replies were favorable. Two respondents expressed reservations. One stated that he hated police, and the other was a lady whose reaction was quoted as follows:

She said that the officers showed her no respect whatsoever. She was drunk at the time I was interviewing her, too. She was drunk at the time of the report.

Sergeant: She was drunk at the time of the initial contact with FCIU. I would say that she's a drunk, just off the top of my head.

Interviewer: She said they came into the room and she didn't have any clothes on and stuff like that. And they weren't courteous — they took her husband's side and everything. And really, I couldn't make out what she was really talking about.

The interviewer describes his impression from the study as follows:

Staff: Have you learned anything out of this?

Interviewer: Well, I've learned that the FCI Unit is a pretty good unit. It's doing a damn good job. And I think more police officers, if they don't have any technical training, should be trained where they can help people more. Because some of the people I interviewed I had known from the past.

Staff: Oh, you knew them personally?

Interviewer: Right. And their opinion of policemen was all negative. And to hear them say something like this —

Staff: Did this surprise you?

Interviewer: Yes, it did.

He reiterated that respondents generally had prior reservations about the police, which had been removed through contact with team members:

I have a part on my questionnaire where I state about the different feeling that they have now after the FCIP had been in, and what they had prior. And it's been improved. They view the police department as a better organization now because of this, and so on.

The respondents were able to recall officers' actions which proved especially welcome. They listed a number of services which they felt had not usually been available from police:

One of my questions also states, "what did the officer actually do for you?" This is where I would get a lot of feedback from the people, and they would express themselves, where the officer would sit them down and talk to them, they would refer them to other agencies. They would give them the law aspect from their standpoint, and in most cases most of the participants were satisfied that this was something that hadn't been done.

Finally, the interviewer inquired into long-range solutions to personal problems:

Staff: Is there anything in there about their personal difficulties having been resolved as opposed to the immediate situation having been settled?

Interviewer: Yes, there is. The last question states that. And they have gotten along 100% better. As a matter of fact, one lady, I couldn't even get out of the room because she wanted to come down here and congratulate the officer that was out there. I think it was Officer ——. Where she says now her husband, he's just beautiful. He was like a marriage counselor himself, the officer was.

The results of this mini-survey may not be conclusive, but they are concordant with the officers' version. Do they agree with observations by referral agencies?

The Referral Agencies: A View from the Bridge

The Oakland concept of family crisis teams placed emphasis on liaison with referral agencies. At the start of this chapter we summarized the first contact with the agencies. Six months later we sought agency reactions to the program.

We discussed FCIU with a representative of Family Services, whom team members rank as cooperative and relevant. Thirty-four referrals have been made to this small agency; twenty-three families have availed themselves of its counseling services.

How does the agency's staff feel about FCIU? The representative tells us that

Six different workers have been involved, have been interviewing. And I think that all six feel, I've been checking around, that it's a very valuable program. We have been tremendously impressed from many directions. Now many of the people we see we would not consider "motivated" clients. Most of them have come in to us with really not a very clear idea of what they wanted. But it seems to us that they've gotten a lot of clarification of exactly what their problem is just from talking to us even for one hour. And we suspect we will see many of these people again, maybe a year later or two years later. The other thing we've got from them is that they are getting a very different view of the police department. I don't believe that we have had a single negative statement about the team that's come out to visit. And we have had numerous positive statements. They've said things like "you know, they sat down and talked to us for a whole hour, and this is the first time a policeman has ever spent this long." Time seems to be the important factor here, that they have time to give them. And also the clients seem to feel that the police were there to help and not there to punish.

Family Services had made a special effort to obtain clients' reactions to the team's service. In response to the inquiry, according to the agency representative, "we really haven't gotten any outstanding negatives." A review of answers to the agency's question yields an impressive number of laudatory comments:

This is the question, "have you received any favorable or unfavorable response from the party regarding the operation or services of the family crisis intervention program?" This one says "Yes, favorable. Both parties were quite impressed with the attitudes and actions of the officers involved in this call. Mr. and Mrs. B. specifically mentioned the sincerity and interest manifested by the officers in their problems, and the willingness to refer them to an agency which they felt could better help them with their problems. Mr. B. said that were it not for these factors he never would have come. . . . Mrs. B. specifically spoke of the time spent with the family and of the officer's wish to be helpful.". . . . "They were beautiful. Mr. P. mentioned the handling of this matter only briefly, stating that for the first time of the many times he's called the police on his wife, he felt that the police officers were interested and concerned and really wanted to help." . . . Mrs. S. was particularly pleased about the police dropping by a second time, and she mentioned the time they were able to be there. The officers were "helpful and understanding."

Do agency personnel get feelings about the police from their other clients?

We get quite a bit. Usually it's a very negative kind of thing. But I think these people have all had contact with the police, practically all of them have had some contact with the police before, and they speak of the difference, the difference being that "gee, these people really wanted to help." This one lady — I'm looking at her name — was terribly impressed; she has a very sick son, and the son didn't get in to see me, and I don't know whatever is going to become of him. But he had a probation officer, and I talked to the probation officer at great length, and let him know some of my impressions, even though they were second-hand. The boy's terribly disturbed. But anyway, what she said was, "you know, they even came back a few nights later to see how things were." And just the feeling that somebody was out there who cared about her and her sick son was very reassuring. So it's been a very good feeling we've gotten.

Many FCIU clients seem to have altered opinions of the police as a result of contact with the teams. Can a similar point be made about agency staff?

There are those, I think, who had preconceived notions. We all have our prejudices, and that's one that an awful lot of people seem to have these days. But I do feel that the staff itself was surprised in the beginning that the police department would tackle this kind of thing, and very pleased that they were. At first the staff in general was a little dubious about getting in on this kind of thing. I think they were — some of the younger staff members — a little afraid that we were going to get violent people. What they have said is that we're getting the same kind of people we'd have gotten anyway, it's just that now we're getting them referred from the police department. There's no difference in the referrals that you make except that they come first to the police. But we get violent people, we get very disturbed people, we get very troubled people, whether they come from the police or from somebody else. But I think the whole feeling about what the police are trying to do has changed.

Changes have taken place in the agency as a result of the FCIU's operation. For one, provisions have been made in the shape of a weekly hour reserved for FCIU referrals:

We know when somebody's been battling on Sunday night, they really should be seen very shortly. Well, we couldn't always see them the next day, but what I asked each worker to do was to hold one hour that week that would be just for this. Now we didn't always fill them. Say on Wednesday if there was a Thursday opening that hadn't been filled, we'd fill it with something else. So it does mean, though, that the agency's holding time. I know you've worked with a lot of different agencies and I don't know how the other agencies have worked this out, but it seemed that the only way we could do it was by holding a bloc of time.

The agency has also found that its referrals called for a reappraisal of concepts and techniques:

We talked at great lengths among ourselves here about what techniques we use with people who "aren't motivated." And are our caseworkers, who are essentially trained to work with motivated clients, able to use the skills they do have or do they need to develop some new and very different skills? And we really haven't arrived at any firm conclusion. What we did arrive at was that we need to talk together more and present to each other more of the cases that have come and question how each other worked, and see if out of that we can get some information that might be helpful to all of us. I think that's one thing I can say, and that is that we have found we're very active in this sort of case, which very often we are not. But if you get a husband and wife in who are screaming at each other in the interview, there's no point in sitting for an hour letting them scream. So that I think already the caseworkers have learned that in this kind of case we might be much more vocal. Maybe

have to interrupt more often, maybe have to call a halt to
the screaming, and say "look, let me get in here for a minute."
So that, yes, I think it has brought to our attention that we
need to sharpen some of our own techniques. That can be
very helpful to us in some of our other cases, too.

The agency has received useful information from police-sponsored
meetings with the other agencies. In the discussion we summarized,
for example, Family Services learned about the availability of a
resource that had been unfamiliar to them:

It was just that I frankly didn't know much about this one,
which was the Wage Earner's Plan, and we do talk with a
lot of people who are having financial problems, and we
refer them to all kinds of places. And I was not aware that
we had not made any referrals to Wage Earner's Plan, but
I came back and circulated information.

Agency representatives have also found personal encounters
with the FCIU profitable, and would like to see more of them:

My only complaint is that I don't think we communicate
enough with the police department. We've had group meetings three times. On the other hand, we don't have time.
You know, nobody has time, and I keep feeling that we
should be getting together more and talking about all this
more.

Specifically, counselors and social workers have expressed interest in meeting team members. The representative notes that
"they wanted to know who were the persons who were actually
out there on the beat, and what they were like." There has been a
demand for contact at the working level.

This development testifies to the viability of a team concept in
the handling of peace keeping crises. Shared clients can link
patrolmen with partners in the human services. As the police
reach out for resources and allies, social agencies come to view
them as welcome bed-fellows. The liaison is one from which everyone stands to gain.

The Police as Referral Agency

The second agency whose impressions we gathered was the

Legal Aid Society, whose contact with our project had pre-dated the birth of the unit. Again the assessment was a positive one. The director of the agency recalls that he has handled numerous referrals, and has found them appropriate. He expressed himself positively about the teams, and praised the FCIU concept:

> It's a wonderful thing. It's better than good. It's really great, I think. So far, I'm impressed. I've got the phone number right here, immediately available. Because I call them that often. So I have nothing but praise for the outfit, so far. And I'm not saying that because I know them personally, because I don't.

Legal Aid has not questioned its clients about the police. The director, however, refers to evidence of positive contacts between officers and black citizens. He indicates that ordinarily his clients have categorized the police as unapproachable:

> Most people, especially black people, they don't think police are human, especially white policemen. That's another world. And once they start talking to them, in a friendship-type of an approach — that they don't want to arrest the man, they want to help him — it throws them off.

Comments made to legal aid staff have included one complaint, and the staff agreed (after investigation) that the team had mishandled the case:

> It's been mostly complimentary. But there was one woman who was really complaining. I can say of one that I know of that the officers were really the shits, if you want to put it bluntly.

The agency took the matter up with the unit, and the representative declared himself satisfied with corrective follow-up action:

> *Staff:* When you call over, do things happen right away, or any feeling we could improve on that?
>
> *Legal Aid Rep:* Well, that one case, that was beautiful, couldn't be better.

Paradoxically, Legal Aid is not much concerned with FCIU as

a source of business. The unit is perceived as a resource and as a referral agency. This function, according to Legal Aid, fills a gap not only for the agency, but for the criminal justice system:

> It's great to be able to say "can you send a police over here? Can you send someone to talk to this guy, he's killing my client." If I concentrate on going in for a restraining order everytime a client asks me for a restraining order, I could jam that Department 15, just me. I could do it, because there's that many. So I just kind of pacify them, cool them off, see if things can wait until I can have my main hearing, eventually getting a restraining order. And then by that time the emotions are already solved, and people go their way, and I don't even need a restraining order. But for immediate relief, I think this police family crisis unit is it.

Legal Aid regards FCIU as a crisis resolution device, and as a means of preventing time-consuming abuse of the courts:

> I know that they're going to go in there and not arrest the man, because maybe that's not what's needed. But they'll talk to him, pacify him, at least where the emotions are high. And then tomorrow or a day later the husband will be back to normal, and save an arrest.

The availability of FCIU is a function that Legal Aid feels must not only be maintained, but expanded:

> So far there is a real need for more. I don't like it that the officers are only there from 5 to 12 — I need it around the day. Remember this one, Jim, this morning? I needed a police unit to go in today, right now, in this particular case where this lady was booted out by her husband, yesterday, spent a night in a motel. She has no money, no relatives. She's afraid to go back to the house. The husband is not that violent that I think that he'll kill her, but at least violent enough to beat her twice in a row now. When was it, Tuesday night, she says, he jumped on her; last night, he jumped on her. That's two in a row. . . . If the police officers trained in this field could talk to the guy, cool him off for a while. If nothing else, at least give me time to prepare the complaint so I can get it in order. That would be great.

Staff: This is something new! Actually, you're starting to make referrals to the police?

Legal Aid Rep: Yeah, because I need immediate relief. She needs it. Maybe they could settle it, maybe they could save me the trouble of going through a divorce proceeding. I see there's a great need for this type of activity, but more so. Not just token amount, like I feel they have now. There's not enough officers involved in this family business.

A search of FCIU records indicates that the referral use of FCI teams has been intensive and effective:

Staff: How many of these kind of referrals would you estimate you get from Legal Aid?

Officer: I would say at least three a week.

Staff: Is it increasing?

Officer: Oh, I would say much more so, because he's realizing now that he's got another tool to work with, so why not use it? He's found a little trust in the police department.

Staff: Do you find it at all getting to be a headache, that he's calling you and really there isn't much you can do —

Officer: No, because they're pretty smart over there. They realize in one instance where we can't do anything, he's not going to turn around with the same particular circumstances and call us again. They're all usually pretty new incidents, and they're the ones, pretty much, that we can handle.

Beside Legal Aid, there are other agencies that have reversed the usual sequence of roles in the referral field:

They have people that they're counseling and one of them goofs up one way or the other so they call, and if it's getting into a police problem — he's beat her up again, or he's beat the kids again, something like that — and they can't really handle it by counseling at that particular moment, then they will call us up. I remember one where we had been up there once before on a family problem, and referred them to Family Services. And Family Services counseled them for a couple of months, and then I guess their counseling session was over with. When they first started it was probably 4 or 5 months ago. And the problem started again, so they called Family Services. And Family Services referred them back to us. We went up there. It was the same problem, but it saves them from going out, and we're aware of the problem too.

The team concept is a changing one. As the police reach into the community, they begin to be perceived as partners. The change is blatant with Legal Aid, who had tended to see police as an adversary. The changed image is that of police as problem-solvers. Concern and expertise are stipulated, and it is assumed that the police seek justice and equity. The next step is an accommodation, a division of labor toward a common goal. Agencies approach each other, share data and request actions. They dovetail and intersect. Each raises the level of the other's service. As a result, the client discovers new and more effective help.

This project presented a wide variety of opportunities for systematizing knowledge and experience. Indeed, our basic hypothesis presumed that a successful learning experience was contingent upon each individual officer's discovery of appropriate ways to cope with interpersonal conflicts on the basis of his own and his fellow officers' knowledge and experience.

This chapter attempts to identify the educational doors that this type of strategy can open. If appropriately utilized, the approach makes the learning process an integral part of job performance and ties together the performance-evaluation-training cycle.

Discovery and Utilization of Experience

Early in the first series of training sessions, our group participants began to recount their own experiences in situations involving interpersonal violence. This "war story" telling led to a rough grouping of approaches. A healthy debate occurred as to whether a person should "take command" of a situation by authoritative moves or whether it was ever possible to "maintain control" by approaching others in a "soft" manner. Even though there was a mandate to avoid designating any strategy as "right" or "wrong", labels where assigned.

This activity almost immediately brought the group into two areas of inquiry which expedited their own developmental process and which eventually contributed to the overall development of the department.

The Critical Incident Questionnaire[1]

The Critical Incident Questionnaire was originally developed in an

---

1. This research strategy was first described by J. C. Flanagan in "The Critical Incident Technique," *Psychological Bulletin*, 51 (1954): 327–358.

attempt to discover where the members of the department fell insofar as their street behavior was concerned. It listed common street situations and gave the man completing the form the opportunity to select and discuss three alternative solutions. The individual answers were not important but the overall pattern of answers was indicative of a general stance (cf. Appendix). The instrument was administered to a variety of different officer groups. Besides indicating the officer's style, it suggested variations between units and, most important for our purposes here, pointed up disagreement with departmental policies and procedures. It therefore served as a tool for the determination of specific training needs.

The Critical Incident Questionnaire has recently been expanded. The department will use the expanded instrument for detailed evaluation of departmental training programs — particularly of recruit training. Recruits will be given the instrument three times during their probationary year so the department may ascertain their position at entry, their stance after formal recruit training, and their approach to policing during the final stages of their first year as regular officers.

Training Tapes

Another activity that grew out of the group's self-analysis was the tape recording of street incidents, which started as a diagnostic tool. Participants were given the opportunity to tape record their own handling of calls such as family disputes, juvenile parties, etc. The critiques were intended to assist the taped officer in understanding his responses and, if necessary, in analyzing flaws in his performance.

As we have seen, the group decided that tapes were potentially useful training aids for both recruits and experienced officers. They began a tape library for the Training Division, and they improved the value of the tapes by their "voice-on-voice" editing and formal critiques.

The tapes were used to supplement presentations in almost every departmental training program. They served to illustrate instructors' teaching points, provided numerous opportunities to spark discussion, offered models for the construction of role playing situations, and finally, gave command and supervisory officers greater insight into the nature of their subordinates' behavior in street situations.

The tapes were well received in both the Recruit Officers' Training Program and in the Field Training Officers' Program; and although there were some difficulties in maintaining officer interest in the development of finished tapes, the officer-students strongly supported their continued use.

Field Training Officer Program

During many of their discussions, the group members indicated their belief that some officers became violence-prone because they were assigned for initial field training to officers who themselves had problems with violence. The participants felt strongly that the department's field training program was inadequate in duration and in the haphazard selection of the training officers. They therefore chose as a work project the design of a more appropriate Field Training Program.

The newly designed Field Training Program featured two elements. First, each probationary officer's progress was to be monitored from the moment of his induction to the completion of his probationary year. His overall performance was to be supervised by a Field Training Coordinator, and particular attention was to be given to the trainee during his participation in the eighteen-week field training period, which replaced the previous six-week program.

Second, the program included a detailed procedure for the selection, training, certification, and assignment of Field Training Officers. The process called for the nomination of candidates by patrolmen. The nominations were submitted to the chain of command for comment. The list, with accumulated comments, was forwarded to the Chief of Police. The selected officers were placed on an eligibility list. These officers were then contacted to ascertain if they wished to participate in the program. They could then attend an orientation and were formally designated as Field Training Officers.

The program was put into effect with the Field Training Coordinator an officer-participant from our first group.

While a number of changes have been made in the program since its inception (a new coordinator, movement of the administrative responsibility for the program to the Training Division, and a change in the selection procedure that gives greater involvement to middle management) there can be no doubt that our group was both catalyst and original designer for a significant change in the department's training effort.

Further, this program in many ways marks acceptance of the

project's philosophical emphasis on the utilization of officer experience in the training process. While every effort was made to select only the "best" officers as training officers, the decision to let participants design the program and direct it during its early stages suggests a willingness to go beyond simple lip service to the concept of participatory management.

Recruit Training Program

In his classic work *Violence and the Police*, William Westly indicates the importance of the recruit school to the aspiring police officer:

> No recruit could explain this to the observer, but the fact remains that the school is his first contact with policemen and the police force, and through it his picture of the world of police work and the role of the police officer begins to develop. For the man himself, the most important function of the school is to provide him with a set of temporary behavioral definitions — that is, whom to arrest, how to quell a disturbance, how to direct traffic, and so on — which are acceptable to the other members of the force and which he can therefore utilize until he begins to direct his actions through experience and the homely axioms of his fellows.[2]

The Oakland Police Department has recognized the accuracy of this observation, and has striven to make its Recruit Officers' Training Course one of the most comprehensive in the country. Although the program has been used as a model for many police agencies, the Chief of Police held grave reservations as to its ability to produce officers who were trained to cope appropriately with the responsibilities and duties required of the modern urban policeman. The Chief felt that the course did a relatively good job in the technical aspects of policing, but that it was far from successful in giving the recruit officer a sound basis for his task in the areas of interpersonal and community relations. His own view of the police role was such that the order maintenance and service responsibilities of the police required greater attention, an attention at least equal to those paid to the fields of crime prevention and control. In light of this, he sought to redesign the department's training offerings.

While a sizeable block of instruction dealing with Community-Police Relations was developed and offered, it did not seem to take

2. Westley, W. A., *Violence and the Police: A Sociological Study of Law, Custom, and Morality* (Cambridge: M.I.T. Press, 1970), p. 156.

the necessary hold on the police recruit officers. The course was subjected to constant alteration in curriculum, and some instructor replacement occurred, but the department seemed unable to undertake really satisfactory revisions in the program.

However, since the advent of the project three specific events have taken place which have had a profound effect on the Recruit Officer Training Course.

First, during the project's initial phase, our officers interviewed the Training Division Commander and began reviewing the recruit school. The major result of this effort was the assumption of a number of blocks of instruction and the introduction of the tape recordings mentioned earlier.

TABLE 1:
Basic Requirements of the
State Commission on Peace Officer Standards and Training
as Compared with
The Oakland Police Academy Curriculum

	Comm. Reg Hrs	60th Sch Hrs	61st Sch Hrs	62nd Sch Hrs	63rd Sch Hrs	64th Sch Hrs
Introduction to policing	10	39	41	42	60	65
Constitutional and criminal law	16	46	46	55	44	50*
Criminal evidence	8		15	15	14	8
Administration of justice	4	7	7	8	8	8
Criminal investigation	34	63	60	60	59	59
Community-police relations	20	53	127	149	159	157*
Patrol procedures	40	75	76	82	91	93
Traffic control	20	49	45	45	36	36
Juvenile procedures	8	9	9	7	14	14*
Defensive tactics	14	43	37	37	37	37
Firearms (police weapons)	12	42	42	42	42	42**
Critical incident simulations (role playing)	0	0	0	0	31	24*
First aid	10	13	13	16	17	17
Field assignments	0	48	40	40	40	40
Examinations	4	10	9	11	15	16
Critiques	0	5	10	13	13	13
Study periods	0	0	0	0	14	15
Graduation exercises	0	3	3	3	3	3

*Indicates courses which include Role Playing exercises utilizing video tapes, replay discussions. These exercises are integrated throughout the school for a total of 64 hours.

**Includes a nine-hour course of instruction in "Non-Lethal Chemical Agents (Tear Gas) Training," which is presented in the school. This course is required by California Penal Code Section 12403 and is authorized as a Technical and Special Course by the Commission on Peace Officer Standards and Training.

Second, a small group of officers were sent to a Police and Community Relations Program offered by the University of California at Los Angeles; two officers in particular, including one of our men, returned sufficiently motivated to attempt changes in the recruit school.

Third and probably most important, the Civil Service Board of the City of Oakland received a grant from the California Council on Criminal Justice in the "Assessment of Police Recruitment, Selection and Training." This grant provided the resources to do a thorough review of the recruit school and, to a degree, to implement the findings.

All of these factors came together to bring about a change in the recruit school. The result was sizeable increases in time: Community-Police Relations was increased from 53 instructional hours to 157 hours, Patrol Procedures was increased from 40 hours to 93 hours, and Introduction to Policing was expanded over sixfold. Table 1 outlines the changes in the program over a period of approximately one year.

The change in the "Community-Police Relations" block was a major key in giving appropriate recognition to the problem of violence in Oakland and in assisting the recruit officer in facing the problem. This instruction block includes a wide variety of subjects and was described in the following manner in the *Sixty-Fourth Recruit School* bulletin:

COMMUNITY-POLICE RELATIONS

The purpose of this course is to instill in each recruit officer an awareness of the social nature and composition of the community he serves and an appreciation of social developments and behavioral patterns affecting himself and citizens with whom he comes into daily contact. Instruction is provided by persons who are most familiar with the subject matter, many of whom are not affiliated with the police service.

Oakland Community: A history of the ethnic and cultural composition of the City, with particular emphasis devoted to the trend in population from a pre-World War II white majority to a projected black majority by 1985. The course also discusses implications of this population shift for all facets of city government, including the police department. The

course will be conducted in various locations throughout the City in order to provide an orientation to the
various cultures represented in the City, and will include discussions with representatives of various community organizations.

Community Field Experience: The recruit officer will
be given an assignment that will place him in different
environments. He will be assigned to solicit assistance
from agencies such as the Welfare Department, Department of Human Resources, Missions and Legal Aid.
The experience is designed to create a better understanding of the perspective of those who use these
services.

Internship: An opportunity will be provided each trainee
to work for one day in a social service agency such as
the Alameda County Welfare Department of the West
Oakland Health Clinic. The purpose of this experience is to expose the recruits to other agencies involved
in providing service.

Star Power: A sociological game which develops
simulated social stratifications to stimulate an understanding of human behavior.

Concepts of Culture: This subject area examines man
and culture, an understanding of other cultures and
the nature of prejudice.

Minority Cultures: These discussions relate to the
various ethnic communities in Oakland. They include an historical frame of reference as the basis for
current postures and the resulting economic, sociological
and psychological factors and their implications for
police work.

The White Middle Class: This session is a panel discussion, representing a variety of viewpoints. It will
include a discussion of expectations, attitudes and the
implications of these viewpoints for police work.

The Counter Culture: An exploration of the origins
and causes of the "anti-establishment" movements. It
deals with the values and aspirations of the counter
culture and their significance in regard to police work.

The Police Culture: An examination of the police
as a distinct culture. It explores the causes and

implications of this culture, as well as the various subcultures within it. The role dilemma of the Black officer, e.g., in relation to the minority and non-minority communities and the non-minority officers, is also discussed.

Crime in America: A discussion of the relationships between the community, the individual and the institutions of society as they relate to crime and crime trends.

Violence in America: This course explores violence as a tradition in the American past. It deals specifically with the causes and possible solutions of urban riots, criminal violence and campus disorders.

Role of Police in Society, Observations: An explanation of police functions with particular emphasis on the obligations, responsibilities and authority of police officers with reference to the use of discretion.

Judgment-Avoiding Conflict: A discussion of the practical aspects relating to citizens under potentially stress-filled situations. Particular attention will be given to day-to-day techniques which the officer may employ to accomplish his tasks in a manner which will afford a minimum of resistance and antagonism from persons with whom he deals. Special emphasis will be given to discussions concerning the psychological aspects of resistance and verbal abuse.

Discretionary Decision-Making: An explanation of the policeman's role in common situations requiring exercise of police discretion.

News Media Relations: An exploration of the role of the press in a free society and of the relationship of the police to mass media.

Social Disorganization: Discussions concerning mental illness, sexual deviation, and alcoholism with emphasis directed to the emotional and behavioral patterns of development of those persons suffering from such psychological disorders.

San Quentin Tour: To provide an on-site exposure to what it's like "on the inside" of a prison.

Panel Discussion (Experienced Officers): Presents an experienced perspective of the material covered in

Community-Police Relations.

Conflict Management Section: Members of the Department's Conflict Management Section will provide insights from their studies into the use of force by and against police. Recruits will be apprised of the successful techniques used by the unit in handling emotional situations without using physical violence.

Closure: These discussions will be used as summary sessions. These meetings are significant not only for the purpose of summarizing material just discussed, but also in order to relate that material to subjects presented earlier in the Recruit School curriculum.

A whole new approach to the teaching of recruits was also adopted. The instructional atmosphere was purposefully changed from a rigidly executed, militarily oriented lecture-based format to an informal, open-discussion, seminar approach. In an effort to emphasize this philosophy, recruit officers attended most of the course dressed in civilian attire. Uniforms were introduced at the end of the program, and only when it became absolutely necessary. Further, the program was moved from the Police Administration Building to a distant and more relaxed setting to avoid the possible contamination of the recruits by the "locker room syndrome." Indeed, the placement of the "community awareness" block of instruction at the beginning of the course was an attempt to give the recruit officers a powerful introduction to their clientele and the environment within which they would fulfill their responsibilities *before* they discussed the specifics of "police work."

Role playing became a vital part of every facet of the training program. Sometimes under the heading of "Critical Incident Simulations" and other times under regular subject matter titles, officers were exposed to and participated in training exercises containing a degree of realism not heretofore possible. For example, local actors and actresses were recruited, and they assisted in the staging of skits portraying common police incidents such as family and landlord-tenant disputes, and juvenile disturbances. Recruit officers took roles in these training experiences, thus gaining insights and feelings not attainable through the less involving instructional techniques.

To this role playing was added the technique of the videotape replay, and recruit officers were given the opportunity to review and critique their own performances immediately and in detail.

The recruit officers also participated in community field experiences which tended to broaden their understanding of the community, and which helped to sensitize them to citizen-contact problems. Early in their training recruit officers were required to spend brief periods in various neighborhoods to develop their level of awareness. These experiences usually involved the trainee in living and / or working in the community without the benefit of financial resources. They might "live off the land" for a day or so or they might participate in an exercise which called for a white rookie officer to go apartment hunting with a black woman posing as his wife.

Recruits also serve a brief internship in a social or criminal justice agency so they might better grasp the complex interrelationships involved.

At the same time that these new elements were introduced into the program, an attempt was made to upgrade the content of the technical police offerings. The result was hopefully a presentation balanced to meet all the needs of the police recruit, which, coupled with the Field Training Program, would result in a well-rounded probationary police officer.

Learning from Experimentation

One additional training opportunity that arose from project activity was learning from field experiments. For example, an important component of our Family Crisis Intervention Program was the isolation and dissemination of successful officer experiences in dealing with disputes. While there was an honest attempt to evaluate the efficacy of the specialized unit, it was generally assumed that the major thrust of the project was to garner useful information on the handling of family calls for eventual dissemination to patrol officers. As a part of this effort, the participating officers were instructed to pay attention to those aspects of their performance which seemed to produce results. They were debriefed on a regular basis and all pertinent information was recorded and processed for future use in training materials and programs. The department is in the process of compiling such materials and preparing the training presentations.

The same general procedure was followed in the Landlord-Tenant Program, with training materials prepared for use by radio dispatchers and patrolmen.

Success or Failure?

Obviously, in terms of training activity generated, our effort proved an unqualified success. It is doubtful that many projects could have such a large number of positive spinoffs. The Oakland Police Department is presently engaging in a wide variety of training programs reflecting the need to add methods of preventing and coping with street violence. While all the credit for this activity does not belong to our officers, their ideas and impetus certainly made a major contribution. This contribution, in fact, is very much part of the training program today. Two of our first generation officers who are now sergeants have co-ordinated the department's in-service training and recruit academy, and are assigned to the Training Division.

Insofar as detailed evaluative material is concerned, other parts of this report make reference to a downward trend in the number of violence related arrests, and a significant reduction in citizen complaints dealing with the use of force, etc. Furthermore, data suggest that there is a difference between the performance of recruit classes, but much of these data are not conclusive or, in a number of cases, the time lapse has not been sufficient for a realistic evaluation.

There are, however, some general comments that can be offered as a result of observation and of interviews with recruits, training officers, and officers who have worked with newly trained officers.

Taking the recruit school first, the recruits who attended the first revised training school, the 61st, were generally favorably impressed by the program. They built a solidarity based not upon an "us" and "they" dichotomy, but upon the philosophy that they were a well trained group of police officers who had a responsibility to "their" community.

There was a considerable difference of opinion as to the best and worst parts of the program. All recruits were enthusiastic about the technical training because it is "new" and maybe "romantic." While few opposed the new "Community-Police Relations" block, there were mixed responses to questions dealing with it. Some replies were based on personal feelings about one's own presumed sophistication. One black officer from Oakland thus said that he had lived the problems discussed in the culture blocks, but that while he himself didn't need the discussion, some of his classmates did. Another white officer felt the subculture material was "useful" although he was not prejudiced at all.

The majority of the recruit officers were supportive of the relaxed learning environment. They found the role playing generally help-ful, but some seemed to be embarrassed by having to perform and a few seemed to feel dramatization was not needed in as many areas of instruction.

The vast majority of the officers we interviewed felt that the recruits were well prepared upon completion of the school, but several stated that the recruits were more aware of what not to do than of what to do. One Field Training Officer put it this way:

> Yeah, there's always been that sort of comment on this type of training. The guys come out on the street, they're afraid to touch anybody, they're afraid to talk to anybody, even in a man-to-man situation. Some of the recruits I've seen have expressed this feeling quite a bit. . . .
>
> The impression is to bend a little too much. I bend. I bend all the time. But it's part of that discretionary power that you build up within yourself. And, like I say, they're afraid to touch anybody. I'm not saying all of them; I'm saying a good percentage of them. Even a good felony stop, they'll be afraid to pat him down. "If I touch him I may end up in Internal Affairs. I shouldn't touch him because he's black and I'm white."

Recruits from a later recruit training program, the 63rd, were not as positive toward the program. There was a strong feeling that community relations was over-emphasized, and they tended to feel that the emphasis had made them reluctant to enforce the law. Many in the group went so far as to advocate more military dis-cipline in the training setting.

Field Training Officers were generally not enthusiastic about the recruit school, but this feeling was not unanimous. It is interesting that while one officer was very impressed with the recruits' ability to talk their way out of a situation, (something he felt his own class could not have done,) another Field Training Officer classified this behavior as an unwillingness to take action. In his opinion, the new officers were too cautious. This latter opinion seemed to be held by the majority of Field Training Officers.

One incident in particular brought together the opposition to the new training program. While on a field visitation with the Public Defender's Office, a recruit inadvertently heard a police officer from another department make prejudiced remarks while waiting to testify. The recruit reported this to the Public Defender and he, in turn, used these remarks to destroy the witness' testimony. Word of this incident spread through the department like wildfire, and numerous officers contacted the Field Training Officers and the Field Training Coordinator wanting to know if it was the program's intention to turn out "finks." Although excuses and explanations were offered and the Training Division established an orientation for beat officers, there is still a large number of police officers who view the new program as subversive to "good police work."

Further, Field Training Officers had mixed emotions about the efficacy of the Recruit Training Program insofar as the adequacy of technical aspects of policing was concerned. They were almost evenly divided on this issue. A large percentage of the Field Training Officers felt that community relations was overemphasized in the recruit school.

Finally, the greatest opposition to the Field Officer Training Program probably results from administrative displacements caused by the program. In order to place the "right" Field Training Officer with the "right" Recruit Officer it is often necessary to assign other officers different partners, beats, and maybe even watches. This necessary practice has caused a great deal of opposition to the program. In some cases, officers have refused to become Field Training Officers because of the possible discomfort it might cause their brother officers. In an effort to overcome opposition some attempt is being made to give recognition to Field Training Officers. Furthermore, steps are under consideration which will deal with the stability problem as part of a department-wide reorganization.

The differences of opinion concerning the usefulness of the Recruit Officer Training Program and to a lesser degree the Field Training Program, particularly by Field Training Officers, did not come as a surprise. As was noted earlier, the Chief and others viewed the efforts at revising the department's training program as an attempt to provide departmental personnel with the training required to successfully fulfill their duties and responsibilities as modern urban police officers. From the Chief's perspective this revision was only one phase in his effort to "turn the department around." He wished to make the department not only technically competent at crime prevention and control, but sensitive to other community needs. Many officers do not agree with this approach. Indeed, there is strong support to be found for maintaining the "status quo." The strength and depth of this feeling was reiterated a year or so after the inception of the training changes.

As a result of an unrelated incident involving the temporary loss of overtime pay, the Oakland Police Officers' Association decided to take a vote of confidence on the Chief of Police. The members of the association voted "no confidence" in the Chief 375-110 and requested that he retire. One stated reason for the opposition was the officers' disagreement with what they perceived as the Chief's attempt to redefine the police role in Oakland. Various governmental and community groups taking a position on the vote, however, supported the Chief, and he is continuing his efforts to modernize the department.

Obviously, the Violence Prevention Program and the training changes that have been discussed here are only part, albeit an important part, of a larger pattern of change. It is not startling under these circumstances that there is some disenchantment. What is remarkable, though, is the degree of progress that has occurred, in the face of resistance, with rank-and-file participation.

11 • What Have We Shown?

At the start of the project, it appeared plausible that five kinds of outcomes could be expected: (1) the seven first-phase officers would demonstrate competence in self-study; (2) these officers would be able to get the 18 second-phase officers to demonstrate similar competence; (3) both groups of officers would decrease the number of citizen-officer conflicts in which they were involved; (4) new programs and changes in the department's organization would occur; and (5) the participants would have an impact on other officers, contributing to a change in the police subculture.

First-phase Officers: Competence in Self-study

The products resulting from the efforts of the initial seven officers document the high level of competence they achieved in the self-study procedures.

> a. The Critical Incident Questionnaire was an ingenious approach to studying citizen-officer conflict situations. It was a definite step beyond the officers' relating of incidents in which they themselves had been engaged. It represented a systematic way to answer the question: do all officers behave alike in situations in which conflict is likely to emerge between an officer and a citizen? The officers moved beyond concern with their own experiences to pose an empirically researchable question. With some help from staff they developed a procedure for obtaining data relevant to the question. They collected and analyzed the data, demonstrated that officers do behave differently in what they say they would do in critical situations. They thus opened the way for systematic inquiry into the nature of differences in police conduct.

b. The tape recording of actual incidents as they occurred in the field was another systematic study procedure for getting at the nature of different approaches by officers to conflict situations. It too documents the ability of the seven officers to engage creatively in the study of their behavior.

c. Self-initiated investigations of radio room procedures and of the field training officer program also provide tangible evidence of self-study proficiency. These studies led to concrete recommendations for procedural changes which were implemented by the department. Some program development and change within the department can thus be traced to the self-study efforts of the officers.

d. A different type of evidence comes from a review of the summary process statements following each study group meeting. These statements show a growing awareness of the dynamics of group participation and of ways the officers increased their perceptiveness by becoming students of their department's performance.

There is evidence that the initial seven officers were able to effectively engage in self-study. What about their ability to get other officers to become self-study participants?

Second-phase Officers: Competence in Self-study

As discussed in previous chapters, we encountered more problems than we had anticipated with the Phase Two self-study groups. Nevertheless, the products of these groups also document achievement of self-study competence.

a. The Officer Review Panel was a brilliant innovation which was initiated by Phase Two officers as part of their study of their own performance. The idea was originally a suggestion by a group member who asked how the study of officer performance engaged in by his group could be applied to other officers who were having more than their share of citizen-officer conflicts. Working from this question, the officers established a quality control procedure which involves daily review of every arrest report for evidence of citizen-officer conflict. Records are filed by officer, allowing the panel coordinator to keep track of performance as it accrues over time for each officer, as well as for the total department and for significant sub-groups within the department. Upon reaching a designated number of incidents, a study is made of the individual's reports and other relevant information. The Chief allows the officers to keep their own records and to work with their fellow officers without his knowledge of the content of the sessions.

With consulting inputs from staff, the officers added to this quality control system a built-in cumulative program-effectiveness evaluation. Officer characteristics (e.g., age on entering the department, minority group status, amount of education) are noted. Prior experience with the Review Panel as either subject or member is also recorded, as is participation in activities seen as plausibly related to street performance (e.g., the field training officer program). These data allow a multivariate analysis, updated as frequently as once a month, to test to what extent the initial character-istics of the officer make any difference in his street per-formance and then, beyond the variance predictable from these initial characteristics, the extent to which participation in the panels or in other interventions contributes to street performance. This kind of analysis also allows one to sum-marize over months of time what is happening to the num-ber of citizen-officer conflicts throughout the entire depart-ment or within any subgroup of the department. This is a very sophisticated example of program development with ongoing systematic monitoring built into it. It supports the conclusion that the Phase Two officers were productive in using the self-study method in approaching their own de-partment's program needs.

b. The Family Crisis Intervention Unit was also developed by the Phase Two officers, although it was stimulated by a presentation by Morton Bard about a pioneer program in New York City. As we have noted, the Oakland model dif-fers in important ways from that of the New York police, the main difference being its self-sufficiency. The program is based on peer selection and professional development through the use of taping procedures and feedback to the peer group as contrasted with the civilian clinical support given the New York officers. The Family Crisis Intervention Unit program also has built-in evaluation procedures.

c. The third type of impact by the Phase Two officers originated with their review of the Recruit Training Program. This
study contributed to revised procedures and content for the
training of new police recruits, including self-study options.

Consistent with the expectations of the project, the Phase Two
officers showed much less resistance to accepting the idea that both
they and the department were having problems than did the Phase
One officers. They were also readier to approach and study these
problems. The one complication was that despite their initial
acceptance of the program as defined by the Phase One officers,
they did not show the intensity of concern nor the task orientation
that was prevalent in Phase One. However, many of the Phase Two
participants obviously developed a feel for self-study.

Citizen-Officer Conflict Reduction

Citizen-officer conflicts were reduced by half for the Phase One
officers following their participation in the project. Conflicts averaged more than two per month for the group of seven officers in the
early part of 1969 compared with one per month in the first five
months of 1970. Follow-up beyond this point is difficult. Four of
the seven officers were promoted to sergeant in the latter half of
1970, thus almost eliminating the possibility of their running into
citizen-officer confrontations.

For Phase Two we developed, with the Phase One officers, an
elaborate experimental-control design to test for modifications in
officer-citizen conflict, both during the running of Phase Two and in
the months following. The 54 officers having the highest number
of citizen-officer conflicts during the year 1968 were ranked in
order of the number of incidents in which they were involved (the
range was 6 to 32). The Phase One officers took the top three officers
on the list, tossed coins, and assigned the odd man from the coin
toss to group C. They repeated this procedure with each succeeding
group of three. Officers in group C, called the "unaware controls,"
were not informed of the project. The remaining 36 officers were
then interviewed to inform them of the project and discuss the
possibility of their participation. The Phase One officers again
tossed coins, taking in order of ranking the two top officers on the
list and assigned one from each pair to an experimental group
(group B) and the other to a control group (group A, the "aware
controls"). The Phase One officers kept track of citizen-officer con-

flicts for all three groups. They hypothesized that the experimentals would be involved in fewer citizen-officer conflicts, both during the study and subsequent to it, than either of the control groups — and that the aware controls, by virtue of their knowledge of the department's interest in violence, would be involved in fewer incidents than would the unaware controls.

Neither hypothesis was confirmed. Analysis of variance over the three months during which the intervention was run, correcting for the decreased time on the street of officers in the experimental group, showed no significant differences among those exposed to the intervention and those in the two control groups. Analysis of variance over the five months following the intervention, holding number of incidents in the five months prior to the intervention constant, also showed no significant differences.

These comparisons do not demonstrate the expected behavioral effects of officer participation in self-study. There is evidence from other data, however, that such participation can significantly influence street performance. Before presenting this, let us consider some of the problems underlying the present analysis. First, the sample from which the three groups were chosen was small (54 officers) and it rapidly decreased. Injuries, resignations, firings, promotions, and assignments to non-street positions left a sizable proportion of the original 54 unavailable for experiences that might lead to reported conflict. Twenty percent were not on the street through all of 1970, the year of the intervention, and thirty percent through the year following.

Table 2 shows the average number of incidents per month per officer for three periods during 1970: the five months prior to the intervention, the three months during which the intervention took place, and the five months following the intervention. It will be seen that in all three groups there is a decrease from the first to the second period, that this decrease is then maintained in the third period for the two control groups but continues for the experimental group. It should be remembered that these variations are well within what could be expected by chance. Moreover, because the numbers of incidents show rather large fluctuations from month to month, both for the department as a whole and for the three groups in our sample, and because of the small number of officers involved, the selection of a cut-off time for follow-up becomes important. The addition (or deletion) of one or two months may alter apparent trends as may the addition of deletion of one or two officers. The cut-off time used for our analysis was selected to retain a maximum number of officers in the samples.

TABLE 2:
Citizen-Officer Conflicts
Before, During, and After Self-Study Intervention

	Before Jan-May 1970	During June-Aug 1970*	After Sept 1970- Jan 1971
Experimental (N = 14)			
Average incidents / officer	4.14	2.29	3.00
Average / month / officer	0.83	0.76	0.60
Aware Control (N = 15)			
Average incidents / officer	3.07	1.60	2.75
Average / month / officer	0.61	0.53	0.55
Unaware Control (N = 14)			
Average incidents / officer	3.57	1.36	2.29
Average / month / officer	0.71	0.45	0.46

*Number for experimental group pro-rated for loss of time on street during self-study meetings.

Second, the intervention may have been experienced differently by different officers. For example, the data indicate that one of the three units in the experimental group (Group Two) showed a worsening of street performance during the period of the intervention, in contrast to improvement in the other two units. Three of the officers in this unit were responsible for half (52%) of the incidents for the entire experimental group during the post-intervention period, compared to a third (33%) of the incidents in the pre-intervention period. Two of these three men engaged in a project which proved very frustrating, which was never put into operation, and which built resentment in the men who worked on it. (One of these two was Officer White.) The third (Spark) was the scapegoat within his team; a tremendous amount of hostility developed between him and his fellow officers. One might say that these three men, rather than participating in a self-study experience which interested and motivated them, experienced frustration and an almost devastating challenge. This possible development obviously needs more study. It does seem that officers can experience negative impact from the peer group experience, and leave the group (at least, initially) more alienated from their department and more hostile to others than if they had not participated in the experience.

A third problem may be the brevity of the intervention itself. An intervention designed to change performance over time has to be an intervention which persists over time. The self-study procedure could get officers to become students of their department's operation. It was able to give them skills which they could use in program development. But unlike the Phase One officers, most of whom had continuing roles in program management following the project, most of the Phase Two officers had no opportunity for engaging in work they had begun during the summer. Correcting their street performance over time may require reinforcement of their initial participatory experience, either through opportunities to become involved, or through a shift in the department's climate in a direction more favorable to problem-solving efforts.

The Officer Review Panel meets these specifications. It was instituted near the beginning of the Phase Two intervention. Since that time over 120 officers participated in the panel, either as subjects (those whose records were reviewed) or as members (those who did the reviewing), and sometimes as both. The panel is a pure self-study experience, offering immediate rewards to both subjects and members. For the former, there is at least immediate peer approval for willingness to participate, and peer support in trying to deal with experiences that may be uncomfortable. For the latter, there is the rewarding role of helper and a possible chance to learn something about oneself without direct confrontation. Panel experience, as an intervention, offers less opportunity for the frustration that arose with participation in our program.

Though brief, panel experience is predicted to have a positive effect on an officer's street behavior. There is evidence that it does. Table 3 compares panel participants with non-participants in the frequency of citizen-officer conflicts for the five months prior to instituting the review panel and the twenty-six months following. Only officers who were on street duty for the entire thirty-one months were used in the comparison.

TABLE 3:
Total Citizen-Officer Conflicts
Before and After Review Panel Participation:
Review Panel Participants vs. Non-participants

	Before: Jan-May 1970	After: June 1970 July 1972		
		Expected	Observed	Exp.-Obs.
Participants (N=72)				
Average incidents/officer	2.39	12.48	7.90	4.58
Average/month/officer	0.48	0.48	0.30	0.18
Non-participants (N=434)				
Average incidents/officer	0.64	3.38	2.44	0.94
Average/month/officer	0.13	0.13	0.09	0.04

Using the five months prior to the panel as a base, the average number of incidents expected for the next twenty-six months was determined. The actual number that occurred was less than the number expected for both the participants and the non-participants. The decrease was much greater, however, for the participating officers, their expected-observed discrepancy being four-and-a-half times that of the non-participating officers. A co-variance analysis shows that a difference of this magnitude has less than a .001 probability of occurring by chance. The original officer study of street conflicts led to the development of an intervention which has significantly reduced the incidence of such conflict.

Though the Review Panel began in June 1970, participation in the panel was spread over the months following. The figures reported for the participants for the "after" period in Table 3 include varying numbers of months prior to participation. More precise measures were obtained by taking each participant's average number of incidents for the actual months prior to and following his participation in the panel. This analysis is reported in Table 4. The average monthly incidents for the participants drop from 0.37 to 0.16 following participation. Monthly averages for the non-participants (using randomly assigned comparable time periods) drop from 0.10 to 0.08. A co-variance analysis shows that the differences among these averages have less than a .01 probability of occurring by chance.

TABLE 4:
Average Monthly Citizen-Officer Conflicts
Before and After Panel Participation:
Participants vs. Non-Participants

	Before Panel[1]	After Panel
Participants (N 88)		
Average	0.37	0.16
Variance	0.13	0.02
Non-Participants (N 434)		
Average	0.10	0.08
Variance	0.03	0.02

[1]In contrast to the figures in Table 3, time before and after participation varies for each participant. Actual months on the street before and after participation are used to determine monthly averages. This allows the inclusion of 16 additional officer-participants who could not be included in the analysis reported in Table 3 because they were not on the street for the full before and after periods.

Time is controlled for the non-participants by proportional random assignment, to correspond to the monthly proportions of participants.

Review Panel participants include both those officers who were engaged as subjects — that is, whose street behavior was under review by panel members — and those who participated as reviewing members only. It was hypothesized that participation as a subject would have a greater impact on street behavior than involvement as a member only. This is supported by the data in Table 5. The average monthly incidents for the subjects drop from 0.63 to 0.21 following participation. Monthly averages for the non-participants (who now include the Panel members-only as well) drop from 0.11 to 0.08. A co-variance analysis shows that these differences have less than a 0.05 probability of occurring by chance.

TABLE 5:
Average Monthly Citizen-Officer Conflicts
Before and After Review Panel Participation:
Subjects vs. Non-Subjects

	Before Panel	After Panel
Subjects (N 37)[1]		
Average	0.63	0.21
Variance	0.13	0.03
Non-Subjects (N 485)		
Average	0.11	0.08
Variance	0.03	0.02

[1]Panel subjects include only those officers whose activities were under review by the panel. The 51 officers who participated as members but not subjects are included in the non-subject group.

New Programs and Organization Change

The Oakland Police Department has been undergoing an accelerating process of program development since its present chief took office three years ago. Concern with letter-of-the-law enforcement has shifted to concern with due process law enforcement. It is difficult, perhaps impossible, to disentangle the specific effects of our project from ongoing change in the department, but some major developments can be traced directly to the project's work.

The department has created a permanent Conflict Management Unit (sometimes called the Violence Prevention Unit), first headed by a sergeant who was an officer in Phase One of the project, and now by a sergeant who was an officer in Phase Two. The unit is concerned with the operation of new programs which have grown out of the violence concerns of the project. The Officer Review Panel is administered by the Conflict Management Unit. Its quality control and evaluation system is seen as a sub-system of the department's total information system. The specific coding and reporting procedures developed in the officer review program are expected to be eventually built into the department's information system.

The Family Crisis Intervention Unit (FCIU) demonstrates how programs initiated in the study groups can have impact on the total department. FCIU is administered as part of the patrol division, but is organized under the cognizance of the sergeant in charge of the Conflict Management Unit; its training and evaluation are conducted under this unit. FCIU is an experimental program. The first six-month trial showed significantly fewer arrests, citations, and reports for calls handled by this unit (5 percent) than for calls handled by other officers (17 percent). Since the unit handled an average of only two family crisis calls per shift during its first phase, major modifications were made in the operation of the second phase which allow for varying times of shifts and other procedures to improve the unit's effectiveness. In addition, FCIU has a commitment to develop strategies for handling crises which will be made available as written training material for the total department. Besides its role in reducing the number of formal charges growing out of family crisis calls, the unit has been favorably received by both clients and fellow officers. In the survey of recipients of FCIU service, 31 of the 41 persons we interviewed rated officer performance as good or excellent. A majority (63%) of the 78 officers polled on the unit's operation saw it as a worthwhile extension of the department's activity.

Operation of the unit has also opened the way for contacts between the department and other agencies. We have seen that both the Family Service and Neighborhood Legal Assistance agencies feel that the program has an impact on their operation and staff, challenges stereotypes about officers and clients, and has increased communication and co-operation with the police.

The Field Training Officer Program, which grew out of a group project, was initiated under the direction of one of the Phase One officers. Other developments stemming from the work of the groups include changes in the procedures used in the radio room to process calls to officers in the field and some of the changes we have reviewed of training offered in recruit classes.

The Chief, through his interest in due process law enforcement, has a legal assistance office in the department. The concerns of this office merge with those developed from this project. Under collaborative sponsorship, the department has set up a Landlord-Tenant

Unit to handle rent and other disputes. A consumer fraud program is presently being planned.

The evaluation procedures developed through the project have created an interest within the department in revising its information system to make it more consistent with needs for quality control and evaluation of new programs. Plans are to build in new information which can be used, along with existing information, to determine the impact of new departmental interventions developed to modify officer performance.

The project has thus played a role in bringing about all kinds of organizational changes within the department. One major change, which is hard to over-emphasize, is the amount of officer participation within the department. In addition, there has been a tremendous increase in the Chief's direct contact with officers in program planning for the department.

Impact on Other Officers

One apparent impact the project had as a training program was to increase the likelihood of the participants being promoted. Four of our initial seven officers have become sergeants, and a fifth is on the sergeant's promotion list. Three of the experimentals have been promoted and one is on the promotion list, compared to one promotion and two on the promotion list for the two control groups combined. As sergeants these men have increased opportunity for influencing the department's operation.

In addition to the potential impact of the officers as supervisors, they have been used in the field in various ways that offer opportunity for impact on their fellow officers. One man was repeatedly assigned to work as a partner with fellow officers who were seen by his supervisor as having special problems in interpersonal relations. Three of our officers were involved in the design and administration of the Field Training Officer's Program. Others now directly participate, as members of the Conflict Management Unit, in recruit training. A fourth means of influence lies in the Officer Review Panel.

It is plausible that the impact on officers we have worked with will eventually spread to other officers with whom there is no direct contact. If these impacts are effective, it follows that citizen-officer conflicts throughout the department should decrease. It is too early to make a definitive statement regarding changes in total department performance, but such an evaluation is built into the continuing project. In the interim, there has been a downward shift in the average monthly numbers of citizen-officer conflicts, from 130 incidents per month for the period July 1970 through June 1971 to 58 per month for the period July through December of 1971. Citizen complaints against officers also have dropped over these two periods, from an average of 42 to 25 per month.

A procedure has also been established to follow the careers of officers in each graduating recruit class, the argument being that if peer impact is effective, the more recent recruit classes should show fewer incidents compared to those of the total department, than the earlier classes. A system for tabulating citizen-officer conflicts by recruit class per month compared with the total incidents in the department has been established.

Discussion

This project has shown that police officers can use social science methods in approaching their department's major goals and concerns. Men without formal training have not only designed ingenious interventions, but also devised creative approaches to the evaluation of impact. At least one of these double innovations (the review panel) demonstrates that short term training received in the project has significant impact on subsequent performance.

With technical assistance, the men moved from developing ideas and translating them into practice, to designing quality control and evaluation systems that determine the impact of their programs upon the conduct of men in the field. Many of these officers are now in significant positions within the department. Several are in program operating roles which they have helped to create.

The question of the direct impact of participation in this project upon the street performance of the officer participants cannot be unambiguously answered. It is obvious that the original seven officers markedly reduced the number of their street conflicts. In the second phase it is our revised hypothesis that the reduction of street behavior is related to the effectiveness of the self-study experience. One of the three self-study units was seen as markedly less effective, and we know that a good deal of hostility and frustration was expressed by the officers in this group. Our N's are so small that the question still remains as to how much, if any, impact can be directly related to the effectiveness of the self-study program. However, it appears that the peer study groups have planted seeds and initiated a climate for change which has shown impact over time. Procedures have been established for continuing review of the performance of participating officers, and of their peers.

Although it is certainly not the only determinant, it seems plausible that this project has contributed to opening up communication and increasing participation within the department. Men working on special projects report directly to the Chief, and there are more discussions involving officers and other members of the staff concerning problems and issues of operation and training. There is also a climate more generally oriented toward increased participation in building something that is different from the way the department is currently constituted. This goal has been expressed by the Chief as building a service-oriented and a social-change-oriented department.

As a direct outgrowth of this project's attention to systematic study and the evaluation of new programs, the department, with the assistance of the officers in the project, is turning its attention to modifying its use of information. This system is now geared mainly to providing arrest data which gives information on aggregates of kinds of arrests. Modifications will permit us to obtain information on the performance of a given officer or group of officers over time, thus allowing an assessment of the impact of new programs. New kinds of information beyond arrest report and citation activity are also being developed in sub-systems for quality control and evaluation arising from this project. We thus have an organization which is changing in its ways of operating and in its approach to change, and which is heavily committed to systematic development, quality control, and evaluation. How much of this change can be directly attributed to the project is impossible to determine. But it would be hard to argue that the project was not a significant component in a changing organizational climate to which the police have become committed.

12 • What Did We Learn?

What have we learned? What do we know now that we didn't know in the spring of 1969? For one thing, we must speak now of "coping competence." We know that the results of participation can be expressed in terms of the individuals' and the organization's ability to cope with forces with which they must contend to survive — that the self-study process can be analyzed from the point of view of how a group and its participants perceive their competence to cope. We have learned that when our officers saw themselves able to deal with self-study demands — and only then — did productive things happen.

In order to maximize the effectiveness of participation strategies we must look at the implications of this discovery for some self-study principles: providing participatory roles; making room for autonomy of action, decision, and choice; building a group culture around a cause to which one can be committed; offering a meaningful future; and allowing natural leaders to emerge.

A Role For Everyone

The inherent value of the officers' full participation in developing the studies they undertook and of the resulting feeling that they were working for themselves (rather than someone else) held up as an ingredient of an effective model. However, participation was not uniformly high throughout the project. The waxing and waning of enthusiasm for the group and its purpose appeared related to the likelihood of producing a product. It was hard for the group to plan and to state expectations as a result of planning, even though staff tried to provide structure by delineating the scope and direction of the group's activities. The staff's circumscription of goals could be felt as a challenge to the coping competence of both the individual members and the group as a whole. A commitment to a goal presupposes the perceived ability to achieve expected outcomes. We demonstrated the difference between talking bravely about initiating procedures and taking the risky first steps of actual production. A blatant example was the problem with follow-through on the taping of street incidents. Everyone expressed interest, if not enthusiasm, and a commitment to carry through (including sermons directed at other group members); but the actual production of tapes seemed to succumb to ever-present self-produced snags.

We can think of several ways to keep study group members actively participating and less afraid of getting into deep waters with attempts to be productive.

1. We need to optimize effective participation by taking advantage of the individual's style, skills, and abilities. When we move into something new, we must concentrate where personal competence is the strongest. One example was our capitalizing on Waterman's knowledge of electronics to develop the field of tape recording and the voice-on-voice recording (an emergent product) of critical incidents. Another example was our use of Jack's writing skill and analytic capacity as we moved into the field training officer program. Another was developing Bill's role as an instructor, group leader and salesman. Casting Bill as a project administrator was not an example of taking advantage of individual style, skills and abilities; but placing Kent in this role was.

2. Participation in project work must be constantly and clearly defined. Rather than having group members standing around watching someone like Jack work, one must creatively assign specific roles to available skills; ideally, no more than two persons should work together on clearly defined tasks. Dissatisfaction with planning and abstractions might be neutralized by keeping thinking tied down to specific tasks and actual functions. All project work — including planning functions — could maximize specificity and objectivity.

3. We encountered some difficulty obtaining full participation in planning, particularly for Phase Two. Though some of this may have been due to our rigidity in imposing our own outline of objectives (which we assumed the group had accepted) we could have paid more attention to an action

approach to planning. Role playing of situations to be anticipated and discussing the implications of how these are handled would be one way to minimize the abstractness of planning.

4. It can help bridge the gap between conceptualizing and specific action to bring force field analysis to bear on every project. Instead of talking generally about planning we must talk about the forces with which we contend, and work from these to specific problems, specific tasks, and specific roles.

5. The use of summary reviews and rotating summarizers for each work session proved a valuable technique. It not only encouraged participation in the task but helped define the study group process itself: sharing the problems, sharing corrective actions, and epitomizing the role of a participant in a program's development. However, the use of the taped summaries and staff (or consultants') inputs could be improved. We could use formal summaries not only with the total group but with any task forces; in these summaries, we could tie down specific roles and tasks which, again, would tend to keep content more task-oriented and less discursive. Specifically, one can make certain that each recorded summary has a section on "expecteds" and on who is committed to doing what.

Being Your Own Man

Creating an environment in which our officers had room to express their interests in their own ways proved essential in developing the initial self-study climate. In Phase Two the same game was inappropriately continued: autonomy was over-played at the expense of more relevant principles within the self-study model. To quote the words of the opening session: "It's wide open. You are free to study anything you want to study, to do anything you want to do." This stance moved the group's emphasis from concern with the study of violence to program issues of all kinds. In retrospect it seems that in our planning with the Phase One officers and in the operation of Phase Two we could have defined the parameters of the self-study task more clearly and worked for autonomy *within* a commitment to think through issues which would relate directly to reducing violence between citizens and police officers.

There is continual pressure to justify looseness or lack of structure as an interest in allowing autonomy to express itself. We need to give more attention to environmental structure that allows autonomy to be something other than laissez faire sloppiness. Complete openness makes it harder to set goals and to know when you have reached them, and it does not contribute to developing coping skills. We operated far from the extreme of a non-directed program, and we are well aware that whatever we attempted with our groups is neither sensitivity training nor extreme permissiveness. But we failed in the defining of borders and the setting of limits. We feel confident that room for self-expression, the working out of goals and objectives (within a larger set of goals and objectives) which allow for optimal use of a person's own style, can be achieved.

Culture vs. Counter Culture

Coping competence requires an inter-personal or social base. Coping competence relates to how much support you need and how much support you feel you have among significant others, particularly among your peers. For those of us who live long enough, coping competence no longer presupposes the feeling that you can charge up the hill single-handedly. In risking change one needs to feel a part of the equivalent of ten stouthearted men. Once the ten (or twenty-four) stouthearted men have become effective, we can more easily obtain ten (or ten thousand) more. One way of defining the motives of our officers was in terms of their feelings of being a part of something worth doing with which they could cope. Building a group culture that would allow these feelings to develop was a central task for the initial group. The central theme of the culture was that street officers had knowledge and skills which could be used in improving their department's effectiveness. A secondary concern (consistent with this theme) was to show that officers could be supportive to each other by reducing the probability of others getting hurt or fired.

We could have done more, structurally, to keep those who joined the group continuing to feel a part of it. This includes not only our own group members but those who joined us by becoming review panel participants or team members of the Family Crisis Intervention Unit, the Landlord-Tenant Program, or the Field Training Officer Program. We held meetings in which we made an attempt to get the group members' ideas as to what was going on, what could go on, and what were the implications of the direction being taken. It would have been appropriate to intersperse with our formal meetings more informal gatherings of this kind. We could also have held (and we would recommend) periodic formal meetings designed specifically to help with group identification and the cohesiveness of the group culture.

The belief that an officer with the aid of a few others and with a reasonable opportunity structure could have an influence on the way the department operates is seriously challenged by the prevailing locker room values and beliefs. An early interview of the group with members of the Crime Prevention Unit following the latter's involvement with the Hell's Angels dramatized the conflicting pressures of the new self-study culture and the locker room culture. In developing new cultural identity there are concerns about peer acceptance and concerns about one's emerging role in the organization. The new culture demands a new set of peer acceptances and a belief in the viability of an identity that allows a man to do something about the gripes he has against his organization rather than an identity in which he sees himself as a victim of the organization.

Any effort to bring about a change in cultural identity must take into account the intensity of life and time commitment within the culture. What are the time and work commitments necessary for building a new culture? How early can one bring on overt confrontation between the locker room culture and the newly formed culture? It may well be that we erred seriously by encouraging an encounter with main-line (hard core) officers as early as we did. This doubt fits a general principle of letting new groups of clients have time to form their own identity before they interact with groups representing opposing sets of forces out of their past.

The culture vs. counter-culture dynamics highlight the need to develop coping competence within the framework of the new culture. In order for the officer to be able to give up the minimal security he has in his identity with the larger culture (i.e., the police locker room), he must have some feeling of his ability to contribute as a member of the new one.

This still does not handle the issue of why one wants to move from one kind of identity to another, from one set of culture values to another. We assume that there are always pressures within any culture for needed change. These pressures are expressed as dissatisfaction with things as they are, but they result in little more than alienation as long as people feel helpless to produce change. We would argue that readiness to assume new roles is already present in those who are both strong and "poor losers,"[1] those who have not yet acquiesced in the limitations placed on their lives. Opportunities to become competent in actually bringing about change serves to mobilize this existing readiness.

Carrying the Torch

The new group culture needs to be built around specific content. The "cause" in our case was seen at first as keeping oneself and other officers from getting hurt or fired. The cause came later to be defined more broadly, though this varied somewhat from officer to officer. Generally we would say that commitment to a cause facilitates the emergence of new identity and group culture, and that this new identity and culture supports (but does not insure) the competence to handle new tasks and roles.

There are three ways we attempted to facilitate joining a cause. First, we picked strong officers, as perceived by peers. Basic strength facilitates the move to a new cause because a strong man is less dependent on the support of the majority and established roles. He can better afford to take on a new cause, and to deviate from the majority position. Second, once the nucleus is formed, these men make it easier for others to join their strength, to venture out on a new path, even without coping strength of their own.

As a third strategy, starting with the study of the officers' experiences (critical incidents) allowed us to approach an area where the officers had the most to contribute, where their competence could be most effective. They were able to contribute to our theme by providing their expertise from knowledge of incidents on the street in which violence had occurred. It was from working with such experiences that we derived a surprising amount of early creativity. In connection with this experience we evolved our critical incident emphasis and the tape recording methodology.

We tried a fourth way to facilitate the sense of joining a cause. Expeditions to other cities for presentations were intended to emphasize the big picture concerning the project, the importance it could carry for police work in general, and the contributions it could make to dealing with other problems facing our culture. Although there is no doubt that the officers became heavily involved at the time of giving their presentations, there was little transfer to productivity upon their return. In retrospect it would appear that an emphasis on building a sense of competence from production out of the task at hand (within more relevant reference groups) would have produced more strength in carrying on the cause than the remote revival element of the presentations was able to furnish.

Throughout the program Joe Mills consistently took on the role of a police officer's police officer who had sufficient personal independence to join or not join our cause depending on the cause's integrity as he perceived it. Toward the end of Phase One, Joe had moved to the position of an advocate for the cause. In Phase Two, however, when working with Bill, obvious antagonism arose between the two men, with Joe saying that Bill in particular and the program in general represented emphasis on low-priority police goals. Joe again became supportive of the cause in his role as street sergeant. For some strong men, commitment dies in an atmosphere of pep-rallies and flag-waving. It seems plausible to us that our efforts to cement a cause by outside trips and the vista of grand opportunities tended to undermine one man's commitment while appealing to the motives of another.

For a third man (Joe Young), joining a cause was linked to his perception of future career opportunities. Joe tried to join our program and obtain a position in Training, both of which he saw as ways to enable him to become sergeant. From this perspective, a cause was not seen as worth joining at the possible expense of a personal career. And we did not succeed to link (in Young's mind) membership in the cause with long term career interests. We were able to retain our man physically, but the tenuousness of his commitment lowered the quality of his performance. Young's case, however, is atypical. His efforts to negotiate career opportunities within the department is in contrast to a general concern of the first seven officers with something they called "officer power." They were personally concerned with the influence officers could have in determining what went on in the department and with how the group might be able to contribute to developing such power.

For officers to have status in their department is a powerful rallying point for developing a cause. Our initial group expressed this concern mainly through their worry about whether or not they could influence the Chief. It made a tremendous impact on this group to be able to discuss with the Chief his locker room image and to convince him to drop into the locker room and to talk informally with the line officers there. Even though the Chief found he was unable to continue this activity at the time, his effort gave the officers a feeling of potency, expressed through their ability to influence the Chief.

In retrospect, it seems plausible that we would have moved more rapidly if we had invoked the Chief's involvement earlier. This could have given the officers a more concrete demonstration that what they were doing was goal-producing. Involvement of the Chief could have shown that he was thinking with the group, would have provided the program with additional organizational status, and would have legitimated the group's involvements with other officers. This does not mean that the Chief should have been a full-time member of the group, but he could have been invited at least every other week, not only as a legitimator, but as a consultant in project planning and development. This also raises the issue of whether we should not have shared with the Chief, if not right at the start, soon afterwards, the strategy of counter culture and new culture interplay and the role he could play in having an influence on the police officer culture. Stated another way, the Chief as legitimator could have been an early partner and resource for idea development and problem posing, and this might have reduced the wallowing and non-contributing anxieties concerning where the Chief stood. There are two questions here: what would have been a more effective role for this Chief? and, what is an effective role for administrators in general when one is trying to develop a self-study strategy within an agency? The Chief's own thoughts in the matter are recorded in our preface.

One other important question is the extent to which officers need communication with their fellow officers. We have demonstrated the usefulness of a nucleus of peer leaders with strengths to develop their own cause without being overwhelmed by the need for immediate approval from other officers. But we must think very hard about (1) how we can neutralize encroachments from the counter-culture, and (2) how we can use the need for communication with fellow officers as a lever to bring about contagion from the new culture. Possibly we are saying that we should have spent more time with the seven officers working with the Chief to get integrity defined. Then we should have moved more strongly to enhance the influence of the first seven men on the second eighteen, and, beyond them, on others. The officers themselves developed field officer training, the review panel and the Family Crisis Intervention Unit. They also proceeded to discuss their program in line-ups and more informally elsewhere. But these may not have exhausted the possibilities of contagion available at that time and over the following years. Could we have ameliorated the local police association's vote of no confidence in the Chief, or did we contribute to the confrontation by making change issues more apparent to the counter culture? In either case, it represents a failing of the program.

Eventual confrontation between an established culture and a growing counter culture may be inevitable. However, a failure of the project lay in not projecting beyond Phase Two and anticipating possible conflict between culture and counter culture.

Beyond The Project

We left the idea of future participation entirely to spontaneous program development and possible roles within it. We could and should have done more. We could have conceptualized linkage roles from the project to other parts of the department, and we could have given our men some sort of formal linkage roles. We may have overplayed a big dream in getting some of the officers interested in how to sell or develop the program nationally when they had not yet entrenched it at home. We would have been on sound ground if we had demonstrated coping successes within the department itself and left the expansionist movement to emerge from fully developed internal strength.

When one engages in self-study, although one needs an immediate problem such as violence as the initial entree into an agency's development, one also needs to have larger goals, reasonably thought-through, concerning the personal careers aspects of change efforts on a continuing basis. By leaving this to chance one fails to capitalize on available strength and precludes any on-going self-study development within the organization.

Who Runs The Show?

The role of leader was a crucial one, particularly among the initial nucleus of seven officers. This, of course, was no surprise in a group selected for their peer leadership potential. We ran into the disappointing but not surprising finding that our seven leaders had trouble sharing leadership in Phase Two. In each group, one of the officers rose to the coping opportunity and took over as leader. The second officer in each case demonstrated his unique adaptation to threatening perceptions of his coping competence. One became an overt rival to the other's leadership, another withdrew, and the third went off into a corner and did his thing. Actually, in the second group, we had the least clear single predominant leadership role.

One suggestion for handling this phenomenon is to form smaller Phase Two groups and to give each of the initial group members his own leadership role. Another suggestion is to spend more time in the later part of Phase One working on functions of the initial nucleus in relation to the Phase Two members. Role playing could help define a sharing of roles or at least a strategy for sharing roles that becomes very explicit in the minds of the initial group. These function-defined roles could vary, as appropriate, for each leadership team.

Another leadership issue occurred in Phase One. One officer in particular became obsessed with the idea of "officer power," not only in relation to the group's ability to express it but with respect to his own involvement. This led to a large amount of productivity on his part. He wrote a paper which he used in a community college course and which he felt clarified thinking within the group concerning officer roles and the participation strategy. He attacked the staff and demanded the right of officers to express their own capabilities without the interference of staff. We sensed a flooding here of accumulated alienation as the officers moved from complaining about their lack of opportunity to experience impact and success to a flood of expression of held-back potential. Certainly the role of Jesus Christ Superstar is qualitatively different from coping competence. Part of coping competence has to be the awareness (and skills to go with the awareness) that the game is not to run the world but to find an active role in a world that's concerned with other forces besides your own — to understand that no man and no group are islands unto themselves, and to be able to keep your feet without being overwhelmed by all those others. The Jesus Christ Superstar phenomenon is perhaps best distinguished from coping competence as an anxious reaction to an opportunity in which one cannot just complain about not having the opportunity to express one's potential. We need build more peer living-learning support for men as they move into these action roles. We could extend, for example, the approach used in the Officer Review Panels into analysis of officer-officer and middle management-officer relationships.

The Phase Two study group which produced the most effective product (the Peer Officer Review Panel) was also the most cohesive. It had the involved leadership of Bill and careful participants' selection because of Bill's concern with finding a group he thought he could work with; it also had the most consistent staff consultation. The second most productive group in terms of the product (the Family Crisis Intervention Unit and contact with outside agencies) had the least cohesiveness, the least organized leadership, and the least amount of consistent consultation. The biggest surprise, however, was the group which ultimately produced no effective product but which initially was extremely impressive as a cohesive well-led group. This group received not too intensive consultation, but had a powerful leader in Hill. The group had good discussions, was well monitored and organized, but as time went on produced little more than reasonable well-disciplined participation.

It appears that leadership demands more than being an impressive leader, and that product effectiveness is an outcome of more than contagion through natural peer leadership. There must be the capacity to put into effect the principles and conditions described in this chapter. An inspiring working model, who demonstrates what effective study group performance is all about by doing it, appears to be more essential than charismatic leadership.

Selection

Our selection procedures, however crude, did allow us to recruit a nucleus of initial strength. It does appear that even brief observations of ability to cope in discussions with peers can allow a reasonable selection for a nucleus of strong group participants.

It also appears that the peer influencing role is a much more basic selection criterion than initial motivation. Another lead for selection is the matter of roles one needs in a group to optimize effectiveness. In our case, there was the stabilizing role of Mills, the non-self-aggrandizing but true-to-the-cause role of Hill, the extremist role of Bill, the task role of Jack. It is still a question whether one needs to or can select for initial roles within the nucleus group or whether with a concentration of peer coping powers appropriate roles will emerge through the dynamics of the group's working together.

Study Group Structure

We need to think of the constraints that operate on the study group program and optimal ways to cope with them: the counter culture, the budget, the board of supervisors, middle management. We mentioned earlier that we should be sure we have the nucleus group's identity and concerns crystallized before it takes on a head-on counter culture confrontation, and that we can do more in planned approaches linking group activities to locker room culture and to the organization in general. (Actually, we expected more overt resentment from the officers representing the locker room culture than was in fact obtained.) "Spreading the word" as an autonomous function has some advantages but too much of it, particularly too early, can boomerang by getting participants concerned about selling products, rather than developing a product that can sell itself. Our approach to middle management should be like that to the locker room: we must make planned moves for participation as we actually develop projects which involve middle-management.

Study Group Process

We feel that at the start, any study group should be concerned with the actual experiences of its participants. The use of critical incidents as a way to approach a problem and to help define it is related to the concept of coping competence. We start where our participants have their greatest strength. They are experts with incident experiences, and the staff at first learns from group members around the major content. The staff's role then becomes one of providing methodological rules and support to help make sense out of the basic knowledge of participants.

Our experience suggests that one must be explicit about moving from the critical incident stage to the analysis stage, then to the implications of analysis to program innovation, and then to a stage of opportunities for action and expression. It seems important to move quickly into additional insight-producing activity. Uncontrolled, self-generated inquiry can lead to anxieties. By starting with personally experienced critical incidents, we foster bridging from the familiar, shared, concrete fact to experiencing the relationship between data and concepts, the awareness of new aspects of familiar situations, and the benefit of learning something new.

In our conflicts with the officers about planning, the group became impatient and needed concrete activity. It is fair to say that planning provides a tremendous challenge to coping competence. The more we can keep planning concrete, the more the feeling of potential mastery is available. If we try to avoid the planning issue completely, and arrange for concrete activity as soon as the group becomes anxious, we discover that energy is dissipated because of lack of planning. Although planning is painful and lowers morale, such anxiety is necessary and the staff must be able to tolerate it. The point here is to keep a challenging uncomfortableness without wallowing in rigidifying panic.

Progress entails conflict among group participants. Possibly the sooner such conflict emerges, the better. Conflict among participants requires openness and trust, and entails a breakdown of pseudo-solidarity which provides a problem-solving experience. One way of putting it is that conflict among the participants can enhance coping competence by letting men face something beyond a defensive alignment with comfortably resisting forces. Facing conflict also takes the focus away from playing to staff as an audience. We must keep a process going in which the anxiety of uncertainty is faced, but in which there is opportunity for reasonable mastery and the development of increasing feelings of directionality. The planned change game requires tolerating ambiguities and learning to mix conceptualizing with the implications of acting on concepts. This is the model we can offer our groups for adoption.

Staff Roles

Staff's role must allow opportunity but insure effectiveness. Staff can encourage the group to run with the ball but must make certain that the ball is moved, even if staff must at times pick it up and run with it themselves. Rotating responsibility for the recorded summaries and formal commitments for each session are examples of a two-step strategy. The opportunity and encouragement is there for the group to provide its own structure, but the staff can play as much of a role as is necessary at each stage for group effectiveness.

Staff provide viable role models. This includes contributing in the stating of a problem, contributing to developing frames of reference for approaching a problem, contributing to the statement of interventions and to the resulting hypotheses, and contributing to ways of getting quality control. Staff can also show, by example, how one uses scholarship in social action. Staff can do homework, bring in relevant material, report it, make it available and show how one links thinking and the use of available knowledge in attacking applied social problems from a social science frame of reference. Staff can also show human attributes which lead to identification with sympathetic concern for each other and mankind. The role should be not one of weakness but of forming relationships which reduce social distance. A demonstration of basic integrity is necessary which comes primarily through the staff's ability to do its share of homework, as well as in thinking during the actual sessions. This integrity is particularly important in developing the original nucleus. Staff must be prepared to work hard and keep alert till the nucleus group gets involved. Continual work is necessary after this point, but initial intensive effort is essential to get the change game going.

Imput From The Outside

There can be no doubt that appropriate stimuli from the outside world can help group members with the process of change and enhance their feelings of developing competence. We draw a distinction here between input from the outside and presentations by others within the culture or organization. It seems plausible that one should move first for input from the different rather than input from the familiar. An example of catalytic inputs from the outside in our project was contact with welfare agency representatives. Having welfare agency people riding with the officers was stimulating and reinforced an incipient service orientation. The inputs from Chief Ferguson of Covina were also stimulating, and provided a model of innovativeness which reinforced the group's own ideas about innovations. The inputs from the Hell's Angels were important compared with the inputs from other officers, which seemed to reinforce links to the *status quo* and to the alienated locker room culture. The inputs from Bard and the New York Family Crisis Program stimulated thinking in Oakland and also provided a feeling of identity with efforts at change in police work generally. Besides the matter of identification with innovation that comes from outside influence, there is also the matter of obtaining material for analysis of one's own activities. Thus the Hell's Angels, in revealing the social structure of their club's organization, helped focus attention on some aspects of the social structure of the police department.

We draw another distinction between imposed input and input required or requested by the group. Whereas the first type of input typically evokes resistance, the second usually arises in the course of group problem solving, as fact-gathering. Persons providing such input are seen as resources to be actively exploited. They are not only more carefully attended to, but are selectively used. They help the group build its sense of competence because they advance group goals. They furnish not only content, but information about how resources can be mobilized and used.

As we try to become more and more explicit about a self-study model, it seems likely that we can move more and more concretely to the strategic use of specific outside inputs. A potent force in self-study development can be the enriching feed-in of outside stimuli.

Where Are We Now?

We have a right to be encouraged with the project's demonstration of effective participation in organization change. However, the process of developing participation now seems more complicated than it appeared when we began. It still seems reasonable to start with a nucleus of strong men with experience in a problem which can be used as a focus for self-study. Beyond this, the following conditions appear to be essential:

1. Opportunities must be available for each member to participate in reaching some concrete goals, and for each to perceive himself and the group as competent to achieve expected outcomes.

2. Freedom for individuals to work out their own way of contributing must be offered within the framework of clearly defined and agreed-upon goals.

3. A group culture must be built which fosters the feeling of being a part of something worth doing and something with which one can cope.

4. The study group process must provide a challenging uncomfortableness without rigidifying panic in facing the problems of organization change.

5. Strategies must be available for coping with the constraints within which groups must operate.

6. Provision must be made for the new culture to plan for and survive confrontations with the existing culture.

7. Strategies must be developed for furthering self-study development within the organization beyond the creation of the new culture nucleus.

8. Opportunities must be given for expanding leadership roles in the expanding new culture.

9. Leaders must be working models of the self-study method in operation.

10. Staff must provide opportunities for self-development but must also provide viable role models by sharing in the work.

11. Inputs from outside resources must be utilized wherever need for them develops out of the group's own efforts at fact-gathering and problem solving.

Epilogue

We have begun to evolve a prescription for change; as we trace its borders, we find them to vary in strength, clarity and need for buttressing. This fact need not surprise us.

The transition from alienation to participation, from passivity to activity, involves learning and consolidation. Like the acquisition of skill, it requires experiences which bridge the transition from clumsiness to ease, and from doubt to assurance. The long-distance runner starts not only with groping and crawling, but with a stationary self-view. The actor must not only experience impact, but learn to view himself as potent and responsible.

This view does not come easily. Decades ago, McGregor noted that change involves a battle against the comforts of dependence and resentments to it. Cynicism and passivity (especially among the alienated) are born of failure; alienation breeds self-doubt, which fears tests and discounts results. Alienation also breeds mistrust, which sees helping hands as threatening gestures. To "neutralize alienation" is a phrase that denotes a shifting, accommodating strategy. The "change agent" must become a "quick-change" agent. At one point invisible and unobtrusive, he must at another be heavily present; at one point supportive, he must at another withdraw; sometimes sustaining, he must become often uninvolved. The junctures matter. To allow a man to "swim" may cause him to sink; to provide structure may make a man a spectator of his own mission.

The road from alienation to agency is bordered by support and by freedom. The graded, sensitive dispensing of these commodities governs not only the progress of change, but its stability and capacity for survival.

Prologue

The story this book has told is incomplete. The initiation of change, with its complexity, presents fewer problems than change maintenance and acceleration. This is critical, for initiating reform is sterile if we fail to keep change alive and cumulating.

The temptation to stability is enormous. Kurt Lewin (among

others) has noted that all forces, including those we manipulate, tend — when moved — to return to roost. History is replete with splendid experiments that joined the dust from which they arose. Brave movements of the past are tomorrow's diehard institutions, as stultifying and unresponsive as their precursors. Idealism curdles, and the sons of the brave spend lives in ritual and routine.

We have seen that the problem of motivating change is one of building confidence, cementing potency, instilling a sense of agency and worth. We build change agents by orchestrating challenges and conquests, trials and comforts, problems and successes along a road bordered by smugness and defeat. The dangers are real, but the errors redeemable.

Change maintenance is much harder. Success harbors seeds of failure. Rewards of change return— not as incentives, but as sources of decay. Change attained becomes terminal, a product, a thing to be savored, packaged, promoted, formalized. The system closes, movement stops, and change dies.

The reason is obvious. Change-initiation is future-oriented, regarding What Is as imperfect, improvable, open to question. The mind explores. But as new ideas are accepted and implemented, What Might Be becomes the unquestioned present, a new orthodoxy, a repository of faith, an investment. Innovators acquire a stake in innovations; for economy's sake, they name, define and formalize; they spread The Word, registering adoptions as signposts to progress.

If we do not take care, our effort must suffer this fate. Our police pioneers will clear their brush, plant seeds, and settle down. They will become stale and resistant to change. They will guard their formulas, their files, and their resources. Theirs will become a dead slot in a sterile chart.

Is this fate inevitable? We think not. The safeguard, we feel, lies in self-study and in its uses. The "uses," here, are critical. Change-related research has a way of being reactive and autonomous. It is reactive because it is evaluative and promotional. As it catalogues success or failure, it leads change agents to shrugs or tears, but not to new and different types of change. Outside evaluation is prescribed, to preclude incest. Research and action run parallel courses; the researcher looks at the change agent, and assesses his work. The change agent may take heart from the outsider's data, or be discouraged by them. But he is not involved. Nor is he guided, instructed, deflected, or impelled.

We hope for research and change more closely linked. We see

research as a component supplying continuous feedback and guidance. We see a link that is prompt, concrete, peremptory — an inescapable antidote to faith.

The human requisite of our model is the change agent-researcher. Innovations must be research-based, and must pose research questions; new services must have mechanisms for feedback and self-inventory. We assume that new facts must lead to new ideas: deficits must produce innovation and new trials, which must be followed by new and different inquiries.

Such is the model and the logic. Will it work for the police? In time, we hope to know. In the interim, this report must end — like all change inventories, with a proloque.

Such is the model and the logic. Will it work? In time, we hope to know. In the interim, this report must end — like all change inventories, with a prologue.

APPENDICES

I • Information Bulletins

Violence Prevention Program

As we know, Oakland police officers are facing increasing levels of violence in the execution of their duties. Building upon the experience garnered in a previously performed study of assaults on Oakland police officers, a program to determine the causes of violence directed against the police has been initiated within the Department by a professional study team composed of Dr. Hans Toch and Mr. Ray Galvin, faculty members of the School of Criminal Justice, State University of New York at Albany. The study team will provide technical assistance and direction for a selected group of officers of this Department who will themselves research the causes of police-directed violence and develop preventive and precautionary procedures which can be used to lessen the incidence of attacks against police. Eventually, a "Violence Prevention Unit" will be created, which will have as its ultimate purpose the reduction of such incidents.

A group consisting of seven patrolmen has been formed to begin the program. These men will serve both as a research unit and as a training unit. Following an initial discussion and orientation period, the seven officers will interview other members of the Department, conduct records searches and undertake related research. Under the direction of the professional study team, the seven members will attempt to identify those situations which typically result in violent attacks on police and the kinds of calls which present the greatest danger of violent attack. The emphasis in the research will be upon *incidents* rather than upon *individuals.*

During the initial phase of the program, large numbers of situations and the entire range of police methods will be compared and evaluated. An attempt will be made to discern recurring patterns of police procedure which seem to lead to a violent response. It is possible that some traditional police practices which are lawful in nature will be found to commonly result in a violent response.

Methods which seem to decrease the likelihood of such violent responses will be identified if possible; many members may have developed techniques which make them less susceptible to attack. The Violence Prevention Program will provide a means to investigate the value of these various techniques and will facilitate the interchange of information among members. At the conclusion of this phase of the program, the seven officers in the group will be in a position to offer recommendations concerning methods and procedures.

The second phase of the program will consist of the training of other members of the Department. During this phase of the program, a Violence Prevention Unit will be organized.

The purpose of the program is to assist all members in predicting violent acts which may be directed against them, and to develop techniques and procedures which can minimize the prevalence of such attacks. The Violence Prevention Unit will inform itself — and ultimately all members of the Department — of the methods which will reduce the likelihood of attack while accomplishing police objectives.

Field Training Program

During his first year of service, a probationary officer is expected to progress from the status of novice to that of competent police officer. The Department has attempted to accomplish this transition through a three-phase process consisting of formal classroom training, a brief supervised field experience and assignment as a regular officer.

The process has suffered from a number of shortcomings, not the least of which has been a lack of centralized planning, direction and control over the developmental phase. To meet these limitations, the Department is presently implementing a Field Training Program based upon the premise that it must designate the highest priority to the development of new officers.

To provide the necessary leadership for the Program, the position of Field Training Coordinator has been created and placed in the Office of the Deputy Chief, Bureau of Field Operations.

The new Field Training Program features two elements which are particularly noteworthy. First, each probationary officer's progress will be monitored from the moment of his induction to the completion of his probationary year. His overall performance will be supervised by the Field Training Coordinator, and particular attention will be given to the trainee during his participation in the newly designed eighteen week field training period. The probationary patrolman will receive his field training experience on the beat under the guidance of beat officers.

Second, the Program includes a detailed procedure for the selection, training, certification and assignment of Field Training Officers. This process calls for the nomination of candidates for the position of Field Training Officer by patrolmen presently assigned to the Patrol Division, the Preventive Services Division and the Youth Services Section. While any qualified patrolman may be nominated, for the present at least only those officers working Patrol beat assignments will participate in the certification process and be designated as Field Training Officers. Should a nominated officer who is not now serving on a Patrol beat assignment transfer to such an assignment he will then become eligible to participate in the certification process and to attain the designation of Field Training Officer.

After nomination, the names will be forwarded to the Field Training Coordinator for compilation. The list of candidates will then be submitted to the chain of command for comment. The entire list with appropriate comments will then be forwarded to the Chief of Police for final review, with the officers selected being given a place on the eligibility list. These officers will be contacted to ascertain if they wish to participate in the Program. If they do, they will undergo an orientation and be formally designated as Field Training Officers. They will then be utilized in this capacity as the need arises.

If probationary officers are to receive the required amount of quality training, it is of the utmost importance that this Program be properly executed. Proper execution depends to a great degree on the extent of cooperation and participation that can be secured from all levels of the Department. It is therefore urged that all officers participate to the fullest extent whenever their assistance is sought.

Family Crisis Intervention Program

The police have, of necessity, assumed responsibility for providing twenty-four hour service for the mediation and solution of family crises that have reached the stage of physical abuse. These disputes are of a complexity and dimension that place undue aggravations upon the time and resources of the beat officer assigned. Approximately one-third of all homicides and even more assaults take place in the family. Even more startling, 22 percent of all policemen killed nationally and about 40 percent of those injured meet their difficulty while intervening in a family disturbance situation.[1] "While family life has a moderating effect upon suicide, it rather stimulates murder."[2]

In order to deal with these problems realistically and effectively, officers must restore order, prevent injury, and, at the same time, assist the disputants in finding lasting solutions to their own problems — solutions that will eliminate the need for repeated police involvement. The approach to these disturbances should thus be that of problem solving — usually by referral — and crisis management and not necessarily that of arrest and prosecution.

It should be noted here that the preferred course, inherent in this Program, is to enhance the professional competence of the officer and to protect his basic identity as a working policeman — *not* to train him as a social worker or psychologist. Police are untrained and ill-equipped to *treat* psychological and social pathology. It is not, moreover, the purpose of this Program to make them so. Officers can be competent, however, to *identify* a vast range of ills — health problems, social hardships, housing problems, employment difficulties and mental illness — all of which, when they lead to turmoil, have been too broadly categorized as "family disputes."

In furtherance of these objectives, the Oakland Police Department on 11 Jan, 71 will institute a Family Crisis Intervention Program (FCIP) on a six-month experimental basis. This bulletin is to inform all personnel of the purpose, structure and goals of this project.

Background: The New York Experience

The original Family Crises Intervention Unit was implemented in mid-1967 by Dr. Morton Bard in the New York City Police Department under an LEAA grant to the City College of New York. The two-year program involved eighteen patrolmen selected from among 45 volunteers on the basis of brief interviews to determine motivation, interest, and suitability for the duties anticipated. Participation in the FCIU offered no reward other than three college credits and an opportunity to become particularly adept in the management of family disputes.

The first month of the Program was devoted to intensive training, involving full-time attendance at lectures, seminars, group discussions, film sessions, workshops, and "learning-by-doing" in professionally performed family-dispute scenes. Thereafter, members worked in uniform around the clock and performed all police functions, but in addition, whenever a known family disturbance occurred in their precinct area, their radio car would be dispatched, regardless of the sector of its occurrence. An integral part of the program, of course, was the utilization of referral agencies.

The program sought "to demonstrate the effective utilization of selected police officers in a program of crime prevention and preventive mental health."[3] This statement subsumes three specific goals: to prevent crime, to make early identification of mental health problems, and to reduce injuries to police officers. *In reducing injuries to police officers,* the New York experience is heartening, indeed, for during the entire two years, not a single injury was sustained by an FCIU member. By contrast, two members of the regular patrol force in the FCIU precinct and one patrolman in the control precinct were injured while intervening in family disputes. *In the early identification of mental health problems,* it is impossible to determine from the data gathered by the program whether the FCIU made any impact. It would be assumed that it did, but there was, unfortunately, no adequate follow-up research conducted to determine whether the referrals were utilized and, if so, utilized effectively. *In the prevention of crime,* again, the data were inconclusive. The only positive finding was that of the five family homicides occurring in the FCIU precinct, not a single one of the families concerned had been known to the FCIU.

The differences between the Oakland FCIP and the New York FCIU will be discussed below.

The Oakland Program

A Statistical Description of Family Disputes in Oakland. Research conducted by the Department shows that in the first six months of 1970 (January-June) officers responded to more than 16,000 family disturbance calls. The expenditure in man hours exceeded 8,000. *Twenty-five percent* of the assignments were return calls. The majority of these called-for services occurred between the hours of 1900 and 0300, Wednesday through Sunday. The calls, finally, occurred predominantly in two geographical areas of the City: Districts Three and Five. (Both districts are densely populated primarily by low income persons who are black or Mexican-American).

Purposes. The Oakland Family Crisis Intervention Program has the following objectives:

1. to improve police capability of restoring order in the family crisis;
2. to assist families in resolving the tensions which give rise to disputes by referring them to appropriate helping agencies;
3. to minimize further police involvement by providing solutions before serious physical injury results;
4. to establish liaison between the police and other community service agencies, which would provide specialized services in the solution of family crises that would otherwise present a continuing police problem;
5. to enhance police-community relations by making more competent services available to the community; and
6. to free beat officers for other police activities by decreasing the number of family disturbances to which they must respond.

Structure: Field Units. The field units (FCIU's) of the Family Crisis Intervention Program will be assigned to the Patrol Division and will consist of two, two-man teams in unmarked vehicles whose primary responsibility will be the family disturbance assignment. Secondarily, the teams will respond to other disturbances of the peace, emergency dispatched assignments, and preventive patrol. Hours of operation will be 1900-0300, Wednesday through Sunday.

It was thought that the value of the Family Crisis Intervention Program could ultimately be best determined if units were placed in those areas of the City having the highest occurrence of family disturbance calls. Accordingly, one team, with radio designation F-3, will be assigned to District Three, while the other, F-5, will operate in District Five. Street supervision will be provided by the regular district sergeants. District Four will be maintained as a "control area," into which these units will not be assigned, except in extreme emergencies.

Through the use of a "Family Disturbance" form completed after each assignment, both field unit members and the staff unit of the

Program will maintain a record of each family dispute handled. Information from these records will be utilized both in the handling of individual disputes and in the overall evaluation of the project.

Structure: Staff Unit. Responsibility for coordinating field unit activities will rest in the experimental Project Section Coordinator of the Violence Prevention Unit, who will

1. implement training programs for unit members;
2. maintain liaison with referral agencies;
3. maintain unit records and statistics;
4. conduct follow-ups with individuals involved in family disturbances to ascertain whether additional services are needed and whether the individual utilized the referral service recommended; and
5. determine the utility and success of agency referrals.

Selection Criteria of Field Unit Members. Selection of field unit personnel was predicated upon the following criteria:

1. The member must have volunteered to work with the Program.
2. The member must have demonstrated a capability of calming disturbances and maintaining control throughout the call with minimal friction between himself and those involved.
3. The member must have demonstrated a willingness to utilize the service and problem-solving approach to the family disturbance.
4. The member must have had recent street experience.

Referral Services. A critical aspect of the Family Crisis Intervention Program will be its utilization of referral services. Families and individuals having a need for additional services will be referred to the agency or agencies most likely capable of resolving the problem. To the extent that these agencies are able to provide effective guidance in the solution of family crisis, the family will be helped meaningfully and called-for police services will be reduced.

The following agencies, listed with a description of relevant services available, have agreed to participate in the program.

1. *Alameda County Health Department.* The Alameda

County Health Department provides an extensive list of services to residents of this county. Their services relevant to Family Crisis Intervention are the enforcement of laws pertaining to unsanitary houses and yards, garbage and sewage disposal, and restaurants and stores where food is sold; psychiatric treatment, depending upon the needs of the patient; Family Planning Clinic (Medi-Cal recipients are referred to private physicians); and medical services such as pregnancy tests, chest X-rays, venereal disease diagnosis and treatment, and public-health nursing.

2. *Alameda County Welfare Department.* The Welfare Department offers financial relief to qualified applicants, as well as emergency food services to persons who have not established qualifications for welfare funds.

3. *Catholic Social Service.* This agency offers professional pre-marital, marriage and family counseling. A program for counseling and medical care is available for the unwed parent. Fee is determined by family income and no restrictions are made on the grounds of income, race, religion, or sex.

4. *Family Service Bureau of the East Bay.* The Bureau provides professional counseling for marital problems, parent-child difficulties, mentally disturbed individuals (including children), and unwed parents. This agency also offers assistance to the aged. Fee is determined by income.

5. *Jewish Family Service.* Services are offered only to members of the Jewish faith: pre-marital and marital counseling; temporary financial aid to meet emergencies; assistance to the aged in such events as death in the family, chronic illness, inadequate income or loneliness; counseling for juvenile problems; and a refugee and child placement service. Fee is determined by income.

6. *Legal Aid Society of Alameda County.* Legal Aid provides legal representation for low income persons without fees in civil cases (for example, divorce, landlord-tenant matters, bankruptcy, and the like).

7. *Synanon Foundation, Inc.* Synanon provides counseling

and complete communal living for persons with what Synanon describes as "character disorders," including drug addiction, alcoholism, chronic gambling and the like. In addition, "Synanon games" are open to non-residents of Synanon and would provide family disputants with an outlet for the release of hostile emotions and might afford solutions to underlying problems.

8. *Wage Earner Plan.* The Wage Earner Plan provides information and remedial suggestions for over indebtedness. This service is of principal value to those who are regularly employed or, at least employable. Fees are set only if the person utilizes the Wage Earner Plan pursuant to Chapter 13 of the Bankruptcy Act, and, in that event, fees are set by the Court and payable to the Wage Earner Plan.

Comparing Oakland's Program with New York's

Oakland's FCIP was inspired by the New York City program. In their underlying goals and modes of operation, they are markedly similar. There are, however, a number of notable differences. First, New York City took a month at considerable expense to provide formal training for its FCIU members. In addition, weekly in-service training sessions were required. Oakland, believing this to be unnecessary, is relying upon the good judgment and experience of officers recommended by peers and chosen through interviews. FCIU members will spend the initial day of the Program in a seminar setting with Department heads and other representatives of the participating referral agencies. Field operations will begin the following day. No other training is provided for, except that frequent group meetings will be held for the purpose of self-evaluation and program development.

Second, because of the complex educational program, New York's FCIU members were frozen in their responsibilities for the full two-year period of operations. By contrast, FCIU members in Oakland are requested but not required to remain for the six-month duration of the project. If a member learns through experience that he is not capable of offering the services he initially anticipated, he can discuss his difficulties with the program coordinator and, if he remains dissatisfied, will then be re-assigned. A number of officers were selected as alternates to fill vacancies occasioned by illness, vacation, or re-assignment.

Third, in New York relevant comparative data were available in only a few select areas: homicide, injury to officers, and the number of return calls. Data were not available to permit a comparison of family assaults during FCIU operations with family assaults before operations. It was impossible, therefore, to determine whether the FCIU had a preventive effect upon family assaults. Oakland's data, however, will allow comparison of the impact of the FCIP upon all violent acts that occur in the home (homicide, assault with a deadly weapon, and battery). In short, although the New York results do not demonstrate failure, they are too inconclusive to demonstrate success. It is hoped that success or failure in Oakland will be more readily apparent.

Unlike Oakland, moreover, New York considered it an invasion of individual rights to conduct follow-up inquiries with the family involved. The program's attempt to acquire information about the effectiveness of referrals was limited to the submission to referral agencies of routine inquiries, which elicited a disappointing number of replies. Oakland, on the contrary, considers it in the best interest of the family to inquire whether that family took advantage of the referral and, if so, whether the referral agency was successful in providing assistance. The follow-ups, in addition, will determine whether the family needs additional aid and will provide valuable data for use in ultimate and on-going program evaluation.

Landlord-Tenant Intervention Program (LTIP)

Summary

As a result of a 16-month experimental Landlord-Tenant Dispute Settlement Program, a new Landlord-Tenant Intervention Unit is now being established in the Conflict Management Section.[4] It is believed to be the first of its kind in the nation.

Rather than dismiss landlord-tenant calls as "civil matters," the Unit will attempt to achieve a settlement of the dispute, often by referring the parties to other agencies, such as the Small Claims Court. By early settlement of the dispute, the Unit is expected to deter violence that otherwise might occur.

The Unit will operate for an experimental period, after which time its operations will be evaluated and its methodology, if found to be effective, utilized throughout the Department.

The Unit is presently operating Monday through Friday, 1000 to 1800 hours, and can be reached at 273-3231.

Introduction

Police departments historically have treated landlord-tenant matters, at least in their initial and non-violent stages, as being "civil only," and often the best efforts of the most competent officers will serve only to accomplish a temporary truce between the parties. At worst, the officer is called to the scene, and having had little or no training in the complexities of landlord-tenant law, he simply becomes another party to the dispute. The result may be an arrest or arrests for disturbing the peace, breaking and entering, malicious mischief, or even more serious offenses.

In late 1969, the Legal Advisor, Mrs. Linda Moody, undertook a limited experimental Landlord-Tenant Dispute Settlement Program designed to prevent the escalation of minor grievances into serious offenses by the mediation of disputes and the accomplishment of settlements that are lawful and equitable to both parties. The program is believed to be the first of its kind in the nation and has operated so effectively that it is being made a part of the Conflict Management Section (formerly the Violence Prevention Unit).

Landlord-tenant disputes have been common in Oakland, as in other large cities. Research here discloses that at least 90 landlord-tenant disputes are reported in Oakland every month. Not infrequently, officers are called by a tenant whose belongings have been seized by the landlord. Although the occurrence may resemble a burglary, officers have been governed in the past by Departmental policy and procedure that such incidents are "civil matters" and that there is nothing the officer can do. Twenty-five minutes later, a call might come in again from the same address: battery or assault with a deadly weapon.

By the same token, a landlord, distraught that his building is rapidly deteriorating because of destructive tenants, has been given the same answer: the matter is civil; police cannot help. New methods employed by the Landlord-Tenant Intervention Program will permit officers to achieve just solutions in cases like the above.

Why Should Police Become Involved?

Oakland Police officers, of course, presently respond to landlord-tenant calls. They have not uniformly, however, — at least as directed by Departmental policy and procedure— utilized a problem-solving approach to these assignments. Several arguments support a change of direction.

First. Officers now answer landlord-tenant calls, which are often regarded as irritants: police are called because there is no one else available. Under present policy, responses are largely a waste of time both for the officer and the person who calls. At worst, the result is a disappointment to the citizen; a negative impression is created. Rather than contributing nothing to the solution of the dispute, officers should be equipped to facilitate a settlement, often attainable with no greater expenditure of time.

Second. Landlord-tenant disputes often lead to violent or otherwise more serious criminal offenses. Our past reporting practices have been insufficient to permit precise findings, though several incidents of serious violence are known. Thus, the Landlord-Tenant Intervention Program will seek both to prevent escalation and to determine the comparative incidence of violence resulting from those landlord-tenant disputes that are processed as "civil matters" only.

Third. The problem-solving approach to landlord-tenant disputes is designed to provide better service, not only to the complainant, but to the person complained against, as well. Most disputants coming to this Department for assistance lack the sophistication or motivation to seek a lawful settlement of the dispute. More often than not, in addition, both the landlord and the tenant are poor and when in need of help, turn automatically to the police. The Landlord-Tenant Intervention Unit, then, like the Family Crisis Intervention Unit,[5] is another development in the efforts of the Police Department to provide a better quality of service by competent police officers so as to best serve and help the citizens of our community.

Finally. Penal Code sections do exist to prohibit most harassment by landlords and tenants; these laws have virtually been ignored in the past.

Common Cases

Although the usual practive of the police has been to regard these cases as civil only, the fact is that Penal Code sections are often applicable. Abuses most commonly perpetrated by landlords fall primarily into five general categories.

1. *Lockout of the tenant, usually accompanied by the lock-in of the tenant's possessions.* A lockout is a misdemeanor prohibited by Section 418 of the Penal Code ("Forcible Entry or Detainer of Land. — Every person using or procuring, encouraging or assisting another to use, any force or violence in entering upon or detaining any lands or other possessions of another, except in cases and in the manner allowed by law, is guilty of a misdemeanor.")

2. *Seizure of the tenant's property.* Seizure of the tenant's property, similarly, is prohibited by Section 418, unless the seizure is made pursuant to a court order. *See* CAL. CIV. CODE 1861a (Supp. '71).[6]

3. *Removal of doors or windows.* Removal of doors or windows, or any other destruction of property, is considered to be malicious mischief, because the tenant's interest (a leasehold interest) is a real property interest[7] within the meaning of Penal Code Section 594.

4. *Trespass.* Occasionally a landlord will enter the tenant's premises without permission. If the entry is reasonable — for example, to inspect a leaking water pipe or to investigate smoke — it is not considered a trespass. Nor is it a trespass if authorized by the terms of the lease. Some entries, however, are made for purposes of harassing the tenant, snooping around, or other unreasonable purpose. These are trespasses. PEN. CODE 602.5 (unauthorized entry of a dwelling).

5. *Termination of services.* Interference with the tenant's ability to attain services, such as gas, electricity, and water, is also a common practice, but these cases, although misdemeanors under the Oakland Municipal Code, fall within the primary jurisdiction of the Oakland Building and Housing Department and are generally re-referred to that agency unless other offenses are involved as well.

Abuses most commonly perpetrated by tenants are:

1. *Destruction of the landlord's property.* Such conduct, of course, constitutes malicious mischief. Cal. Pen. Code 594.

2. *Refusal to pay rent.* Failure to pay rent is not a crime. Any person, however, "who shall knowingly and designedly, by any false or fraudulent representation or pretense, defraud any other person of . . . real . . . property . . . is guilty of theft. . . ." Cal. Pen. Code 484.

3. *Accumulation of garbage.* When a tenant allows garbage to accumulate, the matter is referred to the Oakland Building and Housing Department for disposition under the Oakland Municipal Code.

Methods of Settling Disputes

Effective handling of landlord-tenant disputes requires, of course, an understanding of applicable Penal Code provisions. The objective in such disputes, however, is not to make or encourage an arrest but to achieve a solution of the dispute by explaining to the parties what conduct is not lawful and by suggesting alternative solutions that are lawful. Thus, if a tenant is locked out, the officer would explain to the landlord that a lockout is unlawful (even if the tenant is behind in his rent), explain why it is unlawful, and suggest that the landlord either consult his attorney or go directly to Small Claims Court, which has jurisdiction to evict in almost all cases coming to the attention of this Department.

When the landlord is unwilling to terminate the offense, it would be made clear to him that criminal proceedings can be initiated by the tenant if compliance is not forthcoming. Experience demonstrates that this tactic will virtually always accomplish compliance. In all but one of the 100 cases handled during the experimental period, a result was obtained that was considered equitable and fair: either the landlord complied or was vindicated by the production of extenuating or justifying circumstances, the controversy ended because the tenant moved, or the complainant was referred to another agency. In the one case considered to be a failure, the landlord resided in a distant jurisdiction and immediately left Oakland after culminating the offense.

The Rationale Prohibiting Self Help

In *Jordan v. Talbot*, 55 Cal. 2d 597, 12 Cal. Rptr. 488, 361 P. 2d 20 (1961), the California Supreme Court summarized the law applicable to "self-help" evictions, that is, those evictions achieved by the landlord's own action, usually by force, threat of force, or some other unlawful act: " [A]bsent a voluntary surrender of the premises by the tenant, the landlord [can] enforce his right of reentry only by judicial process, not by self-help. . . . [A] provision in the lease expressly permitting a forcible entry would be void as contrary to the public policy. . . . Regardless of who has the right to possession, orderly procedure and preservation of the peace require that the actual possession shall not be disturbed except by legal process." 55 Cal. 2d at 604-05. The statute prohibiting forcible entries "was intended to prevent bloodshed, violence and breaches of the peace, too likely to result from wrongful entries into the possession of others. . . ." (607).

Although *Jordan v. Talbot* was a decision interpreting the *civil* statute on forcible entry and detainer, *Daluiso v. Boone*, 71 Cal. 2d 484, 78 Cal. Rptr. 707, 455 P. 2d. 811 (1969), makes it clear that Penal Code Section 418 is also applicable in such cases. The Court also added to its rationale prohibiting self help, explaining that under ancient common law

> one entitled to the possession of land was privileged to enter and use such force, short of death or serious bodily harm, as reasonably appeared necessary to the repossession. . . . It soon became obvious, however, that allowing one to recover his land by force contributed greatly to breaches of the public peace and gave "an opportunity to powerful men, under the pretense of feigned titles, forcibly to eject their weaker neighbors, and also by force to retain their wrongful possession. . . ." 71 Cal. 2d at 490-91.

> "It is a general principle that one who is or believes he is injured or deprived of what he is lawfully entitled to must apply to the state for help. Self help is in conflict with the very idea of the social order. It subjects the weaker to risk of the arbitrary will or mistaken belief of the stronger. Hence the law in general forbids it." Quoting 5 POUND, JURISPRUDENCE 142, at 351-52 (1959). 71 Cal. 2d at 500.

The experimental program has yielded the following conclusions. First, constructive police intervention fills, in great measure, the "remedy gap" between civil and criminal law. Civil remedies for illegal lockouts and seizures of property, simply because they take time, are not effective. (For example, a woman who is locked out of her home at night with three children by her side has no time to seek a court injunction. "See a lawyer," is absurd advice. The threat of criminal sanction, however, communicated by a uniformed police officer to a recalcitrant landlord virtually always accomplishes a termination of the offense.) Second, it is thought that a failure to enforce those Penal Code sections applicable to landlord-tenant disputes (see above) would constitute a "double standard." In short, laws are on the books that protect both the landlord and the tenant; the police responsibility to enforce each with equal vigor is beyond question. Third, police involvement serves to accommodate competing interests in an equitable and effective way and, perhaps most important, is preventive of both minor and serious offenses, some violent, that might have occurred if the parties had been left to their own "self-help" devices.

To attain an objective appraisal of dispute-settlement methodology, two University of California students (Robert Foster and Bryan Gaynor) were invited to study the handling of landlord-tenant disputes by the Oakland Police. They determined the incidence of landlord-tenant calls and the nature of the disposition of each case, as handled both by the Patrol Division and in the experimental program. They determined that the experimental program was handling only five percent of the total number of calls, and that the Patrol Division was processing the balance in diverse ways, with a marked inclination to treat each case as a civil matter. [Treatment of cases as civil matters, of course, has been in complete accord with stated Departmental policy, and, thus, entirely proper. See Training Bulletin: "Civil Disputes," III-J, Revised, pp. 4-7 (8 Aug. 69).]

Their research showed, in addition, that calls occurred in a cyclical pattern that peaked in a period roughly between the 26th of one month and the 5th and 6th of the next, and that calls were concentrated in the time period from 9 a.m. and 5 p.m. Landlord-tenant disputes are a daytime phenomenon.

Creation of New Unit

In order to broaden the scope of the experimental program, a new Landlord-Tenant Intervention Program has been established in the Conflict Management Section. The program is designated the Landlord-Tenant Intervention Unit (LTIU); it will handle all landlord-tenant calls in Oakland to the extent that time and availability permits.

This summer the Unit has operated under the supervision of one police officer assigned to the Conflict Management Section and with the assistance of Miss Nancy Sevitch and Mr. Robert Foster, both recent graduates of the University of California funded under a grant from the Center on Administration of Criminal Justice at the University of California, Davis.

A major grant has recently been awarded by the National Institute of Mental Health to the Research Foundation of the State University of New York for "Research on Violence Prevention by Police" in Oakland. The grant will be directed by Hans Toch, as Principal Investigator, and J. Douglas Grant, as Co-Principal Investigator, and includes funds for two police officers to operate the Landlord-Tenant Unit for a six-month experimental period, dividing the City into one demonstration area and one control area. Thereafter, the Unit will be evaluated so that a determination can be made whether its methodology should be utilized throughout the Department.

The goal is to enhance police competence. Officers can develop the ability to identify the causes of landlord-tenant disputes, to refer these disputants to the proper agencies for resolution, and in some cases achieve settlement without the necessity of referral. Results from this program are anticipated to fill the existing remedy gap, render equitable assistance to both parties, and accomplish a fair settlement of the dispute without the necessity of arrest and prosecution. The Department now provides 24-hour, seven-day-a-week service in landlord-tenant disputes. The only difference under the new program will be "better" service, in the sense that solutions will be sought before the dispute has an opportunity to escalate.

Referral Services

A critical aspect of the Program will be its utilization of referral services. Landlords and tenants in need of additional services will be referred to the agency or agencies most likely capable of resolving their problem. To the extent that these agencies are able to provide effective guidance in the solution of landlord-tenant problems, citizens will be given meaningful assistance and calls for police services will be reduced.

The following agencies, listed with a description of relevant services available, have agreed to participate in the program.

1. *Alameda County District Attorney's Office.* The District Attorney's Office will be relied on in those cases where criminal proceedings or citation hearings are called for.

2. *Alameda County Health Department.* The Bureau of Sanitation is responsible for enforcing laws and codes applicable to housing occupancy. It will investigate source and

contributing causes of rats, mice, broken sewers, and give technical advice on insect problems.

3. *Alameda County Welfare Department*. The Welfare Department offers financial relief to qualified applicants, as well as emergency food services to persons who have not established qualifications for Welfare funds.

4. *Alameda County Legal Aid Society*. Legal Aid provides legal representation for low-income persons without fees in civil cases [for example, divorce, landlord-tenant matters, bankruptcy, and the like].

5. *Oakland Building and Housing Department*. The Housing Division can investigate and compel the landlord or the tenant to correct any existing housing code violations.

6. *Oakland-Piedmont Small Claims Court*. The Small Claims Court has jurisdiction to hear civil claims in the amount of $300 or less. The court has jurisdiction to evict in unlawful detainer actions, after default in rent for residential property where the term of tenancy is not greater than month-to-month and where the whole amount is not more than $300. Unlike eviction proceedings brought in the Municipal Court, there is a 21-day waiting period between the judgment date and the date on which the plaintiff can obtain a writ of execution to regain possession of his real property.

[1]Bard, *Family Intervention Police Teams as a Community Mental Health Resource*, 60 J. CRIM. L., C. & P.S. 247, 248 (1969).

[2]E. Durkheim, *Suicide* 354 (1951).

[3]Bard, *Training Police as Specialists in Family Crisis Intervention*, U.S. Dept. of Justice NO. PR 70-1, at 3 (1970).

[4]Formerly, the Violence Prevention Unit.

[5]See Oakland Police Department Information Bulletin, "Family Crisis Intervention Program," (18 Jan. 71).

[6]Landlords are no longer permitted to hold a tenant's property as security for unpaid rent, except with a court order. Cal. Civ. Code 1861, applicable to hotels, motels, inns, boardinghouses, and lodginghouses, was held unconstitutional by the United States District Court. Klim v. Jones, 315 F. Supp. 109 (N.D. Cal. 1970). Cal. Civ. Code 1861a, applicable to apartment houses, apartments, and cottages, has been revised by the 1970 California legislature to require a court order before the landlord enters to take possession of the property.

[7]E.g., San Pedro, L.A. & S.L.R. Co. v. Los Angeles, 180 Cal. 18, 21, 179 P. 393 (1919).

II • Other Departmental Documents

Special Order No. 1400

To: All Members
Subject: Critical Incident Questionnaire

Recently a Critical Incident Questionnaire was completed by a limited number of members of various ranks, including the Chief, at the request of the Violence Prevention Unit.

The results of the Questionnaire suggest that a great degree of confusion exists as regards Departmental policy and, in some cases, interpretation of the law itself. In order to determine how extensive the confusion is, why it exists, and how to correct it, more information is needed from various members of the Department. Therefore, each sergeant and each patrolman in the following organizational units will complete a copy of the Questionnaire and submit it through channels to the Chief's office: Patrol Division, Preventive Services Division, Youth Section of Community Relations and Youth Division.

Each sergeant and patrolman who completes the Questionnaire shall enter his name, rank, serial number and present assignment in the space provided on the form.

The commanding officers of the above named organizational units shall use an alphabetical roster to ensure that each designated member receives and completes a copy of the Questionnaire. A date entry shall be placed after the member's name when he is given the Questionnaire and a date entry shall be placed after his name when the Questionnaire is returned by the member. The alphabetical listing and the Questionnaires (compiled in alphabetical order) shall be forwarded to the Chief's office by the date designated.

By order of

C. R. Gain
Chief of Police

Critical Incident Questionnaire

For each of the following situations, please indicate what you would do. Answer the questions using *only* the information we are providing; do not read into the statements anything that is not within the context of the wording. We know that this may make for some difficult decisions!

Incident 1
Time: 2100
Location: 23rd Avenue & E. 24th Street
Assignment: 415 Comp. refused
Subject: MN, 30
Appearance and Activity: Officer approaches scene and hears
    sound of argument. Officer knocks. Argument stops. Door
    opened by subject wearing T-shirt. Officer asks if police
    needed. Subject says, "No, pig!" and slams door in officer's
    face.

Do you think you would take further action?

If *Yes*, do you think you'd make an arrest?

If you think you'd take action *other than arrest*, what would you be most likely to do?

Incident 2
Time: 2300
Location: 93rd Avenue & B Street
Assignment:
Subject: MN, 15
Appearance and Activity: Officer observes subject loitering on cor-
    ner. Officer stops car, gets out to approach subject. Subject
    runs 75 feet to a house and enters front door.

Do you think you would take further action?

If *yes*, do you think you would make an arrest?

If you think you'd take action *other than arrest* what would you be most likely to do?

Incident 3
Time: 2230
Location: 54th & San Pablo
Assignment:
Subject: 40-50 MN & FN juvs.
Appearance and Activity: Driving by, officer observes 40-50 MN & FN juvs. at the ¼ lb. hamburger stand. Someone in crowd shouts obscenities at officer as he approaches.

Do you think you would take further action?

If *yes*, do you think you would make an arrest?

If you think you'd take action *other than arrest*, what would you be most likely to do?

Incident 4
Time: 0130
Location: 1900 Block San Pablo
Assignment:
Subject: Three sailors
Appearance and Activity: Officer driving in unmarked vehicle observes 3 sailors, obviously under the influence, staggering across the street toward waiting cab. One sailor bumps against officer's vehicle and gives officer the finger.

Do you think you would take further action?

If *yes*, do you think you would make an arrest?

If you think you'd take action *other than arrest*, what would you be most likely to do?

Incident 5
Time: 0100
Location: 85th E. 14th, IFO 85 Club
Assignment:
Subject: 4 Vehicles double parked, all attended. About 20 MN & FN's in front of club.
Appearance and Activity: Officer drives by slowly and is obviously seen by drivers of double-parked cars. Officer continues on and notes in rear view mirror that vehicles are not being moved.

Do you think you would take further action?

If *yes*, do you think you would make an arrest or issue a citation?

If you think you'd take action *other than arrest*, what would you be most likely to do?

Incident 6
Time: 2330
Location: 2500 – 25th Avenue
Assignment:
Subject: 4 MN's in '64 Ford
Appearance and Activity: Officer drives by noting vehicle in street
        with headlights on. After officer passes, vehicle starts to
        drive away slowly.

Do you think you would take further action?

If *yes*, do you think you would make an arrest?

If you think you'd take action *other than arrest*, what would you be most likely to do?

Incident 7
Time: 0200
Location: 1800 – 101st Avenue
Assignment:
Subject: MN in late 20's walking NB on 101st Avenue slowly in high
        frequency 10851 V.C. area.
Appearance and Activity: Officer stops subject, asks for name and
        address. Subject identifies himself as John Smith of 1901
        101st Avenue. Officer explains 10851 problem and says he
        wants to detain subject for further information. Subject says,
        "No, I gave you my name and address," and walks away.

Do you think you would take further action?

If *yes*, do you think you would make an arrest?

If you think you'd take action *other than arrest*, what would you be most likely to do?

Incident 8
Time: 1830
Location: 85th and E. 14th Street

Assignment:
Subject: Young MN
Appearance and Activity: Subject well dressed in suit and tie is
    selling tins of coffee to citizens on sidewalk.

Do you think you would take further action?

If *yes*, do you think you would make an arrest?

If you think you'd take action *other than arrest*, what would you be
most likely to do?

Incident 9
Time: 0400
Location: 59th and Herzog
Assignment:
Subject: MN 39
Appearance and Activity: Subject dressed in work clothing slashing
    tires on 67 Olds jointly owned but driven by wife.

Do you think you would take further action?

If *yes*, do you think you would make an arrest?

If you think you'd take action *other than arrest*, what would you be
most likely to do?

Incident 10
Time: 1400
Location: 10th and Pine
Assignment:
Subject: 4 MN's
Appearance and Activity: Subjects dressed in Panther attire mak-
    ing major repairs on '56 pink Buick on the street, at the curb.
    One is overheard referring to "pig."

Do you think you would take further action?

If *yes*, do you think you would make an arrest?

If you think you'd take action *other than arrest*, what would you be
most likely to do?

Incident 11
Time: 0500
Location: Campbell Village

Assignment 415 F

Subject: MN & FN 25, 2 children FN 1 & 4

Appearance and Activity: Wife obviously beaten by husband, refuses
to sign complaint out of fear of further beating. Husband
states, "It's all over now." Loudly and aggressively insists
that officers leave at once.

Do you think you would take further action?

If *yes*, do you think you would make an arrest?

If you think you'd take action *other than arrest*, what would you be
most likely to do?

Incident 12

Time: 2300

Location: 7th and Willow

Assignment:

Subject: Young MW

Appearance and Activity: Officer conducting investigation of ADW
with cooperative suspect in rear seat of car. Subject comes
up to window and insists on talking to his friend, the suspect. Officer says no; the subject begins yelling to suspect
through the window, and continues after further warning.

Do you think you would take further action?

If *yes*, do you think you would make an arrest?

If you think you'd take action *other than arrest*, what would you be
most likely to do?

The Violence Prevention Unit

Mission

The Violence Prevention Unit has as its major goal the reduction
of violence during police-citizen contacts. Specifically, the Unit
will identify violence producing situations and aid personnel found
in these situations, undertake detailed analyses of circumstances and
individuals, design and implement preventive and remedial approaches for violence reduction, and evaluate the success or failure
of such approaches.

Organization

The Violence Prevention Unit is directly responsible to the Chief of Police. The Unit is organizationally assigned to the Office of the Chief of Police.

The Unit consists of three sections. These are the Action Review Section, the Training Research Section, and the Experimental Projects Section.

The Action Review Section will analyze in a non-punitive manner the activities of individuals who seem to be having difficulties during inter-personal contacts. Its activities will include the identification of such individuals, the review of their handling of inter-personal contacts, the convening of Action Review Panels, the discussion of cases, and the recommendation of remedial actions.

The Training Research Section will engage in a variety of developmental activities. It will plan, execute, and evaluate training programs dealing with violence reduction for clientele both inside and outside the Department. Of particular importance will be the Section's involvement in exploring new training approaches and applying them in the program of violence reduction.

The Experimental Projects Section will design, execute, and evaluate new organizational approaches to the problem of violence. Operational activities in areas where there is a high potential for violence will receive considerable attention.

FUNCTIONAL ORGANIZATION CHART

VIOLENCE PREVENTION UNIT

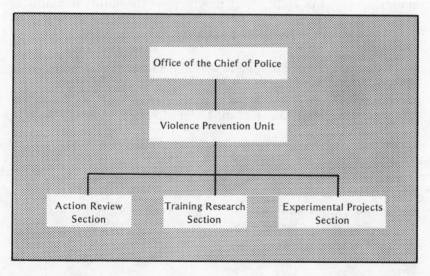

Positions Created as a Result of the Training Program

Title: Supervisor of the Violence Prevention Unit
Civil Service Class Title: Police Sergeant
Civil Service Code Number:
Division and Detail: Office of the Chief of Police, Violence Prevention Unit
Hours Assigned: 0830 – 1630
Number Assigned Position: One
Immediate Supervisor: Chief of Police
Number of Subordinates Supervised: Three

Duties and Responsibilities

The Supervisor of the Violence Prevention Unit plans, organizes, directs, and evaluates the Department's program of violence reduction.

He maintains continuous and effective liaison with all units of the Department. His activities require him to meet and correspond with representatives of governmental agencies, private organizations, and individual citizens.

He participates actively in all of the Unit's programs. He participates in training programs, serves as a member of the Action Review Panel, and participates in the development and execution of experimental projects.

He supervises and coordinates the activities of three patrolmen.

This officer is supervised by the Chief of Police. The position requires supervisory ability, verbal skills, and the ability to maintain effective inter-personal relationships. This officer should have ability as a small group leader and as an instructor.

Title: Coordinator of Training Research Section
Civil Service Class Title: Police Patrolman
Civil Service Code Number:
Division and Detail: Office of the Chief of Police, Violence Prevention Unit
Hours Assigned: 0830 – 1630
Number Assigned Position: One
Immediate Supervisor: Supervisor, Violence Prevention Unit

Duties and Responsibilities

The Coordinator of the Training Research Section is responsible for all the activities of his unit.

He maintains continuous and effective liaison with all units of the Department and representatives of public and private bodies insofar as the activities of his unit are concerned.

He plans, executes, and evaluates Departmental training efforts dealing with violence prevention; coordinates the Department's continued activities utilizing the self-study method of training for violence reduction; experiments with new training methods; coordinates the Violence Prevention Unit's tape recording program; maintains complete records on his section's activities.

He participates in the other functions of the Violence Prevention Unit as necessary.

This officer is supervised by the Supervisor of the Violence Prevention Unit. The position requires considerable verbal skill and the ability to maintain effective inter-personal relationships. This officer should also have ability as a small group leader and as an instructor.

Title: Coordinator of Action Review Section
Civil Service Class Title: Police Patrolman
Civil Service Code Number:
Division and Detail: Office of the Chief of Police, Violence Prevention Unit
Hours Assigned: 0830 – 1630
Number Assigned Position: One
Immediate Supervisor: Supervisor, Violence Prevention Unit

Duties and Responsibilities

The Coordinator of the Action Review Section is responsible for all the activities of his unit.

He maintains continuous and effective liaison with all units of the Department concerning the functions of his unit.

He reviews all records and reports necessary for initiating Action Review Panels; approves volunteer panel subjects or otherwise selects officers to be reviewed; initiates and conducts background investigations of the subjects to be interviewed; selects and notifies the officers to be assigned to the panels; serves as chairman of the review panels; completes post-interview reports; executes the necessary follow-up procedures; maintains complete records on his section's activities.

He participates in other functions of the Violence Prevention Unit as necessary.

This officer is supervised by the Supervisor of the Violence Pre-

vention Unit. The position requires considerable verbal skill and
the ability to maintain effective inter-personal relationships. This
officer should have ability as a small group leader.

Title: Coordinator of Experimental Projects Section
Civil Service Class Title: Police Patrolman
Civil Service Code Number:
Division and Detail: Office of the Chief of Police, Violence Preven-
    tion Unit
Hours Assigned: 0830 – 1630
Number Assigned Position: One
Immediate Supervisor: Supervisor, Violence Prevention Unit

Duties and Responsibilities

The Coordinator of the Experimental Projects Section is responsible for all the activities of his unit.

He maintains continuous and effective liaison with all units of
the Department and representatives of public and private bodies
insofar as the activities of his unit are concerned.

He designs, executes, and evaluates experimental projects, particularly of an operational nature, to improve the Department's
ability to reduce violence in police-citizen contacts (e.g., the proposed Family Crisis Intervention Unit). He maintains complete
records on his section's activities.

He participates in other functions of the Violence Prevention
Unit as necessary.

This officer is supervised by the Supervisor of the Violence Prevention Unit. The position requires considerable verbal skill and the
ability to maintain effective inter-personal relationships. This
officer should have some knowledge of research methods.

III • Patrolmen Opinion Survey Relating to the Family Crisis Unit

Questions:	Response Distribution		
1. Have Family Crisis Intervention Program teams been available to handle a reasonable amount of family disturbances during the hours they are in operation? (Please comment.)	Positive	49	63%
	Negative	11	14%
	Unknown	18	23%
2. Do you have more time to perform other patrol functions since the implementation of the Family Crisis Intervention Program? (Please comment.)	Positive	42	54%
	Negative	15	19%
	Unknown	21	27%
3. Have Family Crisis Intervention Program teams provided you with cover or assistance on any assignments you have handled? (Please comment.)	Positive	54	69%
	Negative	10	13%
	Unknown	14	18%
4. (a) Would a Family Crisis Intervention Program team have been an asset on any of the family disturbances you have handled?	Positive	53	68%
	Negative	17	22%
(b) Have you utilized the referral agencies or have you referred any disputants to the Family Crisis Intervention Units? (Please comment.)	Unknown	8	10%
	Positive	48	62%
	Negative	22	28%
5. Based on your knowledge of the operation of the Family Crisis Intervention Program teams, would you recommend the expansion of the program to include one Family Crisis Intervention Program team in each district of the city? (Please comment.)	Unknown	8	10%
	Positive	53	68%
	Negative	11	14%
	Unknown	14	18%

Summary

Responses to the questionnaire showed majority acceptance (63%) of FCIU's performance as a crisis intervention unit (Question 1). Many comments expressed a desire for time to perform patrol functions other than domestic disputes and were receptive to the contribution of the FCIU in allowing for that time (Question 2). On the whole, patrol officers saw a need and a use for the crisis intervention team (Question 4).

This survey has also shown that despite the positive impression made by the FCIU, there exists a stereotype of an overwhelming number of family disputes, in and out of the experimental area (Question 1). Some officers in light of the estimated magnitude of the problem, evaluated the intervention program as unresponsive and thus ineffective (13% of Question 3). Others saw the scope of the problem as an incentive to employ and expand the experimental unit (Question 5).

The responses determined to be non-ascertainable were due to the officer's lack of contact with the F.C.I.U.

IV • Detailed Analysis of Critical Incident Questionnaire Results

Out of a discussion among our first group of officers about what constitutes good police practice came the suggestion that incidents commonly faced by police officers could be described, that one could get the responses of officers who were perceived as good policemen, and that these responses could then be used to characterize good police practice. The officers worked as a group developing twelve incidents to form a pilot questionnaire. These incidents were derived from the officers' own experiences. They were defined sharply enough to bring out crucial elements which the officers collectively considered essential in raising issues that could differentiate between those who would get themselves into potentially violent-type trouble and those who would be able to manage difficult situations with less opportunity for violence. The respondent was asked to indicate for each incident whether he would take any action, would make an arrest, or would take some action other than an arrest.

The questionnaire was filled out by the Chief of Police, and his permission was obtained to administer it to a pilot sample of the department's personnel as part of the research in developing the instrument. The sample, which was not representative, included 9 men on the command staff, 22 recruit officers, 16 officers in the Crime Prevention Unit, and 30 experienced (two or more years) patrol officers.

The questionnaire items were analyzed first by assigning an aggressive action score to each response (two points if the officer stated he would make an arrest, one point if he would take action other than an arrest, and zero if he would take no action at all). Besides searching for differences in total score among the four subgroups, comparisons were made between and among the groups for behavior on specific items. Very tentative efforts were also made to develop categories which would identify themes or styles of a given officer or group of officers from a review of the total responses to the questionnaire. An example of such a theme would be stalling by requesting more information when an officer is faced with the need to make a definite decision.

Crude and spotty as the initial administration of the questionnaire was, it was immediately evident that officers varied considerably in their responses. Within every group there was much variation in the total "aggressive action score," those in the command group being the most consistent in their way of responding. There was also variation between groups. The Crime Prevention Unit had the highest average score, 13.3, compared to 11.8 for the patrol officers, 11.2 for the recruits, 11.2 for the command staff, and 5.0 for the Chief. The Chief's score was by far the most consistent with that anticipated by the group as the appropriate response from police officers with low violence potential.

The Revised Questionnaire

Findings from the administration of the pilot questionnaire led to the Chief's authorizing its administration to virtually all of the department's uniformed personnel, 516 of the approximately 700 men in the department. This included all sergeants and patrolmen in the Patrol and Preventive Services Divisions and in the Youth Section of the Community Relations and Youth Division. Also included were a group of civilians who work, together with uniformed personnel, in the radio room, and a group of reserve officers, men who work part-time for the department. A copy of the questionnaire and the order for its administration are included in Appendix I.

On the basis of experience with pilot administration of the questionnaire, our officers developed a number of possible response categories for each item. Each of these categories was assigned a score from 1 to 5, the higher score indicating the increasing risk of physical confrontation. Since some incidents were judged to hold more potential for violent interaction than others, the range of possible scores was not the same for all incidents; only two, for example, had response alternatives that were scored 5. A total violence potential score was obtained by summing responses on all 12 items.

Responses to each item were tabulated for both the total group and for subgroups of staff based upon rank, years of experience, and work assignment. A correlation of total score on the odd-numbered items with total score on the even-numbered items was used as a measure of reliability. A validity measure was obtained by correlating the violence potential score on all 12 items with the number of violations of Sections 148 (misdemeanor resisting arrest) and 243 (felony assault on a police officer) of the Penal Code which the officer had reported during the preceding year. Finally, a matrix of inter-item correlations was obtained to determine whether response to the items represented a general behavior tendency or several relatively independent areas of behavior.

The results of the analysis of questionnaire responses are presented here in three parts: (1) distributions of responses over each incident, (2) reliability and validity, and (3) incident clusters.

Distribution of Responses by Incident

How much agreement is there among members of the police department as to the appropriate action to take in street incidents which have a potential to evoke violent behavior? We will look at the data in terms of four sub-questions.

A. To the extent that the responses of the Chief represent the policy he lays down for good police work, how closely is his department in tune with that policy? In the following we will look at the responses to each item of 423 full-time members of the department (men who answered the questionnaire in both the pilot and present studies are not included, nor are men who serve as reserve officers). The tables give the incident as it appeared in the questionnaire and the per cent of persons who give each of several identified responses. Responses given by the Chief are indicated by an asterisk.

342

TABLE A-1. Incident 1: MN, 30 Officer approaches scene and hears sound of argument. Officer knocks. Argument stops. Door opened by subject wearing T-shirt, Officer asks if police needed. Subject says, "No, pig!" and slams door in officer's face.

	% All full-time personnel (N = 423)
1. No action.*	45
2. Knock again, if no reply leave scene, or attempt to locate original complainant, remain at scene to ascertain if breach of peace is committed, ask radio for information.	19
3. In some unspecified manner advise persons inside that they are disturbing the peace.	12
4. Check desire of other party to the argument, method of entry unspecified.	23
5. If breach of the peace is committed upon re-entry, unspecified appropriate action taken.	1

Less than half of the personnel (45%) agree with the Chief that the situation requires no further action. More than half (55%) would attempt further involvement. A fourth (24%: responses 4 and 5) would attempt entry into the premises, action that might be justified but is of doubtful legality.

TABLE A-2. Incident 2: MN 15. Officer observes subject loitering on corner. Officer stops car, gets out to approach subject. Subject runs 75 feet to a house and enters front door.

	% All full-time personnel (N = 423)
1. No action.*	29
2. Check scene for crime, further action unspecified.	6
3. Ascertain from others if juvenile lives at address.	9
4. Check scene for crime, attempt to contact subject at his home, further action unspecified.	26
5. Question subject on reason for running, run F.C., etc. or, instruct parent in control of juvenile, proper method of raising children, etc.	25
6. Demand explanation for behavior.	5

Barely a third of the personnel (29%) agree with the Chief that no further police action is required. Two-thirds (71%) proceed on the assumption that the 15-year-old's actions warrant investigation, with the further explicit or implicit assumption that a crime has been committed. More than half (56%: responses 4, 5, and 6) would attempt contact with the boy and detain him long enough for interrogation, again an action of questionable legality.

TABLE A-3. Incident 3: Driving by, officer observes 40-50 MN & FN juvs. at the ¼ lb. hamburger stand. Someone in crowd shouts obscenities at officer as he approaches.

	% All full-time personnel (N = 423)
1, No action.*	58
2. Stay in vicinity, inform radio of situation, observe.	20
3. Make investigation, call for cover cars, give verbal advice to person or persons.	6
4. Attempt dispersal of crowd, with or without cover.	10
5. Arrest perpetrator(s).	7

Again the Chief states that no police action is required. Slightly more than half (58%) of the staff responding agree with him. The responses of the remainder are scattered over the other four alternatives, all of which suggest that the situation is observed by the officers as likely to erupt into trouble. A fourth of the personnel (23%: responses 3, 4, and 5) would attempt direct encounters with the juveniles involved.

TABLE A-4. Incident 4: Officer driving in unmarked vehicle observes 3 sailors obviously under the influence, staggering across the street toward waiting cab. One sailor bumps against officer's vehicle and gives the officer the finger.

	% All full-time personnel (N = 423)
1. No action.*	11
2. Wait to see if sailors get in taxi, further action unspecified.	7
3. Ascertain if they are returning to base, and let them go.	10
4. Escort sailors to taxi, and/or give advice, obtain information from subjects, further action unspecified, or, hold for A.F.P., call A.F.P.	52
5. Arrest, call for A.F.P. not specified.	19

The Chief states he would take no further action; 11% of the staff responding agree with him. Adding in category 2, which also implies no action, the agreement with the Chief rises to 18%. Four-fifths of the personnel (31%: responses 3, 4, and 5) would make contact with the sailors. A fifth (19%) would arrest them.

TABLE A-5. Incident 5: Four vehicles double parked, all attended. About 20 MN & FNs in front of club. Officer drives by slowly and is obviously seen by drivers of double-parked cars. Officer continues on and notes in rear view mirror that vehicles are not being moved.

	% All full-time personnel (N = 423)
1. No action.	8
2. Ask owners to move cars; further action unspecified.	11
3. Give verbal warning, further action unspecified.	6
4. Give tickets, no verbal warning, or give verbal warning, ticket those not heeding it.*	70
5. Give tickets, no warning, F.C. drivers, check for warrants and and stolen cars.	6

Almost all personnel (93%) agree that some action is required. Two thirds (70%) respond as does the Chief: they would ticket the cars, with or without prior verbal warning. In contrast to the first four incidents, a clear violation of law is involved with clear and relatively circumscribed action on the part of the police specified (requests or warning that cars be moved and/or traffic citations). For this reason perhaps, there is more unanimity of response on this item than on the others so far reported.

TABLE A-6. Incident 6: Four MN's in '64 Ford. Officer drives by noting vehicle in street with headlights on. After officer passes, vehicle starts to drive away slowly.

	% *All full-time personnel* (N = 423)
1. No action.*	40
2. Check with radio regarding stolen car, etc., no car stop, make F.C. without car stop, follow car.	26
3. Stop car, question and check driver, make F.C., etc.	17
4. Stop car, question and check driver and all occupants, check information through radio, make F.C. etc.	17

The Chief states that no action is required and 40% of the personnel agree with him. A third (34%: responses 3 and 4), however, would stop the car and detain the driver for questioning long enough to make a field report.

TABLE A-7. Incident 7: MN in late 20s walking NB on 101st Ave. slowly in high frequency 10851 V.C. area. Officer stops subject, asks for name and address. Subject identifies himself as John Smith of 1901 101st Avenue. Officer explains 10851 problem and says he wants to detain subject for further information. Subject says, "No, I gave you my name and address," and walks away.

	% All full-time personnel (N = 423)
1. No action.*	34
2. Check area for signs of crime, observe area.	1
3. Make F.C. on present informa- mation, follow home.	18
4. F.C. unspecified.	9
5. Detain subject for further infor- mation, method of detaining unspecified, offer ride home, etc.	28
6. Detain subject forcibly if neces- sary to obtain information.	6
7. Detain subject forcibly to obtain information; if unsatisfactory arrest subject.	3

Only a third of the personnel (34%) agree with the Chief that no action is required. Another third (37%: responses 5, 6, and 7) would specifically detain the subject, an action that is illegal in these circumstances and that suggests either lack of knowledge of the law or a willful disregard for it.

TABLE A-8. Incident 8: Young MN. Subject well dressed in suit and tie is selling tins of coffee to citizens on sidewalk.

	% All full-time personnel (N = 423)
1. No action.	8
2. Ask for I.D., F.C. subject, further action unspecified.	9
3. Ask for peddler's license and I.D., explain law, if no license cite.	36
4. Ask for peddler's license and/or I.D., attempt to find out where subject got coffee, F.C. subject.*	41
5. Arrest or cite, no questions asked of subject.	6

Here as in item 5 a specific law violation is involved. Only 8% of the personnel state they would take no action. The majority (77%: responses 3 and 4), including the Chief, would explain the law to the subject and cite or make a field report on him.

TABLE A-9. Incident 9: MW 39. Subject dressed in work clothing slashing tires on '67 Olds jointly owned but driven by wife.

	% All full-time personnel (N = 423)
1. No action.	35
2. Contact wife and ask what she wants done, get her version.	15
3. Talk to one or both parties, preserve the peace, method unspecified, or talk to husband regarding his actions or sobriety, F.C. subject, or make crime report, or assist wife to leave premises.*	40
4. Stop destruction of property, method unspecified, talk to parties or separate parties.	7
5. Arrest subject.	4

In this item a helping and assisting role rather than law enforcement or crime detection becomes part of affirmative police action. Almost two-thirds of the personnel (62%: responses 2, 3, and 4) agree with the Chief that some kind of peace-keeping activity should be attempted. A third (35%) would take no action in this situation.

TABLE A-10. Incident 10: Four MNs. Subjects dressed in Panther attire making major repairs on '56 pink Buick on the street, at the curb. One is overheard referring to "pig."

	% All full-time personnel (N = 423)
1. No action.	19
2. License plate check.	2
3. Explain law regarding repairs in street, allow time to comply.*	17
4. Explain law regarding repairs in street, further action unspecified, or explain law and cite persons.	23
5. Citation.	24
6. Cite persons, check ownership, warrant checks on others, tow car away, get cover units.	15

The Chief and 40% (responses 3 and 4) of the personnel state that they would explain the law violation involved; some of these would allow time to comply and some would issue a citation. About the same number (39%: responses 5 and 6) would cite immediately, 15% taking the further action of checking ownership and preparing for trouble. A fifth (19%) would take no action in this situation.

TABLE A-11. Incident 11: MN and FN 25, 2 children FN 1 and 4. Wife obviously beaten by husband, refuses to sign complaint out of fear of further beating. Husband states, "It's all over now." Loudly and aggressively insists that officers leave at once.

	% All full-time personnel (N = 423)
1. No action.	40
2. Talk to husband, give advice and/or warnings, make crime report, or talk to husband and wife, separate them.*	30
3. Attempt to talk to wife regardless of husband's wishes, make crime report, stand by.	15
4. Talk to wife, if necessary arrest husband, explain law to wife, preserve the peace.	6
5. Arrest husband.	8

Responses here are nearly equally divided among three alternatives: taking no action (40%), intervening by attempting a peace-keeping role (30%, including the Chief), and intervening with the implied use of force if necessary (29%: responses 3, 4, and 5). This last alternative raises legal complications if the wife has made no actual complaint.

TABLE A-12. Incident 12: Young MW. Officer conducting investigation of ADW cooperative suspect in rear seat of car. Subject comes up to window and insists on talking to his friend, the suspect. Officer says no; the subject begins yelling to suspect through the window and continues after further warning.

	% All full-time personnel (N = 423)
1. No action, leave scene.*	21
2. Talk to subject about ceasing, if uncooperative leave scene.	4
3. Talk to subject about ceasing, make threat, further action unspecified, or talk to subject about ceasing, give chance to comply, if uncooperative, arrest.	18
4. Arrest subject.	57

Here only a fifth of the personnel (21%) agree with the Chief that no action is necessary; 25% (responses 1 and 2) suggest driving away as a means of handling the potential conflict. Over half (57%) would make an arrest. This item tends to show excessive aggressive reaction to lack of respect for the police. It may also show a lack of awareness of alternative behaviors: moving the car as a way to handle the situation instead of complicating the interrogation by acting upon the second suspect appears logically plausible but probably not in the behavior repertoire of most personnel (73%: responses 3 and 4).

If one can characterize the policy of the Chief from his responses to his questionnaire, it would be a policy to intervene in cases of specific law violations (items 5, 8, and 10), to attempt a helping and/or peace-keeping role in family disputes (items 9 and 11), and to keep hands off in situations that only seem suspicious but offer no actual evidence of criminal activity (items 2, 6 and 7) or that primarily involve provocative behavior toward police officers (items 1, 3, 4, and 12). Agreement with the Chief's position tends to be greater on the first two types of items than on the last two. The department's staff as a whole are apparently more ready to take action, in more kinds of situations, than is the Chief. An exception is the case of family disputes. A sizeable proportion of the staff state they would take no action in these situations (35%, item 9; 41%, item 11).

B. The case has been made that there is considerable variation among police personnel as to what actions are appropriate in a variety of situations to which they are commonly exposed. The stand taken by the Chief is supported by varying numbers of the men under him, ranging from less than a fifth to about three-quarters. Several hypotheses can be raised concerning the reason for this variation. One is that in a department of this size communication between the Chief and his officers is limited and word does not come directly from the Chief to those responsible for carrying out his policy on the street. Differences might thus be expected on the basis of rank. In the following set of tables item responses given by a group of 36 sergeants and a group of 353 regular patrol officers are presented. Men with ranks above sergeant were not included in the study, with the exception of the Deputy Chief, whose responses are indicated by a double asterisk. As before, the responses of the Chief are indicated by a single asterisk.

TABLE B-1. Incident 1: MN, 30. Officer approaches scene and hears sound of argument. Officer knocks. Argument stops. Door opened by subject wearing T-shirt. Officer asks if police needed. Subject says, "No, pig!" and slams door in officer's face.

	% Sergeants (N = 36)	% Oficers (N = 353)
1. No action.*	31	45
2. Knock again; if no reply leave scene, or attempt to locate original complainant, remain at scene to ascertain if breach of peace is committed; ask radio for information.**	28	20
3. In some unspecified manner advise persons inside that they are disturbing the peace.	3	13
4. Check desire of other party to the argument, method of entry unspecified.	39	21
5. If breach of the peace is committed upon re-entry, unspecified appropriate action taken.	0	1

Contrary to prediction, the officers are more likely to agree with the Chief that no action is required than are the sergeants (45%, 31%). Substantially more of the sergeants state they would attempt entry into the premises (39%: responses 4 and 5) than do the regular officers (22%).

TABLE B-2. Incident 2: MN 15. Officer observes subject loitering on corner. Officer stops car, gets out to approach subject. Subject runs 75 feet to a house and enters front door.

	% Sergeants (N = 36)	% Officers (N = 353)
1. No action.*	44	26
2. Check scene for crime; further action unspecified.	8	5
3. Ascertain from others if juvenile lives at address.	25	8
4. Check scene for crime, attempt to contact subject at his home, further action unspecified.	8	28
5. Question subject on reason for running, run F.C., etc. or instruct parent in control of juvenile, proper method of raising children, etc.	14	26
6. Demand explanation for behavior.	0	6

In this item the sergeants do, as predicted, agree more often with the Chief; 44% state that no action is required, compared to 26% of the regular officers. The majority of the officers would attempt to detain and question the subject (60%: items 4, 5, and 6); this action would be taken by only 22% of the sergeants.

TABLE B-3. Incident 3: Driving by, officer observes 40-5-MN & FN juvs. at the ¼ lb. hamburger stand. Someone in crowd shouts obscenities at officer as he approaches.

	% Sergeants (N = 36)	% Officers (N = 353)
1. No action.*	64	57
2. Stay in vicinity, inform radio of situation, observe.	25	20
3. Make investigation, call for cover cars, give verbal advice to person or persons.	6	7
4. Attempt dispersal of crowd, with or without cover.	6	9
5. Arrest perpetrator(s).	0	8

Differences here are in the predicted direction, but they are small. The sergeants are more likely to take no action than are the officers (64%, 57%), less likely to engage in direct contact with the juveniles (12%, 24%: responses 3, 4, and 5).

TABLE B-4. Incident 4: Officer driving in unmarked vehicle observes three sailors obviously under the influence, staggering across the street toward waiting cab. One sailor bumps against officer's vehicle and gives the officer the finger.

	% Sergeants (N = 36)	% Officers (N = 353)
1. No action.*	11	11
2. Wait to see if sailors get in taxi, further action unspecified.**	6	7
3. Ascertain if they are returning to base, and let them go.	14	10
4. Escort sailors to taxi, and/or give advice, obtain information from subjects, further action unspecified, or, hold for A.F.P., or call A.F.P.	53	51
5. Arrest, call for A.F.P. not specified.	17	21

There are virtually no differences in the responses of the sergeant and officer groups to this item.

TABLE B-5. Incident 5: Four vehicles double parked, all attended. About 20 MN and FN's in front of club. Officer drives by slowly and is obviously seen by drivers of double-parked cars. Officer continues on and notes in rear view mirror that vehicles are not being moved.

	% Sergeants (N = 36)	% Officers (N = 353)
1. No action.	11	6
2. Ask owners to move cars; further action unspecified.	19	10
3. Give verbal warning, further action unspecified.	8	5
4. Give tickets, no verbal warning, or give verbal warning, ticket those not heeding it. *	58	72
5. Give tickets, no warning, F.C. drivers, check for warrants and stolen cars.**	3	6

The officers are more likely to respond that they would ticket the cars than are the sergeants (78%, 61%: responses 4 and 5), a response that is in line with their general tendency to take more authoritative action, but that this time puts them in closer agreement with both the Chief and his Deputy.

TABLE B-6. Incident 6: Four MN's in '64 Ford. Officer drives by noting vehicle in street with headlights on. After officer passes, vehicle starts to drive away slowly.

	% Sergeants (N = 36)	% Officers (N = 353)
1. No action. *	56	38
2. Check with radio regarding stolen car etc., no car stop, make F.C. without car stop, follow car.	31	25
3. Stop car, question and check driver and all occupants, check information through radio, make F.C. etc.	0	18

Differences on this item are striking. Substantially more of the sergeants endorse the position taken by the Chief than do the officers (56%, 38%). A third of the officer group state they would stop the car and question the driver (36%: responses 3 and 3.5), compared with only 14% of the sergeants.

TABLE B-7. Incident 7: MN in late 20's walking NB on 101st Ave. slowly in high frequency 10851 V.C. area. Officer stops subject, asks for name and address.Subject identifies himself as John Smith of 1901, 101st Ave. Officer explains 10851 problem and says he wants to detain subject for further information. Subject says, "No, I gave you my name and address," and walks away.

	% Sergeants (N = 36)	% Officers (N = 353)
1. No action.*	47	32
2. Check area for signs of crime; observe area.	0	2
3. Make F.C. on present information, follow home.	28	18
4. F.C. unspecified.	8	9
5. Detain subject for further information, method of detaining unspecified, offer ride home, etc.	14	29
6. Detain subject forcibly if necessary to obtain information.	3	7
7. Detain subject forcibly to obtain information; if unsatisfactory, arrest subject.	0	3

The sergeants again are in greater agreement with the "no action" position taken by the Chief (47%, 32%), and are less likely to attempt to detain the subject (17%, 39%: responses 5, 6, and 7).

TABLE B-8. Incident 8: Young MN. Subject well dressed in suit and tie is selling tins of coffee to citizens on sidewalk.

	% Sergeants (N = 36)	% Officers (N = 353)
1. No action.	6	8
2. Ask for I.D., F.C. subject, further action unspecified.*	6	9
3. Ask for peddler's license and I.D., explain law; if no license, cite.	39	35
4. Ask for peddler's license and/ or I.D., attempt to find out where subject got coffee, F.C. subject.	42	41
5. Arrest or cite; no questions asked of subject.	8	6

Differences on this item are minor.

TABLE B-9. Incident 9: MW 39. Subject dressed in work clothing slashing tires on '67 Olds jointly owned but driven by wife.

	% Sergeants (N = 36)	% Officers (N = 353)
1. No action.	25	35
2. Contact wife and ask what she wants done, get her version.	14	16
3. Talk to one or both parties, preserve the peace, method unspecified, or talk to husband regarding his actions or sobriety; F.C. subject, or make crime report, or assist wife leave premises; preserve the peace.	42	39
4. Stop destruction of property, method unspecified; talk to parties or separate parties.	17	6
5. Arrest subject.	3	4

The mediating role endorsed by the Chief (responses 2, 3, and 4) is taken more often by the sergeant than by the officer group (73%, 61%). The officers more often report that they would take no action (35%, 25%).

TABLE B-10. Incident 10: Four MN's. Subjects dressed in Panther attire making major repairs on '56 pink Buick on the street, at the curb. One is overheard referring to "pig".

	% Sergeants (N = 36)	% Officers (N = 353)
1. No action.	22	19
2. License plate check.	3	2
3. Explain law regarding repairs in street, allow time to comply.*	11	18
4. Explain law regarding repairs in street, further action unspecified, or explain law regarding repairs in street, cite persons.	39	22
5. Citation.	17	27
6. Cite persons, check ownership, warrant checks on others, tow car away, get cover units.	8	12

The majority of both groups agree that action should be taken. The sergeants, however, are more likely to first explain the law violation involved to the subjects than to cite them directly (50%: responses 3 and 4, compared to 25%: responses 5 and 6). For the officer group, the reverse is true: 40% would first explain the law, 49% would cite immediately.

TABLE B-11. Incident 11: MN and FN 25, 2 children FN 1 and 4. Wife obviously beaten by husband, refuses to sign complaint out of fear of further beating. Husband states, "It's all over now." Loudly and aggressively insists that officers leave at once.

	% Sergeants (N = 36)	% Officers (N = 353)
1. No action.	39	38
2. Talk to husband, give advice and/or warnings, make crime report, or talk to* ** husband and wife, separate them.	36	31
3. Attempt to talk to wife regardless of husband's wishes, make crime report, stand by.	14	16
4. Talk to wife; if necessary arrest husband, explain law to wife, preserve the peace.	0	7
5. Arrest husband.	11	8

Differences are small, but in the expected direction. A somewhat larger proportion of the sergeant group would attempt a peace-keeping role (36%, compared to 31% for the officers), a somewhat smaller proportion would intervene with the implied use of force (25% compared with 31% of the officers: responses 3, 4, and 5).

TABLE B-12. Incident 12: Young MW. Officer conducting investigation of ADW with cooperative suspect in rear seat of car. Subject comes up to window and insists on talking to his friend, the suspect. Officer says no; the subject begins yelling to suspect through the window and continues after further warning.

	% Sergeants (N = 36)	% Officers (N = 353)
1. No action, leave scene.* **	25	20
2. Talk to subject about ceasing; if uncooperative, leave scene.	11	4
3. Talk to subject about ceasing, make threat, further action unspecified, or talk to subject about ceasing, give chance to comply; if uncooperative, arrest.	17	19
4. Arrest subject.	47	58

The sergeants are more likely to avoid a confrontation by leaving the scene than are the officers (36%, 24%: responses 1 and 2), in line with the position taken by the Chief. They are less likely to threaten or arrest the subject (64%, 77%: responses 3 and 4).

It is clear, first of all, that the Chief and his Deputy are in close agreement. The same responses are given by the two to eight of the twelve items; on the other four items (1, 4, 5, and 8) their responses are not far apart. As predicted, on most items a larger proportion of the sergeant group agrees with the position endorsed by the Chief than does the officer group, lending some credence to the initial hypothesis — but the proportion of agreement even with the sergeants is not generally high. Differences between the two groups are largest on those items in which a suspicion of crime, without real evidence and without provocative behavior toward police, is involved (items 2, 6, and 7); in these situations, the sergeants are far less ready to act than are the officers. On the four items in which the subjects make insulting remarks to the police, differences are small (items 3 and 12), nonexistent (item 4), or in a reverse direction (item 1). On two of the items involving specific law violations (5 and 10) the sergeants are less likely to take action than are the officers, thus putting the officers in closer agreement with the Chief, and on the third item (8) there is no real difference between the two groups. Items involving family conflicts (9 and 11) find the sergeants more often attempting a peace-keeping function, as does the Chief, than do the officers, but the differences are not very large.

C. A second hypothesis about the basis for variation in response to the questionnaire is based on the assumption that judgment about good police practice is affected (improved) by experience. The men responding to the questionnaire were divided into two groups: those with more than two years of service (279 men) and those with two years or less (112 men). A small number of civilian employees, included in the larger sample, were excluded here. A third group of 34 reserve officers was included. These men, who work only one or two nights a week or on weekends, have had both limited exposure to police work and limited training. It was hypothesized that the men with the most experience would more often give responses denoting good police practice (as represented by the responses of the Chief) than would those with less experience; that is, the responses of the officers with more than two years of service would be most like those of the Chief, the responses of the reserve officers would be least like his. The following tables give the per cent of persons in each of these three groups who give each of the coded responses. Again, the response given by the Chief is indicated by an asterisk.

TABLE C-1. Incident 1: MN, 30. Officer approaches scene and hears sound of argument. Officer knocks. Argument stops. Door opened by subject wearing T-shirt. Officer asks if police needed. Subject says, "No, pig!" and slams door in officer's face.

	% over 2 years service (N = 279)	% 2 yrs. and less service (N = 112)	% reserve (N = 34)
1. No action*	47	37	65
2. Knock again, if no reply leave scene, or attempt to locate original complainant; remain at scene to ascertain if breach of peace is committed, ask radio for information.	21	20	9
3. In some unspecified manner advise persons inside that they are disturbing the peace.	11	16	12
4. Check desire of other party to the argument, method of entry unspecified.	21	26	15
5. If breach of the peace is committed upon re-entry, unspecified appropriate action taken.	1	2	0

As predicted, the officers with more than two years of service responded more often as did the Chief than those with two years or less. The differences, however, are small; 47% of the former group state they would take no action compared to 37% of the latter. The more experienced officers are also less likely to state they would attempt entry than the less experienced officers (22%, 28%: responses 4 and 5), though again the difference is not large. Contrary to expectation, the reserve officer group is in much higher agreement with the Chief than either of the others; two-thirds of them (65%) choosing the "no action" alternative.

TABLE C-2. Incident 2: MN 15. Officer observes subject loitering on corner. Officer stops car, gets out to approach subject. Subject runs 75 feet to a house and enters front door.

	% over 2 years service (N = 279)	% 2 yrs. and less service (N = 112)	% reserve (N = 34)
1. No action.*	30	23	47
2. Check scene for crime, further action unspecified.	6	4	9
3. Ascertain from others if juvenile lives at address.	12	6	15
4. Check scene for crime, attempt to contact subject at his home, further action unspecified.	25	29	12
5. Question subject on reason for running, run F.C., etc., or, instruct parent in control of juvenile, proper method of raising children, etc.	24	27	18
6. Demand explanation for behavior.	3	11	0

The response pattern is similar to that in the preceding item. Of the more experienced officers 30% agree with the Chief that no action is required by the situation; 52% (responses 4, 5, and 6) would attempt to contact and detain the subject. For the less experienced officers the figures are 23% and 67%. Half of the reserves (47%) agree with the Chief's position; only a third would attempt contact (30%).

TABLE C-3. Incident 3: Driving by, officer observes 40 – 50 MN and FN juvs. at the ¼ lb. hamburger stand. Someone in the crowd shouts obscenities at officer as he approaches.

	% over 2 years service (N = 279)	% 2 yrs. and less service (N = 112)	% reserve (N = 34)
1. No action.*	56	63	50
2. Stay in vicinity, inform radio of situation, observe.	22	13	32
3. Make investigation, call for cover cars, give verbal advice to person or persons.	8	4	15
4. Attempt dispersal of crowd, with or without cover.	8	10	3
5. Arrest perpetrator(s).	6	9	0

On this item, the less experienced officers are most likely to agree with the Chief that no action is required, the reserve officers least so. Of more interest, however, are the alternatives chosen by those officers who feel obliged to take some action in the situation. Of the reserves, most would stay nearby but not attempt to get involved (32%); almost none (3%: responses 4 and 5) would attempt to break up the crowd. The less experienced officers are most like to attempt crowd dispersal, with or without making arrests (19%); 13% would stand nearby, but without direct involvement with the subjects. The responses of the more experienced officers lie somewhere between those of the other two groups.

TABLE C-4. Incident 4: Officer driving in unmarked vehicle observes 3 sailors obviously under the influence, staggering across the street toward waiting cab. One sailor bumps against officer's vehicle and gives the officer the finger.

	% over 2 years service (N = 279)	% 2 yrs. and less service (N = 112)	% reserve (N = 34)
1. No action.*	11	12	24
2. Wait to see if sailors get in taxi, further action unspecified.	6	12	26
3. Ascertain if they are returning to base, and let them go.	10	13	9
4. Escort sailors to taxi, and/or give advice; obtain information from subjects, further action unspecified, or, hold for A.F.P., or call A.F.P.	53	44	24
5. Arrest; call for A.F.P. not specified.	20	20	18

The reserve officers are again more likely than the other two groups to agree with the position taken by the Chief. They are least likely to detain the sailors for questioning, advice giving or detention (51%; responses 3, 4, and 5). These actions are most often taken by the more experienced officers (83%), somewhat less often by the less experienced men (77%).

TABLE C-5. Incident 5: Four vehicles double parked, all attended. About 20 MN&FN's in front of club. Officer drives by slowly and is obviously seen by drivers of double-parked cars. Officer notes in rear view mirror that vehicles are not being moved.

	% over 2 years service (N = 279)	% 2 yrs. and less service (N = 112)	% reserves (N = 34)
1. No action.	9	2	15
2. Ask owners to move cars; further action unspecified.	10	12	12
3. Give verbal warning, further action unspecified.	6	3	15
4. Give tickets, no verbal warning, or give verbal warning, ticket those not heeding it. *	68	80	59
5. Give tickets, no warning; F.C. drivers, check for warrants and stolen cars.	7	4	0

On this item, with a clear law violation involved, the less experienced officers are most likely to take aggressive action (84% : responses 4 and 5), as does the Chief; the reserve officer least likely to do so (59%). Though few in any group suggest the situation calls for no action, this response is more frequent among the reserves than among the other two groups.

TABLE C-6. Incident 6: Four MN's in '64 Ford. Officer drives by noting vehicle in street with headlights on. After officer passes, vehicle starts to drive away slowly.

	% over 2 years service (N = 279)	% 2 yrs. and less service (N = 112)	% reserve (N = 34)
1. No action. *	44	31	47
2. Check with radio regarding stolen car etc. No car stop, make F.C. without car stop, follow car.	26	25	38
3. Stop car, question and check driver, make F.C. etc.	16	22	3
4. Stop car, question and check driver and all occupants, check information through radio, make F.C. etc.	14	21	12

The more experienced officers (44%) and the reserve officers (47%) agree more often with the Chief's position than do the less experienced officers (31%). Nearly half of the less experienced group would detain the driver (43%: responses 3 and 4), compared to 30% of the more experienced officers and 15% of the reserve officers.

TABLE C-7. Incident 7: MN in late 20's walking NB on 101st Ave. slowly in high frequency 10851 V.C. area. Officer stops subject, asks for name and address. Subject identifies himself as John Smith of 1901 101st Ave. Officer explains 10851 problem and says he wants to detain subject for further information. Subject says, "No, I gave you may name and address," and walks away.

	% over 2 years service (N=279)	% 2 yrs. and less service (N=112)	% reserve (N=34)
1. No action. *	35	30	26
2. Check area for signs of crime, observe area.	2	1	3
3. Make F.C. on present information, follow home.	19	17	32
4. F.C. unspecified.	10	6	0
5. Detain subject for further information (method unspecified), offer ride home, etc.	25	33	12
6. Detain subject forcibly if necessary to obtain information.	6	8	18
7. Detain subject forcibly to obtain information, if unsatisfactory arrest subject.	2	4	9

Responses in support of the Chief's position are in the predicted direction, though the differences are small: 35% of the more experienced officers, 30% of the less experienced officers, and 26% of the reserve officers agree with the Chief. The group of less experienced officers is most likely to attempt detention of the subject (46%: responses 5, 6, and 7); 39% of the reserve officers do so, and 34% of the more experienced officers.

TABLE C-8. Incident 8: Young MN. Subject well dressed in suit and tie is selling tins of coffee to citizens on sidewalk.

	% over 2 years service (N=279)	% yrs. and less service (N=112)	% reserve (N=34)
1. No action.	7	10	18
2. Ask for I.D., F.C. subject, further action unspecified.	8	12	18
3. Ask for peddler's license and I.D., explain law; if no license, cite.	37	33	53
4. Ask for peddler's license and / or I.D., attempt to find out where subject got coffee, F.C. subject. *	42	38	12
5. Arrest or cite; no questions asked of subject.	6	8	0

Here, with a specific law violation involved, the main differences occur between the reserves and the other two groups of officers. The reserves are most likely of the three to show apparent ignorance of the law (18% would take no action, compared to 7% and 10% of the more and less experienced officers); 65% of them (responses 3 and 4) would ask for a license, compared to 79% and 71% of the more and less experienced groups.

TABLE C-9. Incident 9: MW 39. Subject dressed in work clothing slashing tires on '67 Olds jointly owned but driven by wife.

	% over 2 years service (N=279)	% 2 yrs. and less service (N=112)	% reserves (N=34)
1. No action.	33	37	65
2. Contact wife and ask what she wants done, get her version.	16	15	12
3. Talk to one or both parties, preserve the peace, method unspecified, or talk to husband regarding his actions or sobriety; F.C. subject, or make crime report, or assist wife leave premises, preserve the peace.*	41	38	24
4. Stop destruction of property, method unspecified; talk to parties or separate parties.	8	4	0
5. Arrest subject.	3	6	0

In this item again, the main differences lie between the reserves on one
hand and the two groups of regular officers on the other. About a third
of the more and the less experienced officers (33%, 37%) would not get
involved in the situation, while nearly two-thirds (65%, 57%) would
attempt a peace-keeping role, as would the Chief. For the reserve
officers, the figures are reversed; two-thirds (65%) would take no action,
the remaining third (36%) would try to negotiate between the two parties
to the dispute.

TABLE C-10. Incident 10: Four MN's. Subjects dressed in Panther attire making major repairs on '56 pink Buick on the street, at the curb. One is overheard referring to "pig."

	% over 2 years service (N = 279)	% 2 yrs. and less service (N = 112)	% reserves (N = 34)
1. No action.	17	24	38
2. License plate check.	2	3	3
3. Explain law regarding repairs in street, allow time to comply.*	19	15	24
4. Explain law regarding repairs in street, further action unspecified, or explain law regarding repairs in street, cite persons.	25	20	18
5. Citation.	24	29	18
6. Cite persons, check ownership, warrant checks on others; tow car away, get cover units.	12	10	6

This item also involves a specific law violation. Again, the reserves are most likely to take no action (38%), compared to 17% and 24% of the more and less experienced officers. The more experienced officers are most likely to follow the Chief in explaining the law to the persons involved, with or without issuing a citation (44%: responses 3 and 4); comparable figures for the less experienced officers are 35%, for the reserves 36%. About the same proportion of each group (36%, 38% and 34%: responses 5 and 6) would cite the subjects.

TABLE C-11. Incident 11: MN and FN 25, 2 children FN 1 and 4. Wife obviously beaten by husband, refuses to sign complaint out of fear of further beating. Husband states, "It's all over now." Loudly and aggressively insists that officers leave at once.

	% over 2 years service (N = 279)	% 2 yrs. and less service (N = 112)	% reserves (N = 34)
1. No action.	37	40	56
2. Talk to husband, give advice and/or warnings, make crime report, or talk to husband and wife, separate them.*	33	30	18
3. Attempt to talk to wife regardless of husband's wishes, make crime report, stand by.	16	15	12
4. Talk to wife, if necessary arrest husband; explain law to wife, preserve the peace.	6	7	15
5. Arrest husband.	9	8	0

The responses of the more and less experienced officers to this item are quite similar. About a third would take no action (37%, 40%), another third would try a peace-keeping role (33%, 30%), and another third would intervene forcefully if required (31%, 30%: responses 3, 4, and 5). The reserve officers however, are far more likely to take no action in this situation (56%), far less likely to attempt a peace-keeping role (18%). As with the other two groups, about a third (27%) would intervene with force.

TABLE C-12. Incident 12: Young MW. Officer conducting investigation of ADW with cooperative suspect in rear seat of car. Subject comes up to window and insists on talking to his friend, the suspect. Officer says no; the subject begins yelling to suspect through the window and continues after further warning.

	% over 2 years service (N = 279)	% 2 yrs. and less service (N = 112)	% reserves (N = 34)
1. No action, leave scene. *	23	15	35
2. Talk to subject about ceasing; if uncooperative, leave scene.	5	3	0
3. Talk to subject about ceasing, make threat, further action unspecified, or talk to subject about ceasing, give chance to comply; if uncooperative, arrest.	20	15	18
4. Arrest subject.	52	64	47

The reserves are most likely to agree with the Chief that no action is necessary (35%), the less experienced officers least likely (15%). Similarly, the reserve officers are least likely to make an arrest (47%), compared to 64% of the least experienced officers. The responses of the more experienced officers lie between those of the other two groups.

The more experienced officers more often agree with the position taken by the Chief than the less experienced officers (in 9 of the 12 items) though the differences are generally small and in several cases negligible (as in the two items dealing with family crises, 9 and 11). This finding of limited differences based on experience may be a function of the crude definition of "more" and "less" experience. Of course, if experience brings no corrective feedback, if may not be reasonable to suppose that differences in response based on experience would be large. The reserve officers seem to represent a special case. They respond far more like the Chief does than the two groups of regular officers in 5 of the 7 items in which he would take no action, but they are the most likely of the three groups to take no action in all situations (exceptions are items 3 and 7). This is especially striking on the two items (9 and 11) involving family disputes. This group of officers, with less training than the regular officers and with far less exposure to police-citizen interactions and to contacts with other officers, tend to be more conservative about using police authority, appear to have less knowledge of the law, and more often call for additional information before acting (items 3 and 6). This response may be largely a function of the very circumscribed definition of the reserve officer's role and authority.

D. Sizeable differences between the responses of the Chief and of the men who work for him have been demonstrated. It was hypothesized that higher-ranking staff would be more likely to respond as does the Chief than line officers. This hypothesis receives considerable support from the data, though the relationship is clearer in some types of situations than in others. It was further hypothesized that men with greater amounts of experience on the police force would be more likely to respond as does the Chief than men who have had relatively little experience. This relationship was not demonstrated in any clear-cut way. Other variables— for example, a readiness to become involved in confrontations — also appear to be important. Experience needs to be looked at in terms of types of situations; and perhaps also in terms of types of experience. For example, patrol officers, who have the most frequent and direct contact with citizens, might be expected to respond differently than men whose work is less likely to involve them in the initial stages of contact. For this purpose, the men were divided in the following work assignment groups: Patrol officers, CPU (Crime Prevention Unit), radio room staff (three-quarters of this group consists of civilian employees), officers assigned to the Youth Section, patrol wagon officers, and officers assigned to Community Relations. In the analysis reported below, only the first four groups are considered; they include both officers and sergeants, in a ratio of approximately 10 to 1. Numbers in the patrol wagon and Community Relations groups were too small for analysis (11 and 4 respectively) and are omitted. Also omitted are a small group of other staff assigned to a variety of departmental tasks. As above, the responses of the Chief are indicated by an asterisk.

TABLE D-1. Incident 1: MN, 30. Officer approaches scene and hears sound of argument. Officer knocks. Argument stops. Door opened by subject wearing T-shirt. Officer asks if police needed. Subject says, "No, pig!" and slams door in officer's face.

	% Patrol (N=251)	% CPU (N=54)	% Radio Room (N=41)	% Youth Section (N=34)
1. No action. *	50	32	56	21
2. Knock again; if no reply leave scene, or attempt to locate original complainant; remain at scene to ascertain if breach of peace is committed, ask radio for information.	16	33	7	24
3. In some unspecified manner advise persons inside that they are disturbing the peace.	12	11	5	15
4. Check desire of other party to the argument, method of entry unspecified.	21	22	32	38
5. If breach of the peace is committed upon re-entry, unspecified appropriate action taken.	1	2	0	3

Agreement with the Chief that no further action is required is highest among the patrol officers and those employed in the radio room, less frequent among those assigned to the CPU, lowest among those assigned to the Youth Section. A larger proportion of this last group (41%: responses 4 and 5) would attempt entry — a behavior of questionable legality — than any other group. The proportion of responses of those assigned to the radio room is also high (32%), those assigned to patrol and the CPU the lowest (22%, 24%).

TABLE D-2. Incident 2: MN 15. Officer observes subject loitering on corner. Officer stops car, gets out to approach subject. Subject runs 75 feet to a house and enters front door.

	% Patrol (N = 251)	% CPU (N = 54)	% Radio Room (N = 41)	% Youth Section (N = 34)
1. No action.*	29	26	39	18
2. Check scene for crime, further action unspecified.	6	7	12	3
3. Ascertain from others if juvenile lives at address.	8	13	0	18
4. Check scene for crime, attempt to contact subject at his home, further action unspecified.	24	30	22	32
5. Question subject on reason for running, run F.C., etc., or, instruct parent in control of juvenile, proper method of raising children, etc.	28	15	27	26
6. Demand explanation for behavior.	5	9	0	3

Those in the radio room most often endorse the position taken by the Chief (39%), those in the Youth Section least often (18%). Men in the Youth Section are more likely to attempt to contact the subject for investigation than any other group (61%: responses 4, 5, and 6, compared to 49% for radio room, 55% for CPU, and 57% for patrol).

TABLE D-3. Incident 3: Driving by, officer observes 40–50 MN and FN juvs. at the ¼ lb. hamburger stand. Someone in crowd shouts obscenities at officer as he approaches.

	% Patrol (N=251)	% CPU (N=54)	% Radio Room (N=41)	% Youth Section (N=34)
1. No action.*	59	56	54	47
2. Stay in vicinity, inform radio of situation, observe.	19	19	27	26
3. Make investigation, call for cover cars, give verbal advice to person or persons.	7	11	2	6
4. Attempt dispersal of crowd, with or without cover.	8	7	15	15
5. Arrest perpetrator(s).	8	7	2	6

In this situation, which also involved juveniles, the men in the Youth Section are again least likely to endorse the "no action" position of the Chief, most likely to attempt direct intervention with the subjects (27%: responses 3, 4, and 5), compared to 25% for CPU, 23% for patrol, and 19% for radio room). Differences among the groups, however, are not large.

TABLE D-4. Incident 4: Officer driving in unmarked vehicle observes 3 sailors obviously under the influence, staggering across the street toward waiting cab. One sailor bumps against officer's vehicle and gives the officer the finger.

	% Patrol (N = 251)	% CPU (N = 54)	% Radio Room (N = 41)	% Youth Section (N = 34)
1. No action. *	10	15	10	6
2. Wait to see if sailors get in taxi, further action unspecified.	7	6	15	0
3. Ascertain if they are returning to base, and let them go.	12	13	0	6
4. Escort sailors to taxi, and/or give advice; obtain information from subjects, further action unspecified, or, hold for A.F.P., or call A.F.P.	52	43	68	65
5. Arrest, call for A.F.P. not specified.	19	24	7	24

Again, differences are largest between the radio room staff and those in the Youth Section, 95% of the latter advocating some kind of intervention (responses 3, 4, and 5) compared to 75% of the former. The other two groups are somewhat closer to the position taken by staff in the radio room than that taken by the Youth Section staff.

TABLE D-5. Incident 5: Four Vehicles double parked all attended. About 20 MN & FN's in front of club. Officer drives by slowly and is obviously seen by drivers of double-parked cars. Officer continues on and notes in rear view mirror that vehicles are not being moved.

	% Patrol (N = 251)	% CPU (N = 54)	% Radio Room (N = 41)	% Youth Section (N = 34)
1. No action.	8	2	12	15
2. Ask owners to move cars; further action.	10	6	7	15
3. Give verbal warning, further action unspecified.	5	2	22	6
4. Give tickets, no verbal warning, or give verbal warning, ticket those not heeding it. *	72	83	56	59
5. Give tickets, no warning; F.C. drivers, check for warrants and stolen cars.	6	7	2	6

This item involves a specific law violation. The radio room staff are the least likely of the four groups to ticket the cars (58%: responses 4 and 5). Responses of the Youth Section staff in this case are quite similar (65%). These two groups more often than the other two state they would take no action. Almost all of the men in the CPU would ticket the cars (90%), almost none would take no action (2%). On this item they are thus in most agreement with the Chief.

TABLE D-6. Incident 6: Four MN's in '64 Ford, officer drives by noting vehicle in street with headlights on. After officer passes, vehicle starts to drive away slowly.

	% Patrol (N=251)	% CPU (N=54)	% Radio Room (N=41)	% Youth Section (N=34)
1. No action.*	36	50	32	41
2. Check with radio regarding stolen car, etc., No car stop, make F.C. without car stop, follow car.	27	22	39	32
3. Stop car, question and check driver, make F.C., etc.	22	15	5	15
4. Stop car, question and check driver and all occupants, check information through radio, make F.C. etc.	16	13	24	12

Again, a higher proportion of the CPU staff are in agreement with the Chief that no action is necessary (50%) than any of the other three groups. The patrol officers most often state they would stop the car and question the subjects (38%: responses 3 and 4, compared to 29% for radio room, 28% for CPU, and 27% for Youth Section).

TABLE D-7. Incident 7: MN in late 20's walking NB on 101st Ave. slowly in high frequency 10851 V.C. area. Officer stops subject, asks for name and address. Subject identifies himself as John Smith of 1901 101st Ave. Officer explains 10851 problem and says he wants to detain subject for further information. Subject says, "No, I gave you my name and address," and walks away.

	% Patrol (N=251)	% CPU (N=54)	% Radio Room (N=41)	% Youth Section (N=34)
1. No action.*	32	46	34	29
2. Check area for signs of crime, observe area.	1	0	0	3
3. Make F.C. on present information, follow home.	19	17	20	12
4. F.C. unspecified.	9	4	7	18
5. Detain subject for further information, method of detaining unspecified; offer ride home, etc.	28	22	39	38
6. Detain subject forcibly if necessary to obtain information.	7	8	0	0
7. Detain subject forcibly to obtain information; if unsatisfactory, arrest subject.	4	4	0	0

The CPU staff are most likely to take no action, as does the Chief, least likely to attempt to detain the subject (34%: responses 5, 6, and 7). Differences among the other three groups are slight.

TABLE D-8. Incident 8: Young MN. Subject well dressed in suit and tie is selling tins of coffee to citizens on sidewalk.

	% Patrol (N = 251)	% CPU (N = 54)	% Radio Room (N = 41)	% Youth Section (N = 34)
1. No action.	9	9	10	6
2. Ask for I.D., F.C. subject, further action unspecified.	8	11	10	9
3. Ask for peddler's license and I.D., explain law; if no license, cite.	36	28	42	38
4. Ask for peddler's license and/ or I.D., attempt to find out where subject got coffee, F.C. subject. *	39	50	34	41
5. Arrest or cite; no questions asked of subject.	8	2	5	6

Responses of the four groups are similar if categories 3 and 4 are combined (about three-quarters of each group's responses are here). The CPU staff most often gives the specific response selected by the Chief (category 4), which specifies a field contact report.

TABLE D-9. Incident 9: MW 39. Subject dressed in work clothing slashing tires on '67 Olds jointly owned but driven by wife.

	% Patrol (N = 251)	% CPU (N = 54)	% Radio Room (N = 41)	% Youth Section (N = 34)
1. No action.	34	33	46	24
2. Contact wife and ask what she wants done, get her version.	16	13	10	15
3. Talk to one or both parties, preserve the peace, method unspecified, or talk to husband regarding his actions or sobriety; F.C. subject, or make crime report, or assist wife leave premises; preserve the peace.*	39	43	37	47
4. Stop destruction of property, method unspecified; talk to parties or separate parties.	7	6	7	12
5. Arrest subject.	4	6	0	3

Three-fourths of the men in the Youth Section would attempt a peace-keeping role, as would the Chief (74%: responses 2, 3, and 4), compared with only half of those in the radio room (54%). Juvenile officers least often state they would take no action (24%, compared to 46% for the radio room). Responses of men assigned to patrol and to the CPU lie between these two groups.

TABLE D-10. Incident 10: Four MN's. Subjects dressed in Panther attire making major repairs on '56 pink Buick on the street, at the curb. One is overheard referring to "pig."

	% Patrol (N = 251)	% CPU (N = 54)	% Radio Room (N = 41)	% Youth Section (N = 34)
1. No action.	18	28	17	21
2. License plate check.	2	6	0	0
3. Explain law regarding repairs in street, allow time to comply. *	21	4	10	12
4. Explain law regarding repairs in street, further action un-specified, or explain law regarding repairs in street, cite persons.	23	18	17	35
5. Citation.	26	24	2	24
6. Cite persons, check ownership, warrant checks on others, tow car away, get cover units.	10	20	54	9

Responses of men assigned to patrol and those assigned to the Youth Section are similar, and both are more in agreement with the Chief's position of explaining the law (responses 3 and 4) than either of the other two groups. Those assigned to the radio room are most likely to issue citations, without explaining the law (56%: responses 5 and 6). Men in the CPU give these responses with high frequency also (44%), but they are also the most likely to report taking no action.

TABLE D-11. Incident 11: MN and FN 25. 2 children FN 1 and 4. Wife obviously beaten by husband, refuses to sign complaint out of fear of further beating. Husband states, "It's all over now." Loudly and aggressively insists that officers leave at once.

	% Patrol (N = 251)	% CPU (N = 54)	% Radio Room (N = 41)	% Youth Section (N = 34)
1. No action.	38	48	58	21
2. Talk to husband, give advice and/or warnings, make crime report, or talk to husband and wife, separate them.*	30	39	17	29
3. Attempt to talk to wife regardless of husband's wishes, make crime report, stand by.	15	7	15	29
4. Talk to wife; if necessary arrest husband, explain law to wife, preserve the peace.	8	2	2	9
5. Arrest husband.	10	4	7	12

Differences among the groups are large but not in a consistent direction. The CPU group is most likely to endorse the position taken by the Chief, least likely to attempt intervention by force (13%: responses 3, 4, and 5). The majority of those in the radio room would take no action (58%), but a fourth of them (24%) would intervene with force. Those in the Youth Section endorse this latter position most often of the four groups (50%), though a third of these officers support the position taken by the Chief. Men in the patrol group are more likely to take no action (38%) or only take action without an arrest.

TABLE D-12. Incident 12: Young MW. Officer conducting investigation of ABW with cooperative suspect in rear seat of car. Subject comes up to window and insists on talking to his friend, the suspect. Officer says no; the subject begins yelling to suspect through the window and continues after further warning.

	% Patrol (N = 251)	% CPU (N = 54)	% Radio Room (N = 41)	% Youth Section (N = 34)
1. No action, leave scene. *	22	11	15	9
2. Talk to subject about ceasing; if uncooperative, leave scene.	4	4	2	9
3. Talk to subject about ceasing, make threat, further action unspecified, or talk to subject about ceasing, give chance to comply; if uncooperative, arrest.	20	15	12	21
4. Arrest subject.	54	70	71	62

In this case it is the men in the patrol group who are most likely to be in agreement with the Chief. Responses of the other three groups are similar. Over four-fifths of them would threaten or arrest the subject (86% for CPU, 83% for radio room and Youth Section: responses 3, and 4), compared to 75% of the patrol group.

TABLE 6:
Critical Incident Questionnaire
Item inter-correlations
N = 136
(All personnel with complete data)

Item	1	2	3	4	5	6	7	8	9	10	11	12	Priors	Total Score
1		23					20		14		25			45
2			21				17		20					38
3				18			-20	18		19				42
4					15		15		19		20		13	37
5						21				18	19	17	28	41
6							18		14			18		37
7									15		26			55
8									30					20
9										25	14		16	49
10												17		44
11												21		57
12													21	33

Priors														
Total Score												27		
Experience											-21	-30		

The officers assigned to the Youth Section are more likely to take action in more situations than any of the other three groups. They are thus in most disagreement with the Chief on those items in which he judges no action to be an appropriate response (an exception is item 6). They are also more ready to intervene in situations involving crises than are the other groups of officers; this puts them in higher agreement with the Chief, although in item 11 they tend to support a more aggressive kind of action than he does. Responses to items 1, 2, and 11 suggest that they are more likely than others to push police action into areas where it has questionable legal support.

Men in the Crime Prevention Unit most often endorse the Chief's position on 6 of the 12 items (4, 5, 6, 7, 8, and 11). Notable exceptions are item 12 in which 70% state they would arrest the subject, and possibly item 10, in which sizeable proportions support positions both more lenient and more aggressive than that endorsed by the Chief. The responses of the CPU group need not be interpreted as a non-interventionist stance. The unit is defined as engaged in serious crime fighting; it may resist activities viewed as distracting or trivial.

The group assigned to the radio room, which contains both civilians and uniformed officers, is the least likely of the four groups to endorse involvement in family conflicts. On most other items, they tend to take a less aggressive stand than the other groups (an exception is item 10), and it is not surprising that on the two items in which the option appears (3 and 6) they frequently endorse the response category of checking by radio for information.

The patrol group, with more men and with less specialized functions, tends to fall in the middle on responses to most items.

Reliability and Validity

The reliability and validity of the violence potential score derived from responses to all 12 items can be viewed as a test of a general violence prone disposition among police officers. The reliability of the Critical Incident Questionnaire was measured by correlating violence potential scores derived from the odd items with the score derived from the even items. A correlation of .29 was obtained, which suggests that there is little consistency over incidents in general. If an officer gives a response judged to show a high probability of evoking violence in one incident he cannot be expected to give similar responses in all other incidents.

The number of 148 (misdemeanor resisting arrest) and 243 (felony assault on a police officer) violation reports made by the officer over the year prior to taking the questionnaire was used as a validity index for measuring the degree to which the total violence potential score over the 12 incidents agreed with a measure of actual behavior. (It is interesting to note that this measure correlates – .30 with the measure of officer experience — more than two years vs. two years and less — indicating that the more experienced officers report fewer such incidents). The correlation between the behavior measure and the violence potential score was only .27, indicating that the total score, derived over the 12 items, is a poor measure of propensity to become involved in violent confrontations.

The lack of acceptable reliability and validity for the general violence potential score increases the interest in examining responses to individual items and to patterns of items. The question is not so much who will become involved in violent incidents but who will become involved in what kinds of incidents.

The critical incident technique is able to show differences among officers in at least what they say they will do in specific street situations. It seems plausible that an officer would say things that would tend to not reveal actions with a high potential for leading to violence. It therefore becomes all the more significant that there is much variation in response to the items when administered under conditions where there is a premium on the officer stating what he thinks he *should* do.

The analysis of group differences we have reported above suggests the need for further explorations of the dimensions of police practice. It should be possible to design further critical incidents that would tease out dimensions such as ignorance of the law, concern for police status, over-reaction to threats of physical aggressions, willingness to take a helping and assisting role, support for a vigorous law enforcement position, indecisiveness or inability to take further action without calling on extra resources such as information or cover.

Incident Clusters

Table 6 gives the significant correlations of a matrix obtained by intercorrelating the individual item scores. This analysis shows low but significant relationships among several of the items and of five of the items with the criterion of prior 148s and 243s. The five items are 4, 5, 9, 11, and 12. These should certainly be viewed as the most solid incidents for further scale development. However, there are other groupings that show promise. In the discussion of differences among officer groups the questionnaire items were divided roughly on the basis of the behavior of the subjects described in the incidents: specific violations of the law by the subjects (items 5, 8, and 10); suspicious behavior on the part of the subjects without any law violation (items 2, 6, 7); family conflicts (items 9, 11); and provocative behavior by the subjects toward the police (items 1, 3, 4, 12). There is some support for the first three of these item groupings in the intercorrelation matrix. It is also possible to group the items in terms of the kinds of responses made to them — that is, in terms of officer behavior. The inter-correlations and face validity of the items suggest three such scales which could also be used as a base for further development of a multiple-scored set of critical incidents. The three are: lack of knowledge of or disregard for the law as it applies to legal restrictions on police behavior (items 1, 2, 7, 9, 11); reactions to threats to police status (items 3, 4, 5, 6, 7, 10, 11, 12); and reactions to threats of physical aggression (items 1, 7, 9, 11, 12).

These scales are only tentative leads for further investigation of patterning in kinds of responses to kinds of situations which lead to violent behavior.

Summary

Aggressiveness in one incident was found to have a low probability of being related to aggressiveness in other incidents. A more complicated explanation is needed than a general aggressive disposition which leads to a high probability of evoking citizen-police violence. A case can be made for a patterning of kinds of responses by officers and sub-groups of officers to kinds of incidents. More work needs to be done to determine such patternings. Several tentative classifications of items were suggested as leads for further study by the Violence Prevention Unit.